The
WEST
of
All
Possible
Worlds:
Six Contemporary
Canadian Plays

The West of All Possible Worlds

Six Contemporary Canadian Plays

edited and with an introduction by Moira Day

Playwrights Canada Press
Toronto • Canada

Playwrights Canada Press
215 Spadina Avenue, Suite 230, Toronto, Ontario CANADA M5T 2C7
416-703-0013
orders@playwrightscanada.com • www.playwrightscanada.com

Playwrights Canada Press acknowledges the support of the taxpayers of Canada and the province of Ontario through The Canada Council for the Arts and the Ontario Arts Council.

Cover artwork "Wood Tales for Late Nights" and cover design by Derek von Essen.
Production Editing: JLArt

National Library of Canada Cataloguing in Publication

The west of all possible worlds : six contemporary Canadian plays / edited and with an introduction by Moira Day.

Complete contents: Noble savage / by Bob Armstrong -- The invalids / by George Hunka -- Saddles in the rain / by Pam Bustin -- Ka'ma'mo'pi cik/The gathering : the Calling Lakes community play / by Rachael Van Fossen and Darrel Wildcat -- Letters in wartime / by Kenneth Brown and Stephen Scriver -- Einstein's gift / by Vern Thiessen.
Includes bibliographical references and index.
ISBN 0-88754-742-7

1. Canadian drama (English)--Prairie Provinces. 2. Canadian drama (English)--21st century. I. Day, Moira Jean, 1953-

PS8315.5.P73W48 2004   C812'.60809712   C2004-902965-7

First edition: May 2004.
Printed and bound by Printco at Toronto, Canada.

I – MANITOBA

Noble Savage, Savage Noble
For production information contact:
Bob Armstrong, 19 Baldry Bay, Winnipeg, Manitoba R3T 3C5
204-275-5018 bobrose@moderndigital. net

The Invalids
For production information contact:
George Hunka, 673 Campbell Street, Winnipeg, Manitoba R3N 1C4
204-488-7594 shmarr@email.com

II – SASKATCHEWAN

Saddles in the Rain
For production information contact:
Pam Bustin, 103-308 Randolph Ave, Windsor, Ontario N9B 2T6
519-977-1132 pbustin@yahoo.com pam.bustin@sympatico.ca

Ka'ma'mo'pi cik – The Gathering: The Calling Lakes Community Play
For production information contact:
Rachael Van Fossen, Black Theatre Workshop
3680 Jeanne-Mance, Suite 432 Montreal, Quebec H2X 2K5
rvf@sympatico.ca
or
Darrel Wildcat, Box 912, Hobbema, Alberta T0C 1N0
drwcat@hotmail.com

III – ALBERTA

Letters in Wartime
For production information contact:
Kenneth Brown
780-436-1231 theatrepublic@hotmail.com
or
Stephen Scriver, 8707 - 43 Ave Edmonton, Alberta T6K 1B7
780-450-5735 scriver@telusplanet.net

Einstein's Gift
For production information contact:
Charles Northcote, The Core Group, 507 – 3 Church Street, Toronto, Ontario M5E 1M2
416-955-0819 literary@coregroupta.com

Table of Contents

The West of All Possible Worlds
Crossing the Threshold into the 21st Century
by Moira Day

_____ • _____ • _____

_____ **I**

On 1 June 1985, the Association for Canadian Theatre Research (ACTR) honoured Gratien Gélinas with an honorary life membership in recognition of his outstanding contributions to the development of the modern Québec and Canadian theatre. In his acceptance speech to the Association, Gélinas, the creator of the street-wise adolescent urchin, Fridolin (1937-1947) and ground-breaking drama, *Tit-Coq* (1948), commented that one of great joys of being active as a playwright and actor in the contemporary Montréal theatre was that it was still capable of encompassing the full range of voices that were considered to make up the modern Québec theatre. For him, the closing decades of the 20th century were a magical time that saw his own generation, representing the beginnings of that theatre in the 1930s and 40s, working alongside the main playwrights of the Quiet Revolution and the rising generation of the 1970s and 80s – with all of them still contributing to the same rich, multi-faceted theatre scene that they had jointly created.

Gélinas' death at the age of 90 in 1999 in many respects marked the poignant close of what he had regarded as a unique era of "wholeness": one in which the greatest number of dramatic voices composing the 20th century Québec theatre could still be heard live at the same time. Yet his passing also marked the beginning of a new century, and of the rise of a new generation of writers joining the established writers of the late 20th century to respond to the challenges and opportunities of the 21st.

The final year of the 20th century also marked significant passages in the English-Canadian theatre as well, including the deaths of alternative theatre pioneer, George Luscombe of Ontario and pioneering stage and radio playwright, Elsie Park Gowan of Alberta. Like Gélinas, Gowan had personally witnessed most of the extraordinary years of the 20th century, and her passing at the age of 94 marked the ending of a similar era of "wholeness" in the Western Canadian theatre. It meant the end of a time in which the most important dramatic voices of the 1930s and 1940s, notably those of Gowan and Gwen Pharis Ringwood continued to be heard among the first post-war generation of Western Canadian playwrights shaped by the rise of the regional theatre movement of the 60s, the second wave of the 70s and 80s, as nurtured by the alternative theatre movement, and the new wave of the 90s rising out of the emergence of the Fringe and New Works Festival movement.

Yet as in the case of Gélinas, Gowan's passing also marked the beginning of a new century, and of a new era in Western Canadian playwriting: one almost completely shaped by an indigenous professional theatre centered in the Western Canada itself, and incorporating both the more established voices of the 1960s on and the emerging ones of the 21st in the same dynamic professional scene. This anthology features a small selection of the works produced by contemporary playwrights currently working on the Canadian prairies in the early 21st century, though the roots of that tradition run much deeper.

II

In Norm Foster's 1988 farce, *Opening Night*, which portrays an opening night from hell in an imaginary Canadian theatre Somewhere In English-Speaking Canada, it is not the least of the frazzled director's complaints that the play he has been required to direct is a bucolic realistic drama, entitled *Whisper on the Wind* featuring – farmers. "I mean, my God, who wants to see another play about farmers? Nobody does plays about farmers any more"(13). Pressed to justify his decision for agreeing to direct it, he snaps, "any half wit can direct a good play but to direct a bad play like this, well that calls for someone extremely gifted"(13).

As it unfolds before our eyes and that of the pleasant middle-aged couple who are making a rare visit to the theatre to celebrate their 25th anniversary (this completely at the urging of the wife; he would rather stay home and watch hockey or finish furniture as he has for the past twenty-five years) *Whisper on the Wind* appears to demand the services of an undertaker rather than a director. While the play appears to be vaguely set in a mid-West locale of some variety, the wife assures her husband that the notes inform them that it "was written by a Canadian"(35) – and indeed there is a chilling familiarity to the images of prolonged drought, laconic farmers wrestling stoically with the land, fragile womanhood destroyed by the relentless isolation and inhuman grind of farm life, and evangelistic preachers thundering hell-and-brimstone sermons over the radio about the iniquities of city life as opposed to the spiritual purity of a life lived close to Nature. When the long-suffering husband of the anniversary couple, baffled by the tendency of the main character to speak "southern lines through a British accent," asks his wife if she is quite certain the playwright is Canadian, she reassures him, "He must be from Saskatchewan. They all talk like that out there"(41).

However, as the show goes on, the bleak reality of the arid mid-west landscape becomes an increasingly apt metaphor for the director's worst fears of what his own theatrical career will look like after subjecting an audience to two hours and forty minutes of relentless sweating, stump-chopping and butter-churning in the theatre. "You know what this is?" he confides to his companion in a moment of calm and lucidity born of intense suffering, "I'm being punished for something I've done in a previous life. My God, it must have been something unspeakable"(76). Foster's own play being a comedy, the situation can only get better before the drop of the final curtain(s). Nonetheless, *Opening Night* certainly seems to imply that the deepest circles of the theatrical Inferno are reserved for directors stuck in a regional theatre in the midst of a grim prairie landscape producing plays about grim prairie landscapes until either hell or the Canada Council for the Arts freezes over.

Foster's play relies, of course, on the popular image of the definitive prairie play being about the epic relationship between the human being and the land. And like most popular conceptions it does have some basis in truth. Much of the early art, poetry and fiction produced by European settlers on the prairies during the closing years of the 19th century and opening decades of the 20th, tended to portray the Canadian NorthWest in heroic, mythic or romantic terms as one of the last great frontiers unspoiled by urbanization and industrialization – an image that often appealed as much to national and international audiences as it did at home. The image may have become more tough, spare and gritty in the tumultuous period between 1914 and 1945. Bracketed by two world wars and shaped by a Depression and a drought, the period saw the prairies, now subdivided politically and geographically into provinces, begin to develop a consciousness of itself as a distinct culture with economic, social and political parameters of its own. Still, given the comparatively large rural population of the provinces over these decades, it was a growing regional sensibility that remained shaped by the imperatives of land and natural resources, and a different human understanding and utilization of them.

As revealed by the small body of extant early feminist agit-prop and the plays of the Workers' Theatre, Western Canadians attempting to develop a distinct dramatic voice of their own over those years, could—and did—rage over the social, political, and economic inequities and injustices of the times. Still, the dominant school of playwriting taught over the period continued to stress the relationship between the human being and land as being quintessential to the Western Canadian experience. The most influential playwriting programs available over that time: the playwriting course offered by Frederick Koch of North Carolina at the Banff School from 1937-42 and continued under Robert Gard and the Alberta Folklore project from 1942-45, tended to work out of a folk play model that reinforced those tendencies.

While Koch felt that the folk play was flexible enough as an aesthetic form to adapt itself to a variety of styles and subject matter, he did stress that it needed to be "earth-rooted in the life of our common humanity," and reflect "man's desperate struggle for existence"—both physical and spiritual—in the face of a "world of nature" that could both ennoble and destroy humanity (Koch qtd. in Henderson 10-11). The end result, in practical terms, was a line of playwriting that tended to work dominantly in the realistic mode, and to stress the recovery of myth and history in ways that reinforced the Western experience as a heroic epic struggle between human beings and land.

Gowan, one of the most prolific playwrights of the period, felt that it was an approach that had its strengths and weaknesses. During the 1930s, Gowan had strongly defended the "kitchen sink" variety of prairie folk tragedy as a necessary step in the process of breaking away from the colonialization implicit in Western Canadians writing or producing drawing room comedies featuring upper class characters with British accents for a commercial market. Instead, indigenous playwrights needed to begin "building drama on the humour and tragedy, the triumphs and defeats, the magnificent courage of the people of the Canadian West." (Gowan "Powerful") Yet, in an interview in 1991, she confessed that while she felt most playwrights of that time, including herself, had felt a need to write at least one play in the "folk" mode—and some, like Gwen Pharis Ringwood, had done it extremely well—she (Gowan) had also become increasingly aware of the limitations of the form. More precisely, she had come to question the wisdom of continuing to promote the folk play as an essential model for Western Canadian playwriting into the 1940s, at a time when its vision of the West was increasingly out of keeping with the urbanization of prairie society and the progressively complex array of social, political and cultural realities being generated by those changes (Gowan "Spirit" 38-43).

Norm Foster's portrayal of the dusty prairie landscape of the thirties continuing to exert its dark, brooding presence on the stage in defiance of the petty superficialities of the theatre and the world around it, may be a tribute on one level to the lasting appeal of the earlier folk play tradition on the popular imagination as the quintessential "Western" drama. Yet the ultimate breakdown and dissolution of that inner dramatic world into comic chaos and absurdity as the human and technical imperatives of the outer play collide on the same stage with increasingly manic energy, speed and force, also reinforces Gowan's own concern about the earlier tradition possibly beginning to perpetuate a vision of the West increasingly out of conjunction with its realities – both human and technical.

III

By 1991, the same year as Gowan's interview, the technical reality of the Western the-atre had certainly moved well beyond the spartan conditions of the 1920s, '30s and '40s which had seen most of the early playwriting efforts of the time performed by school or community players in school auditoriums, community halls, and makeshift spaces. The founding of the first regional theatres in the West, the Manitoba Theatre Centre (1958) in Winnipeg, the Globe Theatre (1966) in Regina, Persephone Theatre (1974) in Saskatoon, the Citadel Theatre (1965) in Edmonton and Theatre Calgary (1968) represented the start of a dream come true for writers who had always hoped that one day they would be able to see their work professionally produced outside of radio broadcasts, and on a mainstage in their own city. The Globe (Regina) in partic-ular was ahead of its time in appointing Rex Deverell as resident playwright in 1972, and encouraging other local writers to produce work for their stage.

However, the regional theatre model was not generally adaptable to the demands of generating new work, despite the fact that Western playwrights such as Ann Henry, Tom Hendry, Carol Bolt, Ken Mitchell, Rod Langley and Sharon Pollock did see their work occasionally produced in Winnipeg, Edmonton, Regina, Saskatoon and Calgary before 1975.

By contrast, the years between 1970 and 1990, influenced by both a rising tide of nationalism and regionalism as well as a strong government commitment to arts funding especially in the first decade, saw nothing short of a revolution in the state of Western Canadian playwriting over that time. This revolution tended to be driven on four distinct fronts: (1) the development of playwriting programs and courses at the university level (2) the rapid expansion of professional associations dedicated to supporting and developing playwrights on an ongoing basis (3) the development of publishing houses dedicated to exposing Western playwrights to a broader reading audience and (4) the development of a Western alternative theatre system to expose the work of Western playwrights to a broader live audience.

(1) The development of playwriting programs and courses at the university level
Historically the Western provinces have had a tradition of unusually innovative programming in educational and extension drama programs, leading to the establishment in the 1940s of two of the oldest degree-granting Drama Departments in Canada: those at Saskatchewan and Alberta. (Queen's also developed a program the same year as Alberta.) The development and expansion of university theatre programs in all three provinces continued over the 1970s and 1980s with significant results for advanced curricular training in playwriting. In 1968, the University of Alberta in Edmonton began to offer the first MFA program in playwriting in Canada. Courses in playwriting and/or dramaturgy were also subsequently added to the curricula of most of the other major Drama Departments in Alberta, Saskatchewan and Manitoba. Since the 1980s, largely under the influence of Per Brask and other associates such as Alan Williams, the University of Winnipeg in particular has developed a strong specialty in playwriting and dramaturgy with close links to the professional community.

(2) The rapid expansion of professional associations dedicated to supporting and developing playwrights on an ongoing basis
This development addressed the needs of people wanting training opportunities in playwriting beyond or in combination with those available in the school system. It also allowed for the ongoing development of scripts outside a regional theatre system that usually demanded finished or proven work for the mainstage. The Manitoba Association of Playwrights (MAP) was founded in 1979, the Saskatchewan Playwrights' Centre (SPC) in 1982 and the Alberta Playwrights' Network (APN) in 1985 to dramaturge and workshop new local work, give script readings, hold playwriting competitions, and establish contacts between playwrights and theatres potentially interested in producing their work. While all three associations eventually developed annual festivals devoted to workshopping, dramaturging and presenting new plays in a public forum, SPC's week-long Spring Festival of New Plays (1982) by far remains the oldest and best established, with the claim that 27 of the plays developed in its first ten years have since gone on to professional production.

Additionally, in Alberta, the Banff School re-committed itself to its earlier mandate to help develop new Western scripts: in 1974 it developed a Playwrights Colony in Banff that was eventually combined with the Alberta Theatre Projects (ATP) program in 1997 to produce the Banff playRites Colony. Reflecting its strong government commitment to the arts, Alberta Culture began to offer an annual Playwriting Competition for Alberta Playwrights in 1975.

(3) The development of publishing houses dedicated to exposing Western playwrights to a broader reading audience
The publication of scripts increases the possibilities of a play having a life beyond its first production through making it more accessible to an audience likely to read, study or produce it again. Once more, the exposure of prairie playwrights to a wider reading audience was greatly enhanced by the establishment of new presses that embraced the publication of dramatic scripts as a part or whole of their mandate. In 1972, the Playwrights Co-op began to publish and distribute Canadian scripts. It branche into paperbacks as well as copyscripts, re-organizing itself as Playwrights Canada Press in 1984 as part of the new Playwrights Union of Canada (now

Playwrights Guild of Canada), and finally separately incorporated in 2003. *Theatrum* Magazine (1985-95) and *CTR* (1974) both committed themselves to publishing new scripts in their issues. Western scripts were also published by Talonbooks of Vancouver beginning in 1969. Presses specifically founded to publish Western work including plays were subsequently established in Manitoba (Blizzard Press 1988-2002, Scirocco Drama – J. Gordon Shillingford 1993), Saskatchewan (Coteau Books 1975) and Alberta: (NeWest Press 1977, Red Deer Press 1981).

The publication of scripts also had its effect on the number of Western Canadian plays eligible for the Governor General's Award for excellence in literature. Since 1980, the first year that English-language drama was offered as a separate category, three Western Canadian playwrights have won the award: Sharon Pollock of Alberta for *Blood Relations* (1981) and again for *Doc* (1986), one Manitoba playwright, Ian Ross for *fareWel* (1997) and Vern Thiessen, again of Alberta, for *Einstein's Gift* in 2003.

Other nominees who were either born on the prairies or developed as playwrights there for a significant period include: Betty Lambert (*Jennie's Story* 1982), George Ryga (*A Letter to My Son* 1984), Ken Mitchell (*Gone the Burning Sun* 1985), Frank Moher (*Odd Jobs* 1986), Sharon Pollock (*Whiskey Six Cadenza* 1987), Michael D.C. McKinlay (*Walt and Roy* 1987), Wendy Lill (*The Occupation of Heather Rose* 1987, *All Fall Down* 1994, *Glace Bay Miners' Museum* 1996, *Corker* 1999) Tomson Highway (*The Rez Sisters* 1988, *Dry Lips Oughta Move to Kapuskasing* 1989) Maureen Hunter (*Footprints on the Moon* 1988, *Atlantis* 1997), Linda Griffiths (*The Darling Family* 1991, *Alien Creature* 2000), Dianne Warren (*Serpent in the Night Sky* 1992), Raymond Storey (*The Saints and Apostles* 1993), Joanna McClelland Glass (*If We Are Women*, 1994), Brad Fraser (*Poor Superman: A Play With Captions* 1995) Eugene Stickland (*Some Assembly Required* 1995) Bruce McManus (*Selkirk Avenue* 1998), Clem Martini (*A Three Martini Lunch* 2001), and Brian Drader (*PROK* 2003).

(4) The development of a Western alternative theatre system to expose the work of Western playwrights to a broader live audience
The most significant development of the 1970s was the establishment of a complete network of small alternative theatres, many of them dedicated both to (1) doing plays or collective creations dramatizing local history, myth and story, though on more conceptually complex, and technically sophisticated terms than the earlier folk play movement, and (2) supporting each other and the playwrights they developed. The most notable of this second wave included Prairie Theatre Exchange (1973), Agassiz Theatre (1980) and the Popular Theatre Alliance (1986) in Winnipeg; 25th Street Theatre (1972) in Saskatoon; Alberta Theatre Projects (1972) in Calgary; and Theatre 3 (1970), Theatre Network (1975), Northern Light Theatre (1975), Catalyst Theatre (1977) and Workshop West (1978), in Edmonton.

In 1973 Prairie Theatre Exchange (PTE) became the easternmost outpost of a Western Canadian alternative theatre network designed to develop and support new Canadian work in general, but prairie writers in particular. In the three decades that followed, PTE not only hosted or produced work from Saskatchewan and Alberta, but threw open its doors to a rush of Manitoba playwrights who had been almost completely excluded from the Manitoba Theatre Centre (MTC) stage. Over the years, PTE produced the work of such local artists as David King, Deborah Quinn, Carol Bolt,

David Gillies, Alf Silver, Nick Mitchell, Rosemary De Graff, William Horrocks, Gordon McCall, Ted Galay, Patrick Friesen, David Arnason, Sandra Birdsell, Bruce McManus, Rick Chafe, and Alan Williams. Most significantly, it also premiered the early work of Wendy Lill (*The Fighting Days* 1984, *The Occupation of Heather Rose* 1986, and *Memories of You* 1989) and of noted novelist Carol Shields (*Thirteen Hands* 1993, *Fashion, Power, Guilt and the Charity of Families* 1995). The theatre also produced the work of both Governor General's awards nominees from Manitoba: Bruce McManus' *Selkirk Avenue* (1991) and Ian Ross' *fareWel* (1996) and *The Gap* (2001).

Agassiz Theatre, dedicated to producing "alternative theatre" also produced de Graff and Nick Mitchell, but was most noted for producing Maureen Hunter's first scripts: *Poor Uncle Ernie in His Covered Cage* (1986), *Footprints on the Moon* (1988) and *The Queen of Queen Street* (1989). The Popular Theatre Alliance of Manitoba, dedicating itself to producing popular or social action theatre in partnership with the socially marginalized, worked collectively but also premiered work by Harry Rintoul, Allana Lindgren, Bruce McManus, Yvette Nolan, Valorie Bunce, Deborah O'Neil and Margaret Sweatman.

In Saskatchewan, 25th Street Theatre also opened its doors to a rising new generation of playwrights locally, while supplying an important link in the production network between its sister Western alternative theatres. During the 1980s, it exchanged productions with Theatre Network in particular. While 25th established its national reputation with *Paper Wheat* (1977), its collective creation celebrating the rise of the co-operative movement in Saskatchewan, its most important long-term effect lay in its development and production of such Western writers as Layne Coleman, Andras Tahn, Brad Fraser, Ken Mitchell, Joanna McClelland Glass, Don Kerr, Ron Marken, Kim Morrissey, Patricia Joudry and Linda Griffiths. Most notably, it produced early professional productions of the work of Brad Fraser (*Wolf Boy* 1978), Linda Griffiths (*O.D. on Paradise* 1980, *Jessica* [with Maria Campbell] 1982), and Jim Garrard (*Cold Comfort* 1979), playwrights who developed a national profile. It also produced the early work of Ken Mitchell (*Pleasant Street* 1972, *The Plainsman* 1985) and Connie Gault (*Sky* 1989), two of Saskatchewan's most successful continuing playwrights; Dianne Warren's *Serpent in the Night Sky* (1991), Saskatchewan's first play to be nominated for a Governor General's Award in Drama; and the Canadian premiere of Saskatoon-born Joanna McClelland Glass' *Play Memory* (1986).

While Rex Deverell continued his tenure at the Globe Theatre as resident playwright, in Alberta, Sharon Pollock, John Murrell, Gordon Pengilly, Lyle Victor Albert, Conni Massing, Raymond Storey and Frank Moher all served as playwrights or dramaturges in residence in Calgary or Edmonton over those years. Seasoned novelist, W.O. Mitchell, embarked on a second career as a playwright winning the Chalmers award for best Canadian play for *Back to Beulah* in 1977. Wilfred Watson, an award-winning poet, also contributed his distinctively absurdist drama to the growing scene, though mostly on the University stage which tended to be more open to experimentalism.

Over this period, Pollock and Murrell in particular also began to mature into the best-established Western voices of the 70s and early 80s. Murrell was to take the Chalmers Award (est. 1972) for best new Canadian play three times: for *Waiting for the Parade*

(1977), *Farther West* (1982) and *The Faraway Nearby* (1995). He also scored an international hit with *Memoir* (1978) his play about an aging Sarah Bernhardt. Pollock, in turn, was not only produced on both main and alternative stages in Western Canada, but achieved national recognition as the recipient of the Governor General's Award for English-Canadian drama an unprecedented two times: once for *Blood Relations* premiered in Edmonton at Theatre 3 in 1980 and again for *Doc* premiered at Theatre Calgary in 1984.

However, Murrell and Pollock were only two figures in a rapidly rising tide of Albertan playwrights being generated by Alberta Theatre Projects (ATP) in Calgary; and Theatre 3, Theatre Network, Northern Light Theatre, Catalyst Theatre, and Workshop West in Edmonton. Other Albertan playwrights developed in the growing network of regional and alternative theatres across the prairies included Kelly Rebar, Conni Massing, Raymond Storey, Lyle Victor Albert, James DeFelice, Ben Tarver, Mary Humphrey Baldridge, Paddy Campbell, Richard Epp, Warren Graves, Rick McNair, and Sharon Stearns.

The 1970s and 1980s were also years of growth for the local francophone theatres in Winnipeg, Saskatoon and Edmonton, establishing a Western network of support for playwrights and translators working in French. The venerable Cercle Moliére (1925) in Winnipeg embarked on a more aggressive campaign of developing the work of local French-language theatre in 1972. In Saskatoon, Troupe du Jour (1985) also pursued a similar mandate of producing older French classics, in combination with newer scripts and translations. Edmonton's Théâtre Français, in turn, was established in 1970, combining with Boîte à Popicos in 1992 to become UniThéâtre.

Again, increased theatrical production made Western playwrights more eligible for best new play awards tied in to actual production. In addition to W.O. Mitchell and John Murrell, the Chalmers Awards also honoured Betty Lambert in 1984 for *Jennie's Story*, Tomson Highway for *The Rez Sisters* (1987) and *Dry Lips Oughta Move to Kapuskasing* (1990), Edmonton's Brad Fraser for *Unidentified Human Remains and the True Nature of Love* (1991) and *Poor Superman* (1996), and Ronnie Burkett for *Old Friends* (1996) and *Street of Blood* (1999).

At the Dora Mavor Moore Awards established in Toronto in 1979 to award outstanding work in Toronto Theatre, Western voices began to make their presence felt for the first time in 1983 with Linda Griffiths' *O.D. on Paradise* (with Patrick Bryner) taking an award for outstanding new play. *Jessica*, a play by Linda Griffiths in collaboration with Maria Campbell, and also produced at 25th Street Theatre took honours as the best new play in 1986. Tomson Highway, another aboriginal artist, was the next Western-born recipient of the same award for *The Rez Sisters* (1987) and *Dry Lips Oughta Move to Kapuskasing* (1989). In 1988 Stewart Lemoine received a Dora in the small theatre category for *The Vile Governess and Other Psychodramas*. In 1995, Brad Fraser's *Poor Superman* took the outstanding new play in the mid-size category, followed in 1996 by Raymond Storey's *The Glorious Twelfth* in the large theatre category.

By the late 1980s, the combination of increased training, dramaturgical support, publishing and production opportunities contributed to Edmonton initiating its own annual awards for excellence in theatre in 1987 (Elizabeth Sterling Haynes Awards) with Calgary following in 1998 (Betty Mitchell Awards). Names of Alberta playwrights that have been nominated for or honoured by major playwriting awards within their own communities since the late 1980s include Frank Moher, Stewart Lemoine, Raymond Storey, Greg Nelson, Lyle Victor Albert, David Belke, Marty Chan, Mieko Ouchi, Kathleen Rootsaert, Joey Tremblay and Jonathan Christenson, Kenneth Brown and Stephen Scriver, Ron Chambers, Paul Matwychuk, Pamela Boyd, Trevor Schmidt, Sheldon Elter, José Teodoro, Clem Martini, Ron Chambers, Katherine Koller, Daniel Libman, Doug Curtis, Rose Scollard, Stephen Massicotte, Chris Craddock, Scott Sharplin, Gordon Portman, Robert Clinton and Daniela Vlaskalic and Beth Graham.

IV

Over the closing decade of the century and the opening years of the new, the theatre scene began to change again. An era ended at the Globe in 1990 with Rex Deverell finally ending his seventeen-year association with the theatre as playwright-in-residence and moving to Toronto. There were more profound and troubling passages, however. Much of the rapid growth of the Western theatre of 1970s and early 1980s had been aided by relatively prosperous times and unprecedented government support and funding. By the late 1980s, the funding situation had become much bleaker. Blizzard Publishing ceased operations in 2001. Cutbacks in educational funding contributed to the termination of the MFA program in Playwriting at the University of Alberta in the early 1990s. Arts funding for professional theatre also declined sharply. Many of the more established theatres, like ATP, passed through a time of severe financial crisis, but survived through a combination of finding new sources of funding, often from the corporate sector, reassessing their programming, and drawing strongly on the continuing support of a large, loyal audience base built up over the years. Unfortunately others, like Agassiz (Winnipeg) passed out of existence in 1988 to be followed by the Popular Theatre Alliance of Manitoba in 1998. While 25th Street Theatre (Saskatoon) continued to develop a variety of writers over the 1990s, most notably Rod McIntyre, Scott Douglas, Greg Nelson, Mansel Robinson, Archie Crail, Anne Szumigalski, Sharon Butala, Barbara Sapergia, Pam Bustin, Kit Brennan and Dianne Warren, financial hardship forced the theatre to at least temporarily cease active production in 1999. The Phoenix Theatre in Edmonton, which had risen from the ashes of the old Theatre 3 in 1981, went down a second time in 1997, and was amalgamated into a slightly larger version of Theatre Network. Another effect of the recession was that many of the older alternative theatres that had initially pursued mandates of producing new work either for the purposes of promoting social action (Catalyst Theatre, Edmonton, 1977), or developing a specifically Canadian or prairie voice (ATP, Theatre Network) began to adopt a more varied "something for everyone" approach to programming for the mainstage.

Despite this, the Western Canadian playwriting scene continued to expand and prevail over the 1990s and early years of the new century. In some cases, the older regional system began to include more new Western work on its main as well as second stages. Maureen Hunter's later more sweeping epic plays dealing with aspects of the Old World: *Transit of Venus* (1992), *Atlantis* (1996) and *Vinci* (2002) were all done on the MTC mainstage. In Saskatchewan, Regina's Globe Theatre, in addition to developing Rex Deverell, also premiered work by Ken Mitchell, Connie Gault and Floyd Favel Starr. Similarly, in Saskatoon, Persephone under artistic director Tibor Feheregyhazi (1982) has frequently premiered translations by local writers, including David Edney. He has also premiered work by Barbara Sapergia and Geoffrey Ursell as well as the first two plays of Saskatchewan's award-winning short-story writer and novelist, Guy Vanderhaeghe: *I Had a Job I Liked Once* (1991) and *Dancock's Dance* (1995). A production by Regina playwright, Dan Macdonald is also planned for 2004-05. In Edmonton, as part of a new initiative under current artistic director, Bob Baker (1999), to perform more new work by established Alberta writers, the Citadel Theatre recently appointed its first playwright-in-residence, Marty Chan, in 2002 and created the position of Associate Director for Play Development and Dramaturgy (2001) currently held by Vern Thiessen, whose play, *Einstein's Gift* was premiered at the theatre in 2003.

In other cases, new theatres, either partially or completely dedicated to producing new regional work sprang up to fill in gaps in the network. In Saskatchewan, Dancing Sky Theatre at Meacham (1993) was formed "to reflect and involve the people and culture of rural Saskatchewan" and has recently premiered work by Mansel Robinson, James O'Shea and Geoffrey Ursell. In Winnipeg, Theatre Projects Manitoba was founded in 1990 by Reg Skene and the late Harry Rintoul to premiere new work by Manitoba playwrights. Under Rintoul's dynamic five-year tenure as founding artistic director, 12 of the 17 scripts produced by the theatre were by Manitoba playwrights, including Alan Williams, Vern Thiessen, Yvette Nolan, James Durham and Brian Drader. Currently under the direction of Ken Brand, the company has also performed Drader's *PROK* (2001), a nominee for the 2003 Governor General's Award in English-language drama, and more recently, George Hunka's *The Invalids* (2002) and Bob Armstrong's *Noble Savage, Savage Noble* (2003). In Calgary, One Yellow Rabbit (1982) was formed as a collective to do experimental theatre dominantly based on movement and dance. While strongly physical in nature and focused on creating performance rather than literary text, the theatre nonetheless has produced a body of plays by Michael Green and Blake Brooker.

However, the single biggest change has been in the rise of the Fringe Festival Movement. Founded by Brian Paisley in 1982 through Chinook Theatre (now Fringe Theatre Adventures), The Edmonton Fringe remains the largest festival of its kind in Canada, though its sister festivals at Winnipeg (1988) organized by MTC and at Saskatoon (1989) by 25th Street Theatre have also thrived over the years. Between the development of a Fringe circuit over the summer and co-op companies over the winter, a whole new generation of playwrights, especially in Alberta, has developed, largely working outside the traditional theatre hierarchy. In some cases, artists like Joey Tremblay and Jonathan Christenson have produced award-winning work both at the Fringe and in the context of the main season of Catalyst theatre; Trevor Schmidt, who has similarly produced award-winning shorter work at the Fringe, also continues to develop his work over the winter at Northern Light Theatre. Few prairie playwrights have had the luxury of working closely with the same fine-honed acting collective over a sustained period of time. However, the remarkably prolific Stewart Lemoine, has not only appeared regularly at the Fringe since its inception in 1982, but has continued writing and producing for his Teatro di Quindicina Company—one of the six companies included in the New Varscona Theatre group of co-ops—during the winter months. David Belke is another writer whose comical sense of whimsy has been strongly developed over a sustained period of time through the festival movement. Kenneth Brown, who has been appearing regularly at the Fringe with his THEATrePUBLIC since 1984, has scored at least two palpable hits with his *Life After Hockey* (1985) and *Letters in Wartime* (1994) co-written with Stephen Scriver. Both plays have established stage lives well beyond the Fringe at least in part because they were also expanded from their original Fringe short-form into full-length work suitable for mainstage viewing.

Theatres themselves have also relied increasingly on the festival format to allow them to continue fulfilling an earlier mandate to produce experimental new work, even as their main season has become more conservative or mainstream in choices and style. 25th Street has continued to produce the Saskatoon Fringe, and has on top of that initiated the Her-icane Festival of Women's Art. By doing so it has continued its associations with new writers coming out of the prairies. Pam Bustin who had her first play done on the 25th Street mainstage in 1994, had her next two done at the Her-icane Festivals of 2001 and 2003. Workshop West initiated their Springboards New Play Festival in 1995, then under Ron Jenkins (2000) a KaBoom! and "loud n' queer" event. Theatre Network established NeXFest in 1995, and One Yellow Rabbit, its High Performance Rodeo in 1986. However, the largest and most developed of the main season Western playwriting festivals is the playRites Festival started by ATP in Calgary in 1987 to give a full workshop and production to a select group of new plays across the prairies and Canada, and additional readings and workshops for others over the week. Stephen Massicotte's *Mary's Wedding* first done at the Festival in 2002 and then mounted on stages across the country is certainly one of the success stories of the Festival. Other writers developed through playRites include Linda Griffiths, Wendy Lill, Brad Fraser, Conni Massing, Frank Moher, Eugene Stickland, Ron Chambers, Dan Macdonald and Connie Gault.

V

The 1980s and 1990s have also been a time of proliferating new voices from what have traditionally been the margins of Western Canadian society as defined by gender, class, race and ethnicity. As is perhaps appropriate to the three prairie provinces which first gave women the vote in Canada, initiated the famous "Persons Case" and gave Canada its first woman MP, Agnes Macphail, women have also played a strong role in Western Canadian playwriting, from the 19th century on, beginning with Kate Simpson Hayes (1856-1945), Nellie McClung (1873-1951) and Lillian Beynon Thomas (1874-1961) of Manitoba who included drama among their other writings between 1897 and 1932. The torch was then picked up over 1930s-1950s in Saskatchewan by Minnie Bicknell and even more strongly in Alberta by Gwen Pharis Ringwood (1910-1984) and Elsie Park Gowan (1905-1999) before being passed on to Sharon Pollock over the 1960s and 1970s as the first important woman playwright of the professional Western Canadian theatre. Since then, nurtured largely by the regional and alternative theatre scene, playwrights such as Wendy Lill, Linda Griffiths, Maureen Hunter, Conni Massing, Connie Gault and Dianne Warren have attracted attention both locally and nationally.

Over the1990s, yet another wave of professional women playwrights began to emerge more out of the newer co-op, festival and Fringe movements. Once more, Manitoba pioneered in the area of experimental feminist drama: in 1968 the amateur Nellie McClung Players were founded as a feminist troupe to create commissioned work or collective creations that would bring "the spirit and message of the women's movement to wide audiences." Twenty years later, in 1989, Maenad Theatre was founded in Calgary by five women "to develop new works by women." While initially a Fringe company, Maenad soon became the only full-year company on the prairies exclusively committed to producing the work of women playwrights such as Rose Scollard.

In Saskatchewan, a community-based Women's Theatre Collective was established in Saskatoon during the late 1980s, but the Fringe again appears to have been the most successful generator of feminist playwriting. Over 1990 and 1991 the Curtain Razors (Regina) began touring the western Fringe circuits with the work of Regina-based writer Kelley Jo Burke. Burke's third play, *Charming and Rose: True Love,* which was initially developed on the 1992 Western Fringe Circuit, was produced by Nightwood Theatre in 1993, and nominated for both the Chalmers and Dora Mavor Moore awards in 1994.

Similarly, co-ops have sometimes worked closely with already established alternative companies to create new work. Significantly, 25th Street Theatre which has continued to produce the Saskatoon Fringe since 1989, and to run the annual 11-day Her-icane Festival of Women's Art every spring since 1999, also co-produced Pam Bustin's *Saddles in the Rain* with Beata Van Berkom's co-op company, ReaLife Productions in 1994.

At the same time, collectives have also provided prairie playwrights with opportunities to appear in front of international audiences separately from established, mainstream companies. For instance, the Four Mothers, One Sky women playwrights collective, consisting of Kelley Jo Burke, Connie Gault, Rachael Van Fossen and Dianne Warren, travelled to the International Women Playwrights Festival in Galway, Ireland in 1997 with a kind of "retrospective" staged presentation of excerpts from their diverse works. Independent companies functioning outside of the theatrical mainstream have also facilitated forms of socially-conscious alternative the-atre not easily accommodated by standard theatrical structures. Rachael Van Fossen was also founding artistic director of Common Weal Community Arts in Regina which specialized in the production of community plays, including *The Gathering*, in Saskatchewan between 1992 and 1997.

Alternative theatres working closely in conjunction with Festivals also seems to be a continuing theme in the development of feminist or women-centered playwriting in contemporary Winnipeg as well. Saskatchewan-born Hope McIntyre who formed her own company, Sarasvati, in Toronto in 1998, relocated the company to Winnipeg in 2000 and began producing FemFest: A Festival of One-Act plays by Women in 2003.

Edmonton's Brad Fraser, whose early work was mostly premiered in Saskatoon, Edmonton and Calgary, represents another alternative vision or voice shaped by gender issues. His increasing national and international profile with *Unidentified*

Human Remains and the True Nature of Love and *Poor Superman* in combination with the increasing success of other gay playwrights such as Winnipeg's Brian Drader reflects the strong emergence of a new community of voices reflective of a complex, sophisticated view of the world and humanity as seen through a gay perspective.

However, it is not only the boundaries of gender that have been pushed and expanded by the newest wave of writers. The plays of Marty Chan, Padma Viswanathan and Mieko Ouchi have all contributed non-European perspectives of the past and present to the largely eurocentric tradition of Western Canadian playwriting. Similarly Ian Ross' plays are only the tip of a larger iceberg of Aboriginal and Métis theatre emerging in prairie theatre, and represented at least in part by Yvette Nolan and Doug Nepinak in Manitoba, Maria Campbell, Andrea Menard and Floyd Favel Starr in Saskatchewan, and Sheldon Elter, Terry Ivens and Darrel Wildcat in Alberta.

In Manitoba, the Popular Theatre Alliance, with its strong commitment to social change was among the first to begin important collaborations with First Nations and Métis dramatic artists, most notably premiering the work of Yvette Nolan: *Everybody's Business* (1990), *Six Women* (1994), *A Marginal Man* (1994) and *Two Steps Forward, One Look Back* (1994). In 1993, Red Roots Theatre was founded to "promote and foster the development of many local Aboriginal artists." It is currently affiliated with the University of Winnipeg.

In Saskatchewan, early collaborations between First Nations artists and existing theatres of the 1980s, such as 25th Street Theatre and Persephone in Saskatoon and the Globe in Regina led to an emerging body of work focusing on Aboriginal voices dealing with their own issues in their own voices. While the play itself won a Dora award, mutual frustration over the process that had produced *Jessica* at 25th Street Theatre in 1982 led to other experiments in European-First Nations theatrical collaboration. For instance, Persephone sponsored two important collective productions with the Saskatoon Native Survival School: *Uptown Circles* in 1983 and *Papihowin* in 1984.

A particular milestone in the bridging process, however, was marked by the production of *Ka'ma'mo'pi cik / The Gathering* at Fort Qu'Appelle in 1992 which saw playwrights Rachael Van Fossen and Darrel Wildcat working together with several hundred of the local Aboriginal and white community to tell the story of the valley from a multitude of perspectives.

The Calling Lakes Community play was popular enough to be remounted for a second year, but the main thrust of theatre development continued to be in the cities. In the final years of his tenure with 25th Street Theatre (1985-1998), Tom Bentley-Fisher experimented with launching "Beyond the Ruins: A Festival of New Indian and Métis plays" (Spring 1995), and sending *One More Time* by Maria Campbell and Harry W. Daniels on tour to ten centres in Saskatchewan the spring after (1996). The theatre also did productions of Joe Welsh's *Sacred Places* (1997) a play about Métis war veterans, and Greg Daniels' trio of bleak portraits dealing with survival on the margins: *Blind Girl Last Night* (1992), *Percy's Edge* (1995) and *Four Horses* (1998). Significantly, the latter was directed by Regina director/playwright Floyd Favel Starr whose own work, *Lady of the Silences* (1998) and *Governor of the Dew* (1999) had been presented at The Globe Theatre and who was active in establishing Red Tattoo Ensemble in Regina, Takwaki Theatre in Edmonton and the Native Theatre Workshop.

In 1999, the same year that 25th Street Theatre started to concentrate more on festival work than production, a new company with a new purpose was born in Saskatoon: the Saskatchewan Native Theatre Company. Under the artistic direction of Kennetch Charlette the theatre sought to "design, develop and produce professional and community-based performing arts initiatives and productions that support and promote the richness and diversity of Aboriginal cultures." To date, it has fostered the work of local artists such as Mark Dieter, Andrea Menard and Maria Campbell, and done dramatic work with young people both in its main season, on tour and at the Fringe through its "Circle of Voices."

In Alberta, co-ops and companies of young Aboriginal artists are also starting to emerge. Big Sky Theatre (1999) in Edmonton hopes to increase links and connections amongst creative Native and other artists and enhance "awareness and pride" among Alberta's First Nations' peoples "through storytelling, singing, dancing and celebrating together."

VI

As further shaped and influenced by the new voices, both mainstream and alternative in nature, much of contemporary Western Canadian playwriting concentrates on increasingly complex, multi-faceted examinings and re-examinings of the dominant European tradition and its ambivalent heritage as experienced both at home and abroad by "insiders" and "outsiders" to it. Some, like Maureen Hunter (*Transit of Venus, Atlantis, Vinci*) and Rick Chafe (*The Odyssey*) visit mythic pasts where the crossbeams of present-day Western culture and thinking were first laid. Others, like Bob Armstrong (*Noble Savage, Savage Noble*) contemplate the philosophical moment at which the "snake" entered the garden of the New World. Did it arrive hidden in the perfumed sleeves of Enlightenment rationalism (Voltaire) and pastoral utopianism (Rousseau)? Alternatively, had it already slithered in, barely noticed amongst the bustling, day-to-day commerce of the fur trade and of a life and self adapted so exclusively to its service that there is no room to perceive other lives, imperatives and humanities beyond it? Or does the serpent, as old as death itself, lurk somewhere deep inside the internal wilderness of the human soul simply waiting its moment to strike regardless of the external needs and imperatives of the "real" world?

For a number of writers, the internal wilderness of the human soul and the odd creatures—light and dark—that glide through it, is world enough to explore. In many of the plays of Belke and Lemoine the metaphysical universe is a relatively bright, whimsical one. Demonic creatures may abound and violence, tragedy and loss can happen even to good characters, but the overall world of the play, despite its elements of darkness and absurdity, is ultimately too rational, active and idealistic to sink too far into the darker shadows. For others, like Ronnie Burkett, with the later work of his unique, internationally-acclaimed Theatre of Marionettes (1986), and imagistic writers such as Scott Sharplin, Chris Craddock, Paul Matywchuk, and José Teodoro, the universe, despite its comic absurdity, is a darker, sadder more enigmatic place where one is less sure of one's verities – physical or spiritual. In George Hunka's *The Invalids* the sense of insecurity extends beyond the physical and spiritual well-being of the characters to that of the next generation. Most of the characters are gamely struggling to get on with life despite an alarming (and frankly hilarious) catalogue of illnesses and infirmities, that gives a whole new meaning to the phrase "the walking wounded." Yet it seems to be a darker part of their odd "illness" that they are unable to pass life on without either dying themselves, or having the children born damaged or deformed. If the final moments of the play suggest the possibility of life renewing itself nonetheless, it is very much a case of the triumph of hope over experience.

Other writers are pre-occupied with the bustling day-to-day world of the present, and the cost of surviving in it. The results can vary from the hilarity of Tom Wood's *B-Movie: the Play* and Brian Drader's *The Norbals* to the harrowing adolescent worlds of Clem Martini's *Illegal Entry* or James Durham's *Cruel and Unusual Punishment*. By contrast, the world of Pam Bustin's *Saddles in the Rain*, at least initially, seems to dwell in a brighter, healthier more familiar world of family and mother-daughter bonding. However, it is a story, no less than Hunka's, about "illnesses" that profoundly damage and change children, and the lethal power of "the normal"—what is conventionally considered to be both practical and ideal for the most number of people—to cover up and disguise the profoundly abnormal.

Alternatively, do ideas about what constitutes "the normal" in one age hold over to restrict, blind and tyrannize the perceptions and behaviour of the next? Did the serpent indeed arrive hidden in the perfumed sleeves of Enlightenment rationalism and utopianism? Even after thirty years, many playwrights still continue to circle back to key moments in the mythic consciousness of the West, trying to understand those meetings at the crossroads when the perennial desire to pursue "the best of all possible worlds"—personally, socially, politically, metaphysically—led instead to the diminishing or loss of a self and world instead. Some plays, like James Nichol's adaptation of Margaret Laurence's novel, *The Stone Angel,* and Dale Lakevold's adaptation of Martha Ostenso's *The Wild Geese* are haunting portraits of a deeply-felt sense of personal pain, loss and growth sharpened to an edge by the poetical spareness of language and staging. Other playwrights return to formative moments in the social and political structures of the West – the Riel Rebellions (Ken Mitchell, Rod Langley, Laurier Garreau), the arrival of the Doukhobors (Greg Nelson), the granting of women's suffrage in 1916 (Diane Grant, Wendy Lill) the Winnipeg Strike of 1919 (Ann Henry, Margaret Sweatman) the Estevan Strike and riot of 1931 (Rex Deverell), the 1935 On-to-Ottawa Trek and Regina Riots (Mary Ellen Burgess, Carol Bolt, Mansel Robinson) and the rise of Social Credit in Alberta in 1935 (John Murrell, Conni Massing). They return to those crossroads when the possibility of a utopia of the rational and humane rising out of the struggle of conflicting forces presents itself – only for that possibility to be dashed and shattered violently in ways that bend the future down the course of a darker, more limited path. Certainly, Mansel Robinson's *The Heart As it is Lived* traces the tragedies that have plagued the personal lives of two sisters and the plight of the next generation because the two women failed to understand and grasp "the moment" for revolution in Regina in 1935.

Still other playwrights (Don Kerr) affirm the possibilities of the rational and ideal to yet change the world despite everything. The creators of *The Gathering* (Wildcat, Van Fossen) play not only physical but metaphysical games with time and space. On one level the play functions as Romantic theatre on a grand scale incorporating the natural beauty of valley into the staging. At the same time it is both pageant-like in its evocation and celebration of community, and epic in its critiquing of past blindnesses and injustices. By finding a balance between them, the play attempts to reshape and open the present by reshaping and opening the past, this time to include marginalized or silenced voices unheard in the original discourse. Finally, the community play is evocative of popular theatre in suggesting that the process that the community goes through to create the community play itself can also serve as a rehearsal for effecting a similar healing and reconciliation in the larger theatre of the world beyond the play.

With the plays from Alberta, one begins to be swept out into the wider world again. Set in World War II, Brown and Scriver's *Letters in Wartime*, like Massicotte's *Mary's Wedding* and Arnold and Hahn's *Tuesdays and Sundays* is about a deceptively simple romance between two achingly young and innocent lovers. Starting in a quiet, safe pastoral world, the relationship heads into darker and more complex territory that threatens to sweep both the lovers and their older innocent selves and world away. The Old World, far from seeming a source of rationality and idealism, becomes an inferno of fire, death and cynicism instead. Yet the powers of life, rebirth and regeneration remain surprisingly resilient even as the world darkens and grows old.

With Vern Thiessen's *Einstein's Gift* we return to the war years again, but this time on the other side of the Atlantic in Germany – another place and another time where the potentially fatal consequences of pursuing an Enlightenment program of rationality and Utopianism in a foreign 20th century world are explored, dominantly in the life of physicist Fritz Haber and more peripherally in that of his friend, rival and contemporary Albert Einstein. Both are fated to discover that "one day they will take that useless idea and do something with it you never thought of, whether you like it or not"(103). In some ways Einstein's words are the final—though not definitive— answer to the questions raised by Armstrong's Rousseau and Voltaire in the wilds of 18th century Manitoba. Even knowing that human beings do not work with the beauty and precision of music or mathematical calculations, and are never likely to, ultimately putting all schemes of rationalism and Utopianism into doubt "Should I not think? Should every idea I have, every story I tell, every note I play, should every act of faith be silenced because of this? Should it?" (104) *And he begins to work.*

— • —

Similarly, for playwrights in Western Canada the *work*—the very act of writing, in whatever time for whatever space and out of whatever vision—has always been an "act of faith" in the power of words to re-create the world and its possibilities anew. In *The Undiscover'd Country* Scott Douglas presents a sweeping apocalyptic vision of the West, on the verge of entering the 21st century, as a world caught in dynamic flux between the dissolving patterns of the past—light and dark, liberating and confining—and the emerging visions of what is yet to come. In some way, all six plays in this anthology reflect back bits and pieces of that vision of the West as a perpetually "undiscover'd country." The diversity of voices presented here is only the tip of the iceberg of an enormously rich, multi-faceted theatre scene—both physical and conceptual—that both mirrors back and transforms Western space into an ever-increasing variety of imaginative worlds, past, present and yet-to-come: a West of all possible worlds.

Major Works Consulted or Cited

- Anthony, Geraldine, S.C. *Gwen Pharis Ringwood*. Boston: Twayne Publishers, 1981.

- Beauchamp, Hélène et Joël Beddows, ed. *Les theatres professionnels du Canada francophone: entre memoire et rupture*. Sous la direction de Beauchamp. Québec: Les Éditions du Nordir Inc., 2001.

- Benson, Eugene and L.W. Conolly, eds. *The Oxford Companion to Canadian Theatre*. Toronto: Oxford University Press, 1989.

- Bessai, Diane. ed. *Prairie Performance: An Anthology of Short Plays*. Edmonton: NeWest Press, 1980.

- —-. "The Regionalism of Canadian Drama." *Canadian Literature* 85 (Summer, 1980): 7-20.

- Foster, Norm. *Opening Night*. Toronto: Playwrights Guild of Canada, 1988.

- Gowan, Elsie Park. *The Hungry Spirit: Selected Plays and Prose*. Ed. Moira Day. Edmonton: NeWest Press, 1992.

- —-."Powerful Social Force at Banff School."*Edmonton Peoples Weekly*. 14 August 1937. Elsie Park Gowan Papers. University of Alberta Archives. Edmonton.

- Green, Pamela. "Floyd Favel-Starr. Theatre Artist Stretches Limits of Native Drama." *Saskatchewan Sage* (December 1997): 3.

- Griffiths, Linda and Maria Campbell. *The Book of Jessica: A Theatrical Transformation*. Toronto: Coach House, 1989.

- Henderson, Archibald, ed. *Pioneering A People's Theatre*. Chapel Hill: The University of North Carolina Press, 1945.

- Longfield, Kevin. *From Fire to Flood: A History of Theatre in Manitoba*. Winnipeg: Signature Editions, 2001.

- Ringwood, Gwen Pharis. *The Collected Plays of Gwen Pharis Ringwood*. Ed. Enid Delgatty Rutland. Ottawa: Borealis Press, 1982.

- Stuart, E. Ross Stuart. *The History of Prairie Theatre: The Development of Theatre in Alberta, Manitoba and Saskatchewan 1833-1982*. Toronto: Simon and Pierre, 1984.

- Thiessen, Vern. *Einstein's Gift*. Toronto: Playwrights Canada Press, 2003.

Acknowledgements

This anthology would have been impossible without the work of many people. First of all, many thanks to Angela Rebeiro and Playwrights Canada Press for inviting me to edit the anthology. She and the Press have been a fount of information, wisdom and patience throughout the process.

Many thanks also to my academic colleagues whose patient, painstaking work has built up a substantial body of writing and research on Western Canadian Theatre and added many insights to my own over the years. These include most notably Ann Saddlemeyer, Richard Plant, Toby and Oscar Ryan, Alan Filewod, Paula Sperdakos, Chris Johnson, Douglas Arrell, Claire Borody, Kym Bird, Don Kerr, Patrick O'Neill, Louise Forsyth Dwayne Brenna, Deborah Cottreau, Diane Bessai, Anton Wagner, Geraldine Anthony, Ches Skinner, Anne Nothof, Don Perkins, Alex Hawkins, Rosalind Kerr, Jan Selman, and Mary Glenfield.

I would also like to thank the many playwrights who shared their work, advice or insights over the course of the project. These include Hope McIntyre, James Durham, Doug Nepinak, Scott Douglas, Brian Drader, Margaret Sweatman, Rick Chafe, Dale Lakevold, Ken Mitchell, Mansel Robinson, Dan Macdonald, Kelley Jo Burke, Barbara Sapergia, Maria Campbell, Daniel Arnold and Medina Hahn, Stewart Lemoine, Scott Sharplin, Chris Craddock, Paul Matwychuk, Mieko Ouchi, José Teodoro, Trevor Schmidt, Eugene Stickland, Joey Tremblay and Jonathan Christenson. I would particularly like to thank Bob Armstrong, George Hunka, Rachael Van Fossen, Darrel Wildcat, Pam Bustin, Kenneth Brown, Stephen Scriver and Vern Thiessen for all the time and work they put into writing introductions, sending biographies, bibliographies and reviews, supplying extra information and giving valuable feedback on the introductory materials.

I cannot begin to thank all the theatres, archives, and individuals who have patiently answered questions, referred me to other sources, or retrieved information for me often on short notice. Their name is Legion. However, I owe a particular debt of gratitude to Ken Cameron of the Alberta Playwrights' Network, associate Elyne Quan, and James DeFelice, playwright, academic and director for advice, information, and help, both in terms of contacting playwrights in Alberta, and helping me to understand their work in the context of the contemporary provincial scene. My thanks as well to Theatre Alberta for information on their play library and the Citadel Theatre for extra media material on *Einstein's Gift*. I am equally indebted to Ben Henderson of the Saskatchewan Playwrights' Centre, associates Pam Bustin and Margaret Kyle, Sharon Bakker of 25th Street Theatre, and Pamela Haig Bartley at the University of Saskatchewan, as well as Andrew Houston and Mary Blackstone at the University of Regina, for similar advice and guidance. In Manitoba, I received invaluable help of the same kind from Douglas Arrell and Claire Borody at the University of Winnipeg, Chris Johnson at the University of Manitoba, Rory Runnells of the Manitoba Association of Playwrights and Ken Brand of Theatre Projects Manitoba.

Finally, many thanks to my family and friends for their continuing patience and support. Without the unfailing love and generosity of Norman, Kathleen, Domini, and Linnet, and my mother-in-law, Mrs. Frances Gee, in particular, this anthology might very well never have seen the light of day.

—Moira Day

— • —

About the Editor

Moira Day is associate professor of drama and graduate chair at the University of Saskatchewan, Saskatoon, Canada. She is also an adjunct professor in the Women and Gender Studies Department. She has served as both book editor and co-editor for *Theatre Research in Canada/Recherches Théâtrales au Canada*. Her specialty is Western Canadian theatre studies with a particular interest in women pioneers. She has published chapters in books on both the French and English Canadian theatre as well as articles in *Canadian Theatre Review, Theatre Research in Canada, Theatre InSight* and *NeWest Review* and is editor of *The Hungry Spirit*, a collection of plays by Elsie Park Gowan. She has also spoken at conferences within Canada and internationally at Ireland and China. She is currently working on a book on Elizabeth Sterling Haynes, an important pioneer of the Western Canadian theatre.

Noble Savage, Savage Noble

Bob Armstrong

BOB ARMSTRONG was born in Edmonton, and grew up there and in Washington State, Calgary, Mica Creek, B.C., and Winnipeg. Immediately after high school, he studied journalism at Red River Community College and at age 20 moved to Fort McMurray, Alberta, to work as a reporter for *Fort McMurray Today*. Laid off in the early 1980s oil bust, he worked briefly for the Alberta Wilderness Association before going back to school. During the summers while he was studying history at the University of Calgary he worked as a park interpreter at Fish Creek Provincial Park and Kananaskis Country (in which capacity he wrote and performed in many short plays about the environment and history of the area). After graduating from university in 1987, he edited newspapers in Fernie, B.C., and Blairmore, Alberta, in the Crowsnest Pass area. Following a brief fling with grad school at the University of Alberta, he began working in public relations at the University of Calgary, eventually being lured away to the University of Manitoba to be director of public affairs. At the urging of his wife Rosemary, whom he met through the Hostel Outdoor Group, a hiking and skiing club in Calgary, he became involved as an actor in community theatre in Calgary in 1993. In 1994 he took a playwriting course through the Alberta Playwrights' Network, then in 1995 he won first prize in the Alberta Theatre Projects 24-hour playwriting competition. He continued juggling playwriting with his work life in PR—staging productions of his plays in 1997, 1998 and 1999—until 1999, when he left the University of Manitoba to become a full-time freelance writer and playwright. A two-time finalist in the Canadian National Playwriting Competition (2001 and 2002), he had his first two professional productions in 2003: *Penetration*, staged by Lunchbox Theatre in Calgary, and *Noble Savage, Savage Noble*, staged by Theatre Projects Manitoba. He lives in Winnipeg with Rosemary and their son Samuel.

Memories of an Ex-Trail Builder
Bob Armstrong

Picture, if you will, a young man carrying a book as he walks away from camp in a high meadow in the midst of grizzly bear and bighorn sheep country. He's just finished a day cutting brush and building cairns as a volunteer with the Great Divide Trail Association and now, muscles beginning to stiffen, he's going to relax on a wildflower-strewn ridge by reading Wordsworth in the early evening light.

This young man has no idea what half of the poems are about. He's ignorant of their philosophical, literary and historical significance, but he sincerely believes that somehow combining poetry with his rugged wilderness setting will give him a mystical/aesthetic experience that will lift him above the reality of his daily life in the fast-growing city of Calgary.

In the years to come, this belief will guide a good deal of his reading. It will take him on solo backpacking trips, inspire him to try rock and ice climbing, prompt him to join the campus Green Party. He will come to associate cities with conformity, oppression, decay, decadence and poisons. And the wilderness will be a place of heroic individualism, freedom, equality, virtue and generosity.

In time he'll realize, to his discomfort, that he shares his ideas about cities and wilderness with Nazis, neo and otherwise. He will learn enough history, philosophy, economics and science to know that civilization would not exist without cities, that the problems of industrialization and urbanization are precisely that they are too successful at alleviating misery, poverty and illness.

After he graduates from university and leaves Calgary for the small town of Fernie, B.C., he will be feeling far more ambivalent about the move than he would have a few years earlier. He'll still be thrilled by the scenery. But now the isolation and the lack of cultural amenities will wear him down. Years later, when he begins writing plays, this ambivalence will strike him as a worthwhile theme.

Canadians have long defined themselves in Romantic terms. We're the "true north, strong and free." Our national art icons—Tom Thomson, Emily Carr and the Group of Seven—depicted forest and mountain wilderness scenes. Our most beloved national settings are rocky coastlines, northern rivers, snow-capped mountains and isolated prairies.

And yet, more than 80 per cent of us live in cities, mostly within a few hours of the U.S. border. Our academic history is focused almost entirely on the building of institutions and the extension of communication networks. Though we have all been influenced by American-made Western movies, which express a national creation myth of heroic individuals who respond to the challenges of the wilderness, as Canadians we are all taught a national myth of consensus, caution and co-operation.

In short, we are as a nation torn in two directions. We are creatures of the wilderness and of cities. We are governed by individual passions and by reason. We are revolutionary and gradualist.

Broadly speaking, then, we are children of Jean-Jacques Rousseau and of his philosophical nemesis, Voltaire.

I've been intrigued by that idea and that intellectual battle for years. My first play, *Fred Turner Tames the Last Frontier*, was a farce about a small town in the mountains of B.C. struggling to attract tourists to enjoy its beautiful scenery. A few years ago I had a short story published about the commercial uses of images of rural struggle and poverty. More recently, I've been working on a comic novel, *The Epic of Gilgamesh*, about mountain climbers, artists and bureaucrats struggling over the soul of Canada and a plot to build a modernist skyscraper in Banff National Park.

In 1999 I left a career in PR to write full-time and found myself looking for an idea for a play for the next year's Winnipeg Fringe. I thought I'd try to write something based on actual historical figures, with the commercial motivation that such a play would be easier to promote. I knew that I didn't want to do a standard bio-play or, worse still, a bio memory play. I wanted to have some fun with the past, while exploring ideas that were important to me. Voltaire and Rousseau fit the bill: strong characters with a built-in conflict and relevance to a Canadian audience. Recalling Voltaire's famous dismissal of Canada as "a few acres of snow" and Rousseau's paeans to wilderness and aboriginal peoples, I thought it would be fun to plunk them down in the Canadian wilderness, which they never actually visited.

The play developed in several stages over the coming years. The late playwright Harry Rintoul gave me a very kind reference in 1999 after he dramaturged a reading of the first, very short draft. That led me to get a Manitoba Arts Council grant to expand it to a full-length play, which was a finalist for the Theatre B.C. Canadian National Playwriting Competition in 2001. The play was then subject to a roundtable reading in B.C., this time dramaturged by Fran Gebhard, which led to another round of revisions. That draft was then picked up by Ken Brand, the new artistic director of Theatre Projects Manitoba, in 2002. Theatre Projects workshopped the play for a week, directed by Arne McPherson, one of the founders of Winnipeg's Shakespeare in the Ruins company.

During this process, I continually re-examined my characters, working on the balance of comedy and philosophical debate, trying to make the characters real and at the same time farcical. I needed to even up the two main characters so that Rousseau and Voltaire were fairly matched in the debate. I needed to work on the Everyman character—the trader Pierre—so that he could be the moral and emotional centre. I had to look at the comedy and take out parts that detracted from the drama, sketch comedy moments that took characters out of the moment. I leave it to you to decide if I succeeded.

The process was served extremely well by Arne McPherson and by a half dozen of the most talented actors in Manitoba: Ross McMillan, James Forsythe and Robert Borges, who played in the production, and Grahame Ashmore, Gord Tanner and Justin Deeley, who played in the workshop. Even if you don't like the script, rest assured that you'd have liked what these guys did with it.

— • — Selected Bibliography — • —

Stage Plays – *Published*

• *Noble Savage, Savage Noble.* Manitoba Theatre Projects, Winnipeg 2003.

> *Noble Savage, Savage Noble.* In *The West of All Possible Worlds: Six Contemporary Canadian Plays.* Ed. Moira Day. Toronto: Playwrights Canada Press, 2004.

Stage Plays – *Unpublished*

• *Penetration.* (Techno-thriller about computer espionage, anti-globalization politics, trust and deception.) Lunchbox Theatre, Calgary, March 10-29, 2003. Finalist, 2002 Canadian National Playwriting Competition.
• *Flyoverville* (Large ensemble piece about the imperative to leave home in order to succeed in life.) Westwood Collegiate, Winnipeg, May 2001. Winnipeg Fringe Festival, Winnipeg, July 2001.
• *A Maze in Greys* (One-man show about faith in an age of ironic detachment.) Edmonton Fringe Festival, Edmonton, August 2000. Winnipeg Fringe Festival, Winnipeg, July 1999.
• *Schlepping Yuri* (Comedy about class, greed and the post-Cold War world.) Winnipeg Fringe Festival, Winnipeg, July 1998. Calgary One Act Festival, Calgary, February 1997.
• *The Epistle to the Canadians* (Tragicomedy about faith, hypocrisy and social responsibility.) Third prize winner, 1996 Alberta Theatre Projects 24-hour playwriting competition, Calgary, February 1996.
• *Fred Turner Tames the Last Frontier* (Comedy about tourism, wilderness and the uses of history.) Workshopped by Workshop West Theatre, Edmonton, February 1997. First prize winner, Alberta Theatre Projects 24-hour playwriting competition, Calgary, February 1995.

Fiction / Short Stories

• "The Art of Chance Tickle" (Short story about art and rhetoric and the new and old economies.) Runner up, 2000 Literary Awards, *Pagitica in Toronto* [Toronto Literary Magazine]. Published in *Pagitica* 4 (2001): 51-56.

Novels

• *The Epic of Gilgamesh.* Unpublished Novel. 2004.

Periodicals

- "No Guru, No Method at the Canadian Playwriting Competition." *Ellipsis... The Newsletter for Manitoba Playwrights*, Manitoba Association of Playwrights. 19.3 (Fall/Winter 2003): 4-5.
- "*Flyoverville*: Exploring Life and Work Dilemmas Through Theatre" *Manitoba Journal of Counselling*. 28.3 (May 2002): 19-21.
- "Aristotle and the Triple Backflip." *Ellipsis... The Newsletter for Manitoba Playwrights*, Manitoba Association of Playwrights. 17.1 (Spring 2001): 4-6.

Reviews of *Noble Savage, Savage Noble*

Ayers, Tom. "New Play Balances Humour, Philosophy." Neighbours North Section. *Winnipeg Free Press* 24 September 2003: N1.

Prokosh, Kevin. "Playwright Gives Audience Good Time, and a Message." *Winnipeg Free Press* 4 October 2003: C7.

—-. "Playwright Seeks Noble Ending for Professional Theatre Debut." *Winnipeg Free Press* 30 September, 2003: D3.

Noble Savage, Savage Noble was first produced by Theatre Projects Manitoba in October 2003 at Fenwick Hall (Prairie Theatre Exchange), Winnipeg, Manitoba with the following company:

Robert Borges   Pierre
James Forsythe   Voltaire
Ross McMillan   Rousseau

Director: Arne MacPherson
Set design: Grant Guy
Costume design: Libid Zyla
Lighting design: Michael Walton
Stage Manager: Amanda Smart

Characters

François-Marie Arouet (better known as Voltaire)
b. 1694 in France. Brightest mind of 18th century France. Playwright, amateur scientist, philosopher, novelist, wit, frequent exile.

Jean-Jacques Rousseau
b. 1712 in Switzerland. Self-educated vagabond, turned music teacher and composer, turned philosopher and novelist.

Pierre Le Breton
b. 1730 in New France. Trader, trapper, *coureur de bois.*

Setting

The time is 1757. The place is somewhere in the wilds of what is now Western Canada.

Note

Don't take notes. This didn't happen.

Noble Savage, Savage Noble
by Bob Armstrong
—— • —— • ——

<hr>

Scene I

A campsite beside a river in the forests of the Canadian Shield. On the off-chance that the theatre actually has a budget for scenery building, there should be a climbable tree trunk on the edge of the campsite. VOLTAIRE and ROUSSEAU are searching desperately through their bags of gear.

ROUSSEAU
Food.

VOLTAIRE
Ink.

ROUSSEAU
Food. We must have food.

VOLTAIRE
Did those thieves steal my ink as well?

ROUSSEAU
Voltaire, have you been hiding food from me?

VOLTAIRE
Unless Rousseau's used all the ink for his damned diaries.

ROUSSEAU/VOLTAIRE
(simultaneous) Voltaire! Rousseau!

VOLTAIRE
(sees an inkwell among the supplies ROUSSEAU has been ransacking) Ah! There it is. *(VOLTAIRE picks up the inkwell, produces a quill and begins to write.)* Now, where was I?

ROUSSEAU
Voltaire.

VOLTAIRE
(shushing ROUSSEAU with a movement of his hand, then writing) Doctor Pangloss says "all is for the best in the best of all possible worlds." And Candide says–

ROUSSEAU
What happened to all the food?

VOLTAIRE
No. That doesn't scan right.

ROUSSEAU
Voltaire, answer me!

VOLTAIRE
(turning to address ROUSSEAU) We have been over this already. Our guides took the food.... And Candide says, "But we are stranded in a trackless wilderness—"

ROUSSEAU
How can you just sit there?

VOLTAIRE
Writing consumes fewer calories than running about in a panic.

ROUSSEAU
A panic?

VOLTAIRE
Which is not only inefficient, but undignified.

ROUSSEAU
You and your vanity. That is why our guides left. They grew tired of your smug, superior attitude. Your sample collecting and scientific observations. Your habit of reeling off names in Latin to men who barely speak French.

VOLTAIRE
Or perhaps they had had enough of your lyrical swooning over the scenery. Your raging emotionalism.

ROUSSEAU
Emotionalism? We are alone, a thousand miles west of New France and we are about to starve. I should think that some expression of emotion would be called for.

VOLTAIRE
Not if this were a play by Voltaire. *(goes back to writing)* And Candide says "but we are stranded in a trackless wilderness—"

ROUSSEAU
Your detachment appalls me. I, on the other hand, feel the betrayal of our guides and the terror of our predicament. And you'll see. My feelings will save us both. I am in touch with the passions of the natural man. And now I will let those savage instincts free.

VOLTAIRE
"In a trackless waste with no provisions and only the rags on our backs to ward off the chill of this hyperboreal wilderness."

ROUSSEAU
Yes, it all comes back to me now. My childhood in the Alps. Living at one with nature. I shall open up my senses and nature will show us the way to survive.

> ROUSSEAU *is attempting to reach some sort of meditative state that will allow him to find the survival resource he needs.*

VOLTAIRE
"Hyperboreal wilderness?" Hmm. "Wind-scoured northern hell?" *(shrugs)* And Pangloss triumphantly decrees: "And there is the proof that this is the best of all possible worlds. For the agony of our imminent demise by starvation is assuaged by the cold."

l to r: Robert Borges, James Forsythe, Ross McMillan
photo by Ken Brand, courtesy of Theatre Projects Manitoba

ROUSSEAU
What do my senses tell me? What do I hear? A raven. Hmm. What do I see? A rotting stump. No. What's this! Berries!

VOLTAIRE
Berries?

ROUSSEAU
Yes. A partially decomposed mound of berries.

VOLTAIRE
Decomposed?

ROUSSEAU
Voltaire. It appears that some forest creature has been feasting on nature's bounty. I need only follow this creature's tracks to find where it obtained this wholesome harvest.

ROUSSEAU exits. VOLTAIRE returns to writing.

VOLTAIRE
And Candide says, as he collapses in fatigue, "Good Doctor Pangloss, I thank you for your superior insights. How foolish I was not to perceive that this is indeed the best of all possible worlds." Hmm. Best of all possible worlds. Rousseau, am I running that trope into the ground? *(a thought occurs to him)* Rousseau. What forest creature is known for its consumption of berries?

ROUSSEAU
Bear!

VOLTAIRE
What are its identifying characteristics?

ROUSSEAU
(reappearing on stage) It's fucking huge!

> *ROUSSEAU runs back on stage, crosses the stage and exits the other side. VOLTAIRE follows.*

VOLTAIRE
Exit, pursued by a bear.

> *VOLTAIRE runs off.*

(from offstage) Back! Back!

ROUSSEAU
It's still coming.

> *They re-enter from the other side. ROUSSEAU and VOLTAIRE climb up the tree.*

VOLTAIRE
Did you know that, contrary to popular belief, bears are primarily herbivorous? They seldom attack, except to defend their young.

ROUSSEAU
But do they climb?

VOLTAIRE
My understanding is that *Ursus Americanus* does climb, but the mature *Ursus Horibilis*, owing to his long claws and greater body mass, is seldom arboreal.

ROUSSEAU
And which one is this?

VOLTAIRE
Ask me tomorrow. If you can, the answer will be self-evident.

ROUSSEAU
So what do we do now?

VOLTAIRE
We wait until the bear loses interest in us.

ROUSSEAU
Loses interest? If only I could reach my pack.

VOLTAIRE
(examining something on the tree) Indeed. All my specimen jars are down there.

ROUSSEAU
I have a knife in my pack. Then I would teach this bear to respect the name Jean-Jacques Rousseau.

VOLTAIRE
Rousseau. Hand me your snuff box.

ROUSSEAU
My snuff box?

VOLTAIRE
Please. It is important.

> *ROUSSEAU hands a snuff box up to VOLTAIRE. VOLTAIRE opens the snuff box and inserts insects into it.*

ROUSSEAU
What?

VOLTAIRE
Did you know that the most numerous creatures on earth are of the order Coleoptera? Beetles to you.

ROUSSEAU
The Devil take your beetles. What do we do about the bear?

VOLTAIRE
I suspect if we leave his food supply alone, he will leave us alone…. *(looking into the distance offstage)* There. He's gone back to his berry patch.

ROUSSEAU
So now we're back to starving. We may need to devise a way of eating your beetle collection.

VOLTAIRE
I would prefer some tasty, rare medallions of beaver, sautéed in wild onion with a dash of salt.

ROUSSEAU
And where would we get such a meal?

VOLTAIRE
From the beaver colony I have been observing all day. Our challenge, Rousseau, is not finding food, so much as catching it…. If we can devise a method of trapping them we'll have enough food to keep us until the search parties arrive.

> *ROUSSEAU climbs down from the tree.*

Wait. Don't frighten them.

ROUSSEAU
(getting a knife from the pack) Enough waiting.

> *VOLTAIRE climbs down.*

VOLTAIRE
I thought we might wait until they come out of the water, at night. *(figuring out the physics of it, and pondering the technical details through ROUSSEAU's next speech)* If we use that boulder as a counterweight and that large branch as the fulcrum, we just need some sort of spring mechanism.

ROUSSEAU
All I need is my knife and the strength God gave me. I will go into its twig house and kill it with my bare hands if I must. Better that than lie in ambush and hope your trap works. No, I stand defiantly against the cosmos. A man, no more, no less.

VOLTAIRE
Very impressive…. But try standing two paces to your left. The light is more dramatic.

    ROUSSEAU exits, carrying a knife.

(goes back to writing) "All is for the best in the best of all possible worlds." And then, and then… starvation? What? Time for another *deus ex machina*, I fear. *(pause)* Before cold renders him insensate, Candide's lamentations attract the attention of the savages of the region, who rescue our intrepid explorers and take them back to their simple, peaceful village. *(wracking his brains as he ponders his work in progress)* And in the next chapter…. Hmm. A force of Spanish soldiers put the savages to the sword and sell Pangloss and Candide into slavery.

    Sound of water splashing as ROUSSEAU, offstage, attacks the beaver. In the premiere production this was accomplished on-stage, using a beaver hand puppet.

ROUSSEAU
I've got you now!

VOLTAIRE
Keep it down. Some of us are trying to think.

ROUSSEAU
There! And again! *(The beaver bites him, followed by much flailing about.)* Arrrr! Son of a whore! Filthy, brothel spawn! Damn you! Damn you!

VOLTAIRE
Any luck?

ROUSSEAU
The beast bit me.

VOLTAIRE
Well, come along. I'll stoke the flames and dry your clothing.

ROUSSEAU
It's got me again! It's pulling me under! Back! Back!

VOLTAIRE
(trying to think through the plot of his novel) Candide and Pangloss are about to perish when…

ROUSSEAU
Voltaire. Please, pull me out!

VOLTAIRE
At my age?

ROUSSEAU
Get a rope!

> *VOLTAIRE continues writing.*

Voltaire hurry. I'm going to drown.

PIERRE
No you won't.

ROUSSEAU
Thank God.

> *PIERRE enters carrying a nearly drowned ROUSSEAU.*

PIERRE
Because I'm going to kill you. No man disturbs Pierre LeBreton's traps and lives to tell about it. *(throws ROUSSEAU to ground)* Now, get talkin'. What are you doing on my trapline?

VOLTAIRE
Writing *(pointing to ROUSSEAU)* and shivering uncontrollably.

PIERRE
Did Fat Louis send you?

VOLTAIRE
In a manner of speaking, yes.

> *PIERRE takes out a knife.*

PIERRE
I told that fat bastard there'd be blood if he pinched any more of my furs.

ROUSSEAU
We d-d-don't want your f-f-furs.

PIERRE
So you say now.

ROUSSEAU
W-w-we aren't t-t-trappers.

PIERRE
Of course not. You're fur thieves.

ROUSSEAU
Th-th-thieves?

VOLTAIRE
I beg to differ.

PIERRE
There's no use begging. This is my territory, so I have to kill you. It's the way of the frontier.

VOLTAIRE
(*VOLTAIRE is waiting for PIERRE to recognize him. He turns to present PIERRE with his famous profile.*) Surely you recognize me?

PIERRE
Are you related to Gaetan the Innkeeper?

VOLTAIRE
Monsieur LeBreton. I am François-Marie Arouet, known to the world as Voltaire. (*shows his profile again, waiting for recognition*) Do you wish to be known to history as the man who murdered the greatest author of the 18th century?

PIERRE
Author? Here?

VOLTAIRE
You are a reasonable man, endowed with the natural faculties for cognition. My colleague insists that he is neither a fur thief nor an agent of your Fat Louis. Does he look a frontiersman to you? Consider these arms. This spindly chest.

ROUSSEAU
Who are you c-c-calling sp-spindly?

VOLTAIRE
Oh for God's sake dry off or I'll let Pierre kill you.

> ROUSSEAU begins to dry off and put his dry clothing back on. PIERRE, convinced they aren't thieves, relaxes.

His Majesty, King Louis the 15th, has sent us to this God-forsaken waste on a secret mission. Though I fail to see the value of these few acres of snow, His Majesty deems them so important that he will essay anything to keep them in French hands. Anything, that is, short of committing the Royal Treasury.

PIERRE
And you two are here to fight the English?

VOLTAIRE
We are here to induce the savages to do it for us.

PIERRE
Ahh. Ambassadors. But where are your trade goods?

ROUSSEAU
We're not here to trade with the savages. We're here to study them.

VOLTAIRE
Madame Pompadour gave His Majesty the idea. No man is a complete fool so long as he has the wit to find an intelligent mistress. You would know something about that, eh Rousseau?

ROUSSEAU
(ignoring this jibe) France needs the support of these people and knows little or nothing about them.

VOLTAIRE
So why not send the world's two pre-eminent theorists on the nature of man? Are we all possessed of capacities for God-like reason, capable of casting off superstitions and climbing above our ignorance into a state of enlightenment? Or, as my colleague Monsieur Jean-Jacques Rousseau, Citizen of Geneva, would put it, are we all perfect in our state of untutored ignorance, ruled by passions and fleeting sentiment?

ROUSSEAU
That is a gross parody of my views of mankind and you know it.

VOLTAIRE
Yes, now we shall hear him state his views for the next several hours.

ROUSSEAU
I start with the principle that man's will is his own and is only thwarted by the outward pressures of society. That we are born free but are everywhere in chains.

VOLTAIRE
His one good line.... For me, this was an opportunity to examine the *tabula rasa* that is the savage mind. By observing these simple minds, I seek to inquire into the true nature of humanity.

ROUSSEAU
"Inquire into the true nature of humanity".... You came here because of the offer of a pardon for your many blasphemies that go by the name of satire.

VOLTAIRE
And for you this was a chance to stay one step ahead of both your creditors and the fathers of the girls you have despoiled.

ROUSSEAU
You see what I have had to put up with? Trapped in a tent with this slick-tongued slanderer.

PIERRE
Shut your gobs. Both of you. *(a shocked silence from ROUSSEAU and VOLTAIRE)* I still don't know what I'm going to do with you. *(looks around the campsite)* What are you doing here alone?

VOLTAIRE
Our guides evidently couldn't stomach any more of this Swiss oaf than I can.

ROUSSEAU
Swiss oaf? You effete, cosmopolitan, anglophile, Prussian-loving, hypocritical–

VOLTAIRE
So I found exile in Switzerland tiresome. France may be governed by corrupt aristocrats and fanatical clerics, but at least it has decent pastry cooks. And no yodelling.

ROUSSEAU
You may insult me, but you must not insult my country.

PIERRE
I see why your guides left. *(pause)* So after you reach the savages and… study… them, what's supposed to happen?

ROUSSEAU
Why, in a grand alliance from the Mississippi to the Hudson Bay, they will drive the English to the sea once and for all.

PIERRE
I don't like the sound of that. *(picks up knife again)*

ROUSSEAU
What's wrong with you man? The English are your blood enemies.

PIERRE
Maybe so, but they pay better.

ROUSSEAU
Think of your Fatherland.

PIERRE
My father? You keep that drunkard out of it.

ROUSSEAU
Are you not moved by your very nature to fight the English?

VOLTAIRE
Oh, I think I know what moves Pierre…. Pierre, what do the English pay you for one of those beaver pelts?

PIERRE
Why d'you want to know?

VOLTAIRE
Just one of my interests. A new science, called economics.

PIERRE
One English shilling a pelt.

VOLTAIRE
Do you think that's all you're worth?

PIERRE
Maybe I'm worth a lot more.

ROUSSEAU
You can't put a price on a man's soul.

VOLTAIRE
I suggest you keep your peace. *(to PIERRE)* Now Pierre. With the English paying so well, does that attract more trappers to the country?

PIERRE
Gettin' to be so many men on the river you have to come farther west every year.

VOLTAIRE
The law of supply and demand. But as more beavers are trapped, the price per pelt begins to go down, does it not?

PIERRE
Even the English are drivin' a hard bargain.

VOLTAIRE
So if the English are forced from the country, thousands of trappers will go out of business. Soon there will be a shortage of beaver pelts. And the price will rise higher than before.

PIERRE
But I'll need some money to live off, 'til the price goes back up.

VOLTAIRE
In order to further the science of economics, I shall pay you not to trap. If you will agree to accompany us.

PIERRE
Three shillings a pelt.

VOLTAIRE
Pardon me?

PIERRE
You need me more than I need you. Pay me three shillings for every beaver I don't trap.

VOLTAIRE
Again, the law of supply and demand. Now, why don't you show me your canoe? *(VOLTAIRE begins walking toward the river, gestures back to his pack and PIERRE.)* Oh, that's my pack there. Watch you don't break anything. *(continues walking)*

PIERRE
(lifting the pack and following) What do you call this science again?

VOLTAIRE
Economics.

PIERRE
Economics. Next thing you'll be paying a farmer not to grow crops.

   ROUSSEAU hastily lifts his pack and joins them as they exit.

Scene 2

   A few weeks later at another campsite. PIERRE and ROUSSEAU sitting by the fire.

ROUSSEAU
(groans) I cannot sit another moment. *(gets up with some difficulty)* Day after day in that blasted canoe.

PIERRE
Just takes a bit of getting used to.

ROUSSEAU
How much longer Pierre? We have been searching for the savages for weeks.

PIERRE
Plenty of them back in the forest country. Cree and Ojibway.

ROUSSEAU
No, no. I'm not interested in your trading partners. They have been corrupted by commerce. I want to meet savages who remain untouched by our civilization.

PIERRE
Well, then we have to keep going to the grasslands. Go all the way west until we meet the Blackfoot, or head southwest to see the Sioux.

ROUSSEAU
And they live in a state of nature? Tell me everything you know.

PIERRE
Don't know much. The Blackfoot are at war with the Cree. They know it's traders like me have been giving the Cree muskets, so we don't dare go that far west.

ROUSSEAU
And the Sioux? What of them?

PIERRE
It's worth a white man's life to enter the Sioux lands. Ever since La Verendrye took the Ojibway side against them.

ROUSSEAU
So none of your trade goods reach the Sioux or the Blackfoot? None of your firearms or kettles or coloured beads?

PIERRE
Not through white hands, anyway.

ROUSSEAU
My discomfort is a small price to pay for a chance to change the world. We must continue to the grasslands.

PIERRE
Which way? West or southwest?

ROUSSEAU
It makes no difference which savages we meet, so long as they are free of the taint of civilization.

PIERRE
And this is really important to you?

ROUSSEAU
Pierre, do you remember the simple, happy life you led before the restrictions of society held you in thrall?

PIERRE
Eh?

ROUSSEAU
Masters, teachers, landlords. Imposing their rules, restricting your spirit.

PIERRE
Well, I never really had no teachers, but I guess I know what you mean. That's why I run for the woods.

ROUSSEAU
The freedom of nature. Well do I recall my boyhood adventures on the road. Sleeping under the stars. Climbing the hills.

PIERRE
I just had to see around the bend of the river.

ROUSSEAU
And you found this Eden. Where a man can live as God intended.

PIERRE
Oh yeah. Haulin' 180 pound of fur over a portage and livin' on dried peas for two months at a time. That's just what God intended.

ROUSSEAU
Oh.

PIERRE
One good payout and I'm out of here.

ROUSSEAU
So that is why you took up Voltaire's offer to guide us?

PIERRE
See, I got my eye on a tavern. Sit back by the fire, tell lies and watch the money roll in. No more freezing my ass off out here.

ROUSSEAU
You were prepared to kill us to protect your trapping territory. Now you are planning to abandon it forever to become an innkeeper. Do you not see what a slave you have become to property?

PIERRE
Slave? No, I'm gonna be the master for a change.

ROUSSEAU
Property. Property. Would that someone had cried out "do not believe this imposter" when the first man said "this is mine."

PIERRE
It's a nice tavern. Does good business.

ROUSSEAU
(grasping PIERRE's face, hands) Are these the hands of a publican? Should this noble brow be creased in computation of pints of ale? You were made for better things than that Pierre. Your fall saddens me. *(ROUSSEAU begins to cry.)*

PIERRE
Sorry. Is there anything…?

ROUSSEAU
You are a fallen man, Pierre. Fallen from the innocence of nature to the corruption of petty greed and property. This mission could win you back your soul.

PIERRE
I got some chores–

ROUSSEAU
Which is why you must work closely with me. Once we find the savages of the west Voltaire will want to twist their words to his own corrupt ends. But if you act as my translator, I will ensure that the savages' primitive virtue inspires the world.

PIERRE
Listen, I'm just a simple man.

ROUSSEAU
Pierre. I am not a fool. I know that Europe is not ready for my ideas. The French will not abandon their vanities for my life of virtue. But what about the savages? They may see in me and my ideas, a, a manifestation of the common will. An avatar. A philosopher king, who can lead them to hitherto unimagined greatness.

VOLTAIRE
(from offstage) Pierre! My magnifying glass!

ROUSSEAU
By my side, Pierre, you will be a hero. Not a publican.

> VOLTAIRE *appears carrying a specimen jar.* PIERRE *hands* VOLTAIRE *a glass.*

VOLTAIRE
Buffon will be delighted with this. It will make a splendid addition to his Natural History collection.

PIERRE
What is it?

VOLTAIRE
It appears to be a minuscule biting midge. *(inspecting it closely)* Class *Insecta*, family *Chironomidae*, genus *Culex*…

ROUSSEAU
(ROUSSEAU seizes the insect from VOLTAIRE's hand and eats it.) Why does everything have to involve classification, breaking all of the mysteries of nature down to indistinguishable fragments?

VOLTAIRE
Because my dear obscurantist friend, that is how we move closer to the pure truths of the Creator's mind, as revealed by Newton's insights into the universal and unchanging laws of motion.

ROUSSEAU
You think you can measure the mind of God with a compass? Nonsense. Pure truth is like a blast furnace. It must be approached cautiously, with the eyes averted. But we know it is there. We can sense it. We can feel it.

As the argument escalates, PIERRE begins his chores, stitching up a moccasin.

VOLTAIRE
There he is "feeling things" again.

ROUSSEAU
Yes, Voltaire. Feeling. The most important things cannot be "known" – only felt.

VOLTAIRE
Come now–

ROUSSEAU
The sublime beauty of nature. A mother's love for her child. A son's devotion to his father. A people's common bond of blood and fellowship.

VOLTAIRE
And everybody has these profound feelings? Well, then what do we do when your profound feelings don't agree with mine? If we cannot debate things reasonably, Rousseau, we will be left with violence as the only means of settling questions.

ROUSSEAU
I have seen those sterile spectacles you call debates, Voltaire, and I tell you this craven, bloodless "reasoning" you champion is precisely what is wrong with Europe. It robs us of our vitality. It reduces the awesome mysteries of life to a mere calculation.

VOLTAIRE
But my dear Jean Jacques, in enumerating reasons for your belief in the moral superiority of brute strength, you have already refuted the proposition you seek to prove.

ROUSSEAU
Nonsense. When I say that the reason you praise is an empty vessel, I mean that truth is to be found in the lives of simple, uncultured men who live by the sweat of their brows. Men like Pierre.

VOLTAIRE
Our Pierre?

ROUSSEAU
Pierre. Have you ever looked up at the stars and felt you were not alone? Have you ever seen a mother nursing an infant and felt a surge of joy? Have you had moments of understanding and intuition that came to you suddenly, without words?

PIERRE, distracted by ROUSSEAU, pokes his finger with the needle.

PIERRE
Ouch!

ROUSSEAU
See?

VOLTAIRE
Come Pierre, you must have heard our little exchange as you were doing whatever it is you were doing.

PIERRE
Fixing my moccasins.

VOLTAIRE
And lovely moccasins they are. Now while employed in your rustic atelier, surely you have the opportunity to free your mind and consider matters of metaphysics.

ROUSSEAU
We aren't talking about metaphysics.

PIERRE
Can't say that I do.

VOLTAIRE
Well, there's a first time for everything. In your simple and honest heart, which of us do you believe to be correct? Is the truth revealed through the rigourous application of reason? Or is truth simply a matter of sentiment–

ROUSSEAU
Not "sentiment"–

VOLTAIRE
–strongly, even forcefully, felt in the individual?

PIERRE
Never gave it much thought.

VOLTAIRE
To what questions do you concern yourself my good man?

PIERRE
Where I'll sleep. What I'll eat.

ROUSSEAU
Voltaire, you devil, you've no right to use your wiles to prey on a simple soul like this.

VOLTAIRE
You started it…. You aren't a wealthy man are you, Pierre?

PIERRE
If I was rich would I be here?

VOLTAIRE
Well said…. How many children do you have Pierre?

PIERRE
Well, four. Or five. Or, maybe…

VOLTAIRE
Maybe?

PIERRE
Well Marie was swole up already when I left. So it depends, has she had her delivery and was it a single, twins or a stillborn? *(pause)* Of course, there was the ague when I left, and that's hardest on the young ones like our Jean-Pierre, so maybe I just have three now.

VOLTAIRE
Shall we say five children, plus or minus two?

PIERRE
I guess.

VOLTAIRE
Now Pierre, would you say that it is reasonable to assert that a man in your position could stand to earn an extra 10 livres?

PIERRE
Reasonable.

VOLTAIRE
It just happens that I have 10 livres that I will give to any man who says he agrees with the proposition that man arrives at the truth through a process of reason and debate. For 10 livres, would you agree with me?

PIERRE
For 10 livres I'd agree with the Devil.

VOLTAIRE
There, Rousseau, not only do I now have a majority of those present in agreement with my position, I have the voice of rustic simplicity on my side.

ROUSSEAU
You sophist! You know very well that that is not what I meant. You bribed this man. That is not the same as saying that reason led him to that conclusion.

VOLTAIRE
But surely he was acting reasonably. Weren't you Pierre?

ROUSSEAU
I am not interested in how a man behaves to earn 10 livres. I want to know what he feels deep in the core of his being. In his very belly.

VOLTAIRE
How does your belly feel Pierre?

PIERRE
Hungry.

ROUSSEAU
You may be able to fool Pierre, you charlatan, but I remain adamant. A man finds the truth only through the strength of his character. Your "reasoning" and "logic" are impotent against my iron will.

VOLTAIRE
How hungry are you Pierre?

PIERRE
Well…

VOLTAIRE
I have an additional 10 livres for anyone who will beat this Swiss imbecile until he agrees with my proposition – namely that reason trumps strength.

PIERRE
Beat Monsieur Rousseau?

VOLTAIRE
20 livres. But this is a limited-time offer.

> PIERRE shrugs, looks at ROUSSEAU *as if to say "Nothing personal" and begins to beat him.*

Now say it. "Mere strength of character is insufficient in the face of reason."

ROUSSEAU
Ow! Not the hand! Not the hand!

VOLTAIRE
Heed him Pierre. He may yet write something coherent with that hand. Try the groin.

ROUSSEAU
Stop!

VOLTAIRE
Now do you have something to say to me?

ROUSSEAU
Go to Hell.

VOLTAIRE
Try kicking.

> PIERRE winds up to kick.

ROUSSEAU
You win. Mere strength of character is insufficient in the face of reason.

VOLTAIRE
Q.E.D.… I knew you would see reason. (to PIERRE) And some people question the value of a Jesuit education.

Scene 3

> *A portage. PIERRE is carrying a heavy load – ideally, he should be using a bag with a tumpline, a wide carrying strap that goes across the carrier's forehead making it look as if the load is about to break the carrier's neck. VOLTAIRE is walking directly behind. ROUSSEAU is farther back and moving slowly.*

VOLTAIRE
I must say, we have been moving at a snail's pace these past days.

PIERRE
(labouring heavily) That's because we're going upstream.

VOLTAIRE
That sounds like inefficient route planning.

PIERRE
It'll be faster after this portage. We'll go downstream and then we'll be on a lake.

They sit for a short rest. ROUSSEAU catches up, but hangs back a bit.

VOLTAIRE
You need a more ergonomic method of carrying these loads.

PIERRE
What?

VOLTAIRE
This primitive carrying device. You need something that better distributes the load over your frame.

PIERRE
What I need is a country wife.

VOLTAIRE
Marie?

PIERRE
What good would Marie do me here? She can't carry no more than a hundred pound herself.

VOLTAIRE
And for that you need another wife?

PIERRE
A country wife. A savage. You seen those women with their big hips. The wives carry the heavy loads and it frees the men to hunt or fight.

VOLTAIRE
Would a mule not serve the same function?

PIERRE
Only a mule won't fit in no canoe. And it won't keep you warm at night or fix your moccasins for you. No, I need a country wife. Some chief's daughter who can get her father and uncles to bring all their furs to me. It's the way of the land.

VOLTAIRE
Well, if it is a woman you want, then you must speak to my learned friend here.

ROUSSEAU glares.

You see Pierre, this could be your first lesson. Women like a man to be somewhat surly, self-obsessed, even inarticulate. Try that and they'll fall all over you, just the way they fawn over my Swiss friend.

PIERRE
I'll think about that. But it'd be easier to just give the girl's father a musket.

PIERRE gets up during the next speech and puts on his pack and continues the portage.

VOLTAIRE
(During this speech he walks upstage, faces a bush and is evidently relieving himself.) I still say this country could use a series of canals. These blasted rocks are such an impediment to commerce. What do you say Rousseau? Oh I know what you'll say: "No flat and fertile land, however pleasantly situated, can appeal to me. I must have vertiginous crags and rushing torrents that instill a sense of awe." That's what comes of spending your youth tramping about the Alps. Give me the fertile fields and pleasant hedgerows of the Cotswalds. Oh England, such a green and pleasant land. Pity we are always at war with the English. Eh, Rousseau? Or does the ceaseless conflict bring about the sort of Spartan virtue you so greatly admire? *(pause, still no response from ROUSSEAU to this baiting)* Pierre, I think perhaps you went too far teaching our comrade a lesson yesterday. *(finished peeing)* Pierre? *(to ROUSSEAU)* Are you still sulking? It is most unbecoming.

ROUSSEAU
I am not "sulking."

VOLTAIRE
Very well. Are you still plumbing the profound and melancholic depths of your psyche?

ROUSSEAU
Some people, Voltaire, do not consider it needful to deflect all emotion with shields of irony.

VOLTAIRE
And we have a word for these people: bores.

ROUSSEAU glares.

That brute didn't hurt you did he, Jean-Jacques?

ROUSSEAU
Physically, I will recover.

VOLTAIRE feels ROUSSEAU's pulse and forehead and looks closely at his eyes.

VOLTAIRE
Your bowel movements are regular? Your stool of normal consistency?

ROUSSEAU
(reluctantly) Yes.

VOLTAIRE
Nothing appears to be amiss. Yet you do not look well.

ROUSSEAU
It was ever thus. I am high-strung and prone to the vapours. Especially after a blow to my dignity.

VOLTAIRE
You take things too much to heart.

ROUSSEAU
And you?

VOLTAIRE
Not enough, perhaps. An attitude that has sustained me through prison and exile.

ROUSSEAU
Emotions cannot long be hidden before they die.

VOLTAIRE
I have feelings Rousseau.

ROUSSEAU
You still pine for Madame du Chatelet.

VOLTAIRE
But I cannot have her. So instead of bemoaning my fate, I channel my energies into my writing. I allow my personal pain to move me to greater accomplishment.

ROUSSEAU
Your fecundity shames me. I am too inclined to "sulk."

VOLTAIRE
Come now, consider the blinding pace at which you wrote your Discourse on the Arts and Sciences.

ROUSSEAU
I seem to recall your comment on that Discourse. "No one has ever been so witty as you are in trying to turn us into brutes: to read your book makes one long to go on all fours."

VOLTAIRE
I would not take the trouble to level the cannons of my scorn unless I found the work worthy of such weaponry.

ROUSSEAU
You think so? You think my work worthy?

VOLTAIRE
You are an honest, original and courageous thinker.

ROUSSEAU
And an imbecile. My ideas are nonsensical and I am a fraud.

VOLTAIRE
To what do we owe this intellectual *mea culpa*?

ROUSSEAU
Consider Pierre. There is the simple man of nature. Corrupted by a promise of a few livres. You have done me a favour, Voltaire, by showing me how misplaced is my faith in simple decency.

VOLTAIRE
Yes. Life's most important lessons frequently are painful.

ROUSSEAU
Nothing to do now but burn my writings and go back to teaching music.

VOLTAIRE
And you are certain of this? You have had moments of doubt before.

ROUSSEAU
I thought I had touched something in Pierre. How could I see anything worthy in him?

VOLTAIRE
Do not despair Jean-Jacques. The first step in discovering the truth is to discover what is not true. So, now you know that attempting to raise mankind by appealing to primitive virtue will not work.

ROUSSEAU
No. I suppose it won't.

VOLTAIRE
And you can see now, why I have always maintained that mankind needs a gradual, rational process of education and improvement.

ROUSSEAU
Well, I don't know–

VOLTAIRE
Of course. And that is why I always said your ideas were dangerous. Opening the gates for the barbarians.

ROUSSEAU
Barbarians is a strong word–

VOLTAIRE
Now that you agree with me, Jean-Jacques, we might be able to work together. On Pierre. We could work together to educate him. Start with the basics of rational thought. Build on a firm foundation of Newton and Locke. Show the world how even a white savage such as Pierre can be rescued from the brutality of a state of nature.

ROUSSEAU
You want me to work with you? To educate Pierre?

VOLTAIRE
Oh don't be shy. I am sure that there is something you could contribute to the project. And I would be pleased to help you.

ROUSSEAU
Help me?

VOLTAIRE
You have much to learn. All those subjects you neglected during your years as a raging sentimentalist.

ROUSSEAU
Raging sentimentalist? You are mistaken if you think I will help you drum your soulless science into poor Pierre.

VOLTAIRE
But I thought–

ROUSSEAU
No, Voltaire. I will not help you make him a hollowed-out husk of a man.

VOLTAIRE
You ingrate! I offer to help you in your hour of need and this is how you respond.

ROUSSEAU
I see now what your offer means. You would turn my temporary setback into the absolute destruction of all I have worked for. Now I know what I must do. I will redouble my efforts to reach Pierre.

VOLTAIRE
You will, will you? You think he will respond to your preaching? If there is any way to elevate that brute, it is to seek out what vestigial powers of reason remain in him.

ROUSSEAU
Well, then I see we have a challenge. I will awaken his moral senses and bring his natural virtues to the fore.

VOLTAIRE
And I will lay down a foundation of reason and logic.

ROUSSEAU
And when my approach is successful, Voltaire, I expect you to repudiate your decadence and sophistry.

VOLTAIRE
Dream on Rousseau.

ROUSSEAU
Are we agreed?

> *They clasp hands. Midway through the handshake, they see PIERRE approaching without a load.*

Pierre!

VOLTAIRE
I didn't hear you coming. Normally you lumber along like a percheron.

PIERRE
I'm quiet when I'm not carrying a hundred pound of gear.

VOLTAIRE
Is it far?

PIERRE
Just up ahead. Turn left at the poplar with the blaze on the side. You'll see our bags.

VOLTAIRE
Too bad it takes so many trips.

PIERRE
I wonder why that is.

ROUSSEAU
Perhaps Voltaire and I can help next time. I feel my spirits reviving.

PIERRE resumes walking back the way VOLTAIRE and ROUSSEAU have come.

PIERRE
I'll be back in a few minutes with the canoe. Don't strain yourselves waiting for me.

PIERRE exits.

VOLTAIRE
I think I shall enjoy this.

VOLTAIRE and ROUSSEAU exit on the opposite side.

Scene 4

PIERRE and VOLTAIRE portaging. PIERRE is carrying a very heavy bag filled with VOLTAIRE's books, including Newton's Principia. *VOLTAIRE is carrying nothing.*

VOLTAIRE
I don't understand why we are portaging again, Pierre. If we continued on this river, would we not eventually meet savages camped alongside?

PIERRE
I said I knew the river route. I never said it was no King's Highway.

VOLTAIRE
It just seems strange that we should go by such a circuitous path.

PIERRE
Monsieur Voltaire, if I could take you to the savages without all these portages, don't you think I would?

VOLTAIRE
(trying to ingratiate himself) Do you need assistance Pierre?

PIERRE
It wouldn't hurt.

PIERRE stops. VOLTAIRE rummages in the bag and produces a book, carrying it as his contribution. They continue portaging across the stage, and lay down their loads.

Heavy reading.

VOLTAIRE
Yes, but worthwhile.

PIERRE
What's so valuable in those books that they're worth carrying over every portage from Montreal?

VOLTAIRE
Only the key to unlock the mysteries of the ages.

PIERRE
Alchemy?

VOLTAIRE
Newton. Isaac Newton. The great English scientist who discovered the infallible laws governing the universe.

PIERRE
I thought that was Moses.

VOLTAIRE
Not *those* laws.

> *VOLTAIRE closes his book and uses it to demonstrate.*

First law. Inertia. An object at rest remains at rest, unless acted upon by an external force. And the converse, an object in motion remains in motion…. Second law. Force equals mass times acceleration.

PIERRE
I don't see…

VOLTAIRE
Imagine a billiard table–

PIERRE
A what?

VOLTAIRE
Very well. A tennis court.

PIERRE
Tennis?

VOLTAIRE
The point of Newton's laws is that the universe is not random. Everything acts upon everything else in ways that can be understood and predicted. The new science of human nature says that the same must hold for humanity. We are physical entities just like billiard or tennis balls. We all have the same capabilities, senses, physical and emotional needs. So we should be able to predict human behaviour just as we predict the movements of billiard balls.

PIERRE
Right. If you know balls, you know people.

VOLTAIRE
Pierre. This science promises to make us all happier, healthier, and more prosperous.

PIERRE
Hey. I already know your "science of human nature."

VOLTAIRE
What do you mean?

PIERRE
I'm trading for beaver. I know that Fat Louis's lot have already come through and they're offering one kettle for five pelts or a musket for 50. I've traded all my muskets and I don't have that many kettles, but I know that the chief's a vain bugger and always wants to attract another wife to his tent. So I get a little dodge going. Hire some bint to make a fuss about some beads I'm wearing. The more she fusses over them, the more the chief wants them. By the end of the day, I'm getting seven pelts for a kettle so long as I throw in the beads.

VOLTAIRE
I'm sorry, Pierre, but that's just peasant cunning. It may be efficacious in dealing with the rabble, but it is not the science of human nature.

PIERRE
No?

VOLTAIRE
Not even the best minds in Europe would claim to manipulate human behaviour through the science of human nature. Not yet. That's why I am hoping to succeed with the savages. Perhaps their simplicity will facilitate scientific observation.

PIERRE
Simplicity?

VOLTAIRE
Well, of course. Simple folk are easy to understand, and they should be easy to manipulate for good or ill.

PIERRE
Of course. How simple of me.

> PIERRE turns back and is about to exit. Instead, he gets an idea and returns to VOLTAIRE.

PIERRE
Monsieur Rousseau likes simple folk doesn't he?

VOLTAIRE
Of course he does.

PIERRE
But you don't.

VOLTAIRE
I have nothing against...

PIERRE
The rabble?

VOLTAIRE
No, it's the bestial ignorance of the mob that I detest.

PIERRE
So, you like simple people, so long as they aren't simple.

VOLTAIRE
I do not elevate their ignorance the way Monsieur Rousseau does.

PIERRE
I thought you and Monsieur Rousseau was friends now.

VOLTAIRE
Do you know, during my stay near Geneva, he praised the superstitious cretins, whipped up by Calvinist demagogues, who sought to drive me from the city for holding theatrical evenings in my own home?

PIERRE
Carry a grudge do you?

VOLTAIRE
It is not a grudge. This is a deep-seated philosophical disagreement involving irreconcilable views.

PIERRE
Ahh. So you really think he's a prick.

VOLTAIRE
Rousseau's views are dangerous. Praise the common man for his honesty and simple decency and that man will demand to be rewarded for these traits. He will seek a say in the governing of his society, regardless of his lack of property, education, experience or taste. And we will all suffer from the resultant mob rule. Reform, yes. Constitutional limitations on the monarch, of course. But to allow the swinish multitude to rule is to invite the Visigoths into Rome.

PIERRE
So the common man's a swine.

VOLTAIRE
No. Not individually. But collectively. In a mob.

PIERRE
I'm common.

VOLTAIRE
Yes, but you needn't be. You can better yourself. Through reason.

PIERRE
We better get back to portaging. Those bags aren't gonna move themselves.

PIERRE gets up and starts to carry off a bag. VOLTAIRE runs along after.

VOLTAIRE
See? Newton's first law. Inertia. You've already grasped the concept.

_____ **Scene 5**

In camp. ROUSSEAU is grooming himself, he combs his hair, then tosses it to give it a suitably wild and free look.

PIERRE
Excuse me, Monsieur Rousseau.

ROUSSEAU
Yes?

PIERRE
I been thinking about what happened the other day... I just want to say I'm sorry.

ROUSSEAU
Oh. Well. I accept your apology Pierre. But I hope you will reflect on your actions.

PIERRE
Oh I have. Believe me.

ROUSSEAU
And?

PIERRE
Well, I think my actions prove Monsieur Voltaire right.

ROUSSEAU
Voltaire?

PIERRE
He says simple folk are ignorant rabble.

ROUSSEAU
Yes, of course he does.

PIERRE
I'm simple. So I'm ignorant rabble. No wonder I beat you for 20 livres.

ROUSSEAU
You did not beat me because you are simple–

PIERRE
You see, we're not to be trusted. You can't go around saying "those simple folk are so kind and honest" because that's all a lot of balls. Anybody who says that has his head up his ass.

ROUSSEAU
He said that?

PIERRE
Well, not exactly. I couldn't completely follow him, but the gist was we're thick bastards who don't know our asses from our elbows and you can't trust us.

ROUSSEAU
Has the man never heard of Sparta, or the Swiss cantons, for that matter?

PIERRE
Never came up that I recall.

ROUSSEAU
It is a known fact that in societies of simple equality, violence, thievery, drunkenness, gluttony, and lewd behaviour are unknown.

PIERRE
I'll take your word for it.

ROUSSEAU
In a simple, egalitarian society, the common man can trust his fellows. It is inequality that creates envy and jealousy. It gives people reason to lie and cheat and steal.

PIERRE
And beat up some writer?

ROUSSEAU
Yes. You understand.

PIERRE
So I didn't do it because I'm simple.

ROUSSEAU
No. You did it because you are poor and saw the opportunity of being less so.

PIERRE
So then, what I done proves you right. It's money that's ruined me.

ROUSSEAU
Just as it has ruined Voltaire.

PIERRE
Yes. It *has* ruined Voltaire. *(pause)* He sure has a lot of it though, doesn't he?

ROUSSEAU
Oh yes.

PIERRE
How rich is he?… Just out of curiosity…. To know how corrupt he is.

ROUSSEAU
Richer than he needs to be Pierre. The man has a way with speculation.

PIERRE
He has a talent for making money. *(pause)* If you can call that a talent, right?

ROUSSEAU
Let's not concern ourselves with Monsieur Voltaire's talents.

PIERRE
No. Of course not…. What are you good at, Monsieur?

ROUSSEAU
Me? Music. Thinking. Seeing things clearly.

PIERRE
Monsieur Voltaire says you have another talent.

ROUSSEAU
What would that be?

PIERRE
A way with the ladies?

ROUSSEAU
Pierre. That is not a talent. That is merely a consequence of liberating your passions.

PIERRE
You've liberated your passions quite a bit, though, haven't you?

ROUSSEAU
(*flattered*) Voltaire exaggerates. Besides, a gentleman never tells.

PIERRE
Monsieur Rousseau, I would like you to be my teacher. About human nature and philosophy and stuff. And reading and writing.

ROUSSEAU
Pierre. You've seen enough of Voltaire to know that a little more knowledge won't make you a better man.

PIERRE
But you and Voltaire made up didn't you?

ROUSSEAU
We have arrived at a *détente*. But one must ever be vigilant with Monsieur Voltaire. He toys with people for entertainment and much of his learning is pure sophistry.

PIERRE
You're right. Of course. (*short pause*) Sophistry's bullshit, isn't it?

ROUSSEAU
There Pierre, your moral compass already points you in the right direction. You don't need book learning.... Our classroom will be nature. Come with me into the forest. Our teachers will be the meditative owl, the honest, labouring beaver, the joyful, melodious titmouse.

PIERRE
And then some reading and writing?

ROUSSEAU
First, Pierre, the forest.

> ROUSSEAU *leads* PIERRE *out of the camp and into the woods.*

PIERRE
I think I'm becoming a better person already.

Scene 6

VOLTAIRE in camp, looks up and sees PIERRE returning tired and scratched from a walk in the woods.

VOLTAIRE
Where have you been?

PIERRE
Monsieur Rousseau's lesson from nature.

VOLTAIRE
Oh?

PIERRE
He had me follow a pack of wolves to their den to see how the mother defends her cubs, for a lesson on *(from memory)* "self sacrifice and simple nobility of spirit."

VOLTAIRE
And how is the project in self-improvement going?

PIERRE
Monsieur Rousseau wants to teach me morals. But I want to learn about human nature, and law and economics, and reading and writing. That's what I'll need when I'm an innkeeper.

VOLTAIRE
Well, well. Property, education. Soon all you'll need is a bit of hypocrisy and you'll be one of the leading citizens of New France. *(VOLTAIRE laughs, PIERRE, unsure of the joke, laughs along.)*

PIERRE
You know, Monsieur Voltaire, you and Monsieur Rousseau will both need me to translate when we meet the savages. If I like your teaching better, I could do a better job translating for you.

VOLTAIRE
I stand corrected. You could already be one of the leading citizens of New France. If you are ready, then let us resume our lesson. We covered Newton's laws last time. Now why don't we discuss the social and political implications of his breakthroughs?

PIERRE
Monsieur Voltaire?

VOLTAIRE
Yes, Pierre.

PIERRE
Could we start with the reading and writing and do the social and political part later?

VOLTAIRE
Very well, Pierre. Perhaps we should start with grammar. You have been having trouble with the past pluperfect and the future subjunctive.

PIERRE
Monsieur Voltaire?

VOLTAIRE
Yes?

PIERRE
I've noticed that you and Monsieur Rousseau use very... interesting language when you get into an argument.

VOLTAIRE
You wish to build your vocabulary?

PIERRE
I been—I *have* been—thinking of what I'd like to say to Fat Louis next time I see him. What do you call a man who amuses himself with boys?

VOLTAIRE
A pederast.

PIERRE
Pederast. That's good. How about somebody who steals somebody else's ideas?

VOLTAIRE
A plagiarist.

PIERRE
Plagiarist. How about a stupid, farting, water-brained fool with no balls?

VOLTAIRE
Rousseau. Pierre you never heard me say that.

PIERRE
(slyly) You said something?

VOLTAIRE
What is the reason for this interest in colourful language?

PIERRE
It pays to increase your word power.

_____   **Scene 7**
_____

ROUSSEAU is blowing a few notes on a handmade whistle. PIERRE is sitting opposite him.

PIERRE
Excuse me Monsieur Rousseau.

ROUSSEAU
Please, Pierre, interrupting a performance is like jostling a man at prayer.

PIERRE
Sorry.

ROUSSEAU
Now close your eyes and open your ears and your heart.

PIERRE
Sure. Um, Monsieur Rousseau? What's a pederast?

ROUSSEAU
What? Why–

PIERRE
Just curious.

ROUSSEAU
A man who pleasures himself with boys.

PIERRE
Ahh. You can play now.

    ROUSSEAU goes back to playing.

Excuse me. Sorry.

ROUSSEAU
Pierre. We are studying music. That wordless language that reaches deep into the soul, to the innermost core. This is not a time for discussions.

PIERRE
I know.… But… I just wondered, what's a plagiarist?

ROUSSEAU
A plagiarist? Somebody who steals the words and ideas of another. Why are you–

PIERRE
You know, sometimes a word pops into your head and.… Thank you. Oh to know so many big words.

    ROUSSEAU goes back to playing, but with more difficulty after these interruptions. He then hands the whistle to PIERRE.

ROUSSEAU
Now Pierre, you play. Feel the music.

PIERRE
(puts whistle to his lips, pauses) Oh. One more thing.

ROUSSEAU
Pierre. Music is a harsh mistress. She demands concentration.

PIERRE
I know. I'm sorry. But it's just, I don't know these words and I can't ask Monsieur Voltaire.

ROUSSEAU
Monsieur Voltaire? Well, out with it. And then Pierre, we commune with Orpheus.

PIERRE
What's a "hydrocephalic, mongoloid, flatulent, eunuch?"

ROUSSEAU
Where are you getting these words?

PIERRE
I better not say.

ROUSSEAU
What do you mean?

PIERRE
I was practising my reading.

ROUSSEAU
Where did you read words like that?

PIERRE
I shouldn't have read them. It's just the letter fell open and there they were.

ROUSSEAU
What letter?

PIERRE
The dispatch to France. To Monsieur Diderot.

ROUSSEAU
He sent a dispatch to Denis?

PIERRE
Yesterday. When you were napping. An Indian courier come by—sorry, came by—on his way to Fort Frontenac.

ROUSSEAU
And whom was he calling a pederast, plagiarist, hydrocephalic, mongoloid, flatulent, eunuch?

PIERRE
I shouldn't never—shouldn't ever—have seen the letter.

ROUSSEAU
Me? Was he talking about me?

PIERRE
I really can't–

ROUSSEAU
The filthy, pox-ridden guttersnipe!

   VOLTAIRE enters.

PIERRE
Ah, Monsieur Voltaire. We were just talking about you.

ROUSSEAU
You have mocked me for the last time, you scoundrel! I demand satisfaction.

VOLTAIRE
Whatever are you–

ROUSSEAU
I know what you called me yesterday. *(ROUSSEAU steps forward and delivers a ceremonial slap to VOLTAIRE's face.)* I will not be insulted by a clown, no, a literary prostitute who uses his pen to tickle a leering smile from his jaded readers.

VOLTAIRE
You see, Pierre, there's the difference between my colleague and me. He insults me, but I would defend to the death his right to do so.

ROUSSEAU
If you wish to defend anyone's words to the death, defend your own.

VOLTAIRE
Oh, very well. The field of honour at dawn. *(VOLTAIRE goes to leave.)*

ROUSSEAU
Where do you think you're going? I've challenged you.

VOLTAIRE
So you have, but there is a proper style for everything. Pierre, come along, you shall be my second.

ROUSSEAU
Your second?

VOLTAIRE
Of course. Every duelist requires a second, to ensure the appropriate protocol.

ROUSSEAU
Well, who's my second?

VOLTAIRE
Pierre, when you are done attending to my needs, please attend to Monsieur Rousseau here.

ROUSSEAU
Your flippancy offends me even further. I shall withdraw, until we meet for the last time.

> *ROUSSEAU exits.*

VOLTAIRE
And he wonders why none of the smart salons will have him…. Very well, Pierre, I thank you for consenting to your role in this exercise. You are familiar with your duties?

PIERRE
I think so.

VOLTAIRE
You've done it before have you?

PIERRE
A few times…

VOLTAIRE
Good.

PIERRE
You keep him busy from in front and I come in from behind... *(raises knife to indicate stabbing in the back)*

VOLTAIRE
Not quite.... As my second you represent me in discussions concerning the place and choice of weapons. In the event of my demise, you carry my last words and a lock of my hair to the young woman of my choice.

PIERRE
Ahh.... So none of this... *(the knife gesture)*

VOLTAIRE
None. Now, the first order of business is choice of weapons. Ordinarily, I would opt for the elegance of the rapier, but Rousseau is 20 years my junior. So then the situation calls for dueling pistols, don't you think?

PIERRE
Only gun we have is my musket.

VOLTAIRE
Right, then rapiers it is. I may not be a sprightly youth, but I still have a certain finesse.

PIERRE
Rapier's a sword right?

VOLTAIRE
No rapiers? Foils? Sabers?

PIERRE
Tomahawks. *(produces two tomahawks from his bag)*

VOLTAIRE
Be careful with that, you could hurt somebody. *(takes a few little swings)* I may require some instruction on the finer points of tomahawking.

PIERRE
That's for sure.

VOLTAIRE
I'll have you know, I cut a fine figure in my youth.

PIERRE
Maybe so, but tomahawk fighting against Monsieur Rousseau...

VOLTAIRE
What about him?

PIERRE
Never seen a man take to the tomahawk like that.

VOLTAIRE
What?

PIERRE
You should've seen him when I had my run-in with that mother wolf. If Monsieur Rousseau hadn't been there I'd be a dead man.

VOLTAIRE
Rousseau?

PIERRE
Choppin' the wolf's head off in one swing like that. Guess he's been living in a little cottage back in France. Probably chops his own firewood.

VOLTAIRE
So he has youth and strength on his side. But I have the superior intellect. *(begins to practise moves in PIERRE's direction)* I shall employ the Castillian feint, and when he takes the bait... he will be at my mercy.

PIERRE
(Grasping VOLTAIRE's tomahawk wrist with one hand, he holds up his own tomahawk as if to deliver a blow.) Like this?

VOLTAIRE
Oh my. Perhaps the Sicilian Retreat. Allow him to pursue, until I–

PIERRE
Take one between the eyes.

VOLTAIRE
This will never work. Pierre, there must be some tactical maneuver you can suggest.

PIERRE
There is one other way.

VOLTAIRE
Nothing that involves... *(VOLTAIRE mimes the back-stabbing gesture.)*

PIERRE
I'm Monsieur Rousseau's second, right? So I look after his weapon. What if I'm clumsy and careless? What if his tomahawk's blunt, the head's loose and the handle's nearly worn through? He won't be able to hurt nobody. Anybody.

VOLTAIRE
Tamper with a duelist's weapon? I could never show my face again... if Rousseau knew it had been done.

PIERRE
Did I mention that I'd like to have genuine pewter mugs for that tavern I'm going to buy?

> *VOLTAIRE crosses to his side of stage to make his preparations, write his last words, etc. Enter ROUSSEAU. He and PIERRE speak on ROUSSEAU's side of stage.*

ROUSSEAU
Pierre. There you are. I have been thinking. Absurd as it may be, I will accept your services as my second.

PIERRE
I'll do what I can.

ROUSSEAU
So then, it is your job to prepare me for the duel and advise me of the likely strategy to be employed by my opponent.

PIERRE
Can I peach on Monsieur Voltaire like that?

ROUSSEAU
You aren't betraying Voltaire. You are fulfilling your duties as my second.

PIERRE
(*pause, considering this*) Okay. You'll be fighting with tomahawks.

ROUSSEAU
A natural weapon, noble in its simplicity.

PIERRE
I told Monsieur Voltaire about some of the, what do you say, finer points of tomahawk fighting.

ROUSSEAU
As my second, you must tell me as well.

PIERRE
All right. Here's what we do out west. If you've got something good to trade, you get somebody big to step in and save your ass.

ROUSSEAU
He's hired you? The blackguard!

PIERRE
He probably thinks I'll do it for 30 livres, but this time I'm going to hold out for at least 100.

ROUSSEAU
Are you going along with this? Have you learned nothing from our lessons?

PIERRE
For 110, I'll be your man.

ROUSSEAU
You know I haven't that kind of money.

PIERRE
Sorry, then.

ROUSSEAU
Pierre. We are birds of a feather. Men of the soil. Men of nature.

PIERRE
Fallen men.

ROUSSEAU
Wait. Pierre, I have something better than money.

PIERRE
What's better than money?

ROUSSEAU
Voltaire said I was a ladies' man, did he?

PIERRE
And you said he was exaggerating.

ROUSSEAU
Did he tell you that, when I was a young man in Savoy, a wealthy older woman paid all of my bills for 10 years? And Pierre, that certainly was more than 100 livres.

PIERRE
So...

ROUSSEAU
I am going to write down the name of the wealthiest, and least satisfied, woman in all of New France. If you see to it that I survive this encounter, I will introduce you to this creature. Furthermore, I will instruct you in certain techniques taught me by the famous Parisian courtesan Madame du Chatelet. Using the techniques I learned from Madame du Chatelet, you will keep this woman satisfied for years to come. *(writes a name on a piece of paper)* Pleasure, prosperity, and a patroness. On this piece of paper.

PIERRE
Don't you worry about Monsieur Voltaire. Or his tomahawk.

> *PIERRE takes the paper from ROUSSEAU, looks at it as if reading, then crosses to VOLTAIRE.*

VOLTAIRE
Here you are, Pierre. 100 livres.

PIERRE
The price is 200.

VOLTAIRE
Two hundred?

PIERRE
Come on. Tampering with a duelist's weapon?

VOLTAIRE
But Pierre. You need to keep me alive. For my money.

PIERRE
I'm Monsieur Rousseau's man too.

VOLTAIRE
What does he have to offer you?

PIERRE
He's offered to introduce me to this little minx. Says it'll be worth my while.

VOLTAIRE
(reading) Isn't this the niece of the Bishop of Montreal?

PIERRE
And he'll tell me about fancy ways of fucking.

VOLTAIRE
What?

PIERRE
Says he learned it from some noble woman in France. Madame du Chatelet–

VOLTAIRE hears the name, goes into a jealous rage.

VOLTAIRE
Rousseau! Don't you dare suggest Madame du Chatelet was one of your conquests, you foul Huguenot pig! I'll kill you.

ROUSSEAU
Just try it.

They begin to duel, starting with the ritual duelist's salute.

VOLTAIRE
En garde.

PIERRE
Psst. Monsieur Voltaire… I haven't *ixedfay* his *omahawktay.*

ROUSSEAU
Prepare to breathe your last.

PIERRE
Ahem. Monsieur Rousseau.

They begin the duel. VOLTAIRE is trying to use his tomahawk as a rapier or foil. PIERRE gets between them.

PIERRE
Stop. Before somebody gets hurt.

VOLTAIRE
(realizing ROUSSEAU's weapon hasn't been fixed) I have gone too far to stop. Either Rousseau dies or I die.

Before he can respond, an arrow strikes a tree with a loud thunk.

PIERRE
Or maybe we all die.

ROUSSEAU
We've found them.

VOLTAIRE
Correction. They have found us. And they don't seem terribly happy about it.

PIERRE
What did you expect? We trade muskets to their enemies.

ROUSSEAU
Look at them. So bold. So virile. Built like Greek statues. Greetings! I am Jean-Jacques Rousseau, Citizen of the Geneva!

PIERRE
Quiet fool. I need to figure out what they're doing here.

VOLTAIRE
Don't they live here?

PIERRE
They must be a raiding party come to attack the Ojibway. They shouldn't be within a hundred leagues of here.

ROUSSEAU
You've been saying the western savages should be just around the next bend. For days now.

VOLTAIRE
You've been defrauding us.

ROUSSEAU
Fraud? *(it sinks in)* Yes. You were pretending to lead us to the western savages, and all the while you have been leading us in circles.

PIERRE
I figured you'd thank me when I got you back to Quebec alive.

PIERRE steps forward, opens his clothing, drops his knife and shows his empty hands, then prepares to approach the Indians.

ROUSSEAU
What are you doing now?

PIERRE
They haven't killed us, so maybe they'll give me a chance to tell their chief who we are and why we're here. And we'd bloody well better hope he's as reasonable and noble as you say.

ROUSSEAU
Excellent. When you speak to them make sure to tell them about the evils of trade. Today kettles. Tomorrow all the vices of Versailles.

VOLTAIRE
You must report to me everything you see and hear. With sufficient knowledge of their society I will be able to look into their very souls.

PIERRE
I'll do what I can.

Scene 8

VOLTAIRE and ROUSSEAU tied to stakes.

VOLTAIRE
That rogue. Cunning, vicious, underhanded, backstabbing – he'd have a great future at Versailles.

ROUSSEAU
Corrupted like everybody else by the poison of refinement, divorced from his–

VOLTAIRE
Oh, shut your gullet.

ROUSSEAU
You shut up.

VOLTAIRE
Make me.

ROUSSEAU struggles with his bonds. PIERRE enters.

ROUSSEAU
Pierre.

VOLTAIRE
Good old Pierre. I knew you'd come back.

ROUSSEAU
Quickly. Untie us.

PIERRE
I don't think so.

VOLTAIRE
Pierre, I have 1,000 livres sewn into the lining of my frock coat.

PIERRE
Really? You mean this coat? *(PIERRE shows that he's carrying the coat.)*

VOLTAIRE
You – Never mind the cursed coat. I have 10,000 livres I can draw from a money-lender in Quebec if you'll untie me.

PIERRE
I'd be dead before I took a step. See that sentry with the bow?

VOLTAIRE
You could try.

PIERRE
Be reasonable, Monsieur Voltaire.

ROUSSEAU
Reason. Be a man!

PIERRE
And leave a widow and four or five or six orphans.

ROUSSEAU
Coward.

PIERRE
I just came to give you some advice. When they start the fire. First thing. Breathe deep. As deep as you can. Hold it in. The smoke'll knock you out and maybe you won't feel...

ROUSSEAU
They're going to burn us?

PIERRE
It looks that way...

VOLTAIRE
Brutes.

PIERRE
Don't blame them. It's kind of my fault. I told the chief you were wise and powerful medicine men. Said you wanted to look into his soul and stop him from getting trade goods. He said you sounded even worse than those Black Robes he'd heard of.

ROUSSEAU
Liar! You sold us.

PIERRE
He practically forced me to take all those beaver pelts.

VOLTAIRE
Judas.

PIERRE
You know, everybody's getting what they want. The savages get rid of two bad medicine men. I get a load of furs. And you both get to see the man you hate put out of business for good. All's for the best in the best of all possible worlds.

Scene 9

PIERRE smoking a pipe and preparing to hit the trail back to Quebec.

PIERRE
Have they been burned yet? They aren't the first white men to burn on the frontier and won't be the last.

He goes to empty his pipe so he can depart, but an ember hits his hand.

Ow! Shit on the Host! (*shakes off the pain, then thinks as he massages his burn*) If one little ember can hurt like that.... The poor bastards.... Not that death by starvation is a walk in the park. (*takes the stick and touches it to his hand on purpose*) Well, life is full of pain. And I'm not the one burning these poncy buggers. If it hadn't been for me, they'd have died weeks ago. Right? *(pause)* But how would Voltaire put it? I recognize from the pain I feel in my wrist that there's a physical law... fire plus flesh equals pain. And if I try to reason from the existence of physical laws to human laws I must make those laws universal. Not "burning is bad for me but fine for Voltaire," but "burning is bad for all people." *(pause, thinks over things)* Rousseau would call that sophistry. He'd say that I'm standing here, staring at those two pitiful old fops, because I'm moved by some powerful passion. And what is it? What's it telling me to do? *(pause, then he realizes what he must do)* Oh shit.

> *Picks up the tomahawk.*

What did Voltaire say about writing plays? If you have a tomahawk on stage in the first act, somebody had better use it in the second.

> *In premiere production, we see PIERRE sneak up in near darkness with his tomahawk in his hand, then he jumps and swings and stands, seeing what he has done before the stage goes dark.*

Scene 10

> *VOLTAIRE and ROUSSEAU carrying an injured PIERRE, weaving about the stage in exhaustion.*

VOLTAIRE
Watch that root.

ROUSSEAU
Lift your side up.

VOLTAIRE
He's slipping.

ROUSSEAU
Don't drop him.

> *They set him down.*

VOLTAIRE
I cannot go another step. I must rest and eat.

> *VOLTAIRE searches through the bags for food, producing a squash, pot, tomahawk and flint and steel. PIERRE pulls himself partway up while VOLTAIRE is getting food ready.*

How's the leg. Is it getting any better?

> *PIERRE shakes his head and sits.*

(while preparing the meal) Rousseau and I can't do all the paddling. We need you strong and healthy. We need something to control sepsis. There must be some root or leaf that could stimulate healing, purge bad blood. It was only an arrow. Surely, with my knowledge of modern medicine I can overcome a simple stone weapon.

ROUSSEAU
Do you think we've lost them?

PIERRE
They'll follow. And when they find us, we won't know it until it's too late.

ROUSSEAU
But we must have a head start.

PIERRE
But unless you two learn to paddle we won't stay ahead long.

ROUSSEAU
(picking up paddle) J stroke.

> VOLTAIRE lifts his tomahawk and prepares to cleave the squash. ROUSSEAU sees
> what VOLTAIRE is doing and turns away to be sick.

VOLTAIRE
What's wrong now?

ROUSSEAU
It's just… that squash… and the tomahawk. Did you see the sentry's head? It was
just like that when Pierre came to free us.

VOLTAIRE
And a very good thing it was.

ROUSSEAU
He took that tomahawk and he…. He took *that* tomahawk. The tomahawk you are
using to prepare *our meal*…

VOLTAIRE
I did wash it.

> ROUSSEAU heaves again.

PIERRE
(picks up squash) Monsieur Voltaire, do you recall our lessons on Locke?

VOLTAIRE
Yes.

ROUSSEAU
(recovering) Pry, reach, backpaddle.

PIERRE
Locke said that all memories, all the impressions of the senses, the sounds, sights,
smells, tastes, feelings, they're stored in little folds of flesh inside the skull. Am
I right?

VOLTAIRE
I have taught you well.

PIERRE
That sentry. Every deer he hunted, every dance he danced, every time he loved his
wife, it was packed into a ball no larger than this…. What a piece of work is man.

VOLTAIRE and ROUSSEAU look at each other.

VOLTAIRE
(to ROUSSEAU) Did you cover Shakespeare with him?

ROUSSEAU
You're the anglophile.

PIERRE
How noble in reason. How infinite–

VOLTAIRE
Alas poor Butternut. *(VOLTAIRE takes the squash from him and puts it back in the pot.)*

PIERRE
Could you do something for me, Monsieur Voltaire? The money you've offered to pay me, make sure that it gets to my wife. I can't bear the thought of my children ending up foundlings, thrown to the mercy of the world.

VOLTAIRE
It was good enough for Rousseau.

PIERRE
Promise.

VOLTAIRE
I promise.

PIERRE
You are a good man, Jean Marie Arouet, *dit* Voltaire. And you too Jean-Jacques Rousseau. It is to my everlasting shame that I betrayed you.

VOLTAIRE
Yes, well, we'll talk about that when it's time to pay you.

PIERRE
My friends. Too late, I have encountered your brilliance. If only I had developed my mind and soul as you have, I would not be facing eternity with such fear and uncertainty.

VOLTAIRE
Oh, I am sure one faces eternity with fear and uncertainty under any circumstances.

PIERRE
It is good to speak honestly for once.

VOLTAIRE
Yes, it's a tonic isn't it? Now who's for some delicious squash?

He gives up on the fire, starts to gnaw on raw squash, then they hear drumming.

Not what I had in mind for my last meal.

ROUSSEAU
Trapped like rats.

VOLTAIRE
The canoe.

PIERRE
There's no point. They'll have us surrounded.

ROUSSEAU
What are they waiting for?

PIERRE
The chief will want to purify himself. Seek guidance from the spirit world before he comes to kill us.

VOLTAIRE
Primitive superstition. They're as bad as the Spaniards…. Well, nobody is as bad as the Spaniards.

ROUSSEAU
Maybe we can hide.

PIERRE
The only thing to do is make peace with your life and death.

   PIERRE closes his eyes and begins to hum along to the tune of the drumming.

ROUSSEAU
I can't make peace with death by torture.

VOLTAIRE
Well, at my age my heart will give out before they flay me. I hope.

ROUSSEAU
Voltaire. I want you to kill me. Then kill yourself. You will spare yourself much suffering.

VOLTAIRE
I couldn't. You kill me.

ROUSSEAU
No. It was my idea.

VOLTAIRE
I don't want to.

ROUSSEAU
Why not?

VOLTAIRE
And go to Judgment with murder and suicide on my head?

ROUSSEAU
Since when do you believe in the Last Judgment?

VOLTAIRE
I've made a great deal of money over the years betting on propositions that I thought were unlikely. If only Pierre here were a priest I'd ask him for the last rites.

ROUSSEAU
Pierre.

VOLTAIRE
Of course. Pierre. It's all the same to you. You've killed plenty of men. What's two more?

PIERRE
Pardon?

VOLTAIRE
Kill us. You must know some relatively painless way.

ROUSSEAU
From behind please.

PIERRE
Come to me.... Kneel. Close your eyes.

VOLTAIRE
I knew he'd see reason.

PIERRE
I've heard these savages sing death songs to prepare their spirit for the next world. *(pause)* It's been a long time since my last confession. Maybe I should sing something. A song of confession. A song of regret.

VOLTAIRE
A song?

PIERRE
Oh God who made me, hear my words.
I've lived a wasted life.
I've sinned and lied and failed you
And now prepare to die.

VOLTAIRE
You will kill us when you're done?

PIERRE
I regret the killing. That sentry. And two of Fat Louis's men. And a fur thief on the Winnipeg River. And you? What do you regret?

ROUSSEAU
I regret the writing I have not yet done.

PIERRE
And there was that drunk in the tavern in Montreal.

VOLTAIRE
Me too. I had this novel I wanted–

PIERRE
And the Englishman on the Ohio. And the Cree porter on the Ottawa River.

VOLTAIRE
Are you quite done?

PIERRE
That's all.

VOLTAIRE
There was this novel–

PIERRE
And the whoring. I regret–

VOLTAIRE
Enough about you! There was this novel I wanted to finish. A satire. This innocent travels the world with his intellectual hero, Doctor Pangloss. They would keep getting into terrible disasters, and each time they would be delivered from imminent death by some ridiculous *deus ex machina*. It would have been hilarious. Imagine the Marquis de Montcalm marching over that hill with 1000 grenadiers.

ROUSSEAU
I wish I had brought together all of my theories about political and social organization into one magnum opus. It would have shaken Europe to its foundations.

VOLTAIRE
You? A book on politics and society? You're the most politically and socially inept man I know.

ROUSSEAU
Bold words from somebody who has spent half his adult life in exile.

PIERRE
And the pride. The boasting. The greed and dishonesty. All of the miserable, underhanded ways I have behaved. All of these years, I have been doing nothing but adding to the world's stock of suffering – and what has all of my effort amounted to? A little piece of dirt here in the wilderness. I think, my friends, that this is the time for us to cast off our worldly concerns, accept our fate and contemplate the emptiness of our lives, the emptiness of all of our striving. Perhaps we will meet again and be wiser next time.

ROUSSEAU
He's not going to kill us, is he?

    PIERRE begins walking toward the Indian encampment.

Where are you going?

PIERRE
To meet eternity.

VOLTAIRE
Give it my regards.

ROUSSEAU

Sure you won't reconsider? (*He points at the back of his own head as if to say "right here."* PIERRE *refuses it.*) Calls us his friends but can't be bothered killing us.... What do you think death will be like?

VOLTAIRE

Have you ever been to Madame Dupin's salon?

ROUSSEAU

Do you think we'll be able to watch what goes on in the world after we're gone?

VOLTAIRE

I hope so. I've spent sixty years coming up with quotable sayings. I'd like to hear them quoted.

ROUSSEAU

What do you think will happen?

VOLTAIRE

I see the triumph of reason. Maybe not right away. But eventually. All over the world, people will stop fighting over religion – Catholic and Protestant, Christian and Muslim. I see Justice. Progress. Plenty. And I see big things for the Germans. If there's one thing I learned in Prussia from Frederick it's that the Germans will some day be the most rational, civilized, peaceful nation on earth. (*pause*) How about you?

ROUSSEAU

I see mankind living in communion with nature. No more will we pose and preen and seek to disguise our bodies and our souls. And once we have liberated ourselves from the shackles of an artificial society, we will celebrate the world as God created it. No longer will we foul our world with smoke and offal. The air and water and soil will again be as clean as in the Garden of Eden.

VOLTAIRE

It will be wonderful to watch.

ROUSSEAU

I won't even mind the pain.

Suddenly the drumming stops.

VOLTAIRE

That's it. They're attacking.

They hear a noise of someone approaching.

ROUSSEAU

Oh, Jesus and Mary protect me.

PIERRE limps back into camp.

A ghost! Oh God spare me this visitation.

VOLTAIRE slowly walks forward and touches PIERRE.

VOLTAIRE
You both look like you've seen a ghost.

PIERRE
The horror. The horror.

VOLTAIRE
Now that's a good line.

ROUSSEAU
What is it?

PIERRE
Smallpox. I saw the last man die at his drum.

ROUSSEAU
Don't look at me.

VOLTAIRE
I would look at you if it were *syphilis*. All that time they've been chasing us, they've been dying of smallpox.

PIERRE
Burning through them like a prairie fire. One by one.

Scene 11

The bank of a river. ROUSSEAU, VOLTAIRE and PIERRE are sprawled on the ground.

ROUSSEAU
For five days we were doing fine in the canoe. I actually thought we would make it home. But you, Voltaire, who ought to have studied the science of canoeing, you had to stand up and reach for one more bug.

VOLTAIRE
Insect. I told Denis I wanted to write the Entomology section of the Encyclopedia.

ROUSSEAU
No canoe. No food. No way out. Lost in the middle of the wilderness. We're right back where we were when he found us.

VOLTAIRE
We should have saved the seeds from that squash. We could have planted a garden.

ROUSSEAU
We never got a chance to test our theories on human nature and now we're going to starve.

VOLTAIRE
We should have tended our garden. *(pause)* Let me write that down.

ROUSSEAU
(ROUSSEAU searches through the bags of gear and produces VOLTAIRE's insect samples.) Your bugs!

VOLTAIRE
My insect specimens? All my specimens add up to less than a single lamb chop.

ROUSSEAU
When what we need is nice fat leg of mutton.

PIERRE
(delirious) We are all one.

ROUSSEAU
And with three mouths to feed…

VOLTAIRE
How is he?

ROUSSEAU
Worse.

VOLTAIRE
Doesn't look like pox. Probably still just his leg wound.

ROUSSEAU
A wound like that will likely prove fatal.

VOLTAIRE
It will be gangrenous soon if it isn't already.

PIERRE
All one flesh. One spirit.

VOLTAIRE
He's not going to make it.

ROUSSEAU
Unless we amputate.

VOLTAIRE
Excuse me, Dr. Rousseau, but I wouldn't trust you to remove a hang nail. He's dead either way.

ROUSSEAU
If only we could hold out a little longer. There are bound to be some traders along this river.

VOLTAIRE
I fear we've only got a few days ourselves.

ROUSSEAU
Unless we had another food source that could tide us over. Don't the traders head back to Quebec soon?

VOLTAIRE
But where will we get a food source?

ROUSSEAU looks at PIERRE.

No. No. Pierre? No.

ROUSSEAU
Not Pierre. Just his leg.

VOLTAIRE
His leg? Are you sure you don't mean his drumstick?

ROUSSEAU
You said yourself. He's dead either way. And maybe that's not the case. Maybe he'll recover enough to guide us out. He'll thank us.

VOLTAIRE
For eating his leg?

ROUSSEAU
For having the courage to face the unpleasant task head on.

PIERRE
You have lifted the scales from my eyes.

VOLTAIRE
Pardon me?

PIERRE
Now I am enlightened.

ROUSSEAU
Pierre? Pierre? Are you lucid?

PIERRE
Best of all possible worlds.

ROUSSEAU
Pierre. Your leg wound is becoming infected. Your only chance of survival is amputation.

PIERRE
Into your hands. I...

ROUSSEAU
You?

PIERRE
Into your hands I entrust my soul.

ROUSSEAU
That sounds like a yes to me.

VOLTAIRE
What do you care about consent? You're cannibalizing the man.

ROUSSEAU
Just hand me that tomahawk and shut your gob.

ROUSSEAU raises the tomahawk and the light goes out as the tomahawk comes down. We hear a thunk as the light goes out.

Scene 12

VOLTAIRE is sitting and reading. PIERRE is covered in blankets and moaning. ROUSSEAU is offstage, cooking.

ROUSSEAU
Just about ready.

VOLTAIRE
I'm so hungry I could eat a horse.

ROUSSEAU
You're French. You could always eat a horse.

ROUSSEAU comes on stage carrying what looks like a large leg of lamb.

VOLTAIRE
(takes a bite) Just needs a hint of garlic.

Scene 13

A little later in the season and a little colder. ROUSSEAU and VOLTAIRE are wrapped in blankets.

VOLTAIRE
That's the last of it.

ROUSSEAU
You aren't hiding any?

VOLTAIRE
Didn't last as long as we thought.

ROUSSEAU
I'm worried about the infection.

VOLTAIRE
What?

ROUSSEAU
I think it may spread to the other leg.

VOLTAIRE
You mean to say–

ROUSSEAU
Better no legs than no life…. He can get one of those carts…. Look there's a lot of food that's just going to be eaten by the ravens if we don't.

PIERRE
Two canoes. One paddling normal speed. One paddling the speed of light. What happens to time? *(pause)* A beaver. A beaver in a box. And you don't know, has the trap inside gone off yet and killed it? Is it live or dead? A principle of uncertainty.

ROUSSEAU
Listen to that. He's delirious.

VOLTAIRE
Either that or 150 years ahead of his time.

ROUSSEAU
Show me where to cut.

VOLTAIRE
Here. A little further up this time. We wasted a lot of good meat on the thigh.

PIERRE
What if space curves and time runs backwards? What if Newton doesn't work?

VOLTAIRE
See here. I'll have no disparaging Newton.

ROUSSEAU
Right. Mark the spot.

> *They hear drums: snare drums this time.*

Oh God. More savages.

VOLTAIRE
Ssh. Those aren't the savages. Those are military drums. British military drums.

ROUSSEAU
You're sure?

VOLTAIRE
You're the musicologist.

ROUSSEAU
I studied Italian opera.

> *VOLTAIRE sneaks closer and peeks.*

VOLTAIRE
British soldiers.

ROUSSEAU
What do we do?

VOLTAIRE
We give ourselves up. Better a British prison than starving here.

ROUSSEAU
What British prison? I'm not their enemy. I'm Swiss.

VOLTAIRE
You're always Swiss when it's convenient.

ROUSSEAU
And you're always a Citizen of the World when it's convenient. Well Citizen, go and speak to them. You must have learned English when you were in exile. Say we'll tell them everything we know for amnesty.

VOLTAIRE
We don't know anything.

ROUSSEAU
They don't know that.

VOLTAIRE
I'll be back. *(looks back)* I'd put down the tomahawk. The British have this thing about cannibalism. It's only permitted for their Polar explorers. But then it's compulsory.

VOLTAIRE exits.

PIERRE
Rousseau. I've been dreaming. I dreamed I was Jesus Christ at the Last Supper. Telling my disciples to eat of my flesh and drink of my blood. What do you think that means?

ROUSSEAU swallows hard.

I think it means that none of us die. Not really. Matter is neither created nor destroyed. After I am gone and the worms eat my flesh, I will still exist and perhaps some day I will again take a form that attains consciousness. So we are all Jesus. We are all resurrected and achieve eternal life through being devoured.

ROUSSEAU
Right...

PIERRE
The energy that is in us all originated in the same place at the same moment. It is all the same substance. We are not just Brothers, Rousseau. We are one flesh.

ROUSSEAU
In a manner of speaking...

PIERRE
I must thank you both. You have opened my eyes. I see things now I never could have imagined before. I owe it all to you and Voltaire.

ROUSSEAU
Rest, Pierre.

PIERRE goes back to sleep. ROUSSEAU starts to tidy up as if to clear up the evidence of his grisly deed. VOLTAIRE returns.

VOLTAIRE
Good news.

ROUSSEAU
They have food?

VOLTAIRE
Better still. They'll take us back and they won't even arrest us.

ROUSSEAU
No?

VOLTAIRE
I spoke to their captain and told him who we are. He knew all about us. He said we inflict more damage on the French Crown than all the ships of King George's navy. Gather your things.

ROUSSEAU
What about him?

VOLTAIRE
Do you really want to explain?

ROUSSEAU
Not really.

VOLTAIRE
Hurry up. They're on their way back to their colonies.

ROUSSEAU
I hope they feed us.

VOLTAIRE
Of course. But they *are* British. Expect something with kidneys and suet.

ROUSSEAU
You're sure we can't take a little something to go?

They exit.

PIERRE
Reason. Reason is a dead end. We know what is. But do we know what ought to be? Voltaire, I see your path. Your science of human nature will become a tool for those who would enslave and control. Without compassion what is the use of knowledge? Rousseau, your path leads to death and madness. Who would speak against reason but a madman? And I see the madmen you will inspire. Passion and hatred and blood and soil – these will govern your followers, Rousseau.... But what if there is a new Science. Newer than Newton. The universe is not a machine. Not clockwork. There is room in it for reason and for passion. It is order built on chaos. God loves the world even as he plays dice with it.... We must write this down. Voltaire, Rousseau, when we are back in Quebec you will finish teaching me to read and write. And together we will create a new science for a new world.... I am so lucky I met you both. I see so much more clearly now. I can rise above my old

superstitions and greed and fear and behold the world as it is and as it could be. I am so happy…. Come friends. Let me look at your faces once again.

Pause.

Friends?

Curtain.

The end.

The Invalids

a play in three acts

George Hunka

photo by Ryszard Hunka

GEORGE HUNKA lives in Winnipeg, Manitoba. Since graduating from the University of Manitoba, Mr. Hunka has worked for many years as a scenic artist for the Manitoba Theatre Centre, Prairie Theatre Exchange, Le Cercle Molière, and the Canadian Broadcasting Corporation, as well as numerous film and independent theatre productions. He has also worked as a photojournalist for Canadian Publishers. Mr. Hunka is currently a Marketing Manager for a manufacturer of theatrical lighting products. *The Invalids*, Mr. Hunka's first play, was written during a year-long sabbatical on travels through Europe. A second play titled *Sanctuary* was completed during another year-long tour of China, Southeast Asia and Europe.

Introduction to The Invalids
George Hunka

I wrote *The Invalids* while travelling through Europe for one year. The year in Europe gave me the time I needed to write but it also provided an opportunity to see plays all over the continent. For the most part *The Invalids* was written in Eastern Europe and the Balkans where the majority of my time was spent. I have always been interested in the plays of Kantor, Gombrowicz and Havel amongst others and it was the literature, theatre and films of Eastern Europe that had the greatest influence in shaping what I was writing. But it is not art as a political tool that I am most interested in here but art free of commercial constraints, exploring and ultimately challenging ideas about structure, substance and meaning. Stepping out of my own cultural environment and into a foreign and unfamiliar one, gave me another perspective on the place from which I came.

The Invalids is a black comedy set in a small cafe on three different evenings. The play is a triptych. Three actors play six characters. Two characters are patrons of the cafe and the third character is a waiter. Each act is a different evening with a new combination of characters at the table and a different waiter. Each patron of the cafe has an approximate double in one of the waiters. Gothard, a writer, becomes blind after witnessing an eclipse. As a result he can no longer write. The waiter Shmarr was born blind but acquired some vision as the result of a miracle. Shmarr wears an eye patch and has extreme difficulty functioning as a waiter with his limited vision. Vera, an actress and Gothard's lover discovers she is pregnant after Gothard leaves her and later dies during childbirth. The waitress Maria is in her final days of pregnancy and gives birth on stage while working an evening shift at the cafe. Gustav, a professor and playwright, limps and uses crutches for support in the second act and then a cane in the third. He has undergone surgery that was to enable him to walk normally. However not only was the surgery a failure but it actually worsened his condition. The waiter, Maximilian has one of his legs in a cast. He has broken his leg a few days ago and can barely walk yet insists on waiting tables. His situation is worsened when he tries to scratch under the cast with a kitchen knife which breaks at the handle. The blade becomes lodged inside his cast. As the same actor plays both characters in each situation there is a blurring of identity between the two and ultimately the meaning and function of the character is challenged.

Confusion is compounded within the play by certain situations that are ambiguous and ultimately unresolved. Are Vera and Gothard married or not? Who is the little girl next to Shmarr in the theatre? She resembles his daughter but it cannot be his daughter because his daughter is dead. In the third act when Maria tells us about her sister giving birth at her place of work and the baby being delivered by a janitor, is this the same person that Gothard is describing giving birth at his place of work in the first act? Is the little girl that Shmarr adopts after the death of his daughter Vera's child? Questions continually gnaw at the psyche. Reality is hard to grasp. The psychological environment of the stage becomes that of a hallucination or schizophrenic episode.

There is no particular time or place in which the play is set. The only indication that it is in the twentieth century (or later) is the electric light bulb over the table and the telephone backstage. The ambience and attitude of the play as well as the characters' names suggest central Europe in the last half of the twentieth century but I think the play can be placed just about anywhere.

Throughout the play comedy and disturbing imagery overlap. Humour and horror crash against each other with the suddenness of an automobile accident and the audience doesn't know whether to laugh or to gasp. There is talk of a subtly absurd world where the edges of the social fabric are gradually being frayed by disease and deformity. Something very dangerous is happening and children seem to be the main victims. They are born without limbs and necessary organs. They grow into grotesque freaks which cause havoc in school yards as observed by Vera after she discovers she is expecting a child. It's not possible to have children anymore, she desperately tells Gustav. Why this is happening is uncertain but the crisis seems to have a spiritual dimension as suggested by the mystical illnesses that Gustav speaks of in the second act. *The Invalids* ends with a faint sign of hope.

— • — Selected Bibliography — • —

Stage Plays – *Published*

• *The Invalids.* Germinal Stage, Denver, Colorado, USA 2001, Manitoba Theatre Projects, Winnipeg 2002.

> *The Invalids.* In *The West of All Possible Worlds: Six Contemporary Canadian Plays.* Ed. Moira Day. Toronto: Playwrights Canada Press, 2004.

Stage Plays – *Unpublished*

• *Sanctuary.* Typescript. 2004.

Periodicals

"Springtime in Auschwitz." *Outlook.* 1 November – December 15, 1997: 8, 28.

Reviews of *The Invalids*

Denver, Colorado, USA:
Bornstein, Lisa. "*Invalids* Amuses but Confounds." *Rocky Mountain News* 16 November 2001. 11D
Marlowe, David. "*The Invalids* A-." *Out Front.* 21 November 2001.
Moore, John. "Playwright Lives His Dream." *Denver Post* 2 December 2001.
Prokosh, Kevin. "Tina Has Been Jilted by Winnipegers." *Winnipeg Free Press* 6 November 2001: D6.
"Raucous Comedy at Germinal Stage." *House Review* [Germinal Stage].

Winnipeg, Manitoba, Canada:
Enright, Robert. "*The Invalids*: A Review by Robert Enright for CBC Radio (with Terry McLeod)." November, 2002.
Prokosh, Kevin. "Canadian Premiere by the Mystery Man of Winnipeg Theatre." *Winnipeg Free Press.* 29 October 2002: D7.
—-."*The Invalids* a Comical Trip into Absurdity." *Winnipeg Free Press* 1 November 2002: D8.
—-. "In Theatre." The Tabloid. *Winnipeg Free Press* 26 December 2002: 5.
Wilson, Jill. "Waiting for a Go: *The Invalids* Finally Finds Way to Winnipeg Stage." *Uptown* 31 October 2002: 5.
—-. "Playwright Paints it Black." *Uptown* 7 November 2002: 11.

The Invalids was first produced at Germinal Stage, Denver, Colorado, USA, in November 2001 with the following company:

Vera, Maria   Petra Ulrych
Gothard, Shmarr   David Quinn
Maximilian, Gustav   Michael Shalgoub

Director & Designer: Ed Baierlein
Costume Design: Sallie Diamond
Production Manager: Linda A. Barner

— • —

The Invalids was subsequently produced at Theatre Projects Manitoba in the Colin Jackson Studio Theatre, Winnipeg, Manitoba, in October 2002 with the following company:

Vera, Maria   Sharon Bajer
Gothard, Shmarr   Chris Sigurdson
Maximilian, Gustav   Ross McMillan

Director: Chris Gerrard-Pinker
Costume and Prop Design: Barbara Myrvold
Stage Manager: Sylvia Fisher

— • —

The Invalids was originally workshopped at Playwrights' Workshop Montreal in January 2000, directed by Peter Hinton with Danielle Desormeaux, Greg Kramer and Henri Gauthier.

It was translated into Polish by Miroslaw T. Maslowski in July 2003.

Characters

Gothard Frok
Vera Kreff
Gustav Broom
Maximilian: A waiter played by the same actor as Gustav.
Shmarr: A waiter played by the same actor as Gothard.
Maria: A waitress played by the same actress as Vera.

The Invalids
a play in three acts
by George Hunka

———— • ——— • ————

<hr>

ACT I

SCENE: Interior of a small cafe. A winter night. Enter VERA and GOTHARD. VERA is shivering.

VERA
It's dead! There's nobody here…. Why did we come here Got?

GOTHARD
Because it's quiet…. So we can talk.

VERA
You're a blast.

He shows her to a table and helps her off with her coat.

It's cold in here!

He hangs their coats on a coat rack and takes his chair. VERA slips off her shoes and rubs her feet together.

My feet are numb…. The cold always makes my feet numb…. It's my circulation. My veins are too thin.

GOTHARD
Maybe your blood is too thick?

VERA
I don't bleed when I cut myself. That's not normal is it?… Do you know those pills I take before I go to sleep?

GOTHARD
The blue ones?

VERA
The little yellow ones.

GOTHARD
The oval ones?

VERA
The round ones – they're for my circulation. *(searching through her purse)* They help me sleep better…. Are my feet cold in bed?

GOTHARD
Little icicles.

She finds a package of cigarettes and a lighter and puts a cigarette between her lips.

VERA
Sometimes when I get up in the morning… *(flicking the lighter without success)*
I can't feel my legs at all. *(flicking the lighter some more)* Blasted…

> *The cigarette falls from her lips. She replaces it and continues flicking the lighter.*

GOTHARD
I have a light.

> *He rummages around in his pocket and pulls out a pen, keys, a little crumpled napkin, and finally a pack of matches. He proceeds to light a match, however VERA succeeds in producing a flame on her lighter and lights her cigarette.*

(motioning with a lit match) En garde!

VERA
(blows out the match) Touche!

> *She reclines in her chair and savors the cigarette exhaling long great puffs of smoke until she is overcome by heavy coughing.*

GOTHARD
Are you alright?… Vera? *(She nods, still coughing.)* Should I slap your back? *(She shakes her head.)* Are you going to live?

VERA
(rasping) For now.

> *She stops coughing, clears her throat several times and resumes smoking. Meanwhile GOTHARD tries the pen on the napkin to see if it writes. It doesn't, so he gives it several forceful shakes and tries it again without success. He then sucks on the tip for a moment and shakes it even more forcefully.*

What are you doing?

GOTHARD
Nothing.

> *He scribbles wildly on the napkin and the pen begins to write. VERA laughs.*

What?

VERA
You have ink on your mouth.

GOTHARD
Where?

VERA
(pointing) There… on your lower lip.

GOTHARD
Where?

VERA
Here.

Chris
Sigurdson
(standing),
Ross
McMillan
(floor)

*photo by Chris
Gerrard-Pinker.
Courtesy of
Theatre Projects
Manitoba.*

*She finds a compact in her purse and hands it to him. He examines his mouth
in the compact mirror and proceeds to wipe his mouth with the napkin he had
scribbled on. Little pieces of the napkin crumble off and stick to his lips. He spits
them out.*

Whaa!... Don't spit that stuff on the table!

He continues spitting the crumbs onto the floor.

Does it taste good?

GOTHARD
Delicious.

VERA
What were you going to write?

GOTHARD
Huh?

VERA
What were you going to write... just now... on your napkin?

GOTHARD
Nothing.

VERA
I thought that maybe you had an inspiration… for a poem or something.

GOTHARD
I just wanted to see if this pen writes.

VERA
Well now at least you know that it writes on your face. Next time you have an inspiration you can write it on your face… or somewhere else on your body.

GOTHARD
Or on your body.

VERA
Well, if you're going to write on my body your poem will have to be about me.

He wraps his legs around hers under the table.

GOTHARD
I know where I could write a little poem.

VERA
Getting inspired are you? *(pulling her legs away)* I thought we just came here to talk.

GOTHARD
You're a blast.

VERA
Well this is an inspiring place.

GOTHARD
I'm glad you like it.

VERA
This is where you always meet Gustav?

GOTHARD
Sometimes.

VERA
Why?

GOTHARD
Why?

VERA
Why do you always come here?

GOTHARD
It's convenient.

VERA
Do you come here to write?

GOTHARD
No.

VERA
What do you do?

GOTHARD
We come here to talk.

VERA
What do you talk about?

GOTHARD
Nothing…. Anything…. Just talk.

VERA
And tonight you brought me here to… talk!… Is that right?

GOTHARD
I thought it might be nice.

VERA
Hmm…. This place is so small, I feel as if we should be talking in whispers.

GOTHARD
Why?

VERA
Because the waiter might hear us.

GOTHARD
Well then, if it makes you feel more comfortable, talk in a whisper.

She leans over to whisper to him. He turns his ear to her.

VERA
(*in a whisper*) You still have ink on your mouth. (*He wipes his mouth with his sleeve.*)
Here, allow me.

*She takes a napkin out of her purse and carefully wipes his lower lip. GOTHARD
playfully bites her finger. She yanks her finger back quickly, injuring it on his tooth.*

(*loudly*) Owww!

GOTHARD
Shhh!

VERA
You shhh! Oh… look, I'm bleeding!

GOTHARD
Let me see. (*He examines her finger.*) It's just a little scratch.

VERA
(*shouting*) But it hurts!

GOTHARD
There's no need to scream.

VERA
Maybe if somebody hears me we'll finally get some service! *(She applies a napkin to her injured finger.)* I wonder if anyone knows we're here?... Is there a waiter here or not? Maybe he's dead!... What kind of a place is this? It's cold... and dreary... and dead.... What is this, a morgue!

GOTHARD
Do you want to leave?... We can go somewhere else.

VERA
I don't want to go outside again.

GOTHARD
I can call a cab to take us home if you like.

VERA
Well that would really be a blast wouldn't it! You drag me to this sad little hole on the coldest night of the year, then you eat some ink, and a napkin, and part of my finger, and we sit around for a while, and then finally you decide that maybe this wasn't such a good idea after all!... You really are a blast you know! What do you do for an encore?

A loud thump is heard offstage followed by another, and another, etc. Enter MAXIMILIAN. His right leg is in a knee-high walking cast. There is a bandage on his chin, and his nose and forehead are scraped raw.

MAXIMILIAN
Gothard!

GOTHARD
(surprised) Max!

MAXIMILIAN
Gothard Frok!... I thought I heard your voice out here.

GOTHARD
Good God Max!

MAXIMILIAN
I'm sorry to keep you waiting so long. As you can see I'm at a little disadvantage tonight.... I had a little accident.

GOTHARD
A little accident!

MAXIMILIAN
Yes.... I broke my leg walking to work last week.

VERA
How awful!

MAXIMILIAN
I should say!

GOTHARD
Did you fall down a flight of stairs?

MAXIMILIAN
No, no, worse!… Much worse. Do you remember the rain storm last week?

GOTHARD
No.

MAXIMILIAN
The monsoon?

GOTHARD
No…. Maybe it was the day I stayed home from work.

MAXIMILIAN
Well if you did stay home from work it was a good day to do so because it was raining so hard that the streets were flowing with water like rivers! A knee-deep lake formed down at the end of the street by the cathedral. But I walked to work as I do every day. I never let a little rain stop me. My shoes were full of water and the bottoms of my pants were soaked and heavy when a gust of wind suddenly caught my umbrella. As I lurched forward to grab it, I lost my balance and my legs somehow tangled beneath me and I fell forward striking the pavement with my face.

VERA
Oh my!

MAXIMILIAN
I knocked myself out cold. I was lucky I didn't lose any teeth…. However I did bite off the tip of my tongue. See… *(sticks out his tongue)*

GOTHARD
What did you do?

MAXIMILIAN
I lay there like a worm in the rain, slipping in and out of consciousness, my leg broken, my nose broken, my face a bloody pulp, freezing water rushing through my clothes, my favourite umbrella blowing away out of sight. I couldn't do anything, I was helpless. All I could do was scream from the pain and scream for help!… So I screamed and I screamed!… And of course no one could hear me. The rain was like the roar of a waterfall, the streets were empty, there was no one around. There was no one to help me. And when I could scream no more I dug my fingernails into the cracks between the cobblestones and began to pull myself forward, dragging my broken leg behind me trying to find a friendly door to knock on, until I finally passed out from the pain and exhaustion.

GOTHARD
Good God!

MAXIMILIAN
I don't know how long I was unconscious, maybe a few minutes, maybe an hour, maybe all morning. When I regained consciousness, standing over me holding my umbrella, was an old Gypsy woman. I tried to tell her that my leg was broken and to go for help, but she just crossed herself and began to recite Hail Marys in a foreign language… and I just passed out again. The next thing I remember I was lying on a stretcher in the emergency ward at the General Hospital being undressed by a nurse.

GOTHARD
What an ordeal!

MAXIMILIAN
To be sure!

VERA
I would have died!

MAXIMILIAN
I almost did.

GOTHARD
Why are you working tonight Max? Why don't you stay home and let your injuries heal?

MAXIMILIAN
Who would look after the cafe?

GOTHARD
But how can you work – you have a broken leg!

MAXIMILIAN
My doctor said that for the kind of broken leg that I suffered, I can be in a walking cast. I can continue to work even with a broken leg. It will heal as long as it is kept absolutely straight.

GOTHARD
How long do you have to wear it?

MAXIMILIAN
I don't know, nine months, maybe ten.

GOTHARD
Ten months! I've never heard of a broken bone healing for so long.

MAXIMILIAN
Oh broken bones can take years to heal. My nose is broken, but it will probably heal much sooner. Fortunately it doesn't require a cast. I have noticed that it's bent slightly towards the left now.

GOTHARD
Where are your waiters Maria and Shmarr? You could ask one of them to work for you at least for a few days?

MAXIMILIAN
Oh of course I would if I could, but Maria is at home with the flu and Shmarr is on vacation in the mountains.

GOTHARD
Then why don't you just close the cafe for a while until you are well?

MAXIMILIAN
All my customers would go somewhere else. I can't afford to lose them. Once they're gone they're gone – I have to keep my cafe open…. I appreciate your concern Gothard, but I'm not being reckless. I know I look frightening to you right now but

these scrapes and bruises are just flesh wounds, that's all. Well except for the broken leg of course. But it's just a broken leg, it won't kill me. Look I am standing *(takes a few steps)* and I can walk. I can move around just fine in this cast and I can do the job of a waiter. And it's not really very busy this time of year. I just sit around waiting for someone to come in most of the time. I'm usually quite bored.

GOTHARD
How can you afford to stay open?

VERA
We're not going to run you around tonight.

MAXIMILIAN
Oh don't worry about me, I'm a fully functional waiter. I'm completely at your service.... By the way my name is Maximilian and I know that you are Gothard's lovely Vera whom I've heard so much about.

GOTHARD
Oh I'm sorry, I should have introduced you.... Vera this is my friend Maximilian, the owner of the cafe.

VERA
Pleased to meet you.

MAXIMILIAN
The pleasure is mine. *(He takes her hand and kisses it.)* Oh you've injured your finger.

VERA
Got bit me.

MAXIMILIAN
You know I've had the pleasure to see you on stage once.

VERA
Oh really!

MAXIMILIAN
Yes, last winter I think it was?

VERA
In what play? Was it in *The Wound*?

MAXIMILIAN
No I don't think it was *The Wound*.

VERA
Maybe it was in *The Coffin*?

MAXIMILIAN
Yes!... Yes it was *The Coffin*!

VERA
I had a very small part.

MAXIMILIAN
Oh but a very important part I remember.

VERA
The Coffin was a dreary little play, nobody understood it. I'm looking forward to performing in the leading role of a new play soon. A play that Gustav is writing.

MAXIMILIAN
Gustav is writing a new play – that's very exciting!

VERA
It's called *The Flesh Eaters*.

MAXIMILIAN
The Flesh Eaters – well I will have to make a point of seeing this new play now that I know the author and the leading actress. Are you involved in the play as well Gothard?

GOTHARD
I'm… inspiring the leading actress.

VERA
He's a flesh eater.

MAXIMILIAN
I know that you are a writer as well. I see your articles in the paper every day.

VERA
Got's written a novel!

MAXIMILIAN
You've written a novel – is that so!

GOTHARD
It's not really a novel. I don't know what to call it. It's…

VERA
It's stream of consciousness schizophrenia – that's what a publisher called it.

MAXIMILIAN
This is really very exciting! You know, there are so many artists frequenting my cafe now, it's really becoming an artists cafe!

VERA
(*putting a cigarette to her lips*) I guess the weather persuaded most of the artists to stay home this evening.

MAXIMILIAN
Most artists but not the two of you! I can always count on Gothard to drop in with a friend even on the most miserable evenings.

VERA
Got's a blast! (*trying the lighter again without success*) Where are your matches?

GOTHARD *begins to rummage around in his pocket for matches.*

MAXIMILIAN
Here allow me.

> *MAXIMILIAN produces a fancy lighter from his apron and lights VERA's cigarette.*

VERA
Thank you.

MAXIMILIAN
You're welcome.

VERA
I need a new lighter.

GOTHARD
Here... *(handing her the matches)* use these for now.

VERA
Thank you.... Here's a present for you.

> *She gives GOTHARD the lighter. He tries it and it lights.*

GOTHARD
It works.

VERA
Not for me.

MAXIMILIAN
Where is Gustav tonight?

GOTHARD
In the hospital.

MAXIMILIAN
Oh, is he not well?

GOTHARD
He had surgery yesterday, on his hip, to correct that limp of his that's been plaguing him all of his life.

VERA
If it's successful he may not have to use a cane to walk.

GOTHARD
We paid him a visit tonight and then we came by here.

MAXIMILIAN
How is he feeling?

GOTHARD
He seems to be in good spirits although I could see that he was in considerable pain. The operation was a rather complicated procedure.

VERA
Twenty-seven hours on the cutting table.

GOTHARD
His surgeon fainted from exhaustion in the nineteenth hour.

VERA
He had to take a little nap before resuming the surgery.

GOTHARD
He's been postponing this operation for years but I think he finally decided to have it performed while he's still young…. Well you can't call him young any more – but it only becomes more difficult with age.

MAXIMILIAN
Poor Gustav.

GOTHARD
He'll be in the hospital for a couple of weeks and then homebound for several months. I don't think he will be able to do anything for himself. I guess he'll have to get a housekeeper to take care of him. He certainly won't be teaching at the university this winter. At least he'll have time to write his plays and read his dusty old books. I'm sure he's looking forward to that.

MAXIMILIAN
I should pay him a visit, but looking like this I would probably frighten him.

VERA
How is your leg feeling?

MAXIMILIAN
My leg feels fine; I have very little discomfort from the break. My good leg is in more pain than my broken one because I'm transferring all my weight to it. However I am experiencing an insufferable itching under the cast. I'm not aware of it when I'm occupied with serving customers, but when I'm just sitting around doing nothing it begins to burn holes into my skin.

GOTHARD
Pour some spirits on it.

MAXIMILIAN
I poured a whole bottle of vodka on it and it didn't help. And then I tried to scratch down there with a kitchen knife which ended up breaking at the handle and slipping down inside the cast. When I heard you come in I was standing on my head trying to get the knife blade to slide out.

GOTHARD
Did you get it out?

MAXIMILIAN
It's wedged in as tight as a nail.

GOTHARD
What are you going to do?

MAXIMILIAN
I guess I'll have to buy a new kitchen knife.

VERA
Is it uncomfortable?

MAXIMILIAN
Only when I walk.

VERA
You poor man! Why don't you pull up a chair and sit down with us?

MAXIMILIAN
No I'm afraid I can't do that.

VERA
Why not?

MAXIMILIAN
Because I'm the waiter.

VERA
But you have a broken leg – with a knife stuck in it! You shouldn't be walking around at all. Here allow me. *(pulling up a chair from the other table)* Sit down right here. *(putting her hands on his shoulders)* Come on sit down. *(He sits down.)* There isn't that better?

MAXIMILIAN
But now there is no waiter.

VERA
Got will be the waiter.

MAXIMILIAN
But this isn't fair to Gothard.

VERA
Would you be so kind Got?

GOTHARD
I guess I'm elected. *(He begins to get up.)*

MAXIMILIAN
Hold on Gothard! I'm sure you didn't come in here this evening to wait on the waiter…. And what if someone else comes in. I can't expect you to wait on a customer.

VERA
I don't think anyone's going to come in tonight.

MAXIMILIAN
But I'm afraid this arrangement isn't acceptable. *(getting up and replacing the chair)* Because I am the waiter and you are my customers, and it's my job to wait on you. Not the other way around.

VERA
But what about your leg?

MAXIMILIAN
Don't worry about my leg. I am your waiter, there is no other waiter…. So let me do my job. Tell me what can I bring you this evening?

GOTHARD
Are you sure Max?

MAXIMILIAN
I'm sure Gothard. Now tell me what you would like? Would you like a bottle of wine?

GOTHARD
We'll have a bottle of red wine, but just show me where it is and I'll get the glasses and pour it.

MAXIMILIAN
Not another word Gothard! A bottle of red wine coming right up.

Exit MAXIMILIAN hobbling and thumping.

VERA
What a blast!

GOTHARD
Max?

VERA
A waiter with a broken leg!

GOTHARD
Waiters shouldn't have broken legs.

VERA
He should have sat down with us.

GOTHARD
How could you ask him to do that and elect me the waiter?

VERA
I'm sure you would have made a charming waiter.

GOTHARD
And I'm sure Max would have been charming company for you.

VERA
I'm sure he would…. There's something about a man with a limp that I find sort of attractive.

GOTHARD
Maybe I'll just call him back for you?

VERA
Go ahead.

GOTHARD
Max!

VERA
Don't be a twit!

GOTHARD
Don't you find his limping attractive?

VERA
You'll be limping in a moment.

GOTHARD
Do you find Gustav's limping attractive?

VERA
Piss off!

VERA collects her purse and rises from her chair hobbling, her right leg is lifeless.

GOTHARD
Where are you going?

He springs from his chair and grabs her by the arms.

I'm sorry.

He embraces her tightly, kissing her on the cheek.

VERA
Okay, okay.... You're salivating on my face.

GOTHARD
Please sit down.

VERA
I just got up to go to the washroom and you attack me.

GOTHARD
I'm sorry.... I thought you were running off.

VERA
My leg's dead, I have to sit down. (*They both return to their seats.*) I have to take my tablets.

GOTHARD
The ones that make you sleep?

VERA
The ones for my circulation.

GOTHARD
Do you want me to rub your calves?

He kneels down in front of her and begins to rub the underside of her right calf.

VERA
Got.... What are you doing?... Got.... Not in here.... Max will see us!

GOTHARD
What's to see?

VERA
Got stop!

He takes off her shoe and begins to rub her foot.

Oh… that feels so good.

He rubs her foot for a while and then starts to work his way up to her thigh. VERA is sighing deeply.

Oh Got…

He begins to rub his lips up and down her thigh.

Got no!

He ignores her and presses his lips high against her thigh.

Got please stop!

She puts her foot on his chest and gives him a forceful thrust that sends him sprawling onto his back.

Stop!

She collects her purse and rushes off towards the washroom. Halfway downstage she stops and returns for her shoe, puts it on, and exits to the washroom. A loud thump is heard offstage followed by another and another, etc. Enter MAXIMILIAN. He is carrying a tray with two glasses and a bottle of red wine.

MAXIMILIAN
Gothard?… Where are you?… *(sees GOTHARD on the floor)* Oh there you are. Are the chairs not comfortable Gothard?

GOTHARD
The chairs are fine Max.

He returns to his chair. MAXIMILIAN begins to open the wine.

MAXIMILIAN
Are you going to be alone tonight Gothard?

GOTHARD
Vera just stepped into the little room for a moment.

MAXIMILIAN begins to pour the wine.

MAXIMILIAN
We are in luck tonight! This is the last bottle of red wine on the ra… *(in sudden agony)* Arrrgh!

He spills a little wine on the table as he cringes in pain.

GOTHARD
What's wrong Max?

MAXIMILIAN
That knife blade inside my cast is digging into my foo… *(in agony)* Arrrgh!

Cringing in pain he puts down the wine and grabs his cast.

One moment please Gothard.

He lies down on his back and shakes his leg in the air trying to dislodge the knife blade.

Gothard could you tap on my cast please. *(GOTHARD taps on the side of his cast.)* Tap on the foot Gothard. *(GOTHARD taps the foot.)* A little harder. *(GOTHARD taps the cast more forcefully.)* Arrrgh!

Screaming MAXIMILIAN crumples in agony on the floor clutching his cast.

GOTHARD
Oh my God Max!… Are you alright?… I'm going to call an ambulance!

MAXIMILIAN
(writhing in pain on the floor) No, no!… I'm okay – I'm fine.

GOTHARD
Can I help you up?… Here let me help you. *(helps MAXIMILIAN to his feet)*

MAXIMILIAN
Thank you Gothard.

GOTHARD
You really should go to the hospital.

MAXIMILIAN
There's no need to overreact Gothard.

GOTHARD
I think I should call you a cab right now.

MAXIMILIAN
Nonsense Gothard, sit down and let me finish pouring the wine.

GOTHARD
Max…

MAXIMILIAN
Not another word Gothard. Please sit down.

GOTHARD resumes his chair and MAXIMILIAN continues pouring the wine.

Oh my, I've spilled some wine on the tablecloth. I'll get you a fresh one from the…

GOTHARD
Max, don't worry about the tablecloth.

MAXIMILIAN
But I've ruined it.

GOTHARD
The tablecloth is fine.

MAXIMILIAN
The tablecloth is not fine!

GOTHARD
Max…

Enter VERA.

VERA
You put a run in my stocking with your stupid… *(sees MAXIMILIAN)* Maximilian!

MAXIMILIAN
The wine is served!

VERA
(taking her chair) Thank you Max.

MAXIMILIAN
I hope that you can forgive me for my frightening appearance and awkward predicament this evening.

VERA
There's no need to apologize for anything Maximilian. Everything is just fine.

GOTHARD
And you should really go sit down and relax Max.

VERA
Yes, go and rest for a while.

MAXIMILIAN
You're so kind, but you know I've been resting all evening. No one has been in this evening except the two of you. I just sit around reading a silly book and trying to scratch inside my cast with various kitchen utensils. This is what got me into trouble in the first place. This afternoon however…. This afternoon was another story. I had no time to think about scratching. I was rushing around all over the place. I had a blind man come in. Do you remember him Gothard? He comes in every once in a while and sits over there. *(pointing to the other table)* Of course being blind he demands a lot of attention. I have to hang up his coat; show him to his chair; show him to the washroom; show him back to his chair and so forth. It's a great deal of running around for me. Before him I had a customer in a wheelchair; a quadriplegic who couldn't even feed himself. What am I to do with a customer like that? After him I had a real treat – someone vomited on the floor…. And then…. And then of course there's the one-legged boy who's always hanging around begging for food. I gave him a piece of dry bread and shooed him away. In two hours he was back again. If I spoil him by giving him a crumb every time he comes to the door he'll end up living here. And yesterday… yesterday a starving dog wandered in. I had to chase him around for forty-five minutes before I was able to get him out. I finally lured him out with a piece of pastry. He was hanging around outside the door again today. He attacked the blind man when he was leaving and tore his coat. Again I had to lure the dog away with a piece of pastry or he would have devoured the blind man. If he's still hanging around tomorrow maybe I'll take him home with me. So you see I had a busy afternoon but a very slow evening. I'm glad that at least the two of you dropped in. It's very boring for me when there is nothing to do. Now I am going to the kitchen to see if I can remove the knife blade from my cast. You enjoy yourselves and if I can get you anything else later don't hesitate to call me.

GOTHARD
Thank you very much Maximilian.

VERA
We really appreciate your hospitality.

MAXIMILIAN
Enjoy!

MAXIMILIAN begins to exit hobbling and thumping. He is almost offstage when VERA calls after him.

VERA
Oh Maximilian… *(He stops and turns.)* Do you have a candle you could bring us?

MAXIMILIAN
Of course, there's one in the kitchen, I'll bring it right away!

GOTHARD
(rising) I'll get the candle.

MAXIMILIAN
Gothard!… You stay where you are. I will bring the candle.

Exit MAXIMILIAN hobbling and thumping.

GOTHARD
Vera…

VERA
It's nice to have a candle at the table don't you think. I can light my cigarettes from it.

GOTHARD
I don't want to cause him any more unnecessary running around.

VERA
I see that you've messed up the tablecloth already.

GOTHARD
Yes Vera I've messed up the tablecloth.

A loud thump is heard offstage followed by another, and another, etc. Enter MAXIMILIAN carrying a candle and a tablecloth.

Max you don't have to change the tablecloth.

MAXIMILIAN
Nonsense, I spilled wine on it and I'm going to change it. How can I expect you to sit at a table with a dirty tablecloth?

He begins to clear the table and place the wine and glasses etc. on the other table. GOTHARD makes an attempt to help him.

Gothard you stay planted! How many times do I have to tell you that? I can do my jo… *(cringing in pain)*

VERA
Are you alright?

GOTHARD
(getting up) Let me...

MAXIMILIAN
Gothard if you get up again I'm going to hit you.

> He begins to spread the new tablecloth and cringes in pain again. GOTHARD
> ignores his threats and helps him reset the table.

VERA
Maximilian what's wrong?

GOTHARD
The knife blade that's lodged in his cast is digging into his foot.

VERA
My God Max you should sit down!

MAXIMILIAN
I'm fine, really.... Now I'm just going to light the candle.

> He takes the lighter from his apron and flicks it several times without success.

GOTHARD
Oh for.... We'll light the candle Max. Let me help you to the kitchen. (attempts to
take MAXIMILIAN by the arm)

MAXIMILIAN
You really want me to hit you don't you? I can get to the kitchen by myself just fine.

> He begins to exit hobbling and thumping and then realizes that the dirty tablecloth
> is draped over the chair of the other table so he begins to return for it.

GOTHARD
What now?

> He realizes that MAXIMILIAN is returning for the tablecloth so he reaches for it
> and hands it to him.

MAXIMILIAN
Thank you Gothard.

> He begins to exit again hobbling and thumping in excruciating pain.

VERA
Help him Got.

> GOTHARD attempts to help him again. MAXIMILIAN puts up his fists.

MAXIMILIAN
I'm going to hit you if you don't sit down right away.

> Exit MAXIMILIAN hobbling and thumping in excruciating pain.

GOTHARD
What a stubborn gimp.

> *VERA tries to light another cigarette with the matches that GOTHARD gave her. She strikes a match several times without success. GOTHARD produces a flame on the lighter that VERA gave him and lights her cigarette and then the candle. VERA inhales and then begins to cough heavily. She searches her purse hacking and coughing.*

What are you looking for?

> *VERA pulls a little vial from her purse and shakes out two tablets. She pops them into her mouth and washes them down with a swig of wine.*

VERA
Blast!

GOTHARD
What?

VERA
(holding the vial in front of her eyes) Wrong tablets. *(looking in her purse for another vial)* Maybe I left them in – here they are.

> *She shakes out two tablets out of the second vial, pops them into her mouth and washes them down with another swig of wine. She then reclines in her chair and stretches out her legs, flexing her feet.*

GOTHARD
Can you feel your feeties now?

VERA
My pinkies are still numb.

GOTHARD
I'll rub some life into them.

VERA
You know you put a run in my stocking with your stupid claws. *(She shows him her left thigh.)* See.

GOTHARD
Where?

VERA
Here.

GOTHARD
I don't see anything, and by the way that's the wrong leg my dear. *(She searches her other thigh.)* Put your footsie up here *(slapping his knee)* and I'll revive your pretty little pinkies.

VERA
I have a better idea, this is what's going to revive my pinkies. *(picking up her glass)* Cheers! *(She takes a sip.)* Wine always goes straight to my toes. *(wiggling her toes)* See, the colour's coming back to my toes already. *(takes another sip)* My toes love red

wine. *(takes another sip and flutters her feet in the air)* My legs love red wine too. *(takes another sip and bounces up and down)* My boom boom loves red wine. All of me loves red wine! Do you love red wine?

GOTHARD
I love you.

VERA
Why aren't you drinking? Don't you like the wine?

GOTHARD
The wine is fine.

VERA
You haven't even tried it yet.

GOTHARD
It's the same wine I have every time.

VERA
Then cheers! *(She lifts her glass.)* Come on cheers! *(They clink glasses.)*

GOTHARD
Do you know what just occurred to me?… Do you know what tomorrow is?

VERA
Tuesday.

GOTHARD
Our anniversary.

VERA
What anniversary?

GOTHARD
The anniversary of our first time.

VERA
It wasn't on a Tuesday.

GOTHARD
No, it was on a weekend.

VERA
Wasn't it Christmas or something?

GOTHARD
It was my birthday.

VERA
Oh yes, I remember the green cake.

GOTHARD
Isn't it seven years now?

VERA
Six.

GOTHARD
We should be married.

VERA
We are married.

GOTHARD
Not really.

VERA
Really enough.

GOTHARD
But we're not married. We just sort of happened together when you moved in. We've never really…. We've never…

VERA
…had a little ceremony?

GOTHARD
Yes, we've never really had a little ceremony.

VERA
Well maybe we can have a little ceremony right now if you want…. Let's see um… what are some good wedding ceremony words? I know!… Do you Gothard Frok take me Vera Kreff to be your lawfully wedded wife; to have and to hold, to cherish and obey, for better or for worse and all that wonderful stuff?… Say I do…. Come on say I do.

GOTHARD
I do.

VERA
And do I Vera Krok take you Gothard Freff to be my lawfully wedded husband for all the same good and noble reasons?… I do! I hereby join us in… holy matri… mony! I pronounce us man and wife. (*making the sign of the cross with her wine glass*) In the name of the Father, Son, and HHHoly Ghost, Amen. (*She takes a hefty swig.*) You can now kiss the bride.

GOTHARD
Thank you Vera, we should have done this years ago.

VERA
Aren't you going to kiss the bride? (*extending her lips to him*) Come on, your new bride is waiting for a kiss! (*He leans over and kisses her.*) There we go, now we're married just like you wanted, husband and wife. We're a family – a happy little family…. Well, almost. All that's missing are the babies. But they haven't been born yet. We'll have to make at least one baby. We're not really a family without a baby. We're just a husband and wife…. Would you like to make a baby Got? We can't be a family without a baby. Don't you want a little baby? A cute little baby-waby, with a cute little nose and ten little fingers and ten little toes…

GOTHARD
And three little eyes with a horn on its nose.

VERA
I know you don't want a baby at all. You hate babies.

GOTHARD
I don't hate babies.

VERA
Yes you do!

GOTHARD
No I don't.

VERA
I know you do.

GOTHARD
I don't hate babies!

VERA
Then why don't you want one?

GOTHARD
Because I just don't.

VERA
What if I want to have a baby?

GOTHARD
You don't want a baby. You just want to get my goat.

VERA
Maybe someday I will.

GOTHARD
What would we do with a baby?

VERA
(facetiously) Eat it.

GOTHARD
We'd never be able to do anything.

VERA
We don't do anything as it is.

GOTHARD
But we still can. Don't you want to travel? Don't you want to see the world? We've never been to Africa or the far east. We've never seen a pyramid or swam in a tropical ocean. We've never even seen a Greek island…. We still have the whole world to see. Just think of all the things that we can do…. We could buy a couple of horses in Ulan Bator and ride them across Siberia to Baku. We'd never be able to do that with a baby. I want to see the world before we start thinking about children…. And things are different now.

VERA
What's different?

GOTHARD
There's too much risk involved.

VERA
In travelling?

GOTHARD
In having babies.

VERA
What risk?

GOTHARD
The risk involved in having a child.

VERA
What are you talking about?

GOTHARD
There's so many abnormal children born now…. Did you see the child in the wheelchair at the hospital this evening?

VERA
No.

GOTHARD
In the elevator.

VERA
No.

GOTHARD
With the nun.

VERA
I saw a nun.

GOTHARD
You didn't see the child in the wheelchair?

VERA
No.

GOTHARD
Because you didn't know it was a child…. I didn't know it was human until it made a sound.

VERA
Why are you telling me this?

GOTHARD
I almost never see a normal child anymore.

VERA
What are you talking about? There's lots of normal children everywhere.

GOTHARD
Walk by a school yard and see for yourself.

VERA
See what?

GOTHARD
See what the children are like. You'll see that I'm right.

VERA
That's a bunch of crap.

GOTHARD
It's not crap, it's true. In the last few years so many of my acquaintances have had... sick children.

VERA
Who?

GOTHARD
Gustav's sister – she had a still birth two years ago.

VERA
Isn't she extremely old?

GOTHARD
Not really – mid-fifties.

VERA
Well I'm not surprised that a woman in her mid-fifties might have a still birth.

GOTHARD
It was worse than a simple still birth. The baby was born without any muscle or skin over its abdomen. It emerged from its mother minus its vital organs which spilled out inside her womb.

VERA
Are you still proposing to me by the way?

GOTHARD
It's happening all the time now. Still births and deformities are becoming more and more common. Every time I hear that someone had a baby.... Last year a woman at the office went into sudden labour several weeks premature and delivered on the floor into the trembling hands of the janitor as we all stood around and watched.... Do you remember when I told you about that?

VERA
No.

GOTHARD
She gave birth to a baby girl.... A baby girl with no eyes... or eye sockets. Her face was flat from the forehead to the cheeks.

VERA
Baby-hater.

GOTHARD
We ran an article in the paper recently about a doctor who claims that the way a baby cries is an indication of its mental health. A normal baby cries in even rising and falling tones: Whaaaaa, whaaaaa, whaaaaa…. like that. A brain-damaged baby shrieks like a little pig. When we walked through the maternity ward on our way out, do you remember how the babies sounded?

VERA
Babies shriek when you don't change their diapers; they shriek when they're hungry; they shriek when you step on them.

GOTHARD
I'm just saying that according to this doctor, brain-damaged babies shriek instead of cry.

VERA
Did you happen to notice that there were no nurses on that ward? Those babies had empty stomachs and full diapers, that's what was wrong with them.

GOTHARD
By the way, do you remember the doctor I said hello to in the hallway on Gustav's ward?

VERA
The one with the bloody smock?

GOTHARD
No the other one, the bald one with the bump on his forehead. That was Gustav's doctor – Doctor Klott, the one who fainted during surgery. He's the father of a little hermaphrodite. It's neither a boy nor a girl. And Shmarr the other waiter that works here – his daughter has no brain…. And do you recall the little boy we see in the basement all the time? The one who's always getting into our laundry basket. Have you ever noticed the conspicuous absence of fingers on his hands?

VERA
Oh shut up already!

GOTHARD
That's why I don't want children.

VERA
What do you want?

GOTHARD
A wife.

VERA
You don't want a wife.

GOTHARD
What do I want then?

VERA
If you want a wife I can get out of your way.

GOTHARD
That's very considerate of you Vera.

VERA
You're so unrealistic Got.

GOTHARD
About what?

VERA
About us. Don't you see that by now?

GOTHARD
Yes…. Yes I do.

VERA
Good. *(She fills her wine glass.)* You're so full of crazy ideas all the time…. We're out of wine by the way. *(shouting)* Gustav!

GOTHARD
What are you doing?

VERA
Gustav!

GOTHARD
Are you losing your mind my dear?

VERA
Oh…. I'm drunk. I mean Max. *(shouting)* Max!

GOTHARD
What do you need Max for?

VERA
I want another bottle of wine. *(shouting)* Max!

GOTHARD
Why don't I get you some coffee.

VERA
Wine! *(shouting)* Max!

GOTHARD
Okay – okay Vera, let's not disturb Max. I'll get another bottle of wine.

VERA
Red!

GOTHARD
Red.

> Exit GOTHARD. VERA gulps down half of his wine. She then pulls up her skirt and begins to search both thighs for the run in her stocking. Next she searches her purse until she finds a nail file with which she makes a run in her stocking. Enter GOTHARD carrying a bottle of red wine.

VERA
That's a different wine.

GOTHARD
(*scratching at the seal*) It's the same wine my dear.

VERA
You're a different waiter.

GOTHARD
Yes, I am a different waiter. Could you pass me that nail file?

> *She hands him the nail file which he uses to remove the seal.*

VERA
Do you want to kiss my legs?

GOTHARD
I'm busy right now dear.

> *He tries to push the cork into the bottle with his thumb.*

VERA
What are you doing?

GOTHARD
I'm trying to push the cork into the bottle.

VERA
Why?

GOTHARD
To open the bottle.

VERA
Why don't you use a corkscrew?

GOTHARD
(*frustrated*) I couldn't find one.

> *He starts to dig the cork out with the nail file scattering cork crumbs all over the table.*

VERA
You're making a big mess.

> *Using the back of his pen GOTHARD tries forcing the cork into the bottle again and succeeds. Wine gushes from the bottle.*

GOTHARD
Shit!

VERA
You're a blast. You've spoiled our tablecloth again. What kind of a waiter are you?

GOTHARD
(*pouring the wine*) The only available waiter my dear…. Cheers! (*They both take a sip.*)

VERA
(spitting) There's cork crumbs in my glass! You filled my glass first and poured all the cork crumbs into it. I want your glass.

She takes his glass and gives him hers.

Blah! *(spitting)* There's crumbs in your glass too!

She gives back his glass and takes hers. They both pick the crumbs out of their glasses. GOTHARD wipes off his pen and tries it out on his napkin to see if it writes.

What are you writing?

GOTHARD
A little poem.

VERA
About what?

GOTHARD
About you my dear.

VERA
How wonderful! *(He puts down his pen.)* What?... Is that all? Why did you stop writing?

GOTHARD
I'm finished.

VERA
Let me see. *(snatching the napkin from him)* It's just a scribble. This is your poem about me? I'm insulted! It looks like you were just testing out your pen.

GOTHARD
It writes.

VERA
You're not a writer you're a pen tester.

GOTHARD
A ten pester.

VERA
All that time you spend at your desk working on your stupid manuscript – you're just testing out your pen. Isn't that so?

GOTHARD
It isn't so.

VERA
Your whole career as a writer has been testing out your pen. You could publish a book of pen test scribbles.

GOTHARD
I'm going to. I found a publisher who is interested in my pen test scribbles.

VERA
The one who called it stream of consciousness schizophrenia?

GOTHARD
The one who thought it was brilliant.

VERA
You could title it *The Brilliant Memoirs Of The Only Available Waiter*.

GOTHARD
I'm a successful waiter.

VERA
I can tell by the way you served the wine.

GOTHARD
(correcting himself) I mean writer.

VERA
You are a waiter – writer.

GOTHARD
I make a good living writing.

VERA
You're a proofreader – waiter – writer.

GOTHARD
I'm an assistant editor for a major newspaper.

VERA
A glorified proofreader!

GOTHARD
I write a variety column.

VERA
You write muffin recipes.

GOTHARD
I have no idea how to make muffins Vera.

VERA
Muffin man!

GOTHARD
I think I have a good job, don't you?… Of course I aspire to something greater.

VERA
A greater – waiter – writer…

GOTHARD
Just like yourself as an actress.

VERA
…baby hater – alligator!

GOTHARD
You're an alligator.

VERA
Refrigerator.

GOTHARD
Menstruater!

VERA
Masturbator!

GOTHARD
You fancy yourself an actress.

VERA
Mattress.

GOTHARD
But all you've had is three little bit parts.

VERA
I've had seven parts!

GOTHARD
In amateur productions.

VERA
Five were professional!

GOTHARD
You're a mattress without a part.

VERA
Did you just blow a fart?

GOTHARD
Yes – yes I did. *(picking up the wine bottle)* Would you like some more wine my dear?

VERA
Please.

    He pours her some wine. She gulps down a mouthful.

GOTHARD
You're lucky...

VERA
Pukey pucky!

GOTHARD
...to have a greater – waiter – writer...

VERA
Baby-hater.

GOTHARD
...to fall back on.

VERA
To throw up on.

GOTHARD
(angry) Knock it off already Vera!

VERA
Oh…. I see…. I see it now!

GOTHARD
What?

VERA
I see what's happening here.

GOTHARD
What's happening?

VERA
You are a muffin man!… Do you think I need you to fall back on? I'm not falling. Do you want me to start pulling my own weight now?… Do you want me to start pulling my own weight, is that it?… Because I don't want to get married?

GOTHARD
I didn't say that!

VERA
(loudly) But that's what you're implying!

GOTHARD
No I'm not!

VERA
Yes you are!… Do you want half the rent?

GOTHARD
Don't be silly!

VERA
I'll give you half the rent.

> *Takes money from her purse and throws it at him.*

GOTHARD
Thank you Vera.

VERA
(shouting) You're a farting little muffin man!

GOTHARD
Please lower your voice Vera.

VERA
(shouting) You're a worm!

GOTHARD
Very good Vera – I'm a worm.

VERA
(*shouting*) You're a maggot!

> *She collects her purse, rises out of her chair and knocks over the empty wine bottle. GOTHARD catches it.*

Stick that up your muffin ass!

> *She begins to stagger towards the door. GOTHARD springs from his chair and grabs her by the shoulder.*

GOTHARD
Vera!

VERA
Let me go!

GOTHARD
Where?

VERA
(*struggling*) Anywhere…. Let me go!

GOTHARD
If you run out there you'll freeze to death in a snow drift or that crazy dog will maul you.

VERA
Let go!

GOTHARD
I'm not going to let you run outside.

VERA
I want to move out!

GOTHARD
You don't want to move out.

VERA
(*still struggling*) Yes I do!

GOTHARD
No you don't…. Listen to me Vera…. I wasn't…. Hold still and listen to me! (*She complies.*) I wasn't…. I wasn't implying that I want you to pull your own weight. I don't want half the rent. I don't want your money. I don't know how you got words twisted around to make you think that. I don't need your money. You don't cost me anything anyways…. I have to pay the rent whether you're there or not. I don't know what to do with the money that I have…. I want you…. (*kisses her on the forehead*) You know that… don't you…. Will you sit down?… Please sit down…. Alright?

VERA
(*struggling*) No!

GOTHARD
Vera please!… Stop making a scene…. I'll call a cab to take us home…. Okay?

VERA
Go home, I'll stay here.

She sits down and immediately swigs down the contents of her glass and pours herself another one. She lights a cigarette on the candle, inhales deeply and starts coughing heavily.

GOTHARD
Are you alright?

VERA
No.

GOTHARD
Do you want some coffee? *(She doesn't reply.)* I'll get you some coffee.

VERA
I don't want any coffee.

GOTHARD picks up the scattered money, places it in a little pile before her and pours himself some more wine.

GOTHARD
I've been thinking.... I've been thinking about... leaving.... I want to leave my job at the paper. *(The lights flicker.)* I've been thinking about leaving... *(The lights flicker again.)* for a long time.... I want to leave my jo... *(The lights go out leaving only the candle burning.)* What now? *(VERA blows out the candle.)* What did you do that for?

VERA
I don't want to see you.

After a long pause the lights come back on.

GOTHARD
I want to leave my job at the paper...

VERA
You said that already.

GOTHARD
I want to go away.... I want to travel.... I've saved some money... *(The lights flicker.)* I want to go to Nepal... or Mongolia. *(pause)* I could support myself writing travel articles. *(pause)* I want to go travelling so that I can finish writing my book.

VERA
See you in Katmandu!

GOTHARD
I have to get away because I'll never finish writing my book here. There are too many distractions.

VERA
Like me.

GOTHARD
I want to give my notice at the office in the next few weeks. *(pause)* I'm going to apply for a passport.

VERA
I've changed my mind Got – I want to get married.

GOTHARD
We'll have to give up the apartment.

VERA
We can get married in Bombay!

GOTHARD
I'll have to store my things somewhere.

VERA
We can honeymoon in the Himalayas! We'll climb K-2! We'll ride a Llama to Tibet and live like ascetics in caves with Buddhist monks eating only rice and meditating all day long, won't that be a blast!

GOTHARD
Maybe I can store my things with Gustav?

VERA
Why didn't we think of this before! We'll travel all over the world! They'll make a movie about us!

> *A horrific scream is heard from MAXIMILIAN offstage.*

GOTHARD
Good God!… What has he done to himself now? *(shouting)* Max!… I'd better go check on him.

> *Exit GOTHARD. VERA blows a few long puffs of smoke, butts out her cigarette and swigs down the last of the wine from her glass. She then collects her things, slowly puts on her coat and casually walks out the door. Long pause. Enter GOTHARD. He rushes into the room in a panic.*

Call an ambulance! Where's the phone? *(sees that VERA is not in the room)* Vera? *(rushes into the washroom)* Vera!… Vera!

> *Discovering that she is not there, he dashes out the front door to look for her.*

(shouting) Vera!… Vera!… Veeerrraaaaa!

> *Enter MAXIMILIAN supporting himself on a broom barely able to walk, his cast leaking blood all over the floor.*

MAXIMILIAN
Gothard!… Gothard?

> *He sees the open door. Frigid air is blowing in to the room. He hobbles over to the door, closes it, then hobbles over to a chair and slumps down in it. GOTHARD runs back into the cafe shivering and extremely distressed.*

Did you call a taxi Gothard?

GOTHARD
I'm calling an ambulance! *(running around in a frenzy)* Where is the phone?

MAXIMILIAN
Just call a taxi Gothard.

GOTHARD
You'll bleed to death!

MAXIMILIAN
I'll be fine. Just call a taxi Gothard.

GOTHARD
Where's the phone?

MAXIMILIAN
In the back by the hot plate.

> *Exit GOTHARD. MAXIMILIAN lifts himself off the chair with the help of his broom.*

Just call a taxi Gothard.

> *Exit MAXIMILIAN supporting himself on the broom, his cast leaving a trail of blood. The lights flicker and blackout. Curtain.*

ACT II

SCENE: Interior of the same cafe a few months later. Night. Enter VERA and GUSTAV. GUSTAV is on crutches; his left leg is lifeless. VERA, folding away an umbrella, opens the door and holds it for him.

GUSTAV
(grunting as he crosses the threshold) That was almost painless.

VERA
Except for the freezing rain.

GUSTAV
And the little tumble I took on the stairs.

VERA
And crushing my foot with your crutch.

GUSTAV
(looking at her foot) Oh dear I put an ugly smudge on your shoe.

VERA
If it was my other shoe I'd be upset.

GUSTAV
My first big adventure.

VERA
Poor boy, you had to stay indoors all winter.

She hangs her coat. He leans his crutches against the wall and balances precariously on his good leg.

You shouldn't be standing unaided like that.

GUSTAV
I'm like a flamingo on my good leg.

VERA
(taking his coat and hanging it) And like a penguin on both.

GUSTAV
I'll just waddle over to the chair.

He attempts to walk to his chair unaided, takes a few steps and collapses.

VERA
Gustav!

She runs to his side and begins to help him up.

GUSTAV
(holding his nose) You're not going to let me lie down for a moment are you?

VERA
Are you alright? *(helping him to his feet)* Did you bump your beak? *(He nods.)* You stupid bird, did you think you were ready to fly?

GUSTAV
The doctor told this stupid bird that he should gradually start practicing.

VERA
He didn't mean belly-flopping onto the floor, did he?

GUSTAV
At least not in public.... Hold me for a moment.

> *She holds him as he leans over her shoulder and swings his leg back and forth lifelessly.*

VERA
What are you doing?

GUSTAV
Checking for damage. *(burying his face in her hair)*

VERA
Is everything still working?

GUSTAV
As far as I can tell. *(inhaling deeply)* Mmmm.... I love the smell of your hair. The whole apartment smells like this since you came to stay. It's still all so new to me.

> *He kisses her gently on the lips. VERA suddenly rips herself away from him wiping her mouth.*

VERA
You're bleeding!

> *Gustav covers his nose, loses his balance and collapses onto his back.*

Gustav!

> *She jumps to his side and helps him sit up.*

Oh God Gustav, are you alright?... Let me find a handkerchief. *(searching her purse)* Here.

> *He applies it to his nose. She finds some tissue paper in her purse and wipes the blood from her lips.*

GUSTAV
I'm sorry.

VERA
Let me see. *(She examines his nose.)* Hold that there for now.

GUSTAV
Help me to the chair please Vera.

> *She takes him under the arm and lifts him to the chair. She takes another tissue from her purse and wipes the blood from his neck and chest.*

VERA
I think we should take you to the washroom to clean you up.... Here put your arm over my shoulder and hop along.

She places GUSTAV's arm over her shoulder and lifts him out of his chair. He is holding the handkerchief under his nose with the other hand. Exit VERA and GUSTAV. Enter SHMARR wearing an eye patch. He lifts his eye patch and peers around the room in an unnatural way as if peering through a tube. One by one he spots the crutches, the coats, and the bloodied tissues on the table. He snaps his eye patch back over his eye, approaches the table and examines the bloodied tissues. He wraps up the tablecloth with the bloodied tissues and exits. He returns in a moment with a fresh tablecloth and a candle which he places on the table and lights. He flips up his eye patch and looks at the place on the floor where GUSTAV fell. He snaps his eye patch back over his eye, bends over, and wipes up a few spots of blood with his napkin. Exit SHMARR. Enter VERA and GUSTAV. GUSTAV is being supported by VERA and holding a tissue under his nose.

Look, the waiter brought us a candle.

She helps GUSTAV into his chair, sits down herself and takes a package of cigarettes from her purse offering one to him. She then produces a lighter and begins to flick it unsuccessfully.

Blast!… Oh, what am I doing? I don't need this.

She lights her cigarette on the candle.

GUSTAV
(*lifting the tissue from his nose*) Am I still bleeding?

VERA
(*looking closer*) No…. I don't think so. No I don't see anything.

He lights his cigarette on the candle.

Try not to sneeze.

GUSTAV
I'm glad there was nobody here to witness my grand entrance…. I hope the waiter didn't see anything. If Shmarr is the waiter tonight, then I don't have to worry.

VERA
Why, is he blind?

GUSTAV
He wears an eye patch over one eye.

VERA
But he can see, can't he?

GUSTAV
Shmarr has some very strange problems with his vision.

VERA
Has he had a stroke?

GUSTAV
No Shmarr's problem is a little more fantastic than that…. He was born blind. And as he has often told me, for the first seven years of his life he could not see at all… except for one thing.

VERA
What?

GUSTAV
His mother.

VERA
His mother?

GUSTAV
That's what he claims. He could see his mother and nothing else. Alone in a room he would be in total darkness until she came in. He could see what she was wearing – he told me he could sometimes see what she was holding, but he couldn't see what was beside her, or above her, or on the floor below her.

VERA
How is that possible?

GUSTAV
It's not…. Shmarr has baffled doctors from all over the world. They would perform all kinds of experiments on him as a child and apparently it was true; he could see his mother and nothing else. Maybe he had some kind of psychic connection with her. Maybe his blindness was psychological or hysterical. Maybe he just didn't want to see anything else for seven years…. I believe him. There are so many strange afflictions and conditions plaguing people these days. Illnesses that are not only physical or psychological but somehow almost mystical. Doctors even have a name for it, but it escapes me at the moment.

VERA
How did he come to see… everything else?

GUSTAV
Supernaturally of course. The story of how he acquired his sight is even more unusual. Do you want to hear it?… I'll tell you. Shmarr's father passed away before he was born leaving his frail, ailing mother alone to care for a blind baby. She was a very pious woman so she would pray to the Virgin for the restoration of his sight every evening for hours on end. He told me that sometimes she would pray until sunrise keeping him awake with her persistent mumbling. After seven years of relentless prayer—Shmarr said that she never missed a day if you can imagine it—she had a dream that she gave birth to two eyeballs. And these two eye balls she placed into the hollow sockets of her son's face. One she accidentally put in backwards. And so it was from that day on Shmarr was able to see, although cockeyed, you see.

 Enter SHMARR. He walks past GUSTAV and VERA without seeing them.

Shmarr!

Shmarr stops, turns, and flips up his eye patch. He speaks with a slight stutter.

SHMARR
Gustav?… Gustav Broom is that you?

GUSTAV
It's me in the flesh Shmarr.

SHMARR
You're in the flesh!

GUSTAV
That's right.

SHMARR
Where ha-ha...

GUSTAV
Where?

SHMARR
Where ha-have you been... all winter?

GUSTAV
Oh I found another cafe to frequent.

SHMARR
(saddened) Oooooh!

GUSTAV
Nooooo, I'm just kidding Shmarr. This is still my favourite cafe. You haven't seen me because I've been at home all winter recovering from an operation.

SHMARR
Oooooh, oh that's right you had an operation.... But that was a long time ago.... On your leg?

GUSTAV
On my hip. *(showing him where)* Right here.... They cut me from here to there.

SHMARR
Who?

GUSTAV
The surgeons.

SHMARR
Oooh.... Why?

GUSTAV
To correct a deformation in my pelvic joint. It was experimental surgery. It will allow me to walk without my cane. For now I'm walking around on crutches. Actually I should be at home in bed and not walking around at all. This is my first time out of my apartment since I had the operation. After staring at the same wallpaper for three months I couldn't resist the temptation to attempt a little stroll to my favourite neighbourhood cafe.... Did you see my little accident when we entered?

SHMARR
No.

GUSTAV
You didn't see me fall?

SHMARR
No.

VERA
Twice!

SHMARR
Oh my!

GUSTAV
Shmarr, I want you to meet my friend Vera.

    SHMARR lifts his eye patch to look at VERA.

SHMARR
P-P-Pandora!

VERA
Vera – how do you do.

SHMARR
Pleased to meet you Pandora.

VERA
My pleasure – Vera.

SHMARR
Vera – Pandora.

VERA
No – just Vera.

GUSTAV
Vera Kreff.

SHMARR
But your name was Pandora…

GUSTAV
You must have Vera confused with someone else Shmarr.

SHMARR
…i-in *The FFFlesh Eaters*.

GUSTAV
Oh you saw *The Flesh Eaters*!

SHMARR
Oh yes…

VERA
I was Madonna in *The Flesh Eaters*.

SHMARR
Oh yes!… Now I remember – Madonna!

VERA
The playwright's name is Pandora.

GUSTAV
Pandora Fork… That's his name – Pandora Fork.

VERA
Did you like it?

SHMARR
The play?… Oh yes I did, it was wonderful! Your performance was beautiful!… I enjoyed your death scene immensely. I wish I could see it again.

VERA
The death scene?

SHMARR
The whole play. It was the best play I have ever seen!

GUSTAV
And I didn't get to see it at all.

SHMARR
No?

GUSTAV
No, I wasn't mobile yet.

SHMARR
Oh you missed a very good play.

VERA
Do you know who Pandora Fork is?

SHMARR
Oh yes – the playwright.

VERA
That's her pen name. Do you know who she really is?

SHMARR
No.

VERA
(pointing at GUSTAV) Him!

SHMARR
Gustav?

VERA
Gustav Broom is Pandora Fork. He wrote *The Flesh Eaters*.

SHMARR
You're Pandora?

GUSTAV
I'm Pandora in the flesh.

SHMARR
But that's a woman's name. Why do you call yourself Pandora?

GUSTAV
It's my pseudonym. That's the name I use when I write. Pandora is my mother's name, you see. Fork was her mother's maiden name. I borrowed those two names for my pen name. I like to stay anonymous and using a woman's name insures my anonymity. If I ever write something I like maybe I'll put my name on it. But until then I'm Pandora the Fork.

SHMARR
You didn't like *The Flesh Eaters*?

VERA
Gustav's too shy with his talent.

SHMARR
But it was a wonderful play – everybody liked it.

VERA
See.

GUSTAV
Thank you Shmarr, but I'm not so sure it would be so easy for Pandora to have another one of her plays produced in this city. The critics weren't too kind and audience attendance was… unspectacular.

VERA
Oh pooh! The reviews were just fine and audience attendance was average which was very good considering the weather this winter kept everyone indoors.

GUSTAV
Gothard read the play before he went away…. He said it was too constipated.

VERA
Got's an idiot.

SHMARR
I haven't seen Gothard for a long time. Where is he?

VERA
On another planet.

SHMARR
What planet?

VERA
It's not in this solar system.

GUSTAV
Gothard's travelling around the world.

SHMARR
Travelling around the world, how exciting!… Is he travelling with his wife?

GUSTAV
Gothard's not married.

SHMARR
I thought he was.

GUSTAV
No.

SHMARR
I thought he married last year...

GUSTAV
You must be mistaken.

SHMARR
...to that girl.... What was her name?

VERA
Madonna.

GUSTAV
No, he left the girl he was living with...

SHMARR
Why did I think...?

GUSTAV
...then he quit his job at the paper, and went travelling around the world to finish writing a book he's been working on. We're a little worried about him. His letters have been infrequent and very strange. But knowing Gothard, I think he's just playing mind games with us.

VERA
He's lost his mind.

SHMARR
Maybe he's ill?

SHMARR flips up his eye patch and looks closely at GUSTAV's nose.

There is something under your nose.

VERA
You're bleeding again!

GUSTAV fiddles with the bloodied tissue he is holding and wipes the blood from under his nose.

Here I'll find you a clean one. *(She searches her purse.)*

GUSTAV
I bumped my nose when we came in.

SHMARR
Oh I bump my nose all the time.

VERA
I don't have any more.

SHMARR
Here take this napkin, it's clean, you can use it.

GUSTAV
Thank you Shmarr. *(presses the napkin to his nose)*

VERA
Do you want to go to the washroom again?

SHMARR
I can bring you some ice to put on it.

GUSTAV
No no that won't be necessary.

SHMARR
When I get a nosebleed I lie on my back.

VERA
Bring him a clothespin.

SHMARR
I don't think I have a clothespin…. Oh, maybe I do!

GUSTAV
You know what you can bring us Shmarr; a nice chilled bottle of white wine.

VERA
Do you mind if we have red wine Gustav?

GUSTAV
Of course, if that is what you prefer. A bottle of red wine then please Shmarr.

SHMARR
Chilled?

GUSTAV
Do you have a bottle of chilled red wine?

SHMARR
No.

GUSTAV
Well then we'll just have a normal room temperature bottle of red wine.

SHMARR
I could chill the wine for you.

GUSTAV
No that won't be necessary Shmarr.

SHMARR
A bottle of room temperature red wine coming right up.

Exit SHMARR.

VERA
I remember him.

GUSTAV
Shmarr?

VERA
I saw him in the audience.

GUSTAV
At a performance?

VERA
I remember one night about two weeks ago I was distracted, as were some of the other actors, by a man with an eye patch in the second or third row who was constantly rolling his head around. It was very disturbing because I kept glancing at him all the time. I thought at first that maybe he was drunk or insane but then I realized that he was just a poor fellow.

GUSTAV
Just a poor fellow.... Was he with anyone?

VERA
I don't remember.... Why?

GUSTAV
Last summer I was sitting in the park on a sunny Sunday afternoon reading a paper when I saw Shmarr and his wife pushing a stroller in which sat a little girl of about five or six years of age. She was a pretty girl. She was wearing a little navy blue dress and a little navy blue beret. I thought that she was a little too old for the stroller. I was about to call out to Shmarr, just to say hello when suddenly the stroller hit a rut in the pavement which caused the child to lurch forward, face into her knees. When this happened her beret fell off... revealing a concave head; like a pumpkin squashed in on one side. I managed to stifle the gasp that swelled up in my throat but several other onlookers were not so successful. I learned later from Gothard that his daughter was born without a brain.

VERA
Oh God.

GUSTAV
I wasn't prepared for the shock of seeing that poor girl's...

VERA
I don't want to hear any more. *(fumbling for a cigarette)*

GUSTAV
I'm sorry, I didn't mean to disturb you.

VERA
I'm not disturbed. *(offers a cigarette to GUSTAV)*

GUSTAV
No thank you, I'll just sniff this napkin for now.

A bottle is heard breaking offstage.

There goes our wine.

VERA
Should I go check on him?

GUSTAV
Not unless you want to help him clean it up. Shmarr is always breaking something.

VERA
I remember now…. A little girl in a beret…

GUSTAV
What?

VERA
At the performance – in the audience. I remember a little girl in a beret with him.

GUSTAV
His daughter?

VERA
Just sitting there motionless staring at the stage while his head lobbed back and forth beside her.

GUSTAV
I wonder if she liked the play?

VERA
Don't joke like that.

GUSTAV
I'm sorry.

VERA
H-How is it that she can live?… Do you think that she feels anything?

GUSTAV
I don't know.

VERA
I wonder if she knows she's alive?

GUSTAV
I wonder if she is alive?

VERA
Does he ever talk about her?

GUSTAV
He talks about her as if she were a normal child.

VERA
Do you know her name?

The sound of breaking glass is heard offstage again.

What's going on back there?

GUSTAV
I think he just threw the broken glass into the garbage can.

He uncovers his nose and gently wiggles it back and forth.

VERA
Stop that, you'll just make it worse.

GUSTAV
Does it look like it's swelling?

VERA
(examining his nose) No, it looks normal.

GUSTAV
(examining her face peculiarly) I think…

VERA
What?

GUSTAV
I think you might still have a little smudge of blood under your chin.

VERA
(feeling under her chin) Where?

GUSTAV
(pointing) There – right under your mouth.

She takes her compact from her purse, examines her chin in the mirror, and then searches her purse for a handkerchief.

VERA
Blast, I've nothing to wipe with.

She wets the corner of the tablecloth on her tongue and begins to wipe off the blood spot. Enter SHMARR carrying a tray with a bottle of wine, two wine glasses, and a stack of loose tissue paper. He is not wearing his eye patch. Instead the eye that is normally covered by the eye patch is tightly shut.

SHMARR
I brought you some papers for your nose Gustav. *(He places the tray on the table.)*

GUSTAV
Oh thank you Shmarr, that was thoughtful of you.

SHMARR
Are you still bleeding?

Gustav inhales forcefully through his nose a few times and then feels for blood.

GUSTAV
I am now.

He takes a few of the loose tissues and applies them to his nose. He keeps his nose covered throughout the ensuing conversation.

VERA
You're not wearing your eye patch.

SHMARR
I lost it. I was lifting it to examine wine labels and the string broke. The patch flew off somewhere into the wine cabinet and I broke a bottle trying to find it.

VERA
And you didn't find it?

SHMARR
No, and I don't see very well without it. I wear the eye patch over my good eye; the eye that I see with best, but I have no control over it. It just rolls around in my eye socket so I keep it covered. When I want to see something I lift my patch and try to point my eye at what I want to see. In my other eye I don't have such good vision but I do have control over it. This is the eye that I use to navigate with when I'm walking. The other eye, the one I keep covered, I use for seeing detail like checking the time on my watch, only it keeps rolling back, or down, or to the side, so I constantly have to struggle with it to keep it pointed at what I am trying to observe. *(pointing to his left eye)* That is, I have good vision in this eye but I have no control over it. It just rolls around looking at whatever it wants to, so I have to keep it covered. *(pointing to his right eye)* I have control over this eye but unfortunately it doesn't see very well. *(He begins to open the wine.)*

VERA
Gustav told me how you were born blind and miraculously came to see.

GUSTAV
I told Vera how you could only see your mother until the age of seven.

SHMARR
It's true, I could see my mother and nothing else…. God allowed me to see my mother through the years of my blindness because soon after I received my sight he took my mother up to heaven. *(He begins to pour the wine.)* Sometimes when I am by myself in a dark room *(closing his eyes)* I can see my mother – she comes to me. *(He misses the glass and pours wine on the table.)* Oh I'm sorry!

VERA
That's alright.

SHMARR
I'll bring you a new tablecloth.

VERA
There's no need to Shmarr.

GUSTAV
Don't worry about it.

SHMARR
I have trouble judging the placement of objects before me without my eye patch. I'm not very good at keeping my left eye shut and it constantly confuses me.

He covers his left eye with his hand and pours the wine into the glass this time over-filling it.

Oh not again, what's wrong with me?

VERA
That's fine, don't worry about it.

SHMARR
I'm going to change your tablecloth and bring you a new bottle of wine.

SHMARR turns to exit. VERA jumps up and stops him.

VERA
Shmarr don't be silly; everything is fine. A little spilled wine isn't going to hurt us.

SHMARR
But I've made such a mess.

GUSTAV
We would have spilled the wine sooner or later anyways.

SHMARR
I can't expect you to sit at a table like this.

VERA
You've already changed our tablecloth once, didn't you?

SHMARR
Let me try to clean this up a little at least.

He dabs at the spilled wine with his napkin and carefully tries to wipe the base of Vera's glass.

VERA
Here, I'll sip some off the top.

SHMARR
I have not been myself lately.

He bends down to make himself eye level with GUSTAV's glass. VERA jumps up and covers his left eye with her hand as he carefully fills the glass.

GUSTAV
Bravo!

SHMARR
I've been having all kinds of accidents and making all kinds of mistakes. I can't do anything right. I don't know what's wrong with me. This afternoon I forgot to bring a blind customer his tea. He comes in every afternoon at half past one and has a cup of tea with lemon. This afternoon I took his order as usual and forgot to bring him the tea. He sat quietly in his chair for three quarters of an hour waiting for his tea to arrive. Eventually someone else came in and after I had seated them I asked the blind man if he would like me to bring him anything else. He told me that I still hadn't brought him his tea. I apologized profusely and quickly brought him a cup of coffee. After half an hour he was able to get my attention when I was serving

another customer and pointed out to me very politely that I had brought him a cup of coffee instead of tea. These kinds of embarrassing mistakes have become routine with me. A customer orders red wine and I bring him white. Someone else wants vodka straight up – I bring it to them on ice.

GUSTAV
Those are common mistakes Shmarr.

SHMARR
But for me they are more than common, they are constant! Yesterday I was washing a few glasses in the sink. I had the water running and the sink stoppered. The phone rang and I went to answer it. It was my wife calling to remind me to pick up a few things on my way home. I was talking to her on the phone when a customer ran into the back room shouting that water was coming into the cafe from the kitchen. The sink had overflowed and the entire cafe and kitchen had flooded. I had to close the cafe and spent the rest of the day trying to mop up the mess. Maximilian arrived and was of course angry that the cafe was closed in the middle of the afternoon, our busiest time of day. He helped me clean up and I went home all wet and exhausted. On my way home I stopped into a store to buy the few things that my wife had asked me to. I picked up the milk, bread, eggs, and whatever was necessary and walked out of the store without paying. I realized what I had done at my doorstep so I turned around and walked all the way back to the store to pay for the items. The grocer said he saw me walk out without paying but turned his eyes because of my recent loss. I explained to him what kind of day I had at work and that I was in a muddle because of the flood in the cafe and that's why I forgot to pay. Returning home I bumped my grocery bag against a fire hydrant shattering the bottle of milk and seven eggs which of course ruined the bread, so I had to return to the store again for bread and milk and seven eggs. Once home safe and sound I received a phone call from Maximilian that I forgot to leave the keys for him to lock up. So off I was again, back to the cafe to give Maximilian the keys. And to make the day complete, on my way home again it began to rain.

GUSTAV
We all have days like that Shmarr.

VERA
Gustav is having one of those days today.

SHMARR
But I am like this every day. Every day I forget something, or break something, or I can't find something. On Sunday afternoon I went to lay flowers on my daughter's grave at the municipal cemetery. You know how large the cemetery is, it stretches for miles and miles in every direction. There is an east sector and a west sector which are identically laid out. Her grave is in the west sector. Somehow I wandered into the east sector and spent an hour searching for her grave before I realized I was in the wrong sector. When I finally found the right sector, somehow all the graves looked the same to me. I couldn't distinguish her grave from all the others.

VERA
Your daughter has a grave?

SHMARR
Yes, in the west sector of the municipal cemetery.

VERA
Oh my God!

GUSTAV
I didn't know Shmarr…. I'm very sorry.

SHMARR
Tell me – how can I forget where my daughter's grave is?

GUSTAV
When did this happen Shmarr?

SHMARR
On Sunday afternoon.

GUSTAV
I mean when did your daughter… pass away?

SHMARR
On Christmas day. We opened the presents and she was so happy with the great big blue pillow that she got for Christmas. Then she went to sleep and…

GUSTAV
I had no idea Shmarr.

SHMARR
What kind of flowers do you think I could plant on her grave this spring to make it more distinctive?

GUSTAV
Do you have other children Shmarr?

SHMARR
No… but we want to adopt another child again.

GUSTAV
Adopt?

SHMARR
Yes.

GUSTAV
Your daughter… was adopted?

SHMARR
Yes…. I was thinking of planting a flowering shrub, but in the winter a bare shrub doesn't look very attractive sticking out of the snow. I think maybe we will plant antirrhinums.

VERA
Antirrhinums are beautiful.

SHMARR
That is what my wife wanted.

SHMARR jerks his head back several times and then begins making circles in the air with his face.

GUSTAV
Are you alright Shmarr?

SHMARR
My eye has disappeared under my eyelid and I can't seem to dislodge it. *(continuing to shake his head around with increasingly exaggerated gestures)* This happens all the time. When it's covered it doesn't bother me. *(covering his left eye with his hand)* I'm going to look for my eye patch otherwise I'll be walking home like this.

VERA
We're very, very sorry to hear about your daughter.

GUSTAV
Very sorry Shmarr.

SHMARR nods his head sadly and exits.

VERA
I was so befuddled by his absurd story and all his silly accidents that when he started talking about getting lost in the cemetery it didn't click with me that his daughter was actually in the cemetery.

GUSTAV
I had no idea his daughter died…. I had no idea she was adopted.

VERA
Who was the blank-eyed little girl in the beret sitting beside him in the audience…

GUSTAV
I'm intrigued that he adopted such a child.

VERA
…since his daughter died Christmas day?

GUSTAV
When I first saw Shmarr's daughter I just assumed that he passed on a lot of bad genes to her.

VERA
Do you think that there are more children like that now?

GUSTAV
Like what?

VERA
Like Shmarr's daughter.

GUSTAV
What do you mean?

VERA
More sick children.

GUSTAV
I don't know.

VERA
You said there are so many strange afflictions plaguing people now. Those mystical illnesses you were talking about. Children would be particularly vulnerable.

GUSTAV
I was born with an affliction.

VERA
You have a little limp; that's not what I'm talking about…. Your sister, she had an abnormal child.

GUSTAV
My sister had a still birth.

VERA
But the baby was extremely deformed.

GUSTAV
My sister was fifty-nine.

VERA
Got said that most children nowadays are born deformed or sick…. And if they're not born that way they soon develop illnesses and disabilities.

GUSTAV
Gothard doesn't like children.

VERA
Do you like children?

GUSTAV
Of course – why not. I have nothing against children.

VERA
I stopped by a schoolyard the other day and observed the children through the fence. I saw a child on crutches, another was blind, several were missing limbs or fingers. There were some hunchbacks, some dwarves, several bald children, a mongoloid or two, a harelip, a hermaphrodite, an elephant boy, a cyclops with a tail and a vampire boy who ran around biting the other children. One little girl had an epileptic fit. They all gathered around and watched her writhing in the mud. The vampire boy ran up to her and bit her on the cheek. When I tried to count them, the sick children outnumbered the normal ones. When they saw me watching them through the bars of the fence they started to screech and throw stones at me. (*She gulps down half a glass of wine, chokes and then coughs.*) How many children are there like Shmarr's daughter? How many shut-ins are there who are so crippled, or retarded, or paralyzed that they don't attend school? How many die like Shmarr's daughter before they reach puberty? And how many are born dead like your sister's child?

GUSTAV
I don't know, maybe Gothard has a point…. I don't know any children personally.

VERA
It's not possible…. It's not possible to have children anymore.

GUSTAV
It is possible.

VERA
No, it's not possible!

GUSTAV
Does it matter to you?

VERA
Yes!

GUSTAV
Why – were you wanting to be a mommy someday?

VERA
Do you know those pills I take before we go to bed?

GUSTAV
No.

VERA
The little round ones.

GUSTAV
The pink ones?

VERA
The yellow ones. They're for my circulation. They also counteract the pills that I take when I get up in the morning.

GUSTAV
The pink ones?

VERA
The blue ones.

GUSTAV
For your dizzy spells?

VERA
For my period.

GUSTAV
Are you having problems?

VERA
Yes.

GUSTAV
What sort of problems?

VERA
I don't menstruate.

GUSTAV
Well then you should see a doctor.

VERA
I have.

GUSTAV
And…

VERA
And I have a little person growing in my stomach.

GUSTAV
What are you saying?

VERA
I'm going to be a mommy.

GUSTAV
You… you're… h-h-how… how is that possible?

VERA
I just told you how.

GUSTAV
I don't…. I don't understand. Because the yellow pills… no, the blue pills…. You don't menstruate because…

VERA
Because the yellow pills counteracted the blue pills. Anyways it doesn't matter how, does it? I'm expecting.

GUSTAV
A-Are you certain?

VERA
I'm just starting to show.

> She gets up and flattens her dress against her abdomen.

See.

GUSTAV
I don't see anything.

> She grabs his hand and places it on her abdomen.

VERA
There.

GUSTAV
I can't feel anything.

VERA
Right there!

GUSTAV
Maybe you're not expecting?

VERA
I am expecting! I had it confirmed! I'm one hundred percent pregnant! I can feel it in my womb! I feel like barfing when I get up in the morning! There's a baby in here!

GUSTAV
A-Alright I believe you.

VERA
In six months I'm going to be a mommy! *(returning to her chair)* You just don't know what a baby feels like.

GUSTAV
No.... No you're right I don't.... In six months?.... Then I'm not... the father?

VERA
No.... I don't know.... Probably not.

GUSTAV
Is it Gothard's child?

VERA
Probably.

GUSTAV
You're not sure?

VERA
It's probably Got's.

GUSTAV
But it's not somebody else's child?

VERA
No!

GUSTAV
Did he leave because of the child?

VERA
No.

GUSTAV
Did he know that you might be with child?

VERA
No.

GUSTAV
Did you know that you might be with child?... Vera... did you know?

VERA
No!

GUSTAV
What are you going to do?

VERA
I'm going to have a baby.

She gulps down half a glass of wine and begins to swoon.

GUSTAV
Is something wrong?

VERA
I feel very weak suddenly.

GUSTAV
Don't drink if you're feeling sick.

VERA
I'm not going to heave – I just feel weak…

GUSTAV
We can go home now if you like.

VERA
I have to go to the washroom. *(She gets up.)*

GUSTAV
Are you alright?

VERA
I don't know.

Exit VERA.

GUSTAV
(calling after her) Vera…. Vera!

He removes the napkin from his nose and examines it. It's saturated with blood and there's blood on his hands. He stuffs the napkin into the ashtray and takes several tissues, wipes his fingers and his nose and tries to stuff them into the ashtray as well. He takes several more tissues and applies them to his still bleeding nose. He holds the tissues to his nose for a moment and then examines them. They're blood stained so he discards them and takes several fresh tissues which he places against his nose again.

(shouting) Vera!… Vera!… Veraaa!

There is no response from VERA so he lowers himself onto the floor with difficulty and begins to crawl painfully towards the washroom holding the tissues to his nose and dragging his legs behind him. Enter SHMARR. He sees GUSTAV writhing on the floor and flips up his eye patch. Gasping loudly he runs to GUSTAV's assistance. He trips over GUSTAV and comes crashing down on his back. GUSTAV screams wildly in excruciating pain. SHMARR gathers himself up, begins to apologize profusely, and tries to help GUSTAV up. Enter VERA who runs into the room having heard GUSTAV's cries.

VERA
What's happening!… Gustav! Oh my God! Oh my God!

She begins to scream in horror at the sight of GUSTAV bloodied on the floor and SHMARR desperately trying to lift him. She becomes faint from the ensuing confusion and collapses first onto her knees and then completely unconscious onto the floor. SHMARR drops GUSTAV, runs to VERA's side and attempts to lift her.

SHMARR
Madonna!… Madonna!

Curtain.

ACT III

SCENE: Interior of the same cafe eight months later. Enter GUSTAV and GOTHARD. GUSTAV is relying heavily on a cane for support. GOTHARD is blind. He is wearing dark glasses and holding a white cane.

GUSTAV
We're going over the threshold watch your step…. There's nobody here tonight, we can sit wherever we like.

GOTHARD
(pointing) What about that table over there?

GUSTAV
There is no table there…. Where are your gloves by the way?

GOTHARD
I don't know.

GUSTAV
Didn't you take them with you?

GOTHARD
No.

GUSTAV
You couldn't find them?

GOTHARD
No.

GUSTAV
Aren't your hands frozen?

GOTHARD
Yes.

GUSTAV
Why didn't you ask me to find them for you?

GOTHARD
I didn't know I needed them.

GUSTAV
Gothard I don't know how to take care of you. If you need help with something, you have to tell me.

GOTHARD
I need help hanging up my coat.

He removes his coat and hands it to GUSTAV. There is a glove hanging out of the coat pocket.

GUSTAV
Your gloves are in your pocket by the way. *(checking the pockets)* Or at least one of them is. Did you lose the other one?

GOTHARD
I don't know.

> *GUSTAV hangs up the coat. GOTHARD with the aid of his cane attempts to find a chair and bumps up against a table.*

GUSTAV
That's our table, sit down there. The chair is on your right.

> *GOTHARD drops his cane and gropes around on the floor searching for it. He finds it, finds the chair and seats himself. GUSTAV hangs his coat and joins him. GOTHARD removes his glasses and begins to roll his head around, his eyes open wide.*

What are you doing?

GOTHARD
I'm trying to see you.

GUSTAV
How does that motion help you to see me?

GOTHARD
I'm trying to position my head. Like this I can sometimes see the general shape of what's in front of me. I see it right out of the furthest angle of my visual field.

GUSTAV
Can you see anything now?

GOTHARD
Make some kind of motion.

GUSTAV
Shall I wave my arms around?

GOTHARD
Movement is easier for me to detect.

> *GUSTAV waves his hands around as GOTHARD twists his head about and rolls his eyes trying to see him.*

No.... It must be too dark in here. Is there any light in here at all?

GUSTAV
There is a light above us.

> *GOTHARD searches the ceiling for the light, twisting his neck and rolling his eyes.*

GOTHARD
Directly above?

GUSTAV
Right above the table.

GOTHARD
I can't see it.

GUSTAV
It's not a very bright light.

GOTHARD
Is it a bare bulb, or is it behind a glass?

GUSTAV
It's a bare bulb.

GOTHARD
I can usually see the glowing tungsten wire in a bare bulb if it's right before my eyes.

He stands up facing the light and twists his head around trying to see it.

GUSTAV
It's a cloudy bulb and it seems to be covered in greasy brown fingerprints.

GOTHARD
Is it very high up?

GUSTAV
It's a few feet above your head.

GOTHARD
No…. I can't see it. *(resumes his chair)*

GUSTAV
Have you had any improvement in your sight at all?

GOTHARD
Before I wasn't able to see the glowing tungsten wire in a light bulb or anything else from the furthest angle of my visual field…. Have you seen the child recently Gustav?

GUSTAV
On one or two occasions.

GOTHARD
Do you know the family that adopted it?

GUSTAV
Her.

GOTHARD
Hmm?

GUSTAV
Her – the family that adopted her.

GOTHARD
Her.

GUSTAV
She hasn't been adopted yet. She's being cared for temporarily by a foster mother until she can be permanently placed in a foster home. I've been told that there is a suitable family interested in adopting her…. She looks a lot like you, you know.

GOTHARD
Does she have a name?

GUSTAV
I don't know. Vera wanted to call her something.... I forget what.

GOTHARD
Did she see the child before she...?

GUSTAV
No.

GOTHARD
Where is she buried?

> *Enter MARIA. She is pregnant with a large round abdomen and is holding a candle for the table. She speaks with a heavy foreign accent.*

MARIA
Gustav!... Gothard!

GUSTAV
Maria!... It's Maria, Gothard!

MARIA
How long has it been since I've seen the two of you – twenty years? *(She places the candle on the table.)*

GUSTAV
Oh it's been a long time Maria but it hasn't been twenty years. One year maybe.

MARIA
You don't like to come here anymore?

GUSTAV
Of course we like to come here, this is our favourite cafe, but we haven't been able to come here, this is the problem. I've been home-bound recovering from an operation and Gothard has been away for a year travelling around the world.

MARIA
Around the world – how exciting!

GUSTAV
He just came home yesterday.

GOTHARD
This is my Katmandu suntan.

MARIA
Yes it's very nice.... And you Gustav, you had an operation?

GUSTAV
On my hip – almost a year ago now. I still have trouble walking.... And I see you're going to be a mother soon Maria!

MARIA
(hand on abdomen) Yes I have a baby in here!

GUSTAV
Maria's going to be a mother Gothard!

GOTHARD
A mother – congratulations Maria!

GUSTAV
When are you due?

MARIA
Any day now. *(wincing)* Agh…. Oh this is a restless baby!

GUSTAV
Are you all right?

MARIA
I think baby just wants to come out right now. *(talking to her abdomen)* Stay in there baby, it's not time yet! What am I going to do if you fall out on the floor? Heh-heh-heh.

GUSTAV
You shouldn't be here Maria. You should be at home resting – not waiting on people. Where are Maximilian and Shmarr? Why don't they help you?

MARIA
Max is at home with the flu and Shmarr is on vacation.

GUSTAV
But how can you be working – you're almost ready to deliver?

MARIA
Who is going to work tonight if not me? I have to work. Baby is not coming tonight. I can work if baby is not coming – why not? Maybe baby will come tomorrow, maybe the next day. I think baby is just packing its bags tonight that's all.

> She cringes in pain and clutches her abdomen. GUSTAV gets up and offers MARIA his chair. His cane falls to the ground.

GUSTAV
Here, sit down Maria.

MARIA
Oh no no, I'm alright, this is normal…. Agh!

> GUSTAV trembling painfully from the weakness in his leg awkwardly tries to resume his chair, loses strength and collapses onto his knees still clutching the chair for support. MARIA jumps to his aid, helps him into the chair, and picks up his cane.

Are you all right?

GUSTAV
Thank you Maria…. I'm afraid I don't have my strength yet. Look at me, one year after my operation and no improvement. I still can't walk. I can't even stand! The operation was supposed to enable me to walk normally.

MARIA
Why do you want to walk normally?

GUSTAV
I'm not sure that it wasn't all for nothing.

MARIA
Whose blind man's cane is that?

GOTHARD
It's mine.

MARIA
What is it for?

GOTHARD
I wave it in front of me when I walk.

MARIA
Why?

GOTHARD
I'm blind.

MARIA
What do you mean you're blind?

GOTHARD
I can't see... anything.

> *MARIA looks deep into GOTHARD's eyes and wiggles her fingers in front of his face.*

MARIA
(gasping) My God Gothard!... What has happened to you?

GUSTAV
Gothard lost his sight on his travels.

MARIA
How?... Did a cobra spit in your face?

GOTHARD
No.

MARIA
Did you drink poison spirits?

GOTHARD
No, I...

MARIA
Did you look at the sun?

GOTHARD
Yes.

MARIA
You looked at the sun!… And that made you blind?

GOTHARD
Yes.

MARIA
Gothard, Gothard, Gothard why? How could you look at the sun? Even little children know they shouldn't look at the sun. How long did you look at the sun? Can you see anything at all?

GOTHARD
I can sometimes see a little light around the edges…

MARIA
Oh Gothard, how could you be so reckless? Your eyes are so precious…. And you are a writer! How are you going to write?

GOTHARD
I don't have to write anymore.

MARIA
You know Shmarr was blind once. He can help you. He was born blind and now he can see. It was a miracle!

GUSTAV
Gothard's sight is improving gradually, isn't it.

GOTHARD
Gradually.

GUSTAV
He will be staying with me now. We're taking care of each other. He is my legs and I am his eyes.

> *MARIA is suddenly jerked by a violent spasm of pain in her abdomen. She leans on the table for support.*

GUSTAV
Maria what's wrong?

MARIA
The baby is dancing around inside my stomach. Stop dancing baby! I think baby is so happy it wants to be born today. Today is not your birthday baby, you can be born tomorrow, you have to wait.

GUSTAV
What if baby doesn't wait?

MARIA
Well baby has to wait because Mama is working.

GUSTAV
I think we should leave and let you close up and go home, just in case baby decides to be born today.

MARIA
(laughing) Are you afraid I'm going to give birth tonight?

GUSTAV
Yes that is starting to worry me a little.

MARIA
Don't worry about that. Do you think I would be here tonight if I thought I was going to give birth? Of course not, I would be in the hospital. I've been having these pains all day. They are not very bad pains. When a woman is going to have a baby she has very strong pains. Not like my little pains. These pains are normal little pains that a woman has when she has a baby inside. I will know when it is time. I will know.... When my sister had a baby she didn't know. She had her baby right on the floor where she works. A janitor delivered the baby. Now he's the godfather. So I will know, I am not like my sister. Do you know how I was born? I was born in a forest. My mother was gathering firewood in the forest. Only our dog Pimpek was with my mother when I was born. She didn't have an axe with her to cut the cord so Pimpek bit the cord in half and my mother wrapped me up in a sack. Pimpek is my godfather now, heh-heh.... You know I once had a woman that started to have a baby right here in the cafe! We called an ambulance and she gave birth to twins on the way to the hospital. If I give birth this evening I'll make you both godfathers, how's that! And to be fair to both of you I will call the baby Gusthard or maybe Gotstav. Or maybe I'll have twins! (She laughs.) I better bring you a drink before the baby comes. I will light the candle, no?

> She produces a lighter from her apron and lights the candle. GOTHARD's attention is caught by the candle and he stares at it intensely.

There, that's nice, isn't it. Now tell me what can I bring you?

GUSTAV
I think we'll have a half litre of vodka. We're celebrating Gothard's homecoming tonight. Would you like a pot of tea as well Gothard?

GOTHARD
(distracted) Hm?... And a pot of tea please.

MARIA
Lemon and sugar?

GOTHARD
Just lemon, no sugar.

GUSTAV
For me sugar and no lemon.

MARIA
The water for the tea is already hot. I just have to boil it.

> She begins to exit and is stopped in her tracks by another painful spasm. She cringes for a moment and then exits.

GOTHARD
I can see the flame!… *(GUSTAV blocks the flame with his hand.)* It's gone! *(He removes his hand.)* Did you do that?

GUSTAV
It seems that you can see something after all Gothard.

GOTHARD
This is something new!

> *GUSTAV picks up the candle and moves it from side to side.*

You're moving it from left to right.

> *GUSTAV begins making circles in the air with the candle.*

Now you're making circles.

GUSTAV
Can you touch it?

> *GOTHARD reaches out for the flame and GUSTAV pulls it away, and again GOTHARD tries to touch the flame and GUSTAV pulls it away.*

You're not fast enough.

GOTHARD
Do you enjoy teasing a blind man?

GUSTAV
Come on try again – catch it.

> *GOTHARD grasps for the flame and extinguishes it when he touches it, burning himself.*

You can see very well for a blind man Gothard.

GOTHARD
Light the candle again!

GUSTAV
Did you notice I don't smell like smoke anymore? I stopped smoking – I don't have any matches. Maria will have to light it for us again when she returns.

GOTHARD
After I lost my sight I was taken into a monastery by some kind monks where I was always surrounded by candles but never able to see a flame.

GUSTAV
When exactly did you lose your sight Gothard?

GOTHARD
What month is this?

GUSTAV
November.

GOTHARD
November, hmm…. The eclipse was on New Year's Day.

GUSTAV
New Year's Day!

GOTHARD
Yes.

GUSTAV
You've been blind for a year!

GOTHARD
Not a whole year yet.

GUSTAV
Not a whole year!… Gothard, you left everything you had and went abroad to see the world and finish writing your book, but you watch an eclipse and poof you're blind. Now you have no book, no sight… and no Vera.

GOTHARD
Have you ever seen an eclipse Gustav?

GUSTAV
No.

GOTHARD
If you suddenly saw a ring of fire in the sky would you watch it or would you turn away?

GUSTAV
I certainly wouldn't blind myself by it.

GOTHARD
I didn't know I was going to blind myself. I didn't even know it was an eclipse that I was witnessing. I looked out the window of my little mountain hut to see why it had suddenly become so dark in the middle of the afternoon, and there in the sky was a golden ring of fire. I couldn't take my eyes off of this wondrous and unexpected apparition. I was transfixed by the beauty of this strange omen on New Year's Day. I watched it for what seemed like hours, afraid that if I took my eyes off of it, it would disappear. Eventually I became cold, closed the window and turned my eyes away to find that the flaming ring moved with my gaze. Everywhere I looked was the flaming ring. It was in my hut, it was on the wall, it was on the floor; when I lay down to sleep it was burning a hole in the ceiling. All night it spun around above me like a top shooting off colourful flames in all directions. In the morning when I awoke the flaming ring was gone and the whole world was dark. I was alone in the blackness of my little frozen mountain hut. I was alone and blind. I tried to keep track of the days by counting how many times I went to sleep and woke up. I lived off of the little bit of bread and rice that I had. And after what seemed like forty days I was rescued by a little wandering monk who stopped by to seek shelter from a storm. He stayed with me for several weeks cooking and caring for me. At some point in early spring it must have been, he took me back with him

to his monastery where I lived like a monk among other monks until just recently. It was there I finished writing my book.

GUSTAV
You finished writing your book?

GOTHARD
In the monastery.

GUSTAV
Blind?

GOTHARD
I didn't use a pen and paper. I wrote it in my mind. *(pointing to his head)* It's all right here, one thousand one hundred and eleven pages. I memorized it as I wrote it word for word, the entire book. The monks have perfected meditation and concentration over many centuries and I was able to apply what I learned from them to memorizing my book as I wrote it.

GUSTAV
How is anyone to read it if it's only in your head?

GOTHARD
I can recite it.

GUSTAV
Well that's very impressive Gothard but not many people have the time to listen to you chant a thousand page book to them.

GOTHARD
Do you have the time Gustav?

GUSTAV
Well…. I suppose…

GOTHARD
Then I will chant it to you and you will write down what I say.

Enter MARIA carrying a tray with a bottle of vodka, a pot of tea, two shot glasses, sugar, and lemon slices.

MARIA
I had trouble finding the vodka. Shmarr mistook it for wine and put it on the wine rack. *(pouring the tea)* Be careful with the tea it's piping hot. Arrrgh!

She is shaken by an extremely violent spasm and falls on GOTHARD's shoulders for support. GOTHARD jumps to his feet and holds her in his arms.

GOTHARD
Did you burn yourself Maria?

MARIA
No no no, I just had another pain.

GUSTAV
Maria are you sure that we aren't going to become godfathers tonight?

MARIA
Oh no no, it's just a little pain. I am okay, this is normal. Don't worry I'm not going to make you a godfather tonight. I'm sorry Gothard, I didn't mean to fall on you.

She collects herself, GOTHARD resumes his chair, and she carefully pours two shots of vodka.

You know I'm not the only one who is going to be a new mother. Shmarr just adopted a little baby girl, isn't that wonderful! A little orphan girl. Shmarr is so happy! He wanted another baby so much after his first little girl tragically passed away last year. She was severely handicapped and unfortunately that was the cause of her death. But the little girl he adopted today is completely normal. She's only two months old. A beautiful little baby girl.

GOTHARD
Does she have a name?

MARIA
Shmarr named her Madonna.... Shmarr and his wife are ecstatic! They cannot have their own children like me. *(wincing)* Argh!... Another little tummy pain. Just in case I do make a baby tonight, do either of you know what to do? *(laughing)* Don't look so afraid, I'm just kidding!... Oops it's coming! Heh-heh-heh.... I'm going to go to the kitchen and wash some glasses. Don't drink the vodka too fast. Cheers!

Exit MARIA.

GOTHARD
Shmarr's daughter passed away?

GUSTAV
Last Christmas. She was extremely deformed you know.

GOTHARD
I saw her once.

GUSTAV
She lies three plots down and one over from Vera in the municipal cemetery. I've run into Shmarr there on a few occasions. He helps me find the grave when I'm lost. He always has a few flowers to spare for his favourite actress.

GOTHARD
Could you put a lemon in my tea please Gustav.

GUSTAV drops a lemon into GOTHARD's cup and puts sugar into his own.

GUSTAV
By the way I'm not teaching at the university any longer. My position was given to someone more mobile.... Which is just as well, I was getting a little tired of teaching the same thing over and over again year after year.

GOTHARD
What are you going to do?

GUSTAV
Well.... I guess I'll be taking dictation for you Gothard. *(lifting his shot glass)* Cheers!

GOTHARD
Cheers!

> *They both swallow the contents of their shot glasses and wash the vodka down with a sip of tea.*

GUSTAV
(putting his hand to his mouth) My God this tea is hot!

GOTHARD
How long exactly has Vera been in the municipal cemetery?

GUSTAV
(pouring another round) Two months.

GOTHARD
Were you with her in the delivery room… when…?

GUSTAV
No…. I wasn't even in the waiting room. I was at home in bed with the flu. Vera was hospitalized two days prior as a precautionary measure resulting from certain health complications that were plaguing her during the pregnancy. In the meantime I had to arrange for a nurse to attend to me during my illness which nearly found me in the hospital as well. The evening of Vera's death I phoned the hospital to speak with her however Vera was heavily sedated and awaiting imminent delivery so I spoke with the attending doctor; Dr. Klott. Do you remember him – he was my doctor?

GOTHARD
He operated on you?

GUSTAV
Yes, he's a very good doctor. He assured me that Vera was doing fine; that there were no serious complications and that he was expecting a smooth delivery. Vera was sedated because of the intense pain, but that was normal, and there was a small possibility that a Caesarean may be necessary. I was concerned that Vera might have contracted the flu that I was suffering from. However Klott assured me that Vera wasn't displaying any flu like symptoms. She was feverish but only as a result of the pain and that I shouldn't worry. I asked him to phone me as soon as the child was born no matter what the hour. At half past three a.m. I was shaken out of a nightmare by the ringing of the telephone. Delirious with fever I picked up the receiver to hear Klott's sombre voice telling me there had been complications and a Caesarean section had been performed. From the solemn tone of his voice I immediately guessed that something was wrong. I assumed that there was something wrong with the child as is so common these days. The doctor then calmly told me that Vera gave birth to a normal, healthy baby girl however Vera unfortunately did not survive the delivery. In my feverish delirium the telephone call seemed to me just an extension of my nightmare. I took three powerful sleeping pills that Vera kept on the night-table and immediately lost consciousness. I was awakened around noon the next day by two policemen summoned by my nurse, who fearing I had died because I wasn't answering the door, broke down the door and found me still asleep in bed. To see if I was still alive they shook me violently and finally roused me to consciousness. After the horror of the phone call and

learning of Vera's death, compounded by the fever and the medication I had taken, and not to mention being violently shaken out of my sleep by two uniformed strangers, I had a nervous breakdown and lapsed into a state of shock that required three weeks of institutionalization in the psychiatric ward of the General Hospital. Vera was buried following the autopsy and the child was placed in the temporary care of a foster mother pending adoption. *(He pours another round.)* I spent a few weeks on sedatives and now I'm more or less back to normal except for a lingering depression, occasional bouts of insomnia, reoccurring headaches, and persistent nightmares. *(lifting his glass)* Cheers Gothard!

GOTHARD
And what about Vera?

GUSTAV
The doctors that performed the autopsy concluded that several factors contributed to her death. The autopsy found vomit in her windpipe and lungs suggesting that she may have choked to death. Klott noted that there had been excessive bleeding during the Caesarean. It was later discovered that she was given a far too powerful dose of the wrong kind of sedatives and apparently the anaesthetist also made some kind of error with the anaesthetic during the Caesarean. As well it was determined that a vein had burst in her brain flooding the left side of her cerebellum with blood and her heart had been severely weakened by all the medication that she had been taking for her circulation and ovulation and whatnot. Oh and one more thing; she was suffering from a dangerously high fever due to having contracted a particularly nasty strain of the flu.... Miraculously the baby was born strong, healthy, and normal. *(reaching for the bottle)* Another round Gothard?

GOTHARD
We forgot to ask Maria to light the candle again.

A gasping scream is heard offstage and MARIA helpless, frightened, and groaning in pain staggers onstage clutching her abdomen, water streaming down her legs.

MARIA
It's time! It's time! The baby, the baby is coming! The baby is coming! Ooooh God!... It's happening! *(crying)* Oooooh...

GUSTAV
Oh my God!... She's going into labour! We have to do something! Lie down Maria! Lie down on the floor!

GUSTAV tries to get up. In his haste his legs fail him as his cane falls to the floor and he falls on his knees and then onto his side.

Gothard help her!... Help her to the floor!

GOTHARD rises from his chair arms flailing around wildly in the air trying to find MARIA. GUSTAV manages to raise himself to his feet. GOTHARD in the meantime has found MARIA and is trying to lower her to the floor.

Wait! Let's put a tablecloth down first.

He grabs the tablecloth from the other table and sends an ashtray crashing to the floor. MARIA is crying hysterically. GUSTAV getting down on his knees awkwardly spreads the tablecloth out over the floor.

Lie down here Maria! Help her down Gothard!

They both carefully ease MARIA down onto the tablecloth.

I'm going to call an ambulance. You stay with her Gothard and do what you can to help her.

Exit GUSTAV clutching his cane and awkwardly limping on his trembling legs as fast as he can. MARIA is lying on the tablecloth, knees bent, legs apart in a birthing position, crying and gasping in pain. GOTHARD is kneeling next to her, awkwardly trying to comfort her.

GOTHARD
Everything will be alright Maria. Gustav is calling an ambulance. They will be here in a few minutes. Soon you'll be in the hospital in a nice bed.... Stay calm.... Stay calm Maria and breathe deeply. That's important Maria, just stay calm. Help is on it's way. Everything will be fine. I'll be right here all the time.

Enter GUSTAV, panicked and hobbling as fast as his crippled legs will carry him toward the front door.

GUSTAV
The phone!... The phone is dead!... I'll.... I'll get help! I'll stop someone on the street!

Exit GUSTAV through the front door.

(*offstage*) Help!... Police!... Police!... Help poliiiiice!

MARIA is wailing in terror and pain as the baby begins to emerge. GOTHARD horrified by the circumstances is helplessly clutching her hand and trembling violently.

GOTHARD
Oh God!... Oh my God!... Oh God help her!

MARIA screaming wildly and GOTHARD screaming with her, gives one final push and the baby slides out onto the tablecloth.

MARIA
Slap it!... Slap it Gothard! It has to breathe! Slap it!

Gothard gropes around between her legs searching for the baby.

GOTHARD
I see it!... I can see the baby!

He lifts the baby by its legs and slaps its bottom. Blackout. A baby is heard crying.

The end.

Saddles in the Rain

Pam Bustin

PAM BUSTIN was born in the Grey Nun's Hospital in Regina Saskatchewan and raised in a host of small towns across the prairies. She has a BA in Theatre from York University.

Her play *Saddles in the Rain* was a finalist in Theatre BC's National Playwriting Competition (1991) and won the 2002 John V Hicks Award.

In 2001 she performed her show *barefoot* at the Her-icane Caroline Festival of Women's Art (Saskatoon) and at Fringes across western Canada. Her play *The Passage of Georgia O'Keeffe* was presented at the Her-icane Ethel Festival (Saskatoon) and the London Ontario Fringe Festival in 2003. Her radio dramas for the CBC include *The White Car Project*, *Coffee in Lloyd* and *Talking with the Dead*. Her short story "Bad Men who Love Jesus" appeared in *The New Quarterly* 86 (Spring 2003). She is currently at work on a novel, tentatively titled *Mostly Happy*. Pam created and taught *The Way of the Word Warrior* – a 15-week creative writing course for female survivors of child sexual abuse for Tamara's House in Saskatoon and was the instructor of 25th Street Theatre's *Playwright Mentor Program* in 2002-2003.

She is a member of the Saskatchewan Playwrights' Centre, the Saskatchewan Writers Guild and the Playwrights Guild of Canada.

Out of the Drawer: The History of Saddles Thus Far
Pam Bustin

Saddles began on a dare.

I was studying Theatre at York University. Tony Stephenson, my third-year Playwriting Prof, gave us an assignment to write a scene wherein "the person we hated the most in the world justified themselves to us." I wrote a scene about a guy named Jake and a girl named Kat. I left the scene on the kitchen table and went to bed. In the morning my roommate handed me a cuppa coffee and the scene and said "what a BITCH!" Success.

Our final assignment in Tony's class was to write a one-act play. I began a comedy about a broke young writer returning to her hometown *(say... Regina)* and camping out in the gazebo of an established Prairie Poet *(say... never mind)*. Tony said "It's okay – but I think you should write the play about Jake."

I said "There is no play about Jake."

He just smiled and said – "Oh yes there is."

And so there was. I wrote it and stuffed it in a drawer. My first play.

Years pass. I'm back in Saskatchewan dealing with some family STUFF and I get a call from my pal Marion DeVries – *Saddles* has been accepted for the New Ideas Festival at Alumni Theatre (Toronto).

I say "I didn't enter."

Marion says "I did – get your ass back here."

And so I do. We get *Saddles* up on the Alumni stage as the first Gulf War rages.

I send a draft off to Theatre BC's National Playwriting Competition, move back to SK and start waitressing to pay off my student loan. *Saddles* is a finalist in the competition. Friends from TO call to say "congrats." I just think "Didn't win."

I get another call.

"Is this Pam Bustin?"

"Yep."

"Pam Bustin who was in a play called *Poison in Paradise* a million years ago."

"Who the hell is this?"

"Beata."

"BEATA Van BERKOM?"

"Yep."

An old pal had been handed a copy of *Saddles* in Vancouver – by some friend of her roommate. It had Connie Gault's name on it and my phone number. We never did figure THAT out – or how this guy got his hands on the play.

She says "You write this?"

I say "Yep."

She says "I wanna do it. Go back to work on it."

So – I do – with the help of DD Kugler, Patti Shedden and the Saskatchewan Playwrights' Centre.

Saddles was produced in 1994 at 25th Street Theatre in Saskatoon. Beata directed and co-produced the show with her company ReaLife Productions. An excerpt was published in *Taking the Stage* (Playwrights Canada Press).

And now here we are—ten years later—and I finally submit the whole play for publication. Dunno why it took me so long.

Well, maybe I do.

It's one thing to tell a story live – on the breath. It's another thing to put it down – officially – on the page.

Like I said, *Saddles in the Rain* is the first play I ever wrote. Since then, I've had several radio dramas produced on CBC radio, a short story published and I've written and toured a show called *barefoot* that uses storytelling and ritual to delineate and celebrate one woman's journey of healing from Child Sexual Abuse.

I've also got a one woman show called *The Passage of Georgia O'Keeffe*. Near the end of the play Georgia says:

> You want to be an artist – do the work – and get the work out there – even if it makes you take to your bed – even if it makes you feel ILL. Create for yourself – and make the buggers take notice. Let them write what they will – knowing you did what you must.
>
> Once I started painting What I wanted As I wanted, following my own nature – there was no stopping me.
>
> Well… not for long. A little bed rest, a few thoughts of insanity… I carried on.
>
> We work. We must work. It's why we are here. To search. To explore our world – the land – the spirit – the beauty… and to bring it to others – as clear as we can.
>
> Do not let the fear stop you.
>
> You mustn't let them stop you from marking your passage.

That Georgia – she's a feisty one.

Writing scares me sometimes. Not all the time. Sometimes it's a hoot. Sometimes a character just starts chattering away in my head and all I have to do is follow her into a story. But somewhere along the way, she's bound to take a turn into Dark Territory and I'll be dragged along.

Kat scared the hell outta me.

Saddles scared the hell outta me. Writing it made me look at stuff like: Why DO women stay with men who hurt them? What happens between a woman and her daughters when Prince Charming turns into a Dragon? Dark territory.

I never sent *Saddles* anywhere because I thought writing it was enough. Truth be told, I thought writing it for Tony's class was enough. Then Marion took me back in for another pass. Then Beata found it and we got it up on stage. I figured that was more than enough. I did the work and I got it out there. Okay – so not many people saw it – but… I did it. Done. I put it back in its drawer.

Then, R.P. MacIntyre said "Hey – was *Saddles* ever published?"

"Nope."

"Why don't you send it in for the John V Hicks Long Manuscript Award – they're doing plays this year."

And so I did.

And it won – along with Mansel Robinson's *Scorched Ice*.

And then Moira asked if she could take a look at it for this collection.

And here it is.

It's a funny ole world.

I'm thankful to Marion, Beata, Moira and everyone else who urged *Saddles* along. I'm especially thankful to Tony for the dare to write the thing in the first place. I'm glad it's leaving the drawer.

Hope you enjoy it. There's some Darkness – but there's laughs along the way – like always.

Go easy – Pam.

— • — **Selected Bibliography** — • —

Stage Plays – *Published*

• *Saddles in the Rain.* 25th Street Theatre and ReaLife Productions, Saskatoon, 1994.

Saddles in the Rain. In *The West of All Possible Worlds: Six Contemporary Canadian Plays.* Ed. Moira Day. Toronto: Playwrights Canada Press, 2004.

Saddles in the Rain. Copyscript. Toronto: Playwrights Guild of Canada, 2001.

Excerpt Published in *Taking the Stage – Selections from Plays by Canadian Women.* Ed. Cynthia Zimmerman. Toronto: Playwrights Canada Press, 1994.

Stage Plays – *Unpublished*

• *The Passage of Georgia O'Keeffe.* pica-pica productions. Her-icane Ethel Festival of Women's Art (Saskatoon) and London ON International Fringe Festival 2003

• *barefoot.* Theatre with a Crooked Grin. Her-icane Carolyn Festival of Women's Art (Saskatoon), Winnipeg, Saskatoon and Edmonton International Fringe Festivals 2001

barefoot. Copyscript. Toronto: Playwrights Guild of Canada, 2003.

Radio Plays

CBC Radio:
• *Talking with the Dead.* New Wave Festival (Radio 2) and Outfront (Street Corner Drama) 2003
• *The White Car Project.* Summer Festival on Monday Night Playhouse (Radio 2), Outfront 2002
• *Coffee in Lloyd.* Festival of New Voices (Radio 2), Gallery, and Outfront 2001

Fiction – *Short Stories*

• "Bad Men Who Love Jesus." *Bad Men Who Love Jesus – the Issue!* [*The New Quarterly* 86 (Spring 2003)]: 239-242.

Reviews of *Saddles in the Rain*

Fuller, Cam. "Fighting Sexual Abuse: A Play That Had to Be. *StarPhoenix* [Saskatoon] 2 November 1994: D1.

—-. "*Saddles in the Rain:* Riveting, Unforgettable Debut Play." *StarPhoenix* [Saskatoon] 27 November 1994: B3.

Gabruch, Jenny. "Coming Home to 25th Street Mixture of Nostalgia and Change." *Saskatoon Sun* 5 November 1994: 19.

Saddles in the Rain was first co-produced by Realife Productions and 25th Street Theatre in Saskatoon in 1994 with the following company:

Kathryn   Patricia Drake
Kat   Paula Costain
Babber   Juanita Vogelsang
Darlene   Judith Hilderman
Jake   Ian Black

Soundscape created and performed by Ley Ward

Director: Beata van Berkom
Designer: Mark von Eschen
Stage Manager: Sheila Crampton

— • —

Saddles in the Rain was given a public staged reading at the New Ideas Festival in Toronto in 1991 under the direction of Marion DeVries.

Saddles in the Rain was given a public staged reading at the Saskatchewan Playwrights Centre's Spring Festival of New Plays in 1994 with the following company:

Kathryn   Patricia Drake
Kat   Sheryl Gardner
Babber   Eden Phelps
Darlene   Heather Hill
Jake   Lou Wetherall

Director: Ben Henderson
Dramaturgy: DD Kugler and Patti Shedden

Characters

KATHRYN	A young woman
KAT	Kathryn as a child – from 5 to 15
BABBER	Kathryn's sister – from birth to teenager
DARLENE	Kathryn's mom
JAKE	Kathryn's stepfather

Notes

The scenes are written to flow into each other. Blackouts should be used VERY sparingly.

The main areas on the set are Kathryn's apartment in the Big City and the family's house, which represents all the houses they have ever lived in. These "homes" can be just suggested, or as realistic as you want.

Kathryn's apartment should be quite obviously separate and have a very different feel than the family house. A circle is good.

The family house has a bedroom with a door that shuts and a window Kat can climb out of, a kitchen and a living room with a tape deck and television.

There's a huge but portable, velvet Elvis watching over us all. Kat takes the painting off the wall at one point so it needs to be reachable.

There is coffee – lots and lots of coffee.

Acknowledgements

Much thanks to all the actors who read and workshopped the script, to the Saskatchewan Playwrights' Centre for development assistance, to Ben Henderson, DD Kugler and Patty Shedden for dramaturgy, to Beata van Berkom for her faith and to Tony Stephenson for daring me to write it.

Dedication

For Tammy.

Saddles in the Rain
by Pam Bustin

——— • ——— • ———

Prologue

KATHRYN listening.

The whispery voices she hears are her mother, her sister, and herself. The lines overlap – so you can't really make them out.

The song she hears is KAT singing her mermaid song. It is a beautiful, haunting, childlike tune.

If you do the voices live KAT's song is more important than her speaking lines.

Suggestions of lines to choose from:

KAT/KATHRYN
I swear never to tell.
Give me a break.
I can't.
I don't understand.

BABBER
I swear never to tell.
He gone to get her?
You were gone long.
I'm okay.

DARLENE
Your dad's here.
Leave her alone Jake.
I really mean it this time…
We'll get away together.

    KATHRYN speaks. Voices continue under.

KATHRYN
Women's voices whispering.
What language? I cannot hear it through my sleep.
The window is open. The women outside.
It's raining.
A child cries.

A young girl hums. Sings a mermaid song on the fire escape of an east Toronto tenement. Drifting notes to slip away on.
Sitting up, I see her through the window.
Her dress is blue cotton.
Sleeveless.

Hanging in the still air
swinging leg

air ruffles near the hem.

Tanned arms,
head bent to the side,
singing into the dusk.

> *KAT stops singing. Whispers stop.*

KAT
What do you fear the most?

KATHRYN
Death.

KAT
No.

KATHRYN
Knives.

KAT
Why?

KATHRYN
I'm afraid of being cut – what it would feel like.

> *We hear a woman (DARLENE) crying with a moaning oboe accompaniment.*
> *Sniffles and whimpers. Sobs.*

I hate the sound of women crying.
What is that "song" on the radio? I hate that. Hate it.
Reminds me of…
Reminds me of my mother when she thinks I'm asleep.

KATHRYN AND AN UNSEEN MAN
Who would ever find you sexy?
Who would ever love you?

KATHRYN
My father said before he left.

> *Crying stops.*

KAT
What do you fear the most?

KATHRYN
Crying. And growing up to be just like Daddy.

When I was nine I knew a prostitute named Annie. She was my best friend
Michelle's mother. Annie was home to make lunch for Michelle and she was there
after school 'til 8:30 – then she went to work. They weren't on welfare.

She had long red hair that me an' Michelle used to braid. "Plait my hair." she'd say.
So we braided it. Michelle did four braid, six braid, even fish-bone, smooth as
anything.

l to r:
Ley Ward,
Patricia
Drake

*photos by
Grant Kernan,
courtesy of
Pam Bustin,
montage by
Pam Bustin*

Annie didn't wear make-up in the day. Only at night. We picked out eye shadows for her. Blue. Brown. Green for special.

She wore jeans in the day, 'til six-thirty, then she decided what to wear for the night. Special nights meant she would be at the big hotel downtown for the whole night. Those nights she wore long soft gowns and green eye shadow. It meant she wouldn't be home 'til eight in the morning, so the door stayed locked. "Don't stay up too late." she'd say. "There's money on the fridge." Then she hugged Michelle and got into the cab.

Whispers start again.

One time Annie got hurt by someone. I was sleeping over. We were still up watching a movie on channel nine. Annie came in and went straight to her room.

"Mom?"

She didn't answer.

Michelle's voice broke on the second "Mom?"
Her eyes kept blinking.

She went to the bedroom door.
"Mom, you okay? Let me in. You okay? Mom? Open the door Mom. Please."

Annie unlocked the door.
I heard Michelle crying in the bedroom. I kept watching Vincent Price.
When I heard Annie start to cry I put on my coat and left through the front door,
locking it behind me.
I didn't turn off the TV.

Whispers stop.

The next day Annie stayed home. Her face was swollen and she had stitches across
her breasts. Boys on drugs had cut her straight across. Dot connecting.
Michelle and I skipped school and stayed with Annie – watching soaps and drinking
coke on the heated waterbed.
I ran to the seven-eleven for smokes.

What do I fear the most?
The young girl in the blue cotton dress singing mermaid songs into the night.
Michelle.
Annie.
Me.

PART I - Scene One

*Music playing. Something BABBER and KATHRYN would listen to. We see the
three women in pools of light. KATHRYN is in her apartment. DARLENE is at the
kitchen table of her and BABBER's house – drinking coffee. BABBER is sitting on
the couch reading a letter from KATHRYN. Lights fade on KATHRYN. Up on only
BABBER and DARLENE's house. Music continues under dialogue.*

KATHRYN
Hey Bab. How's it goin'?
I know, I know – long time no write. Sorry hon. Just workin' and workin'. Had
a part in a play last month and just got totally absorbed – as usual. Now I'm back
waitressin' trying to pay the rent. Gotta love this town.
Just thinkin' about ya tonight and I wanted to drop a line to say hello.
How's Mom?
Hope school's goin' well.
I miss ya kid.
Maybe I can come out sometime soon – or you can come here on a break. Be good
to see ya.
This play I was in was a...

*BABBER stops reading and goes to her bedroom to call KATHRYN. Lights up on
KATHRYN's place as the phone rings.*

KATHRYN
Hello, sorry my machine isn't on to take your call. Can you handle a real live human?
Hello?

BABBER
Hi.

KATHRYN
Who is this?

BABBER
Babber.

KATHRYN
Bab. Hi.
What's the matter?

BABBER
Uh. Nothin'. Just wanted to talk to you.

KATHRYN
Y'sure?

BABBER
Yeah.
How's Danny?

KATHRYN
Uh. Fine.

BABBER
How you doin'?

KATHRYN
Oh great. I've been unemployed for three days and I'm already fighting the "gonna be a bag lady" anxiety attacks. But I've got an audition tomorrow that looks hopeful so I should be okay. How 'bout you?
Bab?

BABBER
Can you come home?

KATHRYN
What?

BABBER
Come home.

KATHRYN
Bab, what happened?
Shit. What'd he do?

BABBER
I charged him.

KATHRYN
Did he hurt you?

BABBER
Not much.

KATHRYN
Are you at home?

BABBER
Yeah.

KATHRYN
He there?

BABBER
No.

KATHRYN
Mom?

BABBER
Yeah. She's in the kitchen.
She won't help me Kat.

KATHRYN
Shit. I'm sorry Bab. Was this tonight?

BABBER
No. A while ago.

KATHRYN
A while. Why didn't you call me?

BABBER
Dunno.

KATHRYN
Okay I'll be home soon as I can.

BABBER
The hearing's in a week.

KATHRYN
Shit. Okay I'll be there.

BABBER
'Kay.

KATHRYN
Babber. Are you okay?

BABBER
(laughs) I charged him with attempted rape.

KATHRYN
Oh God. Bab. I'm sorry.

BABBER
Just come home.

KATHRYN
I will. I love you Bab.

BABBER
Yeah.
Mom says hi.

KATHRYN
Yeah.
See you soon.

BABBER
Yeah.

Lights down on house as BABBER hangs up. KATHRYN hangs up slowly.

KATHRYN
Shit.

She is almost hyperventilating.

Oh shit.

She gets on the phone.

Answer – answer – answer – answer. Shit.

She throws the phone down. She picks it up again – listening to an answering machine.

Hey, Lynne. It's Kathryn. Uh. Could you please call me when you get in – whatever time. Uh. Bab called. I have to go home and I don't know if... I just need to talk to you. Okay. Bye.

Hangs up.

Oh Jesus. I can't do this. Yes you can. You can Kat. You can. No, you will not call Danny. You will not smash a large object. You will sit and wait for Lynne to call. You will pace and wait. You will...

She roots around and pulls out a black file folder full of writing wrapped in her old saddle blanket. It should be concealed somewhere—under a chair, up on a shelf— hidden. She looks at it and is thrown into a series of rapid-fire memories. The scenes are best played as though they begin in the middle of the action – there should be no blackouts.

PART I - Scene Two

KAT is 15 years old. She's packing a duffel bag. She turns to leave and BABBER, 7 years old, is standing there.

BABBER
Where you goin' Kat?

KAT
Bab. I. I just came by to get my stuff. I'm leaving.

BABBER
Leaving for where?

KAT
LEAVING Bab.

BABBER
Like forever?

KAT
Forever?

BABBER
What do you mean you're leaving?

KAT
Bab. I just can't…

BABBER
What?

KAT
I've been gone for two weeks.

BABBER
I just thought you were…

KAT
I know. I found an apartment. I just came back for some stuff.

BABBER
Why?

KAT
I need my stuff.

BABBER
No – why are you leaving?

KAT
Babber.

BABBER
Don't Kathryn. What about me 'n' Mom?

KAT
That's gotta be up to Mom. What am I supposed to do about it?

BABBER
Stay.

KAT
I can't Babber.

PART I - Scene Three

DARLENE
I can't Kat. He needs me.

KAT
Oh please. What? He needs you to scream at and slap around whenever he feels like it.

DARLENE
Kat don't.

KAT
Mom. It's true. I don't understand.

DARLENE
You will one day. It's just the way it is.

KAT
Bullshit.

DARLENE
Kat.

KAT
Bull fucking shit Mom – you have to leave.

DARLENE
I can't.

KAT
Why?

DARLENE
Because I love him.

KAT
Oh Christ – You're terrified of him. All those times you said we'd leave and then we didn't because you were afraid he'd find us like the first time we left. He found us and cried and we went back and within a week – a week – it was three times worse than before we left. So we never left again, just talked about it. Well I've left, and if you don't leave soon and take Babber…

DARLENE
I can't.

KAT
Can you tell me why?

DARLENE
I… can't.

KAT
Tell me why!

KATHRYN
Once i tried to make her leave
So many times i tried
But then i knew i couldn't bring her back
To me
Once we were close – so close
Just Mom and me
Before.

PART I - Scene Four

    KAT is five years old. DARLENE is humming "Raindrops Keep Fallin' on my Head" the theme to "Butch Cassidy and the Sundance Kid."

KAT
That was the best movie ever – eh?

DARLENE
Yeah, it was pretty good.

KAT
Pretty good? You cried.
Mom, who's sexier – Robert Redford or Elvis?

DARLENE
Kat!

KAT
Oh c'mon Mom. You vote for Elvis, right?

DARLENE
What's wrong with Elvis?

KAT
Nothin'. Only I never seen him ride a horse like the Sundance Kid.

DARLENE
He can ride – He plays a cowboy in a bunch of movies.

KAT
Really.

DARLENE
Sure.

DARLENE begins doin' her Elvis impersonation. KAT joins in. They sing a portion of "Flaming Star." They laugh.

KAT
Okay – they tie then.

PART I - Scene Five

DARLENE is putting on make up. KAT, 5 years old, watches.

KAT
Where you guys goin'?

DARLENE
Prob'ly the Circle J.

KAT
The Circle J. Is there cowboys there?

DARLENE
Yep.

KAT
You gonna dance?

DARLENE
You know it. Honey.

KAT
You goin' with Auntie?

DARLENE
Yep.

KAT
I gotta stay at Grandpa's?

DARLENE
Yep.

KAT
Soon I'll be big enough to stay alone right? When I'm seven.

DARLENE
Maybe when you're ten.

KAT
You look real pretty Mom. I bet you're the prettiest one there and everyone wants to dance with you.

DARLENE
You think so.

KAT
I know so. Promise to tell me everything?

DARLENE
I promise. Ready to go?

KAT
C'n I have lipstick?

DARLENE smiles and puts some on her.

PART I - Scene Six

KAT is six years old. A car horn sounds.

DARLENE
Kat, it's time to go. Your Dad's here.

KAT
Don't wanna go.

DARLENE
He's here.

KAT
I'm sick.

DARLENE
You are not.

KAT
My tummy hurts.

DARLENE
Your father is waiting.

KAT
Why do I always have to go?

DARLENE
You haven't gone in three weeks.

KAT
So.

DARLENE
He wants to see you, Kat.

KAT
Why?

DARLENE
Kathryn.

KAT
He pay you the back payments?

DARLENE
Some. That isn't the point.

KAT
You wanna go out this weekend.

DARLENE
Yes. But that isn't the point either.

KAT
Well, why don't you and me go to the dusk 'til dawn Vampire movies at the Cinema Six?

    Car horn sounds.

DARLENE
I promised your father he could see you this weekend. We'll go to the drive-in next week. C'mon kid. Gimme a break here.

KAT
Okay. Can I just go to Anna's? Then you can go out and I won't be–

DARLENE
You're going with your father.

    KAT grabs something and throws it.

KAT
No! I don't wanna go.

DARLENE
What is wrong with you?

KAT
Nothing.

DARLENE
Is he drinking?

KAT
No.

DARLENE
Then what?

KAT
Nothin'. I'll go.

DARLENE
You don't go around throwing things for no reason. Tell me what's the matter.

KAT
Nothing.

DARLENE
I want you to tell me what's wrong. If he's drinking again or not looking after you properly I'll…

KAT
No. I said I'll go.

PART I - Scene Seven

KAT
You goin' out?

DARLENE
Yep. Like my new shirt?

KAT
Yeah.

DARLENE
What?

KAT
It's kinda flashy.

DARLENE
You don't like it.

KAT
No. It's okay. I kinda like it when I squint my eyes and lean my head this way.

DARLENE
Smarty.

KAT
You look great, Mom. Can I go over to Sharon's?

DARLENE
No. You're stayin' at Grandpa's 'til I pick you up.

KAT
I'll just sleep there.

DARLENE
No. I'll pick you up. I won't be too late. We're just goin' for a couple of beers.

KAT
You seein' that guy?

DARLENE
Which guy?

KAT
That guy from last week.

DARLENE
Frank? No.

KAT
Good. Who ya seein'?

DARLENE
I'm going with Auntie.

KAT
Yeah but…

DARLENE
What?

KAT
If someone is comin' back with you I'd rather stay at Sharon's.

DARLENE
You're going to Grandpa's.

KAT
Why can't I stay at Sharon's?

DARLENE
Because I said so.

KAT
That's so dumb.

DARLENE
Kathryn. C'mon. I don't want your friend's mother talking about me.

KAT
Why would she? I'll just pretend you made liver for supper and I didn't want to eat it and I'm trying to escape you.

DARLENE
Very funny. What's wrong with stayin' at Grandpa's? Bet you can get him to play Lego with you. Grandpa's really good at Lego. You can build another Metropolis all over his living room.

KAT
Yeah. That's pretty fun.

DARLENE
Hey, tell ya what. I think this shirt is too flashy to wear out for a few drinks. I think this is a super heroine shirt. I think you should wear it tonight.

KAT
Serious?

DARLENE
Sure. Then you can build your own secret Fortress of Solitude.

KAT
Cool. *(eyes big – irresistibly cute)* I'll come home real early in the mornin'.

DARLENE
Oh all right. You want lipstick?

KAT
No.

DARLENE
Make you pretty.

KAT
Super Chick don't wear no lipstick.

KATHRYN
When i look in a mirror what do i see
distortions of my self
mirrors covered in raindrops
faces covered in tears
not the face to win the prince
not that i ever wanted to
i never really wanted to

PART I - Scene Eight

KAT is seven years old.

JAKE
Hey there beautiful!

KAT
You talkin' to me?

JAKE
You see anyone else?

KAT
Who're you?

JAKE
Jake.

KAT
I'm Kat.

JAKE
I know. I know your mom.

KAT
Great. You want an award?

JAKE
Watcha doin'?

KAT
Drawin'.

JAKE
Drawing what?

KAT
Horses.

JAKE
Can I see? Hey, you're pretty good. How come you only do heads?

KAT
Ain't so good at bodies yet.

JAKE
You like horses, eh?

KAT
Sure.

JAKE
Ever seen a real one?

KAT
Sure. Lotsa times.

JAKE
Yeah?

KAT
Yeah. At the Ex. I rode a pony once. Someday I'm gonna have my own horse. A big one. I'm gonna have a farm and I'm gonna have ten horses – five 'Paloosas, three Quarter Horses and a pair of Clydes. And each one is gonna have her own special saddle and tack 'n' everything.

JAKE
You sure know a lot about horses.

KAT
Yep.

JAKE
Think you could ride a wild pony?

KAT
Sure.

JAKE
They're pretty tough.

KAT
You seen wild ponies?

> *DARLENE enters and watches them.*

JAKE
Sure. In Alberta. I worked a coupla round-ups.

KAT
No way.

JAKE
Yeah way. Nothin' like it, Beauty, being out on the range.

KAT
There ain't no more wild ponies.

JAKE
There sure are.

KATE
You just catch one then it's yours?

JAKE
If you can catch 'em.

KAT
You can catch 'em?

JAKE
Sure. Mostly I worked with a bunch of cowboys – on big round-ups. But I know them ponies. I watched 'em. I lived with 'em – out there in the middle of nowhere. After a spell you learn their ways. The rules of the herd. I could catch one.

KAT
Maybe. But I dunno if you should.

JAKE
Should what?

KAT
Catch 'em. Maybe you oughtta leave 'em alone.

JAKE
They ain't doin' no good wild.

KAT
Sez you.

JAKE
Can't just let them run around.

KAT
Why not?

JAKE
Horses are meant to be rode.

KAT
I dunno. Maybe some are meant to be wild. So we can see them. I'd like to just see that – wild horses runnin'.

JAKE
I thought you wanted a horse of your own.

KAT
Yeah. Well maybe there'd be one that'd like me. Maybe she'd pick me and decide not to be wild.
What?

JAKE
You been readin' too many Black Beauty books. See, I know horses. First you gotta break them – show them who's boss. Then you can train them and they'll do what you say. It ain't just magic.

KAT
You ever had a horse that was your favourite?

JAKE
Had lotsa horses.

KAT
No. Like a favourite – special one.

JAKE
Yeah. Once when I was a kid.
My friend Eddie lived down on the Rez and he had this ole black 'n' white Pinto. Used to follow me around all the time, thinkin' I had apples hid in my jacket.

KAT
Did ya?

JAKE
Sure.
Patches. That was his name.
Ain't the same thing though. He wasn't wild.

KAT
Yeah, but he picked you. It's the same thing.

    Sees DARLENE.

Hey, Mom, Did you know this guy's a cowboy?

DARLENE
No. I didn't actually. Hello Jake.

JAKE
Hiya hon.

KAT
Yeah. He works round-ups and everything. He says I draw horses really good.

JAKE
Sure does.

DARLENE
That's my Kat.

JAKE
So, how's about we three rustle up some steaks down at the Ponderosa?

KAT
Steak? Yahoo – I'm gettin' my coat!

DARLENE
That's really nice. Kat loves restaurant food.

JAKE
Only the best for my gals.

PART I - Scene Nine

KAT
Okay Mom, sit.

DARLENE
What is this?

KAT
Sit. Sit. We have a show for ya.

JAKE
And now the amazing Katmandu...

KAT
Accompanied by Jakeydo the Great present to you... "Jedediah was a Bulldog"

*They proceed to do their version of "Joy to the World" ("Jeremiah Was a Bullfrog")
by Three Dog Night - just one verse and one chorus. JAKE barks and howls. Part-
way through KAT forgets the words and DARLENE joins in. By the end they are
all, including KATHRYN, singing and laughing.*

Thank you. Thank you. You're a dynamite audience. Luv Y'all! Good night.

DARLENE and JAKE kiss.

Sheesh.

PART I - Scene Ten

KAT
You sure like him huh?

DARLENE
Uh huh.

KAT
So... you marrying him?

DARLENE
Uh huh.

KAT
That's good. I like Jake. He's funny huh?

DARLENE
Uh huh.

KAT sings the "Uh Huhs" from "Summer Nights" by John Travolta/Olivia Newton-John.

KAT
Uh huh. Uh huh. Uh huh. Shooby do wah. Uh huh. I'm glad Mom. Congratulations. You'll be happy.

Smiles and a hug.

DARLENE
We'll all be happy.

PART I - Scene Eleven

JAKE
Yeah. When you were little I used to take you for rides on my bike.

KAT
No way.

JAKE
Sure. I'd pick you up from school and give you a ride home. Way back. Even when you were in Kindergarten.

KAT
Really?

JAKE
Sure. Right, Hon? Back when you were workin' at the Bus Depot.

DARLENE
I guess so.

JAKE
You were livin' over on Fifth Ave. In that apartment above the laundromat.

DARLENE
Yeah.

JAKE
See?

KAT
I don't remember.

JAKE
Sure ya do. I even had a little helmet to match your jacket.

KAT
My purple suede?

JAKE
Sure.

KAT
But that was…

JAKE
What?

KAT
I was real little when I had that jacket.

JAKE
Sure. I gave it to you.

KAT
But we didn't know you yet.

JAKE
Yes you did.

KAT
I don't…

JAKE
You were about four or five – cute little thing, playing tag with your friends in fronta the ole man's house.

KAT
Probably Hide 'n' Seek. We always played that. I was the best hider.

JAKE
That's right. You were hiding in the Caragana bushes out front when I drove up. Made ya jump.

KAT
Yeah.

JAKE
Then I called ya over.

KAT
Yeah?

JAKE
Yeah. And you didn't want to come, but you did finally and I gave ya the jacket.

DARLENE
You wore that jacket 'til you split all the seams and it rotted off your body.

KAT
I loved that jacket.

JAKE
'Course. It was cool – and it was from me – coolest of the cool. Right baby?

DARLENE
Right.

KAT
Right.

KATHRYN
Sometimes i wish i could freeze a moment
and hold it forever inside of me
a moment when everything's okay
and the dark is held at bay
just one moment

> *BABBER is swirled onto the scene. She lays down, in the fetal position. KAT goes to her.*

KAT
Barbara. Hi Barbara. You're so tiny. Tiny little Babber.

> *BABBER holds KAT's finger and smiles.*

I love you little Babber.

PART I - Scene Twelve

> *KAT is nine years old.*

JAKE
Kat. C'mon Beauty, wake up.

KAT
What.

> *She's scared. Grabs BABBER who's sleeping beside her.*

JAKE
We gotta go.

KAT
Huh?

JAKE
C'mon. It's vamoose boogie time. Grab yer stuff.

> *He leaves to the kitchen, where DARLENE is finishing packing a bag of stuff.*

Don't forget the black box under the bed.

DARLENE
I got it.

> *She carries the stuff out, comes back in and has a smoke. KAT wakes up BABBER, and throws some books, clothes and BABBER's stuffed toy into a gym bag.*

JAKE
Got everything you need?

KAT
Sure. But where we goin'?

JAKE
Nokomis.

KAT
Nokomis?

JAKE
Sounds good, eh?

KAT
Sure.
Where's Nokomis?

KATHRYN
Sometimes i sense the change in the wind just before it happens
i can't see the storm clouds yet
but i sure can smell the rain.

PART I - Scene Thirteen

They are all wandering around the stage with flashlights.

DARLENE
We shouldn't do this?

JAKE
Why not? I ain't been caught yet.

DARLENE
I mean with the kids.

JAKE
Hey. It's an adventure. You just keep a lookout and we'll explore a little. Relax.

   KAT bumps something.

Shhh.

KAT
What? You sure nobody lives here?

JAKE
Positive.

KAT
They sure left a lot of stuff.

JAKE
All the better for us.

BABBER
Look what I found.

JAKE
Finders keepers, darlin'.

KAT
I'm gonna check the attic – bet that's where the coolest stuff is.

DARLENE
Jake, someone's coming up the road.

Flashlights out.

PART I - Scene Fourteen

JAKE and DARLENE. KAT watches, unseen. She's ten years old.

JAKE
Just shut up and leave me alone.

DARLENE
Jake I'm just worried.

JAKE
So I'll get another fuckin' job. No big deal. Kent says they need some help at the elevator in Govan. We can move there.

DARLENE
Kat'll have to change schools again.

JAKE
So.

DARLENE
It's hard on a kid, movin' so much.

JAKE
You're the one who's always braggin' how smart she is. It ain't gonna hurt her.

DARLENE
I'm just sayin'.

JAKE
So send the little bitch to Regina to live with your old man so she can stay in the same school. I don't give a fuck. We're moving.

DARLENE
Jake. I'm not sending my kid away.

JAKE
Look. I need a job, right? So we move, right? Right?

DARLENE
Right.

PART I - Scene Fifteen

KAT sits at his feet as he talks.

JAKE
Moon shinin' real clear on the water and I'm sittin' there. Just thinkin'.
It's real quiet. Trees casting purple shadows all 'round.
Then I hear this coyote yelp. Real far away. Like he's calling someone. Then it's quiet again. So still I can hear the hum off the lightning bugs.
Then I hear a twig snap. One twig sounds like a shotgun. And there, right across the lake, is a doe.
She dips her head and takes a good long drink. I'm holding my breath, not wantin' to scare her. She lifts her head and I can hear the water drippin' into the lake. She looks right into me with those brown brown eyes.
Eddie's sleepin'.
I just sit there—long time—just lookin' at her. Then the coyote yelps again, and the doe turns and fades back into the woods.

PART I - Scene Sixteen

KAT
What happened?

DARLENE
Nothing.

KAT
Mom, you're hurt.

DARLENE
I shouldn't have bothered him, that's all. He was in a bad mood. I should've left him alone.
He didn't mean it. He was mad 'cause I went out. I should've stayed home.

KAT
You can't stay in all the time.

DARLENE
It's not so bad.

KAT
Mom, what are we gonna do?

DARLENE
What do you mean?

KAT
He hurts you.

DARLENE
I'm okay.

KAT
He's drunk, isn't he?

DARLENE
Kathryn. I shouldn't have bugged him, that's all. He didn't mean anything. He's gone now, so just go and check on your sister. Make sure she's asleep.
Go, I'm okay.

KATHRYN
sometimes, i try to put my arms all the way 'round her
and tell her it's okay.
she forgets if i don't tell her that i love her
so i hug her and say she's beautiful
my beautiful mother love
and when she's lower down – more quieter
i kiss her on the head
and hold her face inside my hands
and make her laugh by pushing back her cheeks
and scrunching up my nose to make a face.
sometimes, if her eye is sore
or she wiped her face, but missed a spot
i spit on the edge of my T-shirt and clean the red off
sure to kiss the bad spot better 'fore she falls asleep
and tell her that the marks don't really show
so much
this time.
i say – shh, shh, my little one
like she does when i get sick.
i say – it's okay. okay
        the bogeyman is gone away
        he won't be back Mom
        not today.

PART I - Scene Seventeen

KAT is asleep. JAKE is standing over her. He leans over her and she wakes up. She freezes. He caresses her face. She is scared but cannot move.

KATHRYN
No.
Shit.

KATHRYN goes back to the hiding spot and pulls out a gun. She wraps herself up in the saddle blanket and stares at the gun.

Oh Jesus. Jesus. Jesus. Jesus…

The phone starts to ring. She ignores it. The rings fade as we move into the memory scene.

PART II - Scene One

"Are You Lonesome Tonight" by Elvis Presley plays. Music, or background noise is constant throughout this memory until the last scene.

Coffee is made. BABBER is asleep in the bedroom. She is about six years old.

KAT comes in wearing a tank top and jeans, carrying a knapsack. She's about fourteen. She's tired. She looks in on BABBER. She stands looking at the picture of Elvis.

KAT
Hiya Hon.

DARLENE enters.

DARLENE
Kathryn.

KAT
Hiya Mom.

They want to hug, but don't.

DARLENE
How are you? You look…

KAT
Ah. A little rough huh?

DARLENE
No. You look fine. Just… tired.

KAT
Yeah.
Jake here?

DARLENE
No. How are you?

KAT
I'm okay Mom. I'm sorry.

DARLENE
Kat, I…. Welcome home honey. *(touches her arm)*
You want some coffee?

KAT
Sure.

DARLENE goes to get it.

DARLENE
A lot of your friends called.

KAT
Yeah? What'd you tell 'em?

DARLENE
Said you were visiting relatives.

DARLENE gives her a coffee.

KAT
Thanks.
Ooh! Hot coffee man. C'mon. I'm gonna go wake de bambino.

She sneaks into the bedroom, gets into bed with BABBER, KAT bumps her and then pretends to be asleep.

BABBER
Mom?

Notices KAT and jumps on her.

KAT
Hey! What days are these when a girl can't even get a little sleep in her own bed?

BABBER
You were gone long!

They wrestle off the bed. BABBER captures KAT and sits on her.

KAT
You keep my saddle polished or what? You take care of my horse? If Cheyenne is skinny I'm gonna have to give her some of this!

Grabs BABBER's cheeks. They wrestle again.

DARLENE
You guys want breakfast?

KAT
Who me? I ate and she doesn't need any.

BABBER escapes into the kitchen.

BABBER
Honeycombs! Gimme mah Honeycombs!

DARLENE
Sure you aren't hungry? I just baked bread.

KAT
Yeah. Smells great, but I'm okay.

BABBER
Honeycombs!

DARLENE
Kat, Jake's gonna be away a while. He's…. He's in Saskatoon.

BABBER has found the Honeycomb and is pouring the cereal all over the table in an attempt to fill her bowl.

BABBER
Honeycombs!

KAT
You jest hold yerself tigither sweet thang 'til ah gits out thar.

> KAT *pours milk in the cereal, cleans the table and puts the Honeycombs back into the box. DARLENE goes to the stereo and puts an old Springsteen (or whatever KAT would've listened to) tape on.*

BABBER
Mom tell ya? Dad got taked away by the cops. They came all the way out here to get him. He was sure mad too and he–

DARLENE
Babber.

> *She lights a smoke.*

KAT
So he in jail or what?

DARLENE
Will be. He's in Saskatoon.

KAT
What'd he do now? No. I don't really care.
Hey, maybe one of these days we'll luck out and he'll actually get to do a stretch at P.A.

DARLENE
Kat.

KAT
He'll get off.

DARLENE
Probably.

KAT
Hey Mom – you smoke too much. *(They smile.)*
So, what's goin' on today?

DARLENE
Bab, go get dressed. *(BABBER goes.)* She missed you.

KAT
Yeah. I missed her too.

DARLENE
Kat, what if we move to Vancouver? You could start school there in September.

KAT
Vancouver.

DARLENE
It's far enough.

KAT
When?

DARLENE
Now. While he's gone.

KAT
What about Cheyenne?

DARLENE
What about her?

KAT
I'm not leaving Cheyenne here.

DARLENE
Christ. Call someone to take her – just 'til we find a place.

KAT
Jake'll get her.

DARLENE
No he won't.

KAT
Mom. I bought her. I broke her. She's mine and I ain't gonna let Jake get her.

DARLENE
What the hell are you talking about? You just took off for a month and left her here
for fuck sakes.

BABBER enters carrying clothes including a large James Dean T-shirt.

BABBER
C'n I wear this?

KAT
Sure.

BABBER
Thanks Kat. *(leaves)*

KAT
Vancouver eh? I could live with that.

DARLENE
We'll take Cheyenne.

KAT
You got money?

DARLENE
Not enough for a car and a horse – but I can get it. I'll go to Mary's. I already talked
to her.
You don't think I can do it.

KAT
I never said that.

DARLENE
I really mean it this time. I'm ready to go. I've got stuff packed for me and Bab. I was just waiting.

KAT
For me.

DARLENE
I couldn't go without you.
I was scared you wouldn't come back this time.
You're right, Kat. We have to leave. I've thought it through. I figure if we head to B.C. he won't be able to find us. I can go back to school out there – get my grade ten and take Hairdressing or something. We can do this.

KAT
Okay. I'm in. What do I have to do?

DARLENE
Pack your stuff. I'll run over to Mary's. When I get back we can hook up the trailer, load up and go. Can you get Bab ready?

KAT
Sure. Oh wait…

She takes a beaded black leather pouch from around her neck.

It's not real Indian Pattern. I wanted to make up my own. It's for keeping treasures in. That's you in the middle.

DARLENE
I'm square.
Thanks. It's beautiful.

KAT
Hey, don't get all sappy on me – just go fill it with treasure.

DARLENE leaves. KAT digs a tape out of her knapsack and puts it on. It's "O Fortuna" from the opera "Carmina Burana" by Carl Orff ("The Siege of Camylarde" on the "Excalibur" movie soundtrack). She tries one of her mom's smokes, chokes. She stands beside her door, strikes a Bette Davis pose with the cigarette.

What – a – dump!

She inhales deeply and begins choking. BABBER has entered and is laughing.

Oh great. *(choke)*

BABBER
I'm tellin'. You smoked.

KAT
Pardon?

BABBER
I'm gonna tell Mom you was smokin' her smokes.

KAT
Oh no you're not.

BABBER
Oh yes I am.

KAT
Oh no you're not.

BABBER
Yes I a-am.

KAT
No you're no-ot. Would you like to know why?

BABBER
'Cuz we gonna duel.

KAT
No…

BABBER
Yeah. 'Cuz if we don't duel I'm tellin'.

KAT
Bab…

BABBER
Tellin' tellin' tellin'…

KAT
Very well.

She draws herself up into a snobbish pose.

I, Lady Peregrine, challenge you Lady…?

BABBER
Lady… Spidey!

KAT
Lady Spidey? *(BABBER nods.)* Oooookay.
I, Lady Peregrine of the Falcons, do hereby challenge you, Lady Spidey of the Webs,
to a duel.

BABBER
A duel you say?

KAT
A duel to the death, m'lady.

BABBER
No. No "to the death."

KAT
So be it. A duel to the deal.

BABBER
I 'cept.

KAT goes to her room and retrieves two yardsticks that have been made into swords. She holds them up to BABBER.

KAT
Choose your weapon Spidey.

BABBER chooses the slightly shorter sword. They've done this a million times and it is a pretty impressive duel.

The rules remain the same. No unfair slinging of webs or calling on the aid of my feathered friends.
EN GARDE!

BABBER gives her a whack.

BABBER
Hah!

KAT
Very good young one, but methinks you haven't been practicing. Whereas I… have!

KAT does some fancy footwork and gets BABBER on the butt. BABBER trips, twisting around to keep her eyes on KAT.

BABBER
Cheatin'!

KAT
Skill, little one, skill. Up! You must watch me and stay standing.

BABBER gets in a hit.

A touch, a touch. I do confess.
Again.

BABBER
By the power of, uh, Wonder Woman!

KAT
Wonder Woman? Your loyalty begs question rogue!

KAT gets in a little tap.

Touche!

KAT keeps escaping 'til BABBER looks like she will give up.

Come, for the second Lady Spidey, you but dally!

BABBER chases KAT with renewed ferocity. KAT starts laughing.

BABBER
EEEEAAAHHHGGG!

She slaps KAT on the side with her sword.

KAT
Ah. I am slain! Oh. I die, sweet Spidey. The strength of thine arm hath cast me to the ground. I cannot live to hear the morning's Lark again. But…. But…

BABBER
No dead scene I said.

KAT
Shall we deal, fair Lady?

BABBER
My dishes for a week!

KAT
A week!

BABBER
Okay. For today's.

KAT
So be it.

KAT starts to do a dramatic death scene.

BABBER
No – dead – scene, bird-face.

KAT
As you wish. Now that the deal has been struck, may I trust you with a confidence?

BABBER
A what?

KAT
A secret.

BABBER
Def'nitely.

KAT
There will be no dishes today.

BABBER
Cheatin'!

KAT
M'lady, you do me dishonour. 'Tis nothing of the kind.

BABBER
Oh that is for sure cheatin' and I wanna new deal.

KAT has turned her back on the harangue and clears her throat to indicate that BABBER has fallen too far out of her role.

KAT
AHEM!

BABBER
You mock me.

KAT
No. By this hand.

> *They fall about laughing.*

Would it suffice thee if I offered to carry your load?

BABBER
What load… pray tell?

KAT
Fair sis, we are about to embark on a daring adventure.

BABBER
For real?

KAT
Soft soft, little one. We have been entrusted with a mission. By the time our Lady, the Queen, returns all must be in readiness, for our departure.

BABBER
Huh?

KAT
We must prepare to flee.

BABBER
Flea?

KAT
Onward – to the undiscovered country with our belongings on our backs.

BABBER
Oh – GO.
Can't we just take the Maverick?

KAT
Look. Are you with me on this or not?

BABBER
Okay. What about… our Lady?

KAT
Mom'll be right back.

BABBER
'Kay. But what about…

KAT
Lady, lady, are you with me or against?

BABBER
With you.

KAT
Then hie to your garret and gather your stuff.

BABBER
Yeah, but…

KAT
Take all of value from the castle walls – make haste!

BABBER
C'n we take the Elvis?

KAT
Absolutely! Go. I'll get it.

> *She takes down the Elvis. BABBER runs to her room, hears a car and looks out the window to see who it is.*

BABBER
It's Daddy. Kat…. It's Daddy.

KAT
What?

BABBER
He's got a new car.

KAT
Shit.

BABBER
(runs out to KAT) What'd you say?

KAT
Nothing.

BABBER
Now he can come on the adventure too.

KAT
Bab. I told you that was a secret.

BABBER
Yeah, but…

KAT
Swear.

> *She holds her thumb out.*

BABBER
Kat.

KAT
Swear.

> *BABBER places her thumb on KAT's as though they are doing a blood swear.*

BABBER
I swear never to tell. I swear.

> *JAKE enters. BABBER runs to him and he swings her up.*

JAKE
Hey Babby! How ya doin'? Ya miss me? Huh?
Where's Mum?

KAT
She's in town.

JAKE
Jesus Christ. Look who's home.

KAT
That's what I was going to say. Get you a cup of coffee?

JAKE
That'd be good. What the hell are you doing with that?

KAT
Dusting.

> *She rehangs the Elvis. She goes to her bag and puts on a sweatshirt, and they all go to the kitchen. KAT pours him a cup of coffee. He watches her closely. When she hands him the coffee he reaches toward her, she dodges. She sits across from him. BABBER sits between them.*

JAKE
When'd you get back?

KAT
This morning.

JAKE
Good timin' Beauty.
Heard you were in Calgary.

KAT
How'd you know that?

JAKE
(laughs) Christ! Babber go shut that off. What the hell is that shit?

KAT
"O Fortuna."

> *BABBER takes off KAT's tape and puts on some Johnny Cash. The first song is "Folsom Prison Blues." KAT smiles. JAKE ignores her. BABBER stays in the living room, playing.*

JAKE
Where's the old lady?

KAT
I told you. In town.

JAKE
F'r what?

KAT
Groceries.

JAKE
Well, she better get her ass back here.

KAT
Why.

JAKE
'Cause we gotta go.

KAT
Where?

JAKE
Outta here f'r fuck sakes! What the hell's wrong with you?

KAT
Nothin'. I'm going for a ride.

JAKE
Where?

KAT
Just wanna take Cheyenne for a run. I'm not going anywhere.

JAKE
Make sure of that.

KAT
What do you think I'm gonna do?

JAKE
Maybe you should stay here.

> *He grabs her.*

KATHRYN
Let go of me.

KAT
With Babber here? That'd be real stupid wouldn't it.

JAKE
Babber, c'mere.

KAT
Don't even think about it… Dad.

JAKE
Why not…. Beauty?

> *BABBER hears a car pull up. Looks to see who it is.*

KAT
You ever do anything to her and I'll...

JAKE
What are you gonna do about it Beauty?

BABBER
'S Mom!

JAKE
Mommy's home. No more time to play. This coffee's shit. Why don't you get me a beer.

     KAT doesn't move. DARLENE enters. She has the pouch hanging around her neck.

DARLENE
Whose car is... Jake.

JAKE
Hiya Hon.

DARLENE
When did you.... You got off.

KAT
Think so?

JAKE
(to KAT) Get the groceries. *(to DARLENE)* You did get groceries, didn't you? That's why you went into town, isn't it?

DARLENE
Yes.

JAKE
You see anyone?

DARLENE
What–

JAKE
(to KAT) Get the groceries! *(She goes.)* Bring them right in. What's that? *(indicating the pouch)*

DARLENE
Oh. Kat made it. *(She tucks it in her shirt.)*

JAKE
Get me a beer. *(She does.)* Pack.

DARLENE
Why?

JAKE
Whaddaya think?

DARLENE
What happened?

JAKE
I just wanna get outta here f'r fuck sakes.
Look. I saw a chance and I took it. They won't miss me til morning.

DARLENE
So we leave by morning.

JAKE
We leave now.

BABBER
We goin' away?

DARLENE
Babber, be quiet.

BABBER
'Kay.

DARLENE
Where are we going?

JAKE
East.

DARLENE
East. East where?

JAKE
I said East for Christ's sake!

DARLENE
You hungry?

> *KAT enters and listens without them seeing her. She puts a bag of stuff on the counter.*

JAKE
Where's my guns?

DARLENE
They took them.

JAKE
Shit. I need a gun.

DARLENE
No you don't. We'll just go. I'll pack right now and we'll go. What do you need a gun for?

KAT
Where we goin'?

DARLENE
East.

KAT
East?

JAKE
East! You just shut the fuck up.

KAT
Sounds like fun. Why don't we just leave the country this time?

DARLENE
Kathryn.

KAT
No, really. C'mon you guys. What the heck. Let's really start over – in a whole new country far far away. We can rob banks or something. We can train Babber to seduce perverted bank managers and we can–

JAKE
Shut up.

DARLENE
Kat. Don't.

JAKE
Pack your shit. Unless you're still packed.
Do it now Beauty.

KAT
I'm not going.

JAKE
We're all going.

KAT
Why?

DARLENE
Kat.

KAT
No really, why? Why'd you come back for us? I don't get it.

JAKE
Because I love you all so much.

  KAT looks at him, looks at her mother.

KAT
Fine. I'll pack.

JAKE
Good plan.

She goes to the bedroom, lies on bed. BABBER lays beside her. DARLENE pours herself a coffee and sits across from JAKE.

DARLENE
You could go ahead and then call us…

JAKE
You don't wanna go?

DARLENE
Of course I want to.

JAKE
Then pack.

DARLENE
Where you going?

JAKE
I need a gun. Pack. I'll be right back.

> *He leaves. DARLENE sits at the table, drinks coffee and starts to cry. She wipes her eyes, lights a smoke. KAT stands in the bedroom door.*

DARLENE
Kat. We're all going.

KAT
Yeah.

> *She gets the bag off of the counter.*

DARLENE
Hey, what's in the bag?

KAT
Shit from your back seat.

DARLENE
Thanks honey.

> *She pulls out the pouch and takes the money out – gives it to KAT.*

You'd better keep this.

KAT
Yeah.

PART II - Scene Two

Lights dim. Up on BABBER in bed. KAT sitting on the floor in the living room making a beaded pouch. She is listening to music. JAKE comes in. He shuts off her music and turns on the TV. He starts watching some cheesy cheesecake sitcom. He's drunk.

JAKE
Yer mom asleep?

KAT
Yep.

JAKE
What're ya doin'?

KAT
Beading.

JAKE
Yeah? Had a friend who did that.

KAT
Eddie.

JAKE
Yeah, Lil Eddie. Told you about him, huh? Full blood Cree – crazy as a wild dog –
but he sure could do carvin' and beadin'. I lived with him and his ole man.

KAT
I know.

JAKE
Yep. After I left home. Went down to Little Eddie's and he and his ole man took me
in. Dad took a fit when he found out I was livin' on the Rez. Come down and tried
to drag me home. Got the shit beat outta him for once. I was what… about…

KAT
Ten.

JAKE
Yeah, ten years old…. Just couldn't stay there no more.
Ole man had me locked up in the back room for days. No food. Dried blood on my
face from the fight we'd had.
Crazy bastard wouldn't even let me out to take a shit. Had a spot in the corner.
Christ.
He got called in to work and Mom came in to bring me some food 'n' clean me up.
She was wailin' and "Oh Holy Motherin'" and I couldn't stand it. I left.

He waits for a response. KAT keeps beading.

She got in trouble for that – lettin' me out while he was gone.
Yep, she got in trouble all right.
Sonny told me she was in the hospital for a week on accounta me. Ole Dad never
took shit from nobody.
Sonny wanted me to come home, but I just stayed with Little Eddie. He was more
my brother than Sonny ever was.
Me 'n' Eddie rode with the Angels y'know.

KAT rolls her eyes in disbelief. Keeps beading.

KAT
Uh huh.

JAKE
Hey, Kat.

KAT
What.

JAKE
You ever meet Eddie?

KAT
No.

JAKE
Nope.
He's dead, eh.

KAT
I know.

JAKE
Youdda liked him, y'know? He was fun.

KAT
Uh huh.

    Silence except for the television.

JAKE
We were runnin' like mad for the bikes. The pavement was wet. I remember.
He reached his first, kicked it into gear and started off.
I was just jumpin' on mine when the bullet hit him. Pulled him right off the bike—
sideways—and the bike kept on goin'. Went a hundred yards, tipped, and kept
sliding along the pavement like a fuckin' movie bike in slow mo.
Christ.
We were only sixteen.
Cops still coming and Eddie screaming "Go. GO!" So I went and left him.
Just left him in a fuckin' rainy parkin' lot.

    Silence except for the television.

You don't understand.

KAT
Understand what?

JAKE
You just think I'm…

KAT
I don't think anything.

JAKE
It ain't been easy, y'know?

Hey. We used to be friends, right? Y'member?

Y'member comin' down to the car wash? We'd work in the back? I taught you how to use them hot guns. C'mon, you 'member.
We'd goof around, waitin' for your mom to come back there lookin' for you? Soaked her every time! *(laugh)*

And, hey, that year we lived in Bulyea, in ole Frank's purple house. What was it your friend Jeanelle used to call me?

KAT
Crazy legs.

JAKE
Yeah – Crazy legs! Cuz I wore those cut-offs all the time and the five of us would go fishin' on the weekend – me, your mom, baby Babber and you and Jeanelle—and when we caught one we'd all dance the Mambo on the shore. Tada-da da da!

> *He is totally caught up in the memory. He's happy. KAT watches him.*

Y'member?

KAT
Yeah. I remember.

JAKE
You had fun then.

KAT
Yeah.

JAKE
So how come it ain't fun anymore?

KAT
I don't know.

JAKE
Your mom go to bingo tonight?

KAT
No. You said you'd be right back.

JAKE
She here?

KAT
She's asleep.

JAKE
She packed?

KAT
Yeah. We're all ready to go.

JAKE
It's late.

KAT
Yeah.

JAKE
We're going early.

KAT
Like always.

JAKE
Don't lip. You are always lippin' off. Christ.

> *He goes off to his room. KAT closes her eyes. She gets up and shuts off the television. She sits down and listens to the silence – the first silence in the house. She stands, looking at the big velvet painting of Elvis on the wall. She takes the picture of JAKE off the TV and smashes it. She listens – no sound. She goes into the bedroom and pulls on her boots. BABBER wakes up.*

BABBER
Whatcha doin'?

KAT
Goin'.

BABBER
Where? 'S time to go?

KAT
Shhhh. No, it isn't time to go. I'm just goin' for a ride on Cheyenne. Don't look at me like that. Okay. Keep this door locked. Okay?

BABBER
Why?

KAT
Just keep it locked. If Jake wakes up and tries to get in – don't open it.

BABBER
Where you goin'?

KAT
For a ride.

BABBER
He's gonna catch you.

KAT
I'm just goin' for a ride.

BABBER
Then…

KAT
He won't even know I'm gone 'til it's too late.

BABBER
You're gonna…

KAT
Yes, Bab. I'm gonna call the fuckin' cops.

BABBER
Kat. Don't go. What if he catches you? What if he comes down and asks for you – what if–

KAT
Don't let him in!

BABBER
What if Mom asks?

KAT
Don't open that door! I'll be back. They won't know. I'll be right back. It'll be all right Babber. I promise.

BABBER
'Kay.

KAT climbs out the window.

Careful.

PART II - Scene Three

There is a crash of thunder and a flash. A fight scene between JAKE and DARLENE is seen in flashes of lightning.

JAKE
WHERE IS SHE?!?!

The sound of the storm increases. In a flash of light we see DARLENE standing in the kitchen at the counter. We hear a car on gravel – hoofbeats – a gunshot and KAT screaming. More storm. When the lights come up we can hear the muted storm outside. BABBER and DARLENE are on the girls' bed. DARLENE's shirt is torn.

(outside) Get out. Get in the fucking house.

JAKE comes in holding KAT by the hair. She's soaking wet and muddy. Her arm is bleeding. She carries the saddle blanket. He throws her on the floor.

Get in there with your mother.

KAT stands up. She doesn't move towards the bedroom.

I said get in there.

He hits her. She recovers and looks at him. DARLENE starts to cry. He throws KAT into the bedroom and leans on the doorframe. KAT stands up again. She must keep standing up. Now that he has them all in one spot he gets very calm – scary, cold, calm. He doesn't have to yell.

KAT
It's okay, Mom.

JAKE
Pretty picture. The whore and her bitches. I oughtta paint you.

BABBER
I didn't let him in.

KAT
'S okay Bab.

JAKE
Shut up. Babber, c'mere.

KAT
What do you want.

JAKE
Was I talkin' to you? Babber's gonna get her daddy a drink.

KAT
I'll get it.

JAKE
No. Little Bab is gonna do it – aren't you sweetheart.

BABBER goes to him. JAKE touches BABBER's hair, caresses her cheek.

Get Daddy a drink, little one.

He yanks her hair. KAT tenses. DARLENE stands up.

DARLENE
Leave her alone, Jake.

JAKE
Oh, like you're gonna stop me. Who the fuck do you think you are suddenly? You're a useless piece of shit – that's what.
It's your fault y'know.
She was goin' to get the fuckin' cops.
You're the cunt that gave her the idea that she's better than us. Always tellin' her how smart she is. Oooooh – she's so fuckin' talented… she's gonna BE someone. Bullshit, Sweety. She's gonna end up just like you.

DARLENE
Shut up.

JAKE
Don't you ever say that to me.

DARLENE
Fuck you, you filthy son of a bitch.

She has a huge butcher knife that she grabbed when we saw her at the kitchen counter – she's ready to use it.

Get out.

JAKE
Oh. You really are stupid aren't you?

DARLENE
I mean it Jake. I'll take this knife and ram it right through your fucking heart. Kat's right… you're… I should've left a long time ago. Just leave – or let us go.

JAKE
Stupid – stupid – stupid – stupid.

>   *He pulls out the gun.*

Put the knife away, Darlene.

>   *It's a standoff 'til he aims the gun at BABBER and smiles.*

You amaze me. You just don't learn – do you? Tell me just how stupid you are.

DARLENE
Please. Don't hurt her.

JAKE
Tell me.

DARLENE
I'm stupid.

>   *He cocks the gun. She drops the knife.*

I'm a stupid worthless piece of shit. Just. Please. Don't.

JAKE
That's better.

>   *He lets up on the gun. Pushes BABBER into the living room. She searches for a bottle.*

See – you can't stop me. You're too fucking weak.
Know what I'm gonna do?
Know what I'd like to do?

>   *He neighs like a horse. BABBER hands him a half-empty bottle of rye.*

BABBER
What happened?

JAKE
Poor Cheyenne fell. You roll good, Beauty.

DARLENE
Oh God.

JAKE
Horrible way to die – getting caught under a falling horse. Waste of a good saddle – wasn't it. Glad you saved the blanket?

>   *BABBER starts to cry.*

Shut up.
Ladies, I have had enough. I'm tired. *(to DARLENE)* Of you and your whorin'
around like a bitch in heat.

DARLENE
What are you–

JAKE
And you, Kitty, with your shit faced attitude – thinking that you matter.
Even you, little Babster – I'm tired of your stupid whinin' face.

Ya think I don't know what's goin' on, eh?
Y'think I don't know that you ain't been goin' to bingo when ya say you are?
Think I don't know why it takes you all fuckin' day to get groceries? Think I don't
know what you're doin'? Who you're doin' it with?
You *(to KAT)* know where she's been goin' – and you think I don't? Christ.

I take care of you. When something goes down, I take the fucking rap and soon as
I'm out the door you're out screwin' around.
You all think you're so damned smart.

Well.
Tell ya what I'm gonna do.
I'm gonna shoot–
1-2-3 and me.

Crazy?

Like you always said Beauty. You get to go last. First, we have some fun. You don't
wanna go with me – so we all stay together.
It's cuz I love you all so much.

KAT
You're…. You are so fucking–

JAKE
Ooooh…. Shouldn't swear, Beauty – someone might think you're part of the family.
Someone might see you for the trash you are. Fuck, you ain't nothin' but a little
useless piece a–

DARLENE
Leave her alone, Jake.

JAKE
Tch. Tch. Tch. You're shirt's ripped darlin'. I think you should change it.
Take it off. C'mon – take it off. Now.
Oh yeah… that's it.

KAT
Mom, don't.

JAKE
Mmmmm…. Lemme see 'em.

KAT
Don't.

JAKE
Yeah. Now c'mere. Kiss me.

KAT
Mom.

JAKE
Shut up.

He reaches to DARLENE, caresses her. He slaps her. She falls.

You stupid slut.

She kicks him. They start struggling and he drops the gun to climb on top of her. BABBER covers her head – she mustn't make a sound. KAT jumps for the gun. She gets it and aims it at JAKE.

KAT
Get off her. Get the fuck away. Good.
Now, you are going to leave—alone—and you know what? You're not going to come back.

JAKE
Beautiful. You play well.
Shoot me.
C'mon, Beauty. Shoot me now – 'cause I'll only come back – you know it. She'll let me 'cause she needs it so bad. She'll let me do – what – I – want.

Who's the fuck here, Beauty? Who's the real Fuck? What's worse – me doin' what I do – or her lettin' me?

KAT
Shut up.

JAKE
Look at her.

KAT
Shut up.

JAKE
Come on, Beauty. Do it. *(smiles)*

You ain't gonna shoot me. You're the same as her. You love it. You ain't ever gonna get away. See – you all need me.

She cocks the gun and is about to shoot him when BABBER starts screaming.

BABBER
Kill him. Kill him, Kat! Kill him.

KAT looks at BABBER. She lowers the gun. KATHRYN breaks into the memory.

KATHRYN
Kill him! Kill him! Kill him you stupid FUCK!

I'm sorry. I'm sorry. I'm sorry. Sorry.

Blackout.

Interval.

PART III

BABBER is about seventeen. She's watching a sitcom. It's a different house, but it has exactly the same furnishings – including the picture of JAKE mended and back on the TV. KATHRYN comes in, wearing a purple jacket, carrying a black knapsack. It contains clothes, the black folder, the saddle blanket and the gun. KAT is with her – like a distant shadow. She moves closer to KATHRYN when things intensify – but other than that she watches from the periphery.

KATHRYN
Hey sweet thing!

BABBER
Hey!

They hug. BABBER shuts off the television. KATHRYN takes off her knapsack and jacket.

KATHRYN
So. How ya doin'?

BABBER
I'm okay. How'd you get here?

KATHRYN
Hitched.

BABBER
Are you crazy?

KATHRYN
Probably. Made good time though. *(smiles)*
I caught a ride with friends.

BABBER
You shit!

KATHRYN
You look just like your picture, y'know?

BABBER
Oh please! You haven't sent one in awhile.

KATHRYN
Sorry. Never get any taken. I always look like shit. Why? I look old or something?

BABBER
It's been awhile.

KATHRYN
That it has.
So. Where's Mom?

BABBER
She's at school.

KATHRYN
Yeah? How's that goin'?

BABBER
She goes more – now that Jake isn't around.

KATHRYN
She still see him?

BABBER
Probably.

KATHRYN
Yeah. Well, how are you?

BABBER
I'm okay.

KATHRYN
What's happening?

BABBER
Court's tomorrow. Mom still says she won't come.

KATHRYN
She doesn't have to?

BABBER
Guess not.

KATHRYN
What happened, Bab?

BABBER
He was drunk.

KATHRYN
He do anything before this?

BABBER
He was drunk.

KATHRYN
Drunk or not – has he done it before?

> *BABBER won't answer.*

Did he hurt you?

BABBER
Just a black eye.

KATHRYN
You get a picture?

BABBER
No. Should I have?

KATHRYN
I don't know.
Why won't Mom go?

BABBER
Doesn't want him to go to jail.

KATHRYN
Jesus.
Was she here?

BABBER
No. She was at bingo.
I ran to a friend's place and we ran to bingo to get her. I made her take me to the cop shop. She took me, but she was mad. Guess she figured I'd be like her and drop the charges the next day.

KATHRYN
Did you come back here that night?

BABBER
No, I stayed at Tracy's 'til he moved out. Mom came home though. She found him passed out naked in the hall.

KATHRYN
She tell the cops that?

BABBER
She ain't telling nobody nothin'.

KATHRYN
Weren't the cops with her?

BABBER
I don't know.

KATHRYN
How'd you get him to leave?

BABBER
Told Mom I wasn't coming home with him here.

KATHRYN
Mom kicked Jake out.

> BABBER lets her think this for awhile.

BABBER
They had a fight.
I came home to get some stuff and found her, took her to the hospital and got a restraining order on him. She just went along with it. Maybe she figures it'll blow over. Maybe she wants him gone. I dunno.

> BABBER lights a smoke. KATHRYN turns off the TV.

KATHRYN
I know.
Bab.
Was this the first time?

BABBER
First time what?

KATHRYN
Don't be...
Is this the first time he tried to...

    BABBER ain't talking.

You aren't gonna tell me, are you?

BABBER
Did you tell me?
Forget it Kat.

KATHRYN
When'd you start smokin'?

BABBER
Forever ago.

KATHRYN
Yeah? I remember when you used to threaten to tell on me for sneakin' butts.

BABBER
Never did though.

KATHRYN
That's only cause we'd always...

BOTH
Duel to the deal!

KATHRYN
You remember that?

BABBER
You mock me!

KATHRYN
No. By this hand. *(laugh)*
That was fun.
Bab. I'm proud that you're doing this. I... I wish I...

    They hear a car.

BABBER
That'll be Mom.
She doesn't know you're coming.

KATHRYN
Great.

DARLENE enters.

KATHRYN
Hiya Mom.

DARLENE
Hello.

KATHRYN
How ya doin'?

DARLENE
Fine. Coffee?

KATHRYN
Sure.

DARLENE
How's school?

KATHRYN
I'm done – finally. So now at least I'm an *edumacated* bum. How's school for you?

DARLENE
I quit a month ago.

BABBER
What?

DARLENE
I quit.

KATHRYN
Why?

DARLENE
Couldn't do it.

KATHRYN
But I thought you wanted to.

DARLENE
What's the use. You're the one with the brains.

BABBER
So, where ya been goin'?

DARLENE
None of your goddamned business! I s'pose she's why you're here.

KATHRYN
Mom, relax.

DARLENE
Why? Because you're here – riding in to save the day?

BABBER
Christ, Give 'er a break. She just got here for fuck sakes.

DARLENE
Watch your mouth.

BABBER
Oh please.

DARLENE
Why can't someone give me a break?

KATHRYN
So…. How about that coffee?

BABBER
I'm outta here.
(to KATHRYN) You can have my bed if you want it. I'll take the couch when I come in.

DARLENE
Oh. Coming home are we?

BABBER
Get off my fuckin' back!

KATHRYN
Babber.

BABBER
Well listen to her.

KATHRYN
Why can't we all…

BABBER
Shut up. You don't have to live with her.

DARLENE
I thought you were glad she came home.

KATHRYN
Bab, stay. I want to talk to you.

BABBER
Fine.

> She goes and sits in front of the television, turns it on. DARLENE goes to the
> kitchen for coffee. KATHRYN follows.

KATHRYN
So.
How are you?

DARLENE
What'd the bitch tell you?

KATHRYN
Mom.

DARLENE
Well I don't know what to do with her anymore – she doesn't listen to me.

KATHRYN
She's a teenager. They don't listen to anyone.

DARLENE
You weren't so bad.

KATHRYN
I left. You didn't have to deal with me. I was probably worse.

    Pause.

So. How are you?

DARLENE
She told you, eh? About Jake?

KATHRYN
Yeah.

DARLENE
So?

KATHRYN
So what?

DARLENE
So what did she tell you?

KATHRYN
What do you think?

DARLENE
He didn't mean anything.

KATHRYN
Yeah. I heard he was drunk. So, what happened – he thought it was you?

DARLENE
Forget it.

KATHRYN
You forgetting it?

DARLENE
Yes I am.

KATHRYN
Won't work.

DARLENE
So – are you supposed to make me testify against him?

KATHRYN
I can't make you do anything.
Could you?

DARLENE
I wasn't here.

KATHRYN
Did you know?

> *DARLENE lights a smoke. There is a long pause 'til KATHRYN takes one too.*

DARLENE
You smoke.

KATHRYN
Off and on. I'm an Artist dontcha know.

DARLENE
Acting?

KATHRYN
Acting and trying to write.

Hey, y'know what I just wrote a piece about? Fat Tara and Cruella DeVil.
Y'know how I always had that fear of going to the bathroom in the dark? I think it is all Fat Tara's fault. Serious.
Y'member that stinky lil house she had on McTavish?
She would never turn on the friggin' light in the basement, so when I had to pee I hadda run down those freakin' dark stairs and turn on the light in the can.
I remember being absolutely terrified – 'cause, for some reason, I thought that when I flushed the toilet – that Cruella DeVil – that woman who slaughtered all those puppies in 101 Dalmatians? I thought that when I flushed the toilet Cruella DeVil would come up out of the bowl and get me. I used to stretch myself out so I could flush the toilet and turn off the light at exactly the same time and then run like hell up the stairs.
I knew she would get me one day. Her, or those vampires under the stairs. Man, I hated Cruella DeVil.

DARLENE
You watch too many movies.

KATHRYN
Mom, you remember the time you brought home that Dalmatian coat?

KAT
Oh shit.

DARLENE
Yeah.

KAT
Don't tell.

KATHRYN
You remember how it disappeared? I never told you this but Babber and I....
Hey Bab!

BABBER
What?

KATHRYN
C'mere.

BABBER
What?

KATHRYN
C'mere! You remember Mom's Dalmatian coat?

They start laughing.

DARLENE
What?

KATHRYN
Didn't you ever miss that coat?

DARLENE
What did you do?

KATHRYN
Well. We found it quite… uh… offensive, and we thought we had to redeem the puppies.

DARLENE
It wasn't made from puppies.

KATHRYN
Thank God. So we had to redeem the dogs.

BABBER
Kathryn said if we buried it, they could rest.

KATHRYN
Right.

DARLENE
You buried my coat?

KATHRYN
Yep. In the yard of 675 Wascana Street.

DARLENE
And you *(to BABBER)* never told?

BABBER
No way. She made me do a blood swear. She sliced our thumbs with that damned Swiss Army knife of hers and we squeezed out a drop of blood to seal the pact with the puppies and then we pressed our thumbs together and swore…

BOTH
Never to tell.

KATHRYN
For two weeks I had visions of you in a bloody Dalmatian coat coming up out of the toilet bowl to get me.

DARLENE
God I hated that coat.

KATHRYN
What?

DARLENE
I told the guy someone stole it.

KATHRYN
You didn't care?

DARLENE
I was just glad I didn't have to wear the damned thing.

KATHRYN
Oh. Great. We go through years of guilt thinking we buried your favourite dead dog coat and you just laugh. Great.

DARLENE
You wrote about that?

KATHRYN
Sure.

DARLENE
And people bought it?

KATHRYN
Nobody actually buys my stuff.

DARLENE
No. I mean – they believed it?

KATHRYN
Course not. They just think I have a twisted imagination.

DARLENE
Well, I'll give them that.

They all move into the living room.

KATHRYN
Anything on?

BABBER
Nah.

KATHRYN notices the picture of JAKE.

KATHRYN
I thought this was gone.

DARLENE
Nope. Well, I'm going to bed. There's blankets in the hall closet.

KATHRYN
I'm still wide awake. Probably watch a movie or two.

DARLENE
Okay. Goodnight.

KATHRYN
Hey Mom.

> *She gives her mom a kiss on the forehead.*

Sleep good.

> *DARLENE leaves. KATHRYN and BABBER sit down to watch TV.*

BABBER
So. How've you been?

KATHRYN
Okay. Still hate the city, but I'll probably hang in a while longer.

BABBER
How's Danny?

KATHRYN
Gone.

BABBER
What?

KATHRYN
It just went away.

BABBER
You sad?

KATHRYN
Sad? *(smiles)* I like to call it Wracking Physical Pain.

BABBER
I thought you loved him.

KATHRYN
I do love him.

BABBER
Then… what's the problem?

KATHRYN
Dunno man. I'm fucked, basically.
It's hard to explain.
I started to lose it. I was bitchy all the time – and I didn't know why. I got all weird and jealous. I was scared. I started having nightmares. Lynne says maybe it was the first time in my life I ever felt safe so all this… shit started to come out… I dunno.

BABBER
Who's Lynne?

KATHRYN
This woman.
My therapist.

BABBER
You have a therapist?

KATHRYN
Yeah. Crazy, eh?

BABBER
I don't get it.

KATHRYN
Me neither.

    KATHRYN starts remembering something disturbing – covers it with a laugh.

BABBER
What's funny?

KATHRYN
Just thinking about this dream I have about Robert Redford.

BABBER
Huh?

KATHRYN
Nothin'.

BABBER
Kat?

KATHRYN
Hmm?

BABBER
Thanks for coming.

KATHRYN
Yeah. Bab. I…

BABBER
Yeah. I know. So what's this dream? You got a thing for Robert Redford?

    There's a knock at the door. BABBER gets it. It's JAKE.

KAT
Shit.

BABBER
What do you want?

JAKE
I need some of my things. Where's your mother?

KATHRYN
She's in bed.

JAKE
Well look who's home.

KATHRYN
Yeah.

BABBER
What do you want?

JAKE
Relax. I just came to get some of my stuff.

BABBER
Why.

JAKE
I need my stuff.

BABBER
You aren't supposed to be here.

JAKE
Then get your mother to gimme my shit and I'll leave.

    She goes. KAT moves closer to KATHRYN.

KATHRYN
You look old.

JAKE
Been a long time.
Can I come in?

KATHRYN
I think not.

    He comes in anyhow.

JAKE
Don't worry. I won't be here long.
Always wondered how you turned out.

KATHRYN
I turned out just fine.

JAKE
No thanks to me.

KATHRYN
Agreed. What do you want?

JAKE
Relax, Beauty.

KATHRYN
My name is Kathryn.

JAKE
Okay Kathryn.
Like I said, I need some stuff. Looks like I might not be back for awhile.

KATHRYN
I can't believe you – coming here – tonight.

JAKE
This is my home.

KATHRYN
This is Mom and Babber's home.

JAKE
Babber? Bar-ba-ra. Now there's a fighter. What is she – seventeen now? Lasted longer with the ole lady than you did, eh?

KATHRYN
I didn't leave because of Mom.

JAKE
Oh, that's right. You ran off to University.

KATHRYN
I was in grade eleven.

JAKE
Whatever. You're still runnin'.

KAT
Shut up.

KATHRYN
You're wrong.

JAKE
Sure.

> *DARLENE and BABBER return. KAT edges back to the periphery. KATHRYN begins to hear the "woman's voices" from the prologue. As things intensify KATHRYN edges over to her knapsack. KAT watches her.*

Hiya Hon.

DARLENE
Here's your clothes.

> *She tosses a bag at his feet. He looks through it – searching for something.*

JAKE
All packed and ready to go, eh? Okay. I need that black box from the bedroom.

DARLENE
What black box?

JAKE
The one under the bed.

DARLENE
It isn't there.

JAKE
What do you mean it isn't there.

DARLENE
It's gone. I threw it out.

JAKE
You stupid bitch.

> *KATHRYN reaches for the bag. KAT cuts her off, stands directly in front of her and stares at her. KATHRYN just stands there. BABBER speaks to JAKE at the same moment as KAT speaks to KATHRYN.*

KAT
No.

BABBER
No. Not anymore.

JAKE
You stay outta this.

BABBER
No. You get out of here. Get – the fuck – out.

> *He goes. The voices in KATHRYN's head begin to fade – by the time BABBER leaves they are silent.*

DARLENE
Bab…

BABBER
Forget about it. I'm going to Tracy's. You want me – call me there. Court's at ten.

> *She grabs her black leather jacket and leaves. KATHRYN, KAT and DARLENE just stand there for a bit. Then DARLENE goes to the kitchen and lights a smoke. KATHRYN goes through her knapsack and finds a pack of smokes. She lights one and sits to smoke. KAT watches. Halfway through the smoke, KATHRYN gets a little woozy. She butts the smoke and just sits.*
>
> *Lights begin to fade on DARLENE as KATHRYN searches through her knapsack and pulls out the black folder full of paper, the saddle blanket and the gun. She looks at the gun and then puts it back in the bag. She walks deliberately clockwise and places each article to form a circle around herself with KAT holding the fourth point (upstage – so she is watching over KATHRYN). She is casting a circle of protection.*
>
> *KATHRYN wraps herself in her coat, falls asleep and dreams. The dream is surreal – romantic to us, horrifying to KATHRYN. It can be done simply, straight or as wildly as you like – playing with the images of their lives – Dalmatians, the coats,*

a baby, a horse, cop sirens, motorcycles, coffee, cigarettes, Elvis, Johnny Cash, Jimmy Dean, Robert Redford, rain and wet leather. Throughout the dream KAT is trying to hold the circle together until the dream blows it apart.

JAKE
Marry me.

DARLENE
Why?

JAKE
You're so beautiful.

DARLENE
You're crazy.

JAKE
Rangy – tang – tang. But I'm here. I came here to get you to marry me.

DARLENE
You don't even know me.

JAKE
Of course I do. Remember.
You said you remembered me.

DARLENE
Jake.

JAKE
Remember me.
I'm the one you loved all along.

DARLENE
I've been married. I don't want...

JAKE
It was a mistake. I was late. Now I'm here.

DARLENE
Why can't we just...

JAKE
No. You will marry me so that I can care for you.
You are the one I am here for.

I left everything for you – remember.

I love you. Remember.

You don't like to be alone.
You can't.
You'll be safe with me.
You all will.
I will care for you all.

He rubs her belly tenderly (as if she's pregnant).

That's why I'm here – for you.
That's why you're here – for me.
You are for me.
Remember?

> *KATHRYN wakes up screaming. She scrambles to the picture of JAKE and smashes it. KAT is thrown back to the periphery. DARLENE runs on.*

DARLENE
What the hell… Christ. Are you bleeding?

KATHRYN
No.

DARLENE
I thought you were through with smashing things.

KATHRYN
Sorry. I don't know why I…
Mom. Why did you marry Jake.

DARLENE
Don't start this now.

KATHRYN
No. I need to know.

DARLENE
Do you remember when I met him, Kat? We were living on Argyle Street across from the Kozars. I was working at the car wash. You were seven years old. He worked with me.
He was fun.

> *As she speaks she begins to pace and almost to trance out into the make-believe. KAT slowly begins to circle them moving counter clockwise saying "Lies. Lies. Lies." She begins very slow and low and it builds until she is screaming.*

We used to sit around and he'd tell stories about how he met me in Virden, Manitoba when I was working at the Dainty Hill Diner.
I was only sixteen.
He would come in for Cokes and I called him Babyface.
He swore that one day he would find me and that we'd be married.

KATHRYN
He was never in Virden, Mom.

DARLENE
And the time we were at old Arnie's and he saw you on the street and gave you the purple leather jacket with the fringe.

KATHRYN
My favourite jacket.

DARLENE
He knew you.
He'd seen me, recognized me and he watched me for years and when you were four he gave you the jacket.
You were...

> *KATHRYN has been caught up and begins to tell the story.*

KATHRYN
Playing in the yard. Hiding from Zeke and Goosey in the Caragana hedge and he was across the street on his Harley. He called me over. Said he was an old friend of yours. I was so shy – I wouldn't come out of the hedge. But then he pulled out the jacket...

DARLENE
Purple suede with extra long fringe. Your favourite jacket.

KATHRYN
Mom, where did I get that jacket?

DARLENE
From Jake.

KATHRYN
I didn't Mom.

DARLENE
You remembered.

KATHRYN
No. I made it up. We made it up.

DARLENE
He knew me in Virden.

KATHRYN
Mom.

DARLENE
He's known me all my life.

KATHRYN
Mom.

DARLENE
He came to me. After Eddie died he had no one else and he came to me and asked me to marry him. He said I was beautiful – that he loved me and that he wanted to take care of us.

> *KAT has begun to scream.*

KATHRYN
MOM! Stop. Stop stop stop STOP!

> *KAT stops.*

DARLENE
What's wrong with you? You asked me – remember?
You want to know why I married him? Because I fell in love.
Is that so impossible for you to understand?
It is, isn't it? What is wrong with you?

KATHRYN
Nothing. Nothing is wrong with me. Nothing is wrong with Me. Oh shit. I wish this was all over. Shit.
Mom, do you remember the night he shot Cheyenne?

DARLENE
Kathryn.

KATHRYN
I coulda killed him, y'know.

DARLENE
No Kat.

KATHRYN
Then... I just left. I ran and left Bab behind.
How could I when I knew what would happen.
I hoped...
I figured "she's HIS kid, it's different" I should have fucking known. Shit. Oh shit.

> She rifles through her black folder and finds a piece. KAT wants to stop her. She can't.

KAT
Don't.

KATHRYN
Here. *(holds the paper out to DARLENE)* Read it.

KAT
No. Please please please please don't show her that. Don't tell!

DARLENE
What is it?

KATHRYN
I wrote it.

> *DARLENE won't take it.*

Fine. I'll read it.

> *KATHRYN reads in an almost monotone – clearly, but totally removed from the story. KAT slowly curls up and begins to cry.*

They are in the basement, at John's, sleeping on the fold out couch. They've been there for the last three weekends, since he got evicted from his room at Mrs. Monroe's. During the week, when he's alone, he sleeps in his car, but on weekends, when his little girl comes to stay with him, they stay at John's. She likes John. He makes her laugh by throwing her up in the air and catching her. She's asleep now, warm against her father's arm. He stares at the red tip of his cigarette in the dark. Her Superman T-shirt is twisted up around her ribs, exposing her stomach. He watches the rise and fall. Her red woolen tights are damp. The basement is hot and dusty. She's five. Still a little plump. He looks at her. Her hand is curled under her head. Her cheeks are full, but pale. They should be pink, like her lips. Soft round lips, opened slightly. She still has a few baby teeth. Her breath is even and sweet. She is sweating; blonde curls stuck to her forehead. He kisses her stomach. Straightens her T-shirt. He pulls her tights to her knees. Her legs are so hot, sweating. He kisses her right thigh birthmark. He removes her tights, slips his fingers inside her blue cotton panties and feels her. He removes the panties, spreads her legs and kisses her, lets his tongue ease inside. One hand supports her lower back, lifts her to his face – so sweet, warm on his tongue. His other hand slips down to grip his penis. Her thighs brush his cheeks, limp. He wishes she would tighten, hold him in place. He thinks of entering her. The thought is enough. He gasps, sticky fingers drip onto the red woolen tights. He moans, presses himself into the sheets between her legs. He moves up to kiss her stomach. He looks at his daughter. Her jaw is clenched. She stares at the ceiling. He starts to cry. She just closes her eyes.

> *DARLENE sits, a little stunned. She goes to the kitchen, lights a smoke. She can't look at KATHRYN.*

DARLENE
That happens, and lotsa times they're younger than five.

KATHRYN
No. Mom. It was me. And Harlan. I was five.

DARLENE
Your father?
Well.
You must have dealt with it if you can write that.

KATHRYN
No. I haven't. That's the problem. I can write about it now and even talk about it now, but I don't feel anything. It's just like a bad movie. Like it happened to someone else.

DARLENE
Well, we've been through hell and back, but we've always come out on top. At least we've still got our insanity.

> *DARLENE cannot hear KAT speak – she is frozen out. KATHRYN hears.*

KAT
Look at me. Me. See me!

I just told you that I was molested by my father when I was five years old and you sit there smiling platitudes at me.
He was my father.

Don't you feel... grief... or... anger?
I know it's over and done, but don't you feel anything?

I want to smash…. Make you read every bit of SHIT in that file – "the chronicles of my childhood." The shit that happened over and over and over – with Harlan, Jake, different boyfriends and one night stands. Men you brought into our house forcing different levels of disgust into me so that now I can't even…

The time I lay in bed and gritted my teeth pretending to be asleep while some asshole who got bored with you tried to shove his cock down my six-year-old throat. He kept coming back all night, making me do it over and over – touch him – touched me.

Why didn't I yell – or sneak out when he went back to your room? I just lay there – terrified.

Why couldn't I tell you?
Why can't you care?
Where did you go?

They sent you so far away I can't find you anymore.

> KATHRYN goes to KAT and comforts her – holds her, forgives her. Together they face DARLENE.

KATHRYN
Sanity.

DARLENE
What?

KATHRYN
At least we have our *sanity.*

DARLENE
That's what I said.

KATHRYN
Mom. I need to know why you stay.

DARLENE
Why.
You tell me Kathryn.
You tell me why you left.

KATHRYN
He hit you in front of Cheryl.

DARLENE
No. He never–

KATHRYN
Never hit any of us when people were watching, right?
Never left any marks unless he got carried away and then we'd just stay inside 'til they were gone, right?
Well one day – a day you probably don't even remember – he hit. No, actually he just pushed you – in front of Cheryl.
That was it.

I knew if I stayed he would kill us. He broke the rule. So I packed and left.

DARLENE
He didn't kill me.

KATHRYN
No.

DARLENE
What if he had?

KATHRYN
How could I stop it? I was fifteen. Maybe I stopped it by leaving.

DARLENE
You just didn't care.

KATHRYN
What?

DARLENE
You don't give a flying fuck what happens to me or to Babber.

KATHRYN
For Christ's sake – listen to yourself!
I gotta get outta here. I'm going to court with Barbara and then I'm gone.
I'm going to talk to her lawyer and see if she wants me to testify.

DARLENE
To what? You weren't here.

KATHRYN
True. But I know what happened.
Don't you understand? He tried to rape your daughter.

DARLENE
No.

KATHRYN
Yes. You know he did.
What are you doing?
You saying Babber is lying? You going to court and say your daughter made it up?

DARLENE
I'm not going.

KATHRYN
Oh. That's great. And if Babber loses and he goes free – you gonna invite him to come home again?

DARLENE
Why are you here?

KATHRYN
Because I don't understand.

DARLENE
That's the problem. No one does.
You blame me for everything, don't you?

KATHRYN
Ah shit.

DARLENE
No, you do. In all your little stories I'm the villain, right? I'm the one to blame. I just can't get it right. I feed my children to animals.

KATHRYN
Mom, I–

DARLENE
You what. Don't mean it that way? But it's true, isn't it?
So what's wrong with me?
Can't you tell me?
You're the one who went to university. You read about it. You're obsessed by it.
Can't you write a book yet on why women stay with men who hurt them? Can't you?
Don't you run away and write this all down and analyze it later with all your little friends? Talk about your fucked-up mother who will put up with anything for a good lay—or a bad lay—as long as she gets something?

KATHRYN
I never–

DARLENE
Shut up.
I'm sick of you.
You come in here spouting bullshit, saying you care. You don't care.

KATHRYN
Stop it.

DARLENE
Why did you come back? To prove to me that I'm the villain you think I am?
I already know that.

KATHRYN
What the hell are you talking about. I'm not blaming you. I'm trying not to blame myself. God, Mom, I don't think…

DARLENE
You do. You do!
Well, if you got away then so can I.
I am sick and tired of everyone talking to me – telling me what IS. Sick and fucking tired of all of you all – hating me – making it my fault.
I can leave y'know.
I will, and no one will ever find me again. No one to find me and bring me back and pretend they care to make me care. I'll just go.

KATHRYN
Fuck, Mom. I left. I ran for my fucking life and it didn't work. It's in me. I can't...
Jesus, Mom – we have to stand beside Babber.

DARLENE
Everything's easy for you.

KATHRYN
Can't you hear me? I'm telling you that–

DARLENE
I'm just saying it ain't that easy.

KATHRYN
I know, Mom.
I came back to make it stop – for me. That's all I can do.

KAT
Come. Oh please, Mom.

> *KATHRYN waits. DARLENE cannot respond. KATHRYN takes her stuff—including the black folder—but leaves the piece she read.*

KATHRYN
I love you, Mom.

> *KATHRYN takes KAT's hand and they leave. KAT keeps looking back at her mother – KATHRYN doesn't. Once they are gone, DARLENE picks up the pages KATHRYN read, and the smashed picture of JAKE underneath them. She sits. She is hidden in darkness.*

Epilogue

> *KATHRYN stands in a flowing blue cotton sleeveless dress. KAT is upstage, raised, singing her song from the prologue. She wears the same type of dress.*

KATHRYN
Women's voices whispering.
I could not hear them through my sleep.
I could not allow them to surface.
Only scattered words and sighs
and mermaid songs that caught me unaware.
They frightened me.
The voices.
Whispered, moaning, screaming voices of women
breaking the silence that I was taught to hold
– clenched tight.

When I was a kid, we moved a lot. Before grade eight I had hit eighteen schools – Saskatchewan, Alberta, Manitoba, even Ontario – for two weeks *(smiles)* but that's another story.

When I was a kid, I had this ritual. No matter how quick we vacated the old place, I'd grab four things – sticks, stones, feathers, or bones from the yard. On the first night in the next place I'd sneak out and lay them around the circumference of the new yard.

She indicates the four directions – clockwise as she did when she cast the protective Circle earlier.

On the outside it looks like a ritual of protection. Which it was. But it wasn't a threat from outside I feared. It was more a ritual of containment. If the terror stayed within the confines I set – we would survive. I could hold the centre – somehow.

I learned my lessons well.

But no more.

KAT begins to move closer.

I have this dream about Robert Redford.
In the dream we're sitting in New York... dunno why New York, but anyway... me 'n' Bob are sitting in this diner, and we're a couple, but we've broken up because he's done something really awful so he's trying to win me back.

Robert Redford is apologizing and begging me to forgive him 'cause he loves me so much and so on and I look past that gorgeous mop of hair and right there on a New York City street I see a saddle hangin' on a fence post in the rain – and that's all I can think of.

Robert fucking Redford is grovelling at my feet and all I can think of is – what the hell is that saddle doing in the rain?

KAT
So, what do you think of when you see a saddle in the rain?

KATHRYN
That somebody better bring it in.

KAT
Why don't you do it? Whatcha scared of – the rain?

KATHRYN
I never thought of that. I just never thought of that.

KATHRYN puts her arm around KAT and they walk off together. Blackout.

The end.

Ka'ma'mo'pi cik /
The Gathering

The Calling Lakes Community Play

Rachael Van Fossen and Darrel Wildcat

l to r:
Darrel Wildcat,
Reginald Newkirk
(Secretary General
of the Baha'i of
Canada), Rachael
Van Fossen.
Accepting the
National Race Unity
Award for The
Gathering, awarded
in March 1993.

photo by Karen Sasani

A professional playwright and theatre director, RACHAEL VAN FOSSEN is currently the Artistic Director of Black Theatre Workshop in Montreal, and teaches in the Theatre and Development programme at Concordia University, an undergraduate specialization for which she helped to design the curriculum. Her other produced plays include A North Side Story (or two), an inner-city community play for North Central Regina, SK in 1995, Dene Suline Ho Ni Ye, for the Dene community of Wollaston Lake, SK in 1994 and City Flats, produced by Common Weal in 1996 and 1997. She is currently working on a full-length play entitled Hooked. Her recent published writing includes contributions to Canadian Theatre Review, and in 2003 a play introduction (co-authored with ahdri zhina mandiela) in Testifyin': Contemporary African Canadian Drama: Volume II, edited by Djanet Sears. Rachael was Founding Artistic Director of Common Weal Community Arts in Regina from 1992-1999, and initiated Common Weal's transition from primarily theatre-based work to a mandate that includes participatory arts practices in a diversity of art forms. She travels nationally and internationally to speak about her work in engaged community arts. Rachael has also produced and directed several radio dramas for the CBC. Rachael lives in Montreal with her partner Gordon Fisch and their children Caitlin and Elijah.

DARREL WILDCAT is a playwright, director, and popular educator of Cree descent, based out of the Ermineskin reserve at Hobbema, Alberta. Darrel was closely involved in the early formation of the Native Theatre School, now known as the Centre for Indigenous Theatre in Ontario. The main focus of his work has been in popular theatre practices for social change, working primarily with Aboriginal peoples across Canada. Most recently Darrel travelled throughout Nunavut designing and leading theatre-based workshops with Indigenous people in the North. Darrel was one of the founding members of the Four Directions Theatre Collective, and served on the first Board of Directors of Common Weal in Saskatchewan. He has also served on several arts council juries, including the jury for the Canada Council for the Arts John Hirsch Prize. His current interest is in using theatre as a means to teach and preserve the Cree language. Darrel has taught theatre at the University of Calgary, and continues to work extensively with young people.

Introduction to Ka'ma'mo'pi cik
Rachael Van Fossen and Darrel Wildcat

Preamble (Rachael Van Fossen)
In 1990 I began to focus my artistic practice in a theatre form known as the community play, a form developed by Ann Jellicoe and Jon Oram of the Colway Theatre Trust in England. This creative process involves a team of professional theatre artists working in collaboration with a geographically defined community, to produce a large-scale theatrical event about the place and the people who live there. To date a handful of other Canadian theatre artists have taken up the wonderful challenges of the community play (of particular note are Dale Hamilton, Ruth Howard and Cathy Stubington, among others). The Canadian community play movement has tended towards plays which deal directly with pressing current social issues, often within a historical framework. Nonetheless the following Colway principles have guided much of the work undertaken in Canada:
- a philosophy and practice of inclusiveness: anyone who wants to take part should feel invited to take part, regardless of previous experience. (In my own practice, this has meant that both the professional artistic team and the primary community organizers must "reflect the community back to itself," and so provide representation from all demographics within that community.)
- while integrity of "process" is vitally important, the artistic "product" is equally important. Community-based artworks should not be considered "cute" or amateurish. (It is nonetheless important to note that the aesthetics and production values of a particular community play will usually reflect some kind of synthesis, or an eclectic mix, of the artists' aesthetic style(s), and an aesthetic appropriate to the community.)
- The project should aim to involve as many community people as possible, in all areas and phases of development and production, working in a collaborative (equal but different) relationship with professional theatre artists. (On the projects I have been involved with, I try to make explicit to the other artists involved that we have at least as much to learn from the community people, as the community will learn from us.)

Reflections on *The Gathering*: Darrel Wildcat and Rachael Van Fossen
Among the Saskatchewan community play projects produced in the 90s, The Calling Lakes project entitled *Ka'ma'mo'pi cik/The Gathering* seems to have most captured the imaginations of academics, students, other theatre artists, and a more general public. In advance of this publication, Darrel Wildcat and I reflected back on our experiences as co-writers and co-directors of the project, way back in Fort Qu'Appelle in 1992.

RVF: I could never have guessed, during that intensive period when we were madly trying to co-author a script for the Calling Lakes Community Play project, that more than ten years later we'd be co-writing an introduction for publication in an anthology. These projects are, after all, intended to be experienced primarily in the performance, and don't necessarily translate well to the page. But then, I wasn't entirely prepared for the high level of interest in that project even at the time, were you?

DW: I was not ready for such an experience! On arriving in Fort Qu'Appelle, my first thoughts were about a project much smaller in scope and impact. Only then did

I start to realize that the project had a meaning for people which was much larger than the script itself. We were talking about these peoples' grandparents and parents, their families. It was wild. The greatest impact of the project was definitely on the people most directly involved: community members on the research team, the steering team, the people working "backstage," people who consented to be interviewed, the actors, and so on. But bit by bit that circle started to grow wider and encompass even more people. Then during the performance run, that circle started to include audience members. For all of these people – Native and non-Native included, the play was a departure point for discussion and dialogue, showing people the actual stories of the "Other" group, and in that way getting rid of some commonly held assumptions.

RVF: It felt like a huge responsibility to "do justice" to the complexities and nuances of the community stories, especially because *The Gathering* was really the first time in the region that Aboriginal peoples and people of European descent worked together, in a very public fashion, on some difficult issues.
A large part of the performance experience also resided in the novelty and the immediacy of the promenade staging, where the audience stood surrounded by six raised outdoor stages.[1] The audience participates more actively in the story, as the action of the play takes place around them, among them, through them, and even over their heads. The audience therefore becomes implicated in the community issues raised. How can we describe this experience for readers of the play in this anthology?

DW: An image that might be useful are those old diner stools – that's how the audience seemed to me, to be spinning, so they had a 360 degree panoramic view. Some people, especially the kids, would actually run from stage to stage to get a "front-row view" every time the action switched. But most people took the panoramic view, letting the surprises surround them.

RVF: When we began our writing process, we needed to find a structure that would allow us to weave together, into a narrative with some kind of unity, the various oral histories the local research team had uncovered. I remember you felt it was crucial not to leave the impression that the history of the Aboriginal peoples began with European contact. So there we were, trying to create a cohesive narrative, beginning with the glaciers, and continuing right up to the present day. The discovery of a shared passion for clowning led to the principle unifying element of our two time-travelling characters, caught in a bitter struggle over control of the land on behalf of "their" people. I also remember some pressure from community members to build the play around "The Legend of the Qu'Appelle", by the 19th Century Mohawk poet Pauline Johnson. The poem ultimately resulted in the play's third "mythically proportioned" character, that of the LegendWoman. How well do you think these characters served the themes and goals of the play?

DW: The clowns were definitely central to the play. Both are strong, recognizable archetypes: Wesakeychuk, the trickster from the oral literature of the Cree people, and the European Fool from the Shakespearean court. Wesakeychuk was especially useful, because he can change shape and form, even gender, so we were able to have both of the clowns become characters in different historical scenes. As for the LegendWoman, I remember some of the people in the community were worried we were going to make fun of her. But I think ultimately we were successful in uncovering the archetype —the Mother Earth figure—that was behind the stereotype.

RVF: I'm sure you have not forgotten some of our "struggles" as co-writers. Ours was not always an easy process, to say the least. It seems to me that we managed not so much to reach "compromise," but rather to agree to maintain, even in our working relationship, the underlying cultural tensions of the play.

DW: One play is not going to make everyone understand everything about each other. But the play did create discourse – not so much a discourse to search for understanding, but to search for some kind of meaning. In any case, it's an impossible thing to ask playwrights to do: "Okay you guys, you playwrights, you make the understanding here." So I think what we tried to do is make meaning, with the stories that the people gave to us.

RVF: Yes, we used juxtaposition of stories, for instance. But we also needed to learn to listen to each other more, as co-writers, rather than either one of us trying to "force" our own agenda on the other one, or (more importantly) on the community. Through this process many people, myself included, learned in a deeper way the difference between white "guilt," and taking responsibility for our history.

DW: Sometimes the listening is ultimately where you find the human element. Meshing those two different oral histories, those different perspectives of different people in the community – that was a difficult thing. That first day we talked, it probably looked like we'd beat each other up verbally. I wanted to tell you something – but maybe we didn't have to tell each other – we had to listen to each other. I was having trouble with the idea of celebrating – what the heck were we supposed to celebrate? What the railroad track meant to one group of people, was not what it meant to other people. These literal railroad lines were also drawing economic and political lines. It's hard for an Aboriginal person to celebrate the "opening up" of Western Canada. You and I didn't disagree about that – we just needed to find a way to allow for discussion, and to reflect the two communities without vilifying either one. I didn't want to water it down and make it fluffy – that was the difficult balance.

RVF: Avoiding vilification was important, since the primary project goal was supposed to be the "bringing together" of people, not to further polarize relations. Interestingly, we ended by finding the celebration in the act itself of trying to find the celebration...

DW: In Act III the two halves of the mudball never actually touched, because we wanted to show the process of reaching out to each other. By the end of the project this act was no longer a fantasy. And I don't think "inclusive" means you'll be able to change peoples' minds in two months. A few people left the project because they were not in the same "place" as where the story was going – not just the story of the play, but the story that other community people wanted to create through the project itself. I remember the grandchildren of one of the Indian Agents, who left because of the representation of Edwards in the play. For people who did choose to stay with the project, it was important that everyone was comfortable with the process and the story.

RVF: Or maybe, sometimes, to be comfortable with being uncomfortable...

DW: The project succeeded pretty well at being accessible to many people. As with everything else, some people have easier access even by the mere fact of having a phone, and some will have less. But people arranged rides for each other to go to rehearsals, and there was a lot of outreach from many people who were involved. You and I interviewed people a lot – for instance the Standing Buffalo women who told their stories of working as domestics ended up basically playing themselves in the production. We interviewed the grandson of J.Z. LaRocque, but couldn't convince him to be an actor, so he gave us permission for someone else to play that role. The play was far from exclusive, that's for sure. The process was very collaborative – we tried to be open to whatever experiences the community people could offer us.

The rest of the artistic team also allowed for a lot of community input. One of the artists might say "We need to bring this up a level artistically," or a community person might say "It's really important to make Charles Pratt less of a 'traitor,' and more of a well-rounded character." It's similar to the popular education work of Freire[2] – the artists are not the only "experts": the community people also have a set of knowledge. The best community-based theatre is when there is a free exchange of knowledge. It definitely takes a certain sensibility in an artist to do this kind of work. You have to have a real comfort level in yourself. We had a good artistic team working on the production, with a broad understanding of what theatre is, and a willingness to explore all those elements. For community people, too – if you've never heard powwow music you need to have a certain openness to it. Artistically the professional team was really strong both in the traditional Aboriginal performance aspects as well as Western practices. For instance, the Kaiswatum Singers—the powwow group—were from the community, but we were lucky to have them because they were also excellent musicians. The more artistic the production is, the more expressive it is, the more effective it is in the end – you actually can give people more information.

RVF: I myself learned a lot working on this project, including a lot of appalling Canadian history that I hadn't previously been exposed to – Canada's own apartheid system of passes and Indian agents, for example. But I also came out of the project with even more passion for creating theatre with people, rather than just about people and for people. Of course this passion is largely because of the social relevance of the work, which makes it really satisfying. But I actually find it more artistically satisfying as well – big images, real peoples' stories – these can make for incredibly powerful art.

DW: The biggest thing I learned was about listening and trying to absorb. Those two words that make up the word "community"—common and unity—I think that really happened for most of us who were involved – a sense of common purpose.

RVF: *A'ko'sai.*

DW: That's it then.

---

[1] Seating was provided for elderly and disabled people.

[2] Freire, Paolo. *Pedagogy of the Oppressed.* New York: Continuum Publishing Company, 1993.

— • — Selected Bibliography — • —

Sources for further reading on the Community Play

Andreasen, John. "Community Plays – A Search for Identity." *Theatre Research International*. 21.1: 72-78.

Butt, Robyn-Marie. "Back to the Source: Community Play Projects." *Theatrum*. Sept-Oct 1994: 13-18.

Caton, Jacolyn. "Urban Issues: Welcome to the Hood." *Performing Arts and Entertainment in Canada* 30 (Winter 1995): 6-9.

de Guevara, Lina. "Sisters/Strangers: A Community Play about Immigrant Women." *Canadian Theatre Review* 90 (1997): 28-31.

Drainie, Bronwyn. "A Last Look at One of the Bridges that Art—and Heart—Built." *Globe and Mail* [Toronto] 22 June 1991: C1.

Howard, Ruth. "Holding On and Letting Go: Designing the Community Play." *Canadian Theatre Review* 90 (1997): 15-19.

Jellicoe, Ann. *Community Plays: How to Put Them On*. London: Methuen, 1987.

Farfan, Penny. "Women Playwrights in Regina." *Canadian Theatre Review* 87 (1996): 55-64.

Kershaw, Baz and Tony Coult. *Engineers of the Imagination: The Welfare State Handbook*. London: Methuen, 1983.

Kershaw, Baz. *The Politics of Performance: Radical Theatre as Cultural Intervention*. New York: Routledge, 1992.

Little, Edward J. and Richard Paul Knowles. "The Unity in Community." *The Theatre of Form and the Production of Meaning*. Montreal: ECW Press, 1999.

Little, Edward. *"The Spirit of Shivaree and the Community Play in Canada." Contemporary Issues in Canadian Drama*. Per Brask, ed. Winnipeg: Blizzard, 1995.

Little, Edward and Ann Wilson, eds. *Canadian Theatre Review* 90 (1997). (Issue on Community Plays)

Little, Edward. "Community Animation and Social Action in *The Spirit of Shivaree*." *Canadian Theatre Review* 67 (1991): 99-104.

—. Aesthetic Morality in the Blyth and District Community Play." *Canadian Theatre Review* 90 (1997): 20-27.

—. "Cultural Democracy in the Enderby and District Community Play." *Canadian Theatre Review* 101 (2000). 56-58.

—. "Theatre and Community: Case Studies of Four Colway-Style Plays Performed in Canada." (PhD Thesis) University of Toronto, 1997.

Little, Edward and Rachael Van Fossen. "Pedagogies, Politics and Practices in Working with Youth." *Canadian Theatre Review* 106 (2001): 5-10.

Mendenhall, Marie. "Stirring Up Tempests in Saskatchewan Communities: Profile of Rachael Van Fossen." *Theatrum* September/October 1994: 11-12.

—. "Theatre with the Power of a Gun." *NeWest Review* February/March 1995: 7-11.

Osachoff, Margaret Gail. "Take That, Pauline Johnson: Natives and Whites Collaborate to Create an Unusual Theatrical Event." *NeWest Review* October/November 1992: 24-25.

Oram, Jon. "The Art of the Community Play." *Canadian Theatre Review* 90 (1997): 5-9.

Selman, Jan and Tim Prentki. *Popular Theatre in Political Context: Britain and Canada in Focus*. Bristol: Intellect Press, 2000.

van Erven, Eugene. *Community Theatre: Global Perspectives*. New York: Routledge, 2001.

Van Fossen, Rachael. "Writing for the Community Play Form." *Canadian Theatre Review* 90 (1997): 10-14.

Van Fossen, Rachael and ahdri zhina mandiela. "Mirroring Duality." *Testifyin': Contemporary African Canadian Drama Volume II*. Toronto: Playwrights Canada Press, 2003.

Van Fossen, Rachael and Edward Little. "Pedagogies, Politics and Practices in Working with Youth." *Canadian Theatre Review* 106 (2001): 5-10.

Reviews of Saskatchewan Community Plays

City Flats. Regina 1996, 1997:
Beatty, Greg. "Message of Hope Delivered." *Regina Leader Post* 1 November 1997: D2.

Brewer, Donna. "Acting Troupe Makes Regina Proud." *Regina Leader Post* 30 March, 1996: A10.

Healy, Don. "*City Flats*." *Regina Sun* 8 October 1997: 4.

Kaminski, Lois-Anna. "*City Flats*: A Review." *Prairie Dog* November, 1997: 9.

King, Randy. "I Just Love Happy Endings." *Regina Free Press* 30 November, 1997.

A North Side Story (or two). Regina 1995:
Pilon, Bernard. "Stories in Regina's Urban Hood." *Regina Leader Post*. 8 Aug, 1995.

Saulteaux, Clint. "*A North Side Story (or two)* Hits National Scene." *Prairie Dog* February, 1996: 19.

The Gathering. Fort Qu'Appelle, 1992:
Cadham, Joan Eyolfson. "First Community Play Truly a Gathering." *Fort Qu'Appelle Times* 25 July 1992: 6.

de la Hey, Mark. "All Together Now." *Western People* 30 July, 1992: 1.

—. "Calling Lakes Community Play." *Briarpatch* June 1992: 29.

Pilon, Bernard. "Play Gives New Life to History." *Regina Leader Post* 16 July, 1992: C2.

—. "A Role for Everyone." *Regina Leader Post* 20 April, 1991: B6.

—. "Venture is Coming Together." *Regina Leader Post* 2 May, 1992: D6.

Wattie, Chris. "Bridging the Gap." *Globe and Mail* [Toronto] 21 Aug 1992: C9.

Ka'ma'mo'pi cik/The Gathering was first produced by the Calling Lakes Community Play Project in 1992 at Fort San, Saskatchewan with the following company:

All cast members played multiple roles:

Elvis Aisaican	M J. Desjarlais	Brenda MacLauchlan
Tera Aisaican	Shane Doucette	Eden Maher
Elizabeth Aitken	Barry Edmonds	Dorinda Maher
George Archer	Jodi Eyolfson	Lavica Mahnke
Marge Barker	Rosemary Eyolfson	Hilary McKay
Joan Bauer	Norma Ferguson	Delores McLeod
Velma Bear	Debbie Graham-Rowe	Clara Pasqua
Sybil Bear	Libby Graham-Rowe	Karen Pasqua
Holly Bedel	Beth Grainger	Joan Peigan
Glynis Bellegarde	Terry Grand	Fifi Piapot
Verne Bellegarde	Chelsea Hamilton	Pam Reynolds
Delvin Bitternose	Darryl Hamilton	Pat Reynolds
Ricky Bitternose	Kenton Hamilton	Bryan Rosnau
Patrick Bird	Kate Hersberger	Lorne Rowell
Juandell Blind	Calinda Hotomani	Shannon Ryder
Jeff Bodnaryk	Justin Ironstar	Cleve Sauer
Shelley Boen	Hazel Jardine	Anne Marie Sauer
Alice Boxall	Naomi Jardine	MaryJo Selenski
Sue Boxall	Kristen Kayseas	Chris Spencer
Thomas Boxall	Curtis Kayseas	Erik Stainsby
Christine Brown	Garry Kerr	Fred Starblanket
Marianne Cameron	Henry Kinsella	Alicia Starblanket
Terry Carrier	Sandra Kitchemonia	Brendan Starr
Bill Cheers	Ken Kuhling	Jeremy Starr
Daniel Cheers	Alana Kuhling	Ashley Turgeon
Doris Dodds	Walter Langman	Rosemary Vernoy
Ron de la Hey	Maureen Mael	Dicky Yuzicappi

Artistic Director: Rachael Van Fossen
Co-Directors: Darrel Wildcat and Rachael Van Fossen
Composer and Musical Director: Billy Morton
Set and Prop Designer: Ruth Howard
Costume Designer: Jo Dibb
Lighting Designer and Production Manager: Ralph Skanes
Production Stage Manager: Richard Agecoutay
Stage Manager: Theresa Hiorns
Choreographer: Maureen Mael
Associate Musical Director: Michelle Kruger
Project Coordinator: Debra Thorne
Musicians: Stephen Cooper, Gord Fisch, Marshall Poitras, Kaiswatum Singers
Métis Dance Coach: Dicky Yuzicappi

— • —

Ka'ma'mo'pi cik/The Gathering was re-mounted in 1993 with co-directors Micheline Chevrier and Lorre Jenson.

Characters (in order of appearance, mostly)

Northern Lights
Legendman
Legendwoman
Fairies, Small People,
  Flying Horse, Laughing
  Sisters, Wetago
Cree civilisation people
Tah'wi
Amisk
Mas'wa'peo
Magpie
Mouse
Badger
Bullboy
Rosebud
Skywoman
Treewoman
Moonwoman (midwife)
Wesakeychuk
The Fool
Government officials
  (minimum 6)
Métis Paddlers
  (minimum 8 men,
  for 4 canoes)
McKay
Desjarlais
LaFramboise
Traders (native and non-
  native – full cast)
Michael Hall

Elizabeth Hall
Fannie Hall
Eleanor West
Nathan West
Plantwoman
Kokum
Hudson Bay Fighters
Northwest Company
  Fighters
Antoine Larocque
Daniel Harmon
Magpie
Surveyors and McIntyre
Mosquitos
Packing Homesteaders
  (flexible numbers)
Homesteader chorus
Fred Gilchrist
Mrs. Gilchrist
Kate Martin
Georgina Binney-Clark
William Hatfield
Sally Hatfield
Mrs. Hatfield
Charles Pratt
Sarah Pratt
Archibald MacDonald
Piapot
Starblanket
Lieutenant Governor
  Morris

Soldiers
Loudvoice
Cote
Gambler
Messenger (a boy)
Ontario Women
Cree Women
Indian Agent Edwards
Yuzicappi
Standing Buffalo
Charlie Sun
Lucie
Marie
Fr Lebret
J.Z. Larocque
Dr Kyle
Nurse Annie
Annette
Antonia
Alice
Jack
Janet
Mona
Fred
Queen Puppeteers (4)
Eagle Puppeteers (3)
Dove Puppeteers (3)
Homesteaders for
  onslaught

Music

Music and Lyrics by Billy Morton, with lyrics for "How Come They Didn't Ask Us"
by Heather Herrell.

Ka'ma'mo'pi cik / The Gathering
by Rachael Van Fossen and Darrel Wildcat

—— • —— • ——

Act I – Prologue

The beautiful hills of the Qu'Appelle Valley provide the setting for the drama and pageantry of the play.

The spectacle begins as the audience moves from the area of the pre-show fair (busking, etc)into an adjacent field somewhat deeper in the hills. Beyond the field is a secluded coulee, accessible only by a narrow path. The full cast, a handful of strolling musicians, and the Northern Lights—costumed cast members on stilts—lead the procession, performing "Welcome to Dreamtime" as they go. The choreographed movement of the Northern Lights is simple and fluid, evoking the mysterious beauty of the Aurora Borealis.

Overture to the play: "Welcome to Dreamtime." Music and lyrics by Billy Morton.

Tell me what you see
When you gaze into the night
Dancing overhead
It is the Northern Lights
Marching back and forth
Across a field of blue
An echo from the past
Calling out to you
Welcome to Dreamtime; Welcome tonight!

Welcome to the heart
Of the Valley of Qu'Appelle
Voices of the past
The wonders they could tell
Fable, legend, lore
Fact and fantasy
Call to one and all
Call to you and me
Welcome to Dreamtime; Welcome tonight!

Watch them if you will
The Creator's gift to you
As ageless as the air
It's really nothing new
Shades of green and gold
Colours on the wing
And if you listen close
You can hear them sing
Welcome to Dreamtime; Welcome tonight!

Follow if you will
A glimpse of paradise
Know what happens once
May never happen twice
Know that what you see
Is never what it seems
But it can bring you all
Closer to your dreams
Welcome to Dreamtime; Welcome tonight!

Welcome to Dreamtime; Welcome tonight!

(solo soprano voice) Welcome to Dreamtime; Welcome tonight!

Scene One

As the audience enters the field, a lone male figure in traditional Cree dress stands above them on the crest of the valley ridge. Down below, clustered near the audience, is a group of masked and wailing mourning women. As the song ends, the young Cree man lets out a war cry and runs downhill toward the mourners.

Hidden among the wailing mourners is a young Aboriginal woman. She is the girl from the poem "The Legend of the Qu'Appelle," by Pauline Johnson. Dressed in a white vinyl fringed dress, and with a brightly coloured feather in her hair, she is reminiscent of the small "squaw" dolls still available in tacky souvenir shops.

The wailing mourners open up to reveal the young woman lying as if dead on a funeral pyre.

The young Cree man, the male character from the famous poem, arrives from the hilltop in a terrible rush, as if late for his cue. He is dressed in traditional fashion.

"The Legend of the Qu'Appelle," by Pauline Johnson.

LEGENDMAN
(catches his breath) I am the one who loved her as my life,
Had watched her grow to sweet young womanhood;
Won the dear privilege to call her wife,
And found the world because of her, was good.
I am the one who heard the spirit voice,
Of which the paleface settlers love to tell;
From whose strange story they have made their choice
Of naming this fair valley the "Qu'Appelle".

I dare not linger on the moment when
My boat I beached beside her teepee door;
I heard the wail of women and of men,
I saw the death-fires lighted on the shore.
To look upon the beauty of her face,
The still closed eyes…

back to
front:
Delvin
Bitternose,
Darryl
Hamilton

*photo by
Richard
Agecoutay, cour-
tesy of Common
Weal
Community
Plays Inc.*

The young woman sits up from her "death bed," and joins in the recitation of the poem.

LEGENDWOMAN AND LEGENDMAN
...THE LIPS THAT KNEW NO BREATH;
TO LOOK, TO LEARN – TO REALIZE MY PLACE
HAD BEEN USURPED BY MY ONE RIVAL – DEATH.

LEGENDWOMAN
(to audience) That's me, the dead one.

The young woman continues the recitation of the poem as the young man listens.

"She called thy name, then passed away," they said,
"Just on the hour whereat the moon arose."
Among the lonely lakes I go no more,
For she who made their beauty is not there;
The paleface rears his teepee on the shore
And says the vale is fairest of the fair.

The paleface loves the haunted lakes they say,
And journeys far to watch their beauty spread
Before his vision; but to me the day,
The night, the seasons are all dead.
I listen, heartsick, while the hunters tell
Why white men named the valley the Qu'Appelle.

Pause.

(to the young man, in Cree) As'tum.

The young man walks to where the young woman stands. He also speaks in Cree.

LEGENDMAN
(in Cree) You are my wife, I have found you, and you must stay with me.

LEGENDWOMAN
(in Cree) You are my husband, and I am your wife. *(She switches to English.)* I am
your wife, but I am also your mother, your sister. I tell you this because the valley
and land is my mother. I must return to her.

LEGENDMAN
(in Cree) I understand, and I accept.

The young man departs.

LEGENDWOMAN
(change of mood) Do you know that poem? Too bad the Indian girl is always the
one who dies, eh? Well, anyway, *tansi*, hello, and welcome. *(She reaches to adjust the
feather in her hair, accidentally pokes herself.)* Ouch! Geez, I hate this costume they
gave me. *(She gives the feather to an audience "plant" who has approached her with a
camera.)* Could you hang onto this for me? Don't be shy. You didn't come here to
watch, did you? To be a spectator? *Wa'te'ne!* Because I could take you on a journey…
(suddenly very solemn) Listen very carefully. You are about to see a birth of peoples,
and of dreams. The birth of our world. The birth of the valley. The births of
different nations. Their Visions. *(beat)* Collisions. *(beat)* Journeys. *(longer beat)*
I am here to lead you on another journey. Welcome to dreamtime – a journey
through time and the valley. My mother– *(She indicates the hills of the valley.)*
I would like to introduce you to my mother, and the dreams she has dreamed.
(drumming and singing from the coulee) Listen, can you hear that? My friends have
come to accompany you.

> With the sound of the drum from the coulee below, children appear from the bushes
> as Little People, Fairies, the Laughing Sisters, Wetago and other creatures. They
> chant and sing "Come with us! Come with us!", enticing the audience along the
> path into the coulee. Adult members of the cast are also on hand to guide and
> welcome the audience as the journey begins.

> The coulee is a magical space, sacred and earthy. The space of the play and of the
> valley.

Scene Two

The audience enters into the hubbub of a Cree civilization scene, pre-contact with Europeans, taking place on all six stages that surround an open "promenade" area where the audience will stand. The Cree civilization is enacted all around and through this promenade area, as well as on the stages. Drumming and singing continue underneath improvised scenes which happen simultaneously. There are scenes of fishing, trapping, tanning and scraping hides, preparations for birthing, a return from a buffalo hunt, an elder counselling two young people who may require discipline, children getting up with their father to fish, children sleeping in, a stick game being played, etc. The audience has walked into everyday life in a pre-colonial era. Audience members are free to roam from stage to stage and area to area, taking in bits of scenes of everyday life as it unfolds around them.

As the last of the audience enters the coulee, a flock of "geese" puppets fly overhead. The LEGENDWOMAN has taken her place on a high platform with steps down either side, and calls attention to a scene of preparations for birth. The other Cree civilization scenes continue quietly underneath.

LEGENDWOMAN
You say you have entered another time. An old era, ancient to us. But take care: what seems old, is new. A birth. Watch.

The midwife MOONWOMAN is walking with ROSEBUD, who is in labour. They are outside a tipi. In front of the tipi are women smudging with sweetgrass. Among the Sweetgrass Women are TREEWOMAN and SKYWOMAN. Another woman places a big branch across the tipi, used for ROSEBUD to hold onto during the birth. The Sweetgrass Women are singing to help ROSEBUD breathe by the beat of the drum. (Note: in performance portions of the scene were spoken in Cree.)

MOONWOMAN
Continue walking, it will help you when it's time.

ROSEBUD
I'm scared and I'm excited. I can feel the baby's head!

MOONWOMAN
Don't think about being scared. Think about the baby you have to bring into the world. Look at all these women. Listen, smell: you have good medicine here.

ROSEBUD
(groan) I guess there's no way out now.

MOONWOMAN
Well there better be a way out for baby. *(rubs her back)* It's going to hurt, you heard that before. *(ROSEBUD groans.)* Breathe, and baby will know which way is out.

The drumming and singing build to a crescendo as ROSEBUD and MOONWOMAN walk into the tipi for the birth. Drumming and singing end abruptly, marking the passage of time. Several hours have passed.

ROSEBUD
(*from inside the tipi*) She is beautiful! She is beautiful! Did you see her, she is beautiful! *Tan'ta Ni'nah'pe'wow.*

> MOONWOMAN *comes out of the tipi with a bundle, which she shows to the other women.*

MOONWOMAN
The baby looks good today.

TREEWOMAN
Today, yes. But I wonder what she will see in her life.

SKYWOMAN
The world is changing – maybe a woman will be chief!

> *The women laugh together, behind their hands.*

MOONWOMAN
(*to an adolescent GIRL*) Go, get Tah'wi. Tell him that he has a daughter.

> *The young GIRL runs through the audience to another stage where TAH'WI and his friend AMISK have been fishing with four young children, named BADGER, BULLBOY, MAGPIE and MOUSE. As the young girl crosses to them, the men are pulling up their net and assessing their catch.*

AMISK
Wow! Look at that catch, Tah'wi!

TAH'WI
You see, I told you they would come.

GIRL
(*rushing up*) Tah'wi. I have just come from Moonwoman and Rosebud…

TAH'WI
Well, what is it…

GIRL
You have a daughter.

TAH'WI
You heard, Amisk? A daughter! At last we have a daughter!

AMISK
Well, go to her, man.

TAH'WI
(*to the girl*) Is it time?

GIRL
I think so, they sent me.

TAH'WI
Well then! Come on…

TAH'WI and the GIRL rush back to the birthing scene. MAGPIE and MOUSE keep audience's attention on fishing scene.

MOUSE
Amisk, where do babies come from?

AMISK
You were a baby once, Mouse, and you were born to your mother, and your mother was born to your Kokum.

MAGPIE
Well then, where did Kokum come from?

BADGER
From her mother, Magpie, what else?

AMISK
Badger is right.

MAGPIE
But where did Kokum's mother come from?

BULLBOY
It must have started somewhere.

MAGPIE
Where did it start?

AMISK
Look, you kids, we're here to catch fish. I'll tell you a story tonight.

MAGPIE
Amisk, we can't fish if we don't know where we come from.

AMISK
(laughing) Oh, I see. Well, sit down then, and listen while I clean the net. *(The children sit around him.)* You know that you're not supposed to talk about the trickster in summer. You tell stories in the winter when he is asleep. But just this one time so you'll learn. Wesakeychuk, eh? Well do you know the story of the big flood, that covered everything?

We hear the drummers of thousands of years. The singing leads the way for WESAKEYCHUK, riding on top of a glacier. On his way in he looks behind him at the valley he has created.

WESAKEYCHUK
Look at that valley – couldn't have done better if I...

He turns forward and bends from his waist, releasing a long and loud fart. Simultaneously, the FOOL enters from behind the glacier and onto a stage. The FOOL is carrying a rucksack.

FOOL
Gross! What was that?

Loud sound effect as the glacier hits a big rock. WESAKEYCHUK almost falls off.

WESAKEYCHUK
Whoa! What was that. *(seeing the audience)* Tansi ekwa kihawaw. Kahki neheowan. Upsis neheowak ota ekwa Mechat monehawak. Tanta homa. Where the heck am I?

FOOL
Hey, you! Where am I?

WESAKEYCHUK
Just a minute. *(looking over the top of the glacier)* It's that rock. *(to audience)* That thing has been following me since I was south of the Duck Mountains east of here. You get going pretty good in one of these newfangled glaciers. Especially compared to what I was using a thousand years ago.

FOOL
Hey, I'm talking to you, Glacierman. I'm lost, where am I?

WESAKEYCHUK
Who are you? *(looks closely)* You look like a fool...

FOOL
Exactly! I am a fool, see? *(reaches into his rucksack)* Knucklebones, Harlequin suit, Red Nose, Big Shoes... I got 'em all. I'm in the theatre, you see, and I've lost my travelling troupe of players... *(looking around)* and somehow this doesn't look like Renaissance Italy, or even England...

WESAKEYCHUK
Look, I don't know what you're doing here, but I'm in the middle of a story, and you aren't in it! Now let me get on with it...

LEGENDWOMAN
(from her high platform) He's in the story, Trickster. *(to FOOL)* You can act?

FOOL
Of course I can act, that's what I do, for cryin' out loud.

LEGENDWOMAN
Look in your bag again, Fool. *(He does.)*

WESAKEYCHUK
(impatient, to LEGENDWOMAN) What's going on here?

FOOL
What's going on here? *(pulling BEAVER costume out)* What the heck is this?

LEGENDWOMAN
(commanding the FOOL) Put it on. *(commanding the TRICKSTER)* Tell the story.

> The two begin to protest. LEGENDWOMAN cuts them off.

It will all work out, in the big picture. Go on!

> The FOOL dons the BEAVER head and takes his place with OTTER and MUSKRAT, crouched behind a large canoe on a stage. The moment WESAKEYCHUK picks up his story again, the "rock" moves from among the audience in the promenade area, onto the stage with OTTER, BEAVER and MUSKRAT.

WESAKEYCHUK
It's that rock. That thing has been following me since I was south of the Duck Mountains east of here. *(beat)* I look over the land and remember a time when there was nothing but water here. Now of course I had nothing to do with this. *(sound of water)* The water came out of the ground and filled the island, Ni'kah'wi', my mother. So! I jumped into the canoe and started to call my brothers and sisters.

WESAKEYCHUK crosses off the glacier toward the animals, chanting to his small hand drum.

FOOL/BEAVER
Do you trust that guy?

MUSKRAT
No way man! Just think of all the things he's done before.

OTTER
This time he's really screwed up. Look at the water.

The animals scramble into the canoe and move as if riding waves.

MUSKRAT
(to WESAKEYCHUK as he arrives) Look brother. We have come on for safety, not to be eaten. Now tell us, what have you done!

WESAKEYCHUK
Well it was kind of an accident. Anyway, here we are! Care for some bark? *(offering some)*

FOOL/BEAVER
Get on with it, Trickster…

WESAKEYCHUK
Okay, well, I kind of flooded the earth.

OTTER
What do you mean you "kind of" flooded the earth? What's not flooded!

WESAKEYCHUK
All right. I flooded the earth. Now don't…

MUSKRAT
What's on your mind besides tricks?

WESAKEYCHUK
Like I was saying, it was more of… an accident…

FOOL/BEAVER
So, like, what do you expect us to do?

MUSKRAT
See! I told you. It was a trick!

WESAKEYCHUK
Brothers and Sisters, let us not argue! We have a chance to make the world here. I can fix this. I'm serious this time. I call you my brothers, honestly. I need your strength and ability to swim. I need our mother's skin.

FOOL/BEAVER
No way!

WESAKEYCHUK
If you would dive and get some mud, from under the water, we can start over. Will you help?

The animals huddle, then emerge.

OTTER
Okay, but you must promise to respect us and never kill us for fun. Plus, your people must always give an offering after your hunt. *(WESAKEYCHUK and OTTER shake hands.)* Now, what must be done.

Drumming as LEGENDWOMAN takes over narration of story.

LEGENDWOMAN
So Wesakeychuk the Trickster…

WESAKEYCHUK
That's me!

LEGENDWOMAN
…took a leather strap, and tied it to the Otter's foot.

WESAKEYCHUK
(does so) Now dive my brother, and swim deep. *(OTTER does so.)*

LEGENDWOMAN
But Otter died from exhaustion.

WESAKEYCHUK pulls OTTER out.

WESAKEYCHUK
Beaver. Your turn. No matter what happens, you will be remembered.

FOOL/BEAVER
You're nuts! Look how deep it is! And it's far…. You can't even see the Duck Mountains…

WESAKEYCHUK
(to LEGENDWOMAN) He's messing up the story!

LEGENDWOMAN
You know what to do. Use another story.

WESAKEYCHUK
Right. *(quickly pulling out his own eyes)* So I grabbed my own eyes and put them back in. *(closing in on BEAVER)* Shall we take out your eyes? See if they'll fit back in after I…

FOOL/BEAVER
Good trick! I, uh, think I can use that somewhere. *(dives into the water)*

LEGENDWOMAN
Beaver swam deep into the water, going farther than Otter, but eventually, Beaver dies. Wesakeychuk pulls on the strap to bring in his little brother.

WESAKEYCHUK
Hmm, nice eyes, oh dead one... Muskrat, your turn. *(putting on the strap)*

LEGENDWOMAN
Muskrat dove far and deep into the water, beyond Otter and Beaver. Deeper and deeper. Reaching the bottom. Grabbing a bit of MUD!

> *MUSKRAT takes a ball of mud from LEGENDWOMAN, who is at the bottom of the "water." This mud ball will be treated with great respect and reverence. WESAKEYCHUK reels in the leather strap.*

WESAKEYCHUK
Yes!

> *WESAKEYCHUK pulls MUSKRAT out. The three animal "corpses" lie side by side.*

Now what am I supposed to do next? This story's not a tragedy.

FOOL/BEAVER
Hey, we're dyin' out here!

WESAKEYCHUK
Oh, yeah.... Blow.

> *WESAKEYCHUK sings. As part of the song, he blows life into the animals.*

LEGENDWOMAN
Wesakeychuk brought the animals back to life. He then took the mud, and with his breath raised Mother Earth from beneath the water.

> *We see WESAKEYCHUK blowing with great ceremony and concentration on the mud ball. As he blows, the "water" withdraws from the promenade area, with a simultaneous unfurling of four lengthy streamers, in the four directions, and the four colours of man.*

WESAKEYCHUK
Wolverine! *(WOLVERINE appears.)* Neya! Run around the land. *(WOLVERINE runs in a large circle, over all stages, accompanied by drumming, and returns.)* A'say, you're back. *(WESAKEYCHUK blows on the mud again.)* Neya! Mena! Run!

LEGENDWOMAN
But this time Wolverine does not return. Wesakeychuk gives a sacred offering of tobacco to the earth, and to the animals, as he has promised.

> *As WESAKEYCHUK begins the ceremony, WOLVERINE climbs onto the glacier and takes off at top speed, with OTTER and MUSKRAT running alongside.*

WESAKEYCHUK
Hey, *chasqwa!*

WESAKEYCHUK chases after the glacier. He nearly forgets the mud ball, and goes back for it.

LEGENDWOMAN
Take care of that mud ball, Trickster.

Returning to get the mud ball, WESAKEYCHUK leaves behind his ceremonial bag.

Scene Three

The FOOL tears off his BEAVER costume as he runs to pick up the ceremonial bag.

FOOL
(holding up the bag) Hey Trickster! You forgot.... Oh geez, he'll never hear me. *(loudly)* You oughta get a muffler on that glacier! *(He looks at the bag.)* Hey, tobacco! Never mind, Trickster, I'll keep your bag.

He pops chewing tobacco into his mouth. The FOOL then looks around as the scenes of Cree civilization continue day-to-day tasks around him, now that the creation story has concluded. He takes a large, loud whistle from his rucksack, and blows on it.

Government Officials! Fall in guys! It's our turn now!

With musical accompaniment reminiscent of old player pianos, groups of Government Officials stream all over the stages, with flyers in hand, raised above their heads and waving like flags. The flyers advertise land for "free" out in the Northwest Territories, for any would-be homesteaders looking to build a new life in the "unconquered," "uninhabited" west. The Government Officials are hucksters, distributing flyers and improvising a hard-sell of the homestead land to the audience.

OFFICIALS
FREE LAND!

FOOL
CHARGE!

The FOOL and all the OFFICIALS charge into the audience with their flyers. The LEGENDWOMAN appears from above, and cuts them off.

LEGENDWOMAN
(very loud) Whoa, whoa! *(The OFFICIALS stop, frightened.)* You're getting way ahead of yourselves. Are the settlers getting hungry – hungry for land! Now get of here! You guys will have your turn.

FOOL
What do you mean? This is part of the story, it really happened.

LEGENDWOMAN
Yes, Fool. But it happens later. These people aren't ready for Future Dreamtime. They have to feel it first. Feeling comes before understanding.

The LEGENDWOMAN claps her hands and the Government OFFICIALS turn on the FOOL.

OFFICIAL #1
(to the FOOL) Idiot! *(hits the FOOL)* Are you trying to make us look like fools?

FOOL
Hey…

OFFICIAL #2
(hitting the FOOL) Calling us in here before it's time? *(hits the FOOL again)*

FOOL
Hey guys, I'm just trying to move the story along.

OFFICIAL #3
(kicking the FOOL) You move along, you piece of worthless excrement! You ass!

FOOL
Hey, that's Fool to you, buddy!

LEGENDWOMAN
Out!

The FOOL runs out with the Government OFFICIALS on his tail.

(to audience) You see the point, don't you? You've got to look at these things in their proper context. Chronological time means nothing – but nonetheless to feel the events as they happen is everything. In the beginning, there was equality…. Remember, the free traders were here first… the voyageurs…

Several canoes enter the promenade area, carried by white Free Traders and Métis Men, all in buckskins. A canoe choreography ensues, through and among the audience. The men sing and their canoes dance.

Métis Paddling Song: "Allons y Nous Pataugeons." Music and lyrics by Billy Morton.

(SOLO) Oh it's a hard life
(ALL) Allons y, nous pataugeons!
(SOLO) I miss my home, I miss my wife
(ALL) Allons y, nous pataugeons!

(SOLO) From the hills we see far
(ALL) Allons y, nous pataugeons!
(SOLO) Wondering where the trees are
(ALL) Allons y, nous pataugeons!

CHORUS
(ALL) Allons y, nous pataugeons!
Pataugeons dans la rivière
Allons y, nous pataugeons!
Pataugeons dans la rivière

(SOLO) Where I go he goes
(ALL) Allons y, nous pataugeons!

(SOLO) Followed by mosquitoes
(ALL) Allons y, nous pataugeons!

> *Repeat chorus.*

(SOLO) We offer you this kind toast *(slower)*
(ALL) Allons y, nous pataugeons!
(SOLO) The devil take the hindmost! *(a tempo)*
(ALL) Allons y, nous pataugeons!

> *Repeat chorus twice.*

> *Canoes exit during the final chorus. Only one canoe remains. It is carried by Neil MCKAY, with DESJARLAIS and LAFRAMBOISE. The FOOL is with the party, but follows behind, dragging a large trunk.*

> *Segue: As the sound of the chorus of paddlers recedes, MCKAY and his men sing the chorus to "The Trading Song." Music and lyrics by Billy Morton.*

CHORUS
You've got something that I want
I've got something that you need
Let's get together and see if we
Can do a little trading
Let's get together and see if we
Can do a little trading

> *MCKAY and his men place their canoe beside one of the stages. The Cree civilization people come to life again with a coyote call from WESAKEYCHUK. The Cree are fascinated, and somewhat fearful, at their first glimpse of the white-skinned people they have heard about from the far east. With the first verse of the song MCKAY's guide DESJARLAIS approaches the Cree. They are negotiating and smoking the pipe. WESAKEYCHUK, in coyote costume, remains to observe the proceedings.*

WESAKEYCHUK
(to MCKAY, who doesn't notice) Whooo are yooooo?

MCKAY
You've got something that I want
I've got something that you need
Let's get together and see if we
Can do a little trading
Let's get together and see if we
Can do a little trading

> *The FOOL and LAFRAMBOISE have come up behind MCKAY with the trunk. MCKAY is trying hard to listen to DESJARLAIS' conversation with TAH'WI and MAS'WA'PEO as his solo chorus ends.*

FOOL
Here Mr. McKay sir. Is this the place?

MCKAY
(startled) Yes, you fool. This is the place. Now, be quiet. Listen!

LAFRAMBOISE
(hitting the FOOL over the head) Yeah, have a little respect!

DESJARLAIS
(to MCKAY) As'tum.

MCKAY
What?

DESJARLAIS
Come. He says we must smoke first.

> MCKAY approaches, and they share the pipe. As they smoke, the FOOL and WESAKEYCHUK sing quietly.

FOOL AND WESAKEYCHUK
Let's get together and see if we
Can do a little trading
Let's get together and see if we
Can do a little trading

DESJARLAIS
(turns to MCKAY) This valley is their winter camp. There's large amounts of fish and protection from winter.

MCKAY
And the trade, Desjarlais, what about the trade?

> At this point the convention should be established that DESJARLAIS is acting as interpreter.

TAH'WI
Your men are known to us. Many people have seen you coming down the river. They say you are an honourable man. The elders say we will trade the buffalo hides. But your men must respect the land and the people that live here.

MCKAY
(extends his hand, TAH'WI just looks at him) On my word, sir, we accept your terms.

FOOL
(jumping up and down with excitement) Start the trading!

WESAKEYCHUK
Respect, he said, fool…

LAFRAMBOISE
(kicking the FOOL) Respect, he said! Idiot…

FOOL
(wounded) Who does this guy McKay think he is, the King of Scotland?

DESJARLAIS
I wouldn't tease him too much about his Scottish background. He has a chip on his shoulder.

FOOL
Yeh, so I get a chip on the butt...

MCKAY
(to DESJARLAIS and TAH'WI) Shall we open the trunk?

TAH'WI
Open the trunk.

> *Reprise of "The Trading Song" and a great flurry of activity as all prepare for the trading.*

MCKAY
(over the music) I want the trunk facing east – that's important to the Indians. Put her up in haste, boys.

> *As the FOOL opens the trunk, singing traders from the rest of the cast appear laden with objects for trade: metal tools, knives, mirrors, blankets, beads and other appropriate items. The Cree civilization people pull out piles of hides, fur, robes, ki'nik'ki'nik', woven porcupine quills, and rattles to trade. During the song, the FOOL is standing at the trunk pulling out trade items and distributing them to people. Everyone is having a good time. This trading song is a big production number, over as suddenly as it began.*

> *"The Trading Song" (reprise). Music and lyrics by Billy Morton.*

You got pemmican

TAH'WI
That's for sure
You got blankets

MCKAY
We need fur.

ALL
Let's get together and see if we
Can do a little trading

You've got something that I want
I've got something that you need
Let's get together and see if we
Can do a little trading
Let's get together and see if we
Can do a little trading

> *As the song ends, MCKAY is left alone, seated with a leather folder on his lap. He is writing a letter to his wife in Montreal. It is winter now, MCKAY is bundled up in a large buffalo hide.*

MCKAY
Dear Mary Ann. I know that this letter will not reach you until almost next year. I write to confirm my love for you. The land here is like the garden of Eden. It holds in abundance buffalo, beaver, fox and wolf. The hides will sell well in the markets of England and Upper Canada. With all its beauty and peace, the land delivers the coldest winter known to civilized man. It's so cold I swear that time freezes, and then you hear for miles. When loneliness takes over, I believe I hear your voice travelling down the St. Lawrence, over the lakes of Huron and Superior, across the plains, and down the Qu'Appelle valley, guiding itself into my heart. There is freedom here, unlike Scotland. These Indians remind me of the clansmen. But how long will their freedom last – before the British empire squeezes them. I have seen their brothers in the east, and the Empire waits for no one. We have learned this well in Scotland, remember. The sun never sets on the Empire. It's because God does not trust them either. I love you like the soul of Scotland. Neil McKay. P.S. I notice there is a romance forming between a young Cree woman called Plant Woman, and one of our young men.

Scene Four

The LEGENDWOMAN shifts focus to ELIZABETH and MICHAEL Hall in their small home in Eramosa Township, Ontario.

LEGENDWOMAN
Things are happening fast, eh? The world is changing. Romance – but that's nothing. *(indicates the Halls' home)* Look at what's on the way. Remember, this is Future Dreamtime...

FOOL
Yeh, sure, jump ahead. I thought you said these things have to happen in order!

LEGENDWOMAN
Quiet Fool! Order in time is meaningless. The readiness is all.

FOOL
Ready for what?

LEGENDWOMAN
Fool, you must learn to listen. These people are ready to understand what's coming. The New World–

The freeze breaks at the Hall household. MICHAEL is reading a flyer and smoking a pipe. ELIZABETH has just finished bathing their youngest daughter FANNIE in a washtub. ELIZABETH is about four months pregnant.

MICHAEL
(standing) Bessie, I want you to read this. *(tries to give her one of the Government OFFICIAL's flyers.)*

FANNIE
But I don't want to go to bed, Mama...

ELIZABETH
Of course you don't want to go to bed, Fannie! But it's time, so off you go!

FANNIE
But Mama...

ELIZABETH
Off you go!

FANNIE exits. ELIZABETH starts to clean up the wash water.

Ack can wash in the morning. And Emma.

MICHAEL
Bessie, they're giving it away!

ELIZABETH
Can't you see that I'm busy, Michael?

MICHAEL
"Good rich farmland. Will yield a fine profit the very first year..." *(placing the flyer on the table)* I'm leaving it on the table, Bessie. Read it, please. *(He exits after FANNIE.)*

ELIZABETH crosses to clear MICHAEL's cup and ashtray from the table, and notices the flyer. She reads it while continuing to clear up.

ELIZABETH
A hundred and sixty acres!

A knock at the door. ELIZABETH crosses to open the door, leaving the flyer on the table. At the door is her best friend ELEANOR West with her sleepy son NATHAN.

Why, come in Eleanor. I haven't known you to be keeping such late hours. Would you care for tea?

ELEANOR
No, thank you, Bess. I just came to bring you over this herb recipe I found. It's supposed to help you keep your baby. I thought since you lost the last one...

ELIZABETH
Lost the last one, but we've got three healthy children, Eleanor. Sit down and I'll fix you a hot cider.

ELEANOR seats NATHAN in a chair by the table, and picks up the flyer.

ELEANOR
Giving away land in the Northwest Territories? The government?

ELIZABETH
Of course. Not that it's theirs to give away.

ELEANOR
We're not going to get into that same argument about the Indians again, are we Bess?

ELIZABETH
(lightly) Oh, probably.

ELEANOR
(a little angry) Well, then I expect your high and mighty principles will keep you from taking "stolen" land in the west!

ELIZABETH
Probably not. *(picks up a broom and starts sweeping)* Michael wants his own farm.

ELEANOR
Bess, you are not moving to the Northwest Territories! I know we have our different opinions, but you are my best friend. I'm telling you there is nothing out there but a few buffalo and a bunch of Indians. And that radical Riel? Fighting the government – I guess he wants to run the country. Anyway, your husband is a dreamer! Those Indians are not about to let your husband plop himself down on any old piece of land he wants to call his own. I read the paper, after all.

ELIZABETH
That's why they make treaties, Eleanor. Anyway, we won't get into that old argument about Riel. You know the Indians around here. They're all right. Not just like us, but peaceful.

ELEANOR
Don't bother us anyway. They stay on their land, we stay on ours. But it's different out there. They're wild.

ELIZABETH
Oh Eleanor, don't be ridiculous!

NATHAN
Mama, I'm tired.

ELEANOR
(gets her shawl) Yes, honey.... Better be getting Nathan home to bed.

ELIZABETH
Yes, Eleanor, you'd better go. Thank you for the recipe. I will have some. We're looking forward to a strapping young boy. *(smiling)* We'll be needing him for the farm, I guess.

ELEANOR
Elizabeth Hall, don't you go talking crazy like that.

ELIZABETH
Never mind, Eleanor. I'll stop by tomorrow with some eggs.

> *ELEANOR exits. ELIZABETH sits down at the table and picks up the flyer again, as the duet for one male and one female voice begins. The chorus is sung by the full cast.*

> *Homesteader song: "Something You Can Hold Onto." Music and lyrics by Billy Morton.*

DUET
We sit here in Ontario
No future here nowhere to go
There's not much land left anymore
And even less if you are poor
The barons own the land and law
From Windsor up to Ottawa
And if you're not the chosen ones
The land goes to the first-born son

I read here in the papers that
Away out there the land is flat
But if you're strong and true and bold
You're looking at a pot of gold
Out west there's land for everyone
And a little less when we'll be done
So if it's true what people say
Wish I was leaving yesterday

CHORUS
A hundred and sixty acres
No one telling you what to do
A place that you can call your own
Something you can hold onto

DUET
We've always dreamed of owning land
To let the dirt sift through your hands
And know it's yours forevermore
You're the only one you're working for
So now it seems the only way
To make those dreams come true today
Is to follow others making hay
A couple thousand miles away

CHORUS
A hundred and sixty acres
No one telling you what to do
A place that you can call your own
Something you can hold onto

A hundred and sixty acres
No one telling you what to do
A place that you can call your own
Something you can hold onto

Scene Five

Shift focus back to MCKAY. The camp looks semi-permanent. The canoe is on its side with a tarpaulin stretched above. The FOOL, DESJARLAIS, and LAFRAMBOISE are sleeping under the tarp. MCKAY is writing another letter to his wife. The weather has warmed up – it's spring. WESAKEYCHUK flies in and joins LEGENDWOMAN observing from above.

WESAKEYCHUK
These settler types are getting ahead of things. We haven't finished the trading.

FOOL
(sitting up from his sleep in the Traders scene) Yah really! This is my best scene – very demanding. I believe I do a good job.

WESAKEYCHUK
Oh yeh, well wait til you see me at the treaty signing!

LEGENDWOMAN
Men will be boys, right…. Okay, take it easy you two. Just watch.

The LEGENDWOMAN indicates another stage where PLANTWOMAN is very agitated, and KOKUM is peeling a root. She throws the root into a boiling pot of water over the fire.

PLANTWOMAN
Kokum, I'm not hungry.

KOKUM
It's not for hunger. It's to calm you down. You know that.

PLANTWOMAN
But I don't want to marry a *mooniash* I have only met once!

KOKUM
For the white trader it is romance. And you can't disgrace Tah'wi. He has made the arrangements. Here, drink this. *(hands her a cup)*

PLANTWOMAN
Well this way I'm disgracing Mas'wa'peo. *(She drinks.)* I want children with Mas'wa'peo.

KOKUM
Mas'wa'peo cannot have children.

PLANTWOMAN
With me he would! I know.

KOKUM
What are you scared of? Making love to a white man? Living with him?

PLANTWOMAN
Everything. How do I dress. What do I say. How do I behave?

KOKUM
You are still Cree. Your children will be Cree, too. Don't forget that your aunt married outside. And that brought us peace for a time.

PLANTWOMAN
(disgusted) The whites are not the same as the Blackfeet.

KOKUM
Tah'wi thinks this is good. I trust his decision, even though he is a man.

PLANTWOMAN
They did not ask me what I wanted!

> *TAH'WI and MAS'WA'PEO are on their way to MCKAY's camp. MAS'WA'PEO tries to block TAH'WI, who is in a hurry to get to MCKAY.*

MAS'WA
Tah'wi, stop! I want a family. We can take the children that have no parent. Plantwoman would love these children because she is one of them. Or maybe… maybe I can have children with Plantwoman.

TAH'WI
You're angry. You think I doubt you or compare you to the *mooniash*. Look, Mas'wa'peo, this marriage will help everybody. These Scots stay with our women. The headman McKay will trust us and treat us fair with the trade. When all this happens the community will benefit. It will bring us together as a family.

> *They are nearly at the camp. MCKAY approaches TAH'WI with his hand stretched out. TAH'WI shakes it confidently.*

MCKAY
Do I call you brother? What is your decision?

TAH'WI
As we agreed…

MAS'WA
The agreement is only between Tah'wi and you, McKay.

TAH'WI
(ignoring MAS'WA'PEO) McKay. You told me there was to be a gift.

MCKAY
Yes.

> *DESJARLAIS hands him a gun. MCKAY extends the gun to TAH'WI. Both men keep their hands on the gun for a moment.*

MCKAY
For you. This will show my happiness for the marriage *(releases the gun)*

TAH'WI
Now I can believe you when you call me brother.

> *All but MAS'WA'PEO shake hands.*

MAS'WA
(quietly) You are making a mistake, Tah'wi.

MCKAY
What makes you say this, brother?

MAS'WA
You are not my brother! We are losing Plantwoman, white man. She knows the medicine of the land. And what do we get! A gun…

MCKAY
This is your future, Mas'wa'peo. The land is changing. You will have greater influence after the marriage.

MAS'WA
You will have greater, influence, McKay. McKay and Company, isn't that what you're after.

TAH'WI
Mas'wa'peo, you are talking with your anger, not your heart. Come. We have been invited for a drink.

MAS'WA
I do not want the white man's trade or his drink. *(exits)*

TAH'WI
He has not learned that it is a new world. We must remake the world to our advantage.

MCKAY
It is inevitable. Come, let's drink to the marriage. *(MCKAY signals LAFRAMBOISE and the FOOL to distribute glasses.)* To your health lads. To your health. Drink hardy. Cheers, friends.

> *The FOOL raises his glass to WESAKEYCHUK who is on another stage with LEGENDWOMAN. WESAKEYCHUK is raising the mud ball.*

FOOL AND WESAKEYCHUK
Cheers, friends.

LEGENDWOMAN
(gently takes the mudball from WESAKEYCHUK) The end of an era… *(gives the mudball back)* …almost.

Scene Six

> *Battle breaks out everywhere. A lean-to shack is on fire. Smoke and the sound of guns fill the air. With shots and whoops a group carrying the Northwest Company flag charge across the playing area, dodging behind audience members as they enact battle with another group carrying the Hudson flag. In this short, intense battle the Northwest flag is torn down, and set on fire. The battle retreats. Occasional gunfire and shots are heard throughout the following scene between*

HARMON and LAROCQUE. HARMON is wounded, recovering from the battle. LAROCQUE, one of the few free traders left, happens upon him, resting and rolling a cigarette.

LAROCQUE
Harmon, you old dog, are you still around here?

They shake hands, happy to see each other.

HARMON
Still here, still ugly. And you, Larocque? How do you survive?

LAROCQUE
Oh, I'm still working on my own. For as long as I can hold out. What are you doing here? You got transferred, right? I thought since the merger you were stuck out in the boonies. Mr. Hudson... Hudson Bay that is.

HARMON
The name's Harmon! Those Hudson bastards haven't won yet! *(hands LAROCQUE a smoke)* I come down to pick up some supplies and visit, then I see the Northwest company still got a chance here. Even an old crusty dog like me got to get out once in a while. *(looking at the ruins)* This was one of the grand old posts of the NorthWest Company. Hudson Bay post down the river. Damn, there used to be good fights.

LAROCQUE
You bet. There was this one time east of here.

HARMON
Exactly! I was there. There I was, alone, defending the post...

LAROCQUE
Hey, I was telling the story...

HARMON
Wait, Larocque. I'm telling a story! You will get your turn. Those bums were comin'. I was ready for 'em. I can still hear it. "Harmon you dirty arse. Get your butt out of that post or we'll burn it and whatever is in front of it!" I was ready for them – one more step...

LAROCQUE
Where did this happen? South Qu'Appelle post? Or was it in your dreams? Anyway, I saw those fights.

HARMON
Oh those Hudson Bay are bastards. You know they burned many a post.

LAROCQUE
Well I can tell you this, I have seen Hudson Bay posts burned down by NorthWest factors.

HARMON
Only in self-defence. Or revenge.

LAROCQUE
Those posts were burnt so your company could have the land. With the land comes the trade, you know that.

HARMON
It belonged to England all the time. It was Charles the first that claimed it. This is our land, we are a company of the empire.

LAROCQUE
Hey, it wasn't English land. That was Cree land.

HARMON
You're wrong, it was Blackfoot land.

LAROCQUE
You see my point.

HARMON
The Empire is not without heart my friend. There will be treaties made with you people.

LAROCQUE
You mean with the Indian people. The halfbreeds in Manitoba, they got nothing.

HARMON
Look chap, you fellows the Métis. You live with us. You're just like us. So we treat you no different. The land is up for grabs!

LAROCQUE
Well, Harmon, maybe I don't know everything. But I know what my Indian brothers believe is true. We are all going to die eventually, right – so who really owns the land? And the priest missionary, he tells us "What is it for a man to have everything in the world if he loses his soul?"

There is a loud explosion not far away. HARMON and LAROCQUE dive for cover as focus shifts.

Scene Seven

TREEWOMAN, SKYWOMAN and MAGPIE enter a field of berries, carrying baskets and buckets.

TREEWOMAN
Which bush do you want?

SKYWOMAN
Take that bush. (*She sits on her upturned bucket beside a bush and takes out her small pipe for a smoke. The other two women pick berries.*) We'll get those berries before they rot on us. Did you hear Plantwoman's husband the white trader has left her?

TREEWOMAN
Serves her right. I wouldn't want to marry a white man.

SKYWOMAN
Me too, a hairy man. If I wanted him hairy, I would make him bear skin pyjamas.

MAGPIE
It's not Plantwoman's fault the white man already had a wife. *(a beat)* Why do people remember my birth as the day the *mooniash* came?

TREEWOMAN
That's when our world started to change. Do you remember a time when there was no mirror or metal?

MAGPIE
No, but I remember when there were more buffalo…

SKYWOMAN
Well, Ki'kah'wi and I remember a time before all those things. That makes us different.

MAGPIE
I'm different, so I'm not a Cree?

SKYWOMAN
(laughing) Cho. You're not WHITE. You are Cree. A new kind of Cree person.

TREEWOMAN
Remember, to be one of us, first believe in the earth, your Mother. Especially now.

MAGPIE
But the land is changing, too. When the buffalo are gone, we will all die.

SKYWOMAN
Si'ta'ka'tis'! We won't die. There is your father and all your relatives. They will look after you and all the children.

TREEWOMAN
Without the buffalo we can still ask the fish, geese and berries to feed us. The earth has always given us what we need. We must believe!

MAGPIE
But if their god is more powerful than the old way, we will all burn in the big fire and live with the devil.

TREEWOMAN
Balance your life and you will live with all the grandfathers and grandmothers. Think of the stories.

SKYWOMAN
Chi'ma'ki'sin'kiya. Listen, and remember what the elders say.

   At the sound of the Surveyors entering MAGPIE turns, afraid.

MAGPIE
Neh'ta!

Scene Eight

LEGENDWOMAN
Look out! Here come the surveyors!

> *Surveyors enter as a group, dressed in orange coveralls. They march in straight lines, singing "Divide and Sub-divide." They place the tripod on the ground and stick in marking sticks, creating an enclosure in the audience promenade area. The FOOL enters with them, in surveyor costume.*

> *Surveyor's Song: "Divide and Sub-divide." Music and lyrics by Billy Morton.*

CHORUS
Divide and sub-divide cut up in quarters
Each time you draw a line you get two borders
Divide and sub-divide cut up in quarters
Each time you draw a line you get two borders

Keep working don't be slow
We are the law since
They passed the Homestead Act
And we'll be a province!

> *Repeat chorus.*

Hammer the stakes in
Quick like a bunny
Settlers are coming soon
And time is money

> *Repeat chorus.*

> *The song breaks as one of the surveyors drops a marker to slap a mosquito. The berry-picking women and WESAKEYCHUK cross into the enclosure. The surveyors neither see nor hear them.*

MCINTYRE
(reading the marker sticks) Steady boys!

SKYWOMAN
Kikway oma Nistasis? What are they doing?

MARKER 1
(slapping) It's these damn mosquitoes.

MARKER 2
(scratching) Are you sure these are mosquitoes? I think they're small birds sir.

WESAKEYCHUK
Mosquitoes, charge!

> *Huge mosquitoes played by children swarm and sting the surveyors.*

MCINTYRE
They're the bloodsucker of the north. Now hold on to that marker. *(In a mosquito panic, he drops the tripod.)*

MARKER 3
Come on, let's hurry it up, we're dying out here!

The mosquitoes dive for one last attack, then buzz off.

MARKER 4
They're gone?

MCINTYRE
We're gone too. Let's go before they bring their offspring along for dessert.
Remember this is going to be one of the Indian reserves. *(does one last check as they
collect equipment)* Tomorrow we'll start the Northwest Mounted Police reserve.

They exit singing the final verse of their song.

Nothing stands in our way
We will deliver
Cut up the land until
We hit a river

Repeat chorus: " Divide and sub-divide" etc.

*Still enclosed in the centre of the markers, the berry-picking women shout at the
exiting surveyors.*

SKYWOMAN
(yelling) What are you doing!

TREEWOMAN
Nobody told us they were coming.

SKYWOMAN
Sticking poles in the ground – that is ridiculous.

TREEWOMAN
Come on, we have to go back and tell the others what we have seen.

They exit.

Scene Nine

*The FOOL stays behind, climbing out of his surveyor outfit, humming the melody
of the song.*

LEGENDWOMAN
(from above) You win this one, Fool. Go on, tell them what's up. What's about to
happen… soon. What's going to happen… when the time is right.

*From his rucksack the FOOL takes out an applause sign and a pedestal. He takes
several bows. He is now the french "clown," the tricky master of ceremonies. His big
moment.*

FOOL
Once again, ladies and gentlemen: FUTURE DREAMTIME! We're really getting to the good part now! Here they are, ladies and gentlemen, preparing their bags, their families, and their constitutions...

WESAKEYCHUK
(heckling) What, self-government already?

FOOL
Not that kind of constitution. I mean their souls, their inner beings, their... these people are preparing themselves for one of the most historic events in our country's great history.... The Settlement of the West! Ladies and gentlemen, in Future Dreamtime, meet our soon to be Homesteaders!

Masses of settlers are preparing for the long journey to the Northwest Territories. Men, women and children appear on all stages as they are packing for the move west to homestead. The families are in locations all over the world. Focus turns to GILCHRISTS on one of the stages. FRED Gilchrist is dragging a large trunk.

MRS. GILCHRIST
Bring it right into the kitchen, Fred. I want to pack the china in that trunk. It's big enough, and sturdy.

FRED
(groaning) And heavy enough. How do you expect me to carry it when the china's inside? I hardly think an ox will be able to drag the load!

MRS. GILCHRIST
Two oxen. You did arrange for two, didn't you? Because I'm taking the sideboard. Familiar things – to make us feel at home.

FRED
Feel at home, eh? Got to build the home first, Sal.

MRS. GILCHRIST
Of course I know that, Fred. Didn't they say we can store the things at the station?

VOICE 1
All I need is my Bible.

VOICE 2
I'll be all right if I can take my violin.

VOICE 3 AND 4
ODESSA, RUSSIA!

VOICE 3
We can own land – it's free for the asking!

VOICE 4
Free land! And we'll be free!

FULL CHORUS
(whispered) Freedom!

Shift to KATE Martin and her mother on one of the stages. KATE is in her travelling clothes. MRS. MARTIN is straightening her collar.

KATE
Yes, mother, of course I'll telegraph right away, soon as I get there. You needn't worry...

MRS. MARTIN
Needn't worry! My daughter, off to live alone – work alone – in Fort Qu'Appelle. Winnipeg's not big enough for my little girl, she has to...

KATE
I'm 22 years old, Mama. Hardly a little girl.

MRS. MARTIN
My little girl, she has to conquer the West, all on her own.

KATE
I don't want to conquer anything. I want to earn fifty dollars a month, which no one is going to pay me for teaching school, or for sewing dresses for the fancy Winnipeg society ladies. And being a telegraph operator isn't something to be ashamed of, is it?

MRS. MARTIN
Katie, I am proud of you, you know that. But you remember when you get out there – lock your doors!

Chorus voices.

VOICE 3
I want adventure! I want to be rich!

VOICE 4
I'm worried about the Indians...

VOICE 5
SCOTLAND. This damn damp cold. Get sick every winter. Folks die. I hear in Canada, in the Northwest Territories, it's a dry cold...

FULL CHORUS
(like wind) WINTER!

Shift to WILLIAM and SALLY Hatfield, in England. They are rushing through the crowd, as a steamer whistle signals departure. WILLIAM's mother runs behind them. Whistle.

WILLIAM
Sally, hurry! We can't miss that boat.

SALLY
Yes, I know, but William, your mother...

WILLIAM
What? Oh yes. Mother, it's going to be a bit of a rush at the quay, I'm sorry.

MRS. HATFIELD
(trying to catch up) That's just the first whistle, Will. It won't be leaving without you.

Chorus voices.

VOICE 6
HUNGARY. Oy! There's opportunity in that land… we'll be rich!

FULL CHORUS
PROSPERITY!

Shift to MRS. GILCHRIST, checking a list.

MRS. GILCHRIST
Oh, sweet heaven, do you suppose the ox cart will carry the piano?

VOICE 7
IRELAND. I'm a widow, with no way to feed my children. In Canada, surely I'll make a living doing something!

VOICE 8
THE UKRAINE. A wheelwright like me will find lots of work in Canada.

FULL CHORUS
(bigger) OPPORTUNITY!

Shift to ELIZABETH Hall, alone reading a letter from her husband.

ELIZABETH
"Dear Bessie, I am still working on the Wisehart farm, but I am making plans for our home on our land. The house won't be ready when you arrive, but as soon as I have some capital saved, be assured that it will all go directly to our own home. Mrs. Wisehart will be arriving in the Spring. I hope our year-long separation will also come to an end my dearest. You needn't worry about the Indians… they are living peaceably on their reserved land, and hardly bother us at all…"

VOICES 9 AND 10
LONDON, ENGLAND.

VOICE 9
Are you out of your mind?

VOICE 10
They're giving away the land out there. I'd be crazy to stay here.

VOICE 9
Land, eh? But I'll wager the beer tastes like horse piss…

FULL CHORUS
LAND. ADVENTURE.

VOICE 5
All I want is freedom to practice my own religion.

VOICE 6
I want to own my own land.

FULL CHORUS
LAND!

Steamer whistle shifts focus to the Hatfields, surrounded by many others, all waving Union Jacks. Cast members in the promenade area wave white hankies.

SALLY
Will, look, your mother's there, I see her! She's waving her hankie, there. *(waves excitedly)*

WILLIAM
I see an ocean of waving white hankies. Oh, by golly, yes! I see her! Goodbye, Mother! *(whistle blows again)* Goodbye, mother. *(to SALLY)* Darling.

SALLY
It's done now. There's no turning back. *(bravely)* What is it, then? Labrador in two weeks?

Steamer whistles as the boat leaves the dock.

MRS. HATFIELD
I'll never see them again.

VOICE 11
RED RIVER SETTLEMENT. Yes, the climate is harsh. There are many hardships. But the Lord keeps me warm, and He keeps me strong, so I may continue my work with the Indians.

FULL CHORUS
FAITH.

VOICE 12
I want a new life in the New World!

FULL CHORUS
A NEW LIFE. FREEDOM. OPPORTUNITY. LAND.

VOICE 13
ONTARIO. My husband is the seventh son. In the territories, we can have our own farm.

FULL CHORUS
LAND!

Shift to KATE Martin, alone.

KATE
Lock my doors. Yes, mother, I intend to lock my doors. Am I… idiotic, really? Is it foolish? I will likely be the only lady—well, the only white lady—for miles around. The only single lady, I should think.

GEORGINA Binney-Clark appears.

GEORGINA
Hang in there dear. If you can manage to stay long enough, there will be one more single white lady.

KATE
Oh, uh…

GEORGINA
You may call me Georgina. I'll be arriving in a few years.

KATE
Oh, I see. You're just working out the details for a homestead?

GEORGINA
Don't be naive, darling. I'll be coming to live with my brother. Women aren't allowed to own the land...

KATE
Oh. Right. I forgot.

GEORGINA
That's quite all right, dear. You'll be more worldly-wise after a few months in the valley, I'm sure. *(starts to go)*

KATE
Oh please wait? Can you tell me, what are the Indians like?

GEORGINA
Why, I have no idea. Perhaps we'll never know. Goodbye.

FULL CHORUS
I WONDER WHAT THE INDIANS ARE LIKE.

> *Full chorus freeze. LEGENDWOMAN strolls into their midst.*

LEGENDWOMAN
They'll have to wait. They have to wait until the treaty is signed.

WESAKEYCHUK
(yelling in the ear of a frozen chorus member) She said, "wait until the treaty is signed!"

> *The chorus comes to life. Fearful, they scatter quickly with improvised comments to and amongst themselves such as "it's not safe out there yet," "I didn't know the treaty wasn't signed yet," "Quick, get the bags unpacked. We'll go when they're ready for us." Panic and anarchy. WESAKEYCHUK thinks this is hilarious.*

Scene Ten

LEGENDWOMAN
Watch, Trickster. This is Sarah Pratt, and her husband Charles Pratt.

WESAKEYCHUK
Charles Pratt? *The* Charles Pratt? We're there, then? 1874 – the treaty?

LEGENDWOMAN
Almost there. This is 1874, in August.

> *SARAH Pratt is tending garden outside the Pratt household. Charles PRATT enters with Bible in hand.*

PRATT

Tansi, Sarah. *(He looks over the garden, pulls some weeds.)* Weeds. I suppose they think we put in this garden especially for them, eh? Think *they* own the garden.

SARAH

Well, the garden is new to us, too, Charles. The vegetables will take strength from the land, when we know better how to tend them.

PRATT

Yes.

SARAH

How was it today? Did the people receive you well?

PRATT

It's difficult. Some listen to the word, most don't. There is hostility, particularly from the medicine men. The traditional ways are still so strong…

SARAH

You must be patient. Even I have doubts sometimes. Don't you? You know you do, Charles. It's scary to think that when we go to heaven, our ancestors won't be there.

PRATT

I'm not worried about our ancestors. Jesus says "There are many rooms in my father's house." Whether or not the leaders of the church choose to believe it. The carrots are gone, look.

SARAH

Oh Charlie, that's our way! They are hungry. How can you possibly expect our people to leave sweet delicious carrots in the earth.

PRATT

Change is inevitable. Look at us, we've changed, haven't we?

He picks up some carrots that have been left lying on the ground.

SARAH

It is our way. We believe in the new god. But it is still a new god. He loves us. We are learning how to love him.

Archibald MACDONALD, the Hudson's Bay clerk approaches.

PRATT

And we love our people too. That's the difficulty.

SARAH

It is, isn't it?

MACDONALD

Good day, Pratt. *(lifting his hat)* Mrs. Pratt.

PRATT

Greetings MacDonald. Sarah, get this man some refreshment, please.

SARAH

Yes. Mr. MacDonald?

MACDONALD
Tea will be lovely, Mrs. Pratt, thank you.

SARAH exits.

MACDONALD
(looking at the garden) Pratt. It's an uphill battle, isn't it?

PRATT
The people are hungry. The buffalo... I'm glad you've come, MacDonald. I've been meaning to talk to you. *(polite pause)*

MACDONALD
Is it about the liquor again? We've been over this before, Pratt. The Indians want to trade for liquor and other things. Economics, pure and simple.

PRATT
Liquor is the tool of the devil. Are you a Christian man?

MACDONALD
Economics, Pratt. Economics will govern this country.

PRATT
CHRIST and economics, Mr. MacDonald.

A Cree family, MOTHER and several children, arrive looking for food. The TRICKSTER is one of them.

PRATT
Sarah!

SARAH enters from the house. MACDONALD and PRATT are silent.

SARAH
(in Cree) Tansi. Your children are hungry? We have fresh meat.

MOTHER
(in Cree) And carrots? We could make a stew...

SARAH
Carrots too. *(switches to English)* The land provides for us. Come in. The rabbit meat is inside.

They exit into the house.

MACDONALD
I'll tell you why I have come Pratt.

PRATT
You have come about the treaty negotiations.

MACDONALD
Yeh. They want you to interpret for the Indians.

PRATT
Interpret for the Indians – and the Queen's men? Don't the Queen's men need an interpreter? Or have you learned to understand the Cree and Saulteaux tongues, like the Oblate fathers?

MACDONALD
The interpreter must naturally translate for both sides. You're the only man for the job, you realize that don't you? There are aren't many around who speak five languages.

PRATT
I see. (a moment) Yes, I agree to interpret for the treaty signing.

MACDONALD
Let the chiefs know that the Queen has their best interests at heart. And… well, we'll work the rest out later. Now, what's this I hear about Piapot?

PRATT
Piapot and Starblanket will not sign.

> Shift to Chief PIAPOT and Chief STARBLANKET, each on separate stages, addressing their bands. PIAPOT holds his rifle, in a pose that recalls the famous photo.

PIAPOT
I will not attend these meetings!

STARBLANKET
My people, Starblanket's band, do not want to live on a reserve!

PIAPOT
It is the same for Piapot's people. We have decided to move west of the hills, where there are still some buffalo to feed the hungry.

STARBLANKET
I don't care if they put me in jail to demonstrate their power over me. They cannot stop me from thinking what I want!

PIAPOT
I agree. The priest is the same as their police. They try and scare us. I know this is not the way to knowledge or the spirit. I listen to the grandfathers.

STARBLANKET
We are not going. We will take care of ourselves.

PIAPOT
Those meetings are not for us. They know that I'm not scared to use this gun. We are leaving.

> Shift back to the Pratt garden. PRATT and MACDONALD are standing. SARAH clears the tea.

MACDONALD
Mrs. Pratt, thank you. Charles, I'll be around in a week or so with the documents. You will have news then, I presume.

PRATT
I will do my best. The chiefs are not always quick to decide. They will want to consult more with their people.

SARAH
They are wise men, the chiefs.

PRATT
Sarah! (She exits into the hut.)

MACDONALD
Goodbye, Charles.

PRATT
Goodbye.

MACDONALD exits. SARAH re-enters.

SARAH
Charles. Do you trust that man?

PRATT
Yes, I trust him. MacDonald is a man who keeps his word.

SARAH
He is also known for keeping a threat. Do you trust him completely? As you trust in Our Lord?

PRATT
No. It is a different kind of trust.

PRATT puts on his hat and crosses to another stage for the treaty negotiations.

Scene Eleven

A military drum. The commissioners are onstage. PRATT takes his place with MACDONALD and LAIRD. MORRIS is the man in charge. Lieut-Col. Osborne Smith is with a party of soldiers, both white and Indian. The FOOL is with them in soldier costume, and a red clown-nose. On a nearby stage are GAMBLER, COTE, LOUDVOICE, and others around a fire. They have just finished smoking a pipe. The scene alternates focus from one group of treaty negotiators to the other. WESAKEYCHUK is a spider, climbing from one stage to another on a spider's web, eavesdropping.

LEGENDWOMAN
At last we're here. The Main Event. The signing of Treaty Four, September, 1874.

All freeze except the TRICKSTER and the FOOL.

WESAKEYCHUK
You may be asking what is the Sioux trickster doing at a Saultaux/Cree treaty negotiation?

FOOL
Yes I am. There are no Sioux Indians here.

WESAKEYCHUK
Exactly. I have come to find out what it's going to be like living here.

FOOL
Oh really? You'll like this guy Morris. Everything is in place now. The land has been laid out for everyone. You'll be well taken care of.

WESAKEYCHUK
What was out of place... before you came... Morris. *(beat)* Anyway, Standing Buffalo and his band of Dakota Sioux, we have some business to take care of in Minnesota first *(gleeful)* the American soldiers are after us because of an incident with a storekeeper. *(beat)* Funny. *Déja vu.*

> *Freeze breaks.*

MORRIS
(pacing the stage) Good God, man, where are these Indians?

MACDONALD
What do you think should be done sir?

MORRIS
Let me talk to our Indian expert. Well, Mr. Pratt.

PRATT
All the communities have not arrived yet.

MORRIS
What do you mean, they haven't arrived? I've seen them camping way the hell the other side. Pratt – go and tell them they're keeping us waiting!

> *PRATT crosses to outside the tipi. The drumbeat moves from military to Cree drumming.*

LOUDVOICE
(puts away the pipe on seeing PRATT) Pratt is here, he has arrived.

PRATT
I have come here to talk to you.

GAMBLER
Who do you represent?

LOUDVOICE
Just as we were told by the people from the east and south, I had a dream one time about a man. I sat on the ground, and I thought that he would join me on the ground. He spread his tent – white, big, and distant. They were in front of me, but they did not sit with me. I kept having to lift my head to them. I laugh about it, because I felt like I had to pray to them.

COTE
Does that mean that they will be far away from us? I am not going anywhere today. We must wait, to talk and listen to all the people.

GAMBLER
Pratt, tell them we must talk longer before we can go to the meeting with Morris. *(stirs the fire)* Remember, we have to be tough. Remember the buffalo's breath.

LOUDVOICE
Pratt you hear what is said. *(PRATT leaves. LOUDVOICE speaks to GAMBLER.)* Yes, be tough. But things are hard. When is the last time you ate buffalo? Do the people have food this winter?

> *Shift. Drums change again. PRATT is back with MORRIS.*

MORRIS
I don't believe this. We travel from Fort Garry to the Qu'Appelle, our gathering place, in fifteen days... and they're not ready!

MACDONALD
Well, to be fair, sir, they have brought their families.

MORRIS
Families... huh. Shows the superiority of the English soldier and system. Pratt, you went to go and see them?

PRATT
Yes, Mr. Morris, they're not ready. They want to talk to all the people who are coming. And there's others who won't come.

MORRIS
Encourage them man! Tell them we have travelled far and deserve the respect of meeting face to face!

> *Shift – drums change.*

COTE
The whiteman keeps coming and taking. He doesn't think of us.

GAMBLER
They keep telling us the Queen will take care of us. Mother Earth takes care of us, not the Queen Mother.

LOUDVOICE
But the buffalo are nearly gone, and there are more *mooniash* coming. We must go and talk to these men, before it is too late.

GAMBLER
So there are more of them coming! When have we ever been the most in this land? The trees and the grass and the insects have always been more. The balance of life. Not numbers. The balance of nature is the law.

LOUDVOICE
The balance is changing, and we are the melting snow... while the whites are the blades of prairie grass that poke through.

GAMBLER
No! We are the breath of the buffalo.

LOUDVOICE
And the buffalo are nearly gone!

Sound of a trumpet.

GAMBLER
So do we leave our brothers, the buffalo?

COTE
Let the Great White Mother blow her horn. We must wait to ask the community leaders who will speak for us.

Scene Twelve

"How Come They Didn't Ask Us?" Music by Billy Morton, lyrics by Heather Herrell.

CREE WOMEN
Who is this Great White Mother
That sends her men alone
To find to barter and buy
What she has never known
What manner of mother is she
That their adoration grows
We hear she won't cook for them
Or even mend their clothes

Chorus:

How come they didn't ask us
We could have told them a thing or two
They have no idea what's real in life
Believe us for a fact we do we do
Believe us for a fact we do

ONTARIO WOMEN
They'll drag us off to some hunk of land
Our heroic settler men
They'll brag about how great it is
While we do our work by hand
We'll haul in snow to wash the clothes
And plant out gardens annual
How come that flat forgotten place
Doesn't come with an owners manual

Chorus:

How come they didn't ask us
We could have told them a thing or two

They have no idea what's real in life
Believe us for a fact we do we do
Believe us for a fact we do

CREE WOMEN
Are there more white women
Are they strong or weak
Will they bear white children
Are they allowed to speak

ONTARIO WOMEN
We hear they stow their babies
In packs upon their backs
We hear they don't wear corsets
That cause their ribs to crack

> *Chorus is sung by each group to the other.*

Where would they be without us

CREE WOMEN
To nurture and to heal

ONTARIO WOMEN
While they eat and talk of changing times

BOTH
We'll be here to make the meals *(laugh)*

We share the common things
We make the home fires glow
We're not so very different
We're the ones who make the home
Maybe we have more in common
Than we ever dreamed

> *Repeat chorus twice, into a jig. At the final chorus, the women cross into the promenade, dancing with each other and then with the audience. The tempo changes to a jig. A large Queen Victoria puppet enters and conducts the dancing. The women follow behind her as "Vicky" crosses in a wide sweep to preside over the treaty signing. The puppet stands behind a banner that reads: "The Queen Loves Her Red Children."*

Scene Thirteen

> *At the treaty signing, the Native men are shaking hands with MORRIS. The Treaty Four Flag Song plays continuously under the scene. When the handshakes are complete, MORRIS sits with officials behind a table. The Cree and Saulteaux are sitting on the ground.*

MORRIS
You have had time to select your spokesmen.

LOUDVOICE
We are ready to negotiate. But first you must answer our questions. We have concerns that are in the way.

MORRIS
The Queen knows what your worries are. The Queen has children all over the world, and she does right with them all. The Queen knows you are poor and that it is hard to find food for your children. The Queen will look after all of these things...

GAMBLER
(standing) You see sitting out there a mixture of Crees, Halfbreeds, Saulteaux and Stonies. All are one, and you were slow in taking the hand of a Halfbreed. All these things are things that are in my way.

MORRIS
The Queen cares for them. You may leave the Halfbreeds in the hands of the Queen who will deal generously and justly with them. She has always cared for her red children as much as her white children. She wants to do something for you...

GAMBLER
Who surveyed this land? Was it done by the Hudson Bay Company? And why are you staying in the Company's house?

COTE
Why did the company receive £300,000 for land from your Queen? The company has stolen this land. We want that money.

All freeze.

WESAKEYCHUK
Hey this dude is on to something. Why does the Hudson Bay get money for land they don't own?

Break freeze.

MORRIS
The Company has a right to have certain lands granted by the Queen, who will do what is fair and just for the Company, the Indians, the Halfbreeds, and the whites. Whatever she promises we will carry out, so that when the buffalo are more scarce, you may be able to do something for yourselves. If you take the Queen's hand she will provide cattle, seed, and land for farming.

Freeze again.

FOOL
Quit whining. Face the facts. The old days are over. Your silly mudball is worthless to you now.

Break freeze.

MORRIS
She will also give you money to buy supplies, for twenty years. She is also ready to give you a school and schoolmaster...

LOUDVOICE
We can't agree to the money granted for supplies. We want the money granted for fifty years, not for twenty.

Freeze.

WESAKEYCHUK
Worthless! No way! This is sacred negotiation. Nation to Nation. People to people.

FOOL
And they call me a fool.

Break.

MORRIS
No, this is outside my power to grant these changes. Are the Queen's red children ready to sign the treaty? At which time terms negotiated will be binding "for as long as the sun shines and the water flows." We ask you to speak, and open your hearts to us.

LOUDVOICE
Before we sign, we want each chief to have a copy of the treaty.

MORRIS
We will send a copy to each chief.

Drumming and singing continues as the chiefs sign. Each shakes hands with MORRIS. The chiefs exit under the escort of Col. Smith and the soldiers. As they exit, a North West Mounted Policeman on horseback is silhouetted on the hills.

WESAKEYCHUK
Kind of funny. These chiefs came independently. Now they sign the treaty, and they leave the meeting under escort of the Queen's army.

WESAKEYCHUK looks down at the mudball in his hands, and tosses it to the FOOL. He then walks offstage into the promenade area, trading his spider costume for the horns of an ox. Alone, MORRIS starts to exit.

FOOL
Hey you, Morris! You forgot the banner!

MORRIS
I don't want that thing.

FOOL
Did I miss something here? I thought this was part of the treaty. You know, the Queen loving her red children and all that.

MORRIS
Fool! Those are just words. It's all in here. *(clutches the treaty paper)* Don't you get it? No compensation, no Indian title to the land. It's ours now. We own it. Now Law and Order has reached this land!

FOOL
But sir, you never told these people anything about surrendering. You just said the Queen loves them and would take care of them.

MORRIS
Please, there are enough missionaries out here. Not another one.

The LEGENDWOMAN appears.

FOOL
(sadly, to the LEGENDWOMAN) Now?

LEGENDWOMAN
Yes, now.

The FOOL pulls out the same whistle and blows it.

Look.

First a lone immigrant arrives on top of the hill. Almost immediately others arrive silhouetted over the crest, armed with pots and pans, noisemakers and tools of all sorts.

LONE PIONEER
Land, free land!

The Lone Pioneer comes charging down the hill, and suddenly they are coming from every direction, banging pots and pans, carrying pitchforks and other settler accoutrements. As they descend, the oxcart passes through the audience carrying ELIZABETH Hall and her children, including a new baby. WESAKEYCHUK is the ox pulling the cart. The FOOL crosses to the cart and leads the ox by the yoke. GOODWIN, the oxcart driver, stands and points ahead.

GOODWIN
Look, Mrs. Hall. The Valley!

FULL CAST
The Valley!

Segue into reprise of "The Surveyors Song."

Scene Fourteen

A cheerful crew of Surveyors enter and go about their work. As the number ends, the Surveyors' tape has created a pathway to the intermission area of the coulee. Surveyors' Song (Reprise) "Divide and Sub-Divide." Music and lyrics by Billy Morton.

CHORUS
Divide and sub-divide, cut up in quarters
Each time you draw a line, you get two borders
Divide and sub-divide, cut up in quarters
Each time you draw a line, you get two borders

Show us the latitude
Straight as your arm is
Show us the longitude
That's where your farm is *(Repeat chorus.)*

ACT II – Scene One

The Treaty Four Flag Song song calls the audience back into the playing area. Segue into "Fire in the Valley," sung by all Aboriginal cast members from a single stage – a show of strength.

"Fire in the Valley." Music and lyrics by Billy Morton.

SOLO
Something is rising can anyone feel it
Am I the only one with the vision
It feels like a fever is growing and growing
And someone must make a decision

NATIVE
Where are we going and why must we follow
The way of life that we are living
The sins of the fathers are brought on the sons
Somewhere these things must be forgiven

CHORUS
There's a fire in the valley tonight
There's a flame and it shifts with the weather
There's a fire in the valley tonight
And it's pulling the people together

SOLO
Just like the first winter storm gets its start
With the first gentle snow of November
The fires that can burn down whate'er man has built
Are started by only an ember

ALL
Gather the people
Gather their strength
Gather the natural forces
Proud we will stand in the wind and the rain
We'll ride with the power of horses

Repeat chorus twice.

Song segues into drumming in mourning of the passing of freedom. LEGENDWOMAN steps forward as the others are leaving the stage.

LEGENDWOMAN
The drums beat in mourning for four days and four nights, marking the dark age of a civilization.

Scene Two

FOOL AND WESAKEYCHUK
Holy moly, here come the trains!

Sound effect of an approaching train, accompanied by steam and breaking sounds. A giant train locomotive is seen arriving at one end of the promenade area. From behind it stream homesteaders, mostly women, with luggage. Among the audience are their husbands, family or friends, waiting on the "platform." Groups of families are re-united in pockets all over the audience.

With a second sound effect, these scenes freeze, and focus shifts to the LEGENDWOMAN.

LEGENDWOMAN
The first train arrived at Qu'Appelle Station twenty miles from the post in Fort Qu'Appelle. Eighteen passenger cars leaving Winnipeg, each one overflowing with settlers. To me, it was like armies of human ants swarming in.

Shift to three Native TEENAGERS, watching from above in fascination.

TEEN 1
Their clothes – how can they move?

TEEN 2
And look at that lady's hair.

TEEN 3
They're going to farm the land? How will they survive?

TEEN 1
I think they'll be needing some help.

TEEN 2
Sure, you just want to meet white women.

Shift to GILCHRIST, alone, as we hear the sounds of crackling fire from all over.

GILCHRIST
(loud and desperate) I walk here to Qu'Appelle station from Dysart—three days—because my oxen both fell through the ice and drowned in a slough – to get all my wife's cherished possessions out of storage. A prairie fire has destroyed everything! We will not let this new land defeat us! We will endure!

Another train sound breaks the freeze and shifts focus back to the train station scene among the audience. With much hustle and bustle, the homesteaders hurry off to catch a stagecoach to Fort Qu'Appelle.

Scene Three

As a prelude to the scene children and homesteaders all over stages and the promenade area, helping to clear the "fields." They recite a short chant together.

Cut the trees
Pull the stumps
Move the rocks
Break the soil

> *Repeat twice, fading as ELIZABETH Hall calls to her children.*

> *At the Hall homestead, ELIZABETH is in charge of the sod hut. MICHAEL is off working on another farm for wages. In front of the sod hut is a scraggly, pitiful little tree, carefully preserved to provide a thin bit of shade on the hot days. In the so-called shady spot is a baby bassinet. On another stage, ACK and EMMA Hall are in the field, picking up rocks and otherwise clearing and preparing for seeding.*

ELIZABETH
(calling) Ack! Emma!

ACK
(lifting a large rock with EMMA's help; neither hears their mother) This land – how can father expect to make a living from this land within a year. We'll never clear enough of this quarter section in time for seeding.

EMMA
Well, why is this land so rocky? Father said it was rich, just waiting to be tilled.

ACK
I s'pose Eramosa farms were rocky too. But not frozen solid most of the year. That's the worst.

EMMA
We're just lucky Father has a bit of a wage from the Wisehart farm.

ELIZABETH
(from the house) Children! Can't hear me. Now how am I going to get that big mattress out that little door to air in the sun? *(to FANNIE, playing with a doll nearby)* A big house, your father said, didn't he Fannie. Hah. Maybe at the turn of the century, if the grain is harvested, if there's a market for it. *(to herself again)* That dreamer. *(She sees someone approaching on foot.)* Oh my, Fannie, a visitor! *(moving quickly, tidying)* ...and the sod of our hut barely dry...

SALLY
Hello Mrs. Hall...

ELIZABETH
Mrs. Hatfield, have you walked all the way from Qu'Appelle? You must be... why, sit right down here in the shade, and Fannie will bring you water. Fannie. *(FANNIE draws water from a barrel by the door of the sod hut.)*

SALLY
(Sitting on a barrel, she drinks. FANNIE exits into the hut.) Thank you, Mrs. Hall. I am tired, but we haven't any horses to spare from the field. Which is why I've come actually.

ELIZABETH
(*distressed*) Oh, Mrs. Hatfield, I'm so sorry, but Michael has taken our only two horses for the work at the Wisehart farm. I haven't any idea when he'll finish there. It could be days.

SALLY
Mrs. Hall, I despise this country! How do you manage? With your children to look after… it's so desolate… the workday never stops, and I haven't any children… yet… and William, I never see him. He's working for someone else, or he's preparing the field for seeding, with all those Indian men hired to help him. And we can't even afford to pay the Indians' wages. Why they're probably making more money from our farming than we are.

ELIZABETH
(*gently*) They work for next to nothing, those men.

SALLY
Well, that is true, but then they're paid what they're worth.

ELIZABETH
(*getting to the point*) You must be missing England, Mrs. Hatfield. You must miss the shops – I know I miss being able to shop in York once a year.

SALLY
Yes, I miss the cities. I miss my family. This "great new life," when does it begin? I would go back to England tomorrow, except William is convinced we'll be rich, and he won't budge from this… desert.

ELIZABETH
There is wealth in the land.

SALLY
How many years of hardship are worth some vague, future wealth?

ELIZABETH
Do you ever visit the Valley, Mrs. Hatfield? I find that its natural beauty restores my faith in God, and in our new life. When I need to, I travel there to meditate on our great good fortune.

SALLY
I visit the post at Fort Qu'Appelle when I can. But the Valley – there are so many Indians. Aren't you afraid when you go there?

ELIZABETH
I've quite enjoyed the few words I have exchanged with the halfbreed men. The women and the Indians, why we never see them. Seems to me they are more isolated than we on their reserve land. (*standing abruptly*) Oh, my heavens. Look, Sally!

   A North West Mounted Policeman rides up on his horse. He does not dismount, but removes his hat.

NWMP
Good afternoon ladies. I'm here to inform you that the Minnesota Sioux, Standing Buffalo's people, have arrived in the area. I don't want you to be alarmed…

SALLY
Not alarmed! The Custer murderers!

NWMP
No, Ma'am. Standing Buffalo's people. It's a different language, even. These Sioux have run into trouble with the Americans, but they're not here to make trouble. They've been quite… tame, almost, in Manitoba. But keep a watch on your livestock. I s'pect they are pretty hungry. Good day, ladies. *(exits)*

SALLY
Elizabeth, I've got to get back to Qu'Appelle! Heavens, I have to watch the chickens, and our geese! The Sioux, why they're thieves, aren't they?

ELIZABETH
Sally, sit down! No one is going to steal your chickens.

SALLY
But Mrs. Hall, I…

ELIZABETH
Not another word about going home. You are exhausted. If you make it back to Qu'Appelle—IF, I say—you won't have an ounce of stamina for chores like watching over your chickens.

SALLY
(remembering chores left undone) Or curing the meat. Tending the garden.

ELIZABETH
Hauling the water. Washing the clothes.

SALLY
Making the soap. Churning the butter. Chopping the wood, by myself! Building the fire. Cooking the meal, if you can call it a meal. Mending the clothes. Fixing the plough.

> *Segue into the "Work Song."*

Scene Four

> The "Work Song," involving nearly the whole cast on stages and among the audience. Characters enter with the instrumental intro. Each character is performing a chore in mime or with a prop.

> "Work Song." Music and lyrics by Billy Morton.

WHITE WOMEN
Every morning before the sun has
Shown its face my day's begun
It's the same thing every day
On it goes 'til they cart me away
But I don't mind
For with the work, the work, the bloody hard work
There's a beautiful thing I find

Plow the field, scatter the seed,
Clothes to wash and chickens to feed,
It's the same thing every day
Things to buy and bills to pay
But I don't mind
For with the work, the work, the struggle and work
We leave some things behind

NATIVE MEN
Set the nets for the fish each day
Check the traplines for the beaver and pray
To the soul that guides the plain
That the buffalo might come again

NATIVE WOMEN
Skin the animals cure the hides
Watch our children and others' besides
Cook the meals and for what it's worth

ALL WOMEN
When we're not doing that
We're giving birth

WHITE MEN
Harvest done, the winter's near,
Sit by the stove with a keg of beer
It's the same thing every day
Watch the wife work the hours away
And I don't mind
We work all spring and summer and fall
To watch the days unwind

ALL
Keep the fires burning bright
Maybe we'll have some peace tonight
It'll soon be time for bed

WOMEN
But not until my husband is fed

ALL
But I don't mind
Even though we work and struggle and work
And a day feels just like ten
When the rooster crows and the sun comes up
We'll start all over again

> As the "Work Song" ends, the FOOL, WESAKEYCHUK, and LOUDVOICE haul
> farm equipment from the song onto a stage.

Scene Five

FOOL
Work, work, work – that was life in the territories.

WESAKEYCHUK
You guys had it easy, Fool.

FOOL
Easy! Are you kidding?

WESAKEYCHUK
(angry) You have freedom! No Indian agents, no pass system…

A loud yell of frustration from LOUDVOICE, struggling with farming equipment.

LEGENDWOMAN
Watch, Fool.

WESAKEYCHUK
It's Loudvoice, the proud hunter. Look at him now.

LOUDVOICE
This damn equipment. First the Indian Agent makes you cut all the trees down. Then we have to take all the stones out of the ground. We burn sweetgrass, and give thanks to the earth. But it's not the same. The ground is naked. We have stripped the earth. *(He sighs and continues with the work of repairing a harness.)* We must feed the community.

FOOL
The land is changing. It is inevitable.

WESAKEYCHUK
Do you see how the Queen takes care of her red children?

LOUDVOICE
Here comes the biggest agent of change.

LEGENDWOMAN
Edwards, the Indian agent.

Enter AGENT Edwards. He strides in like he owns the place. Thinks of himself as a really friendly, generous guy. Slaps LOUDVOICE on the back.

AGENT
So how's the little woman and the papoose?

LOUDVOICE
What do you want?

AGENT
I want to talk to you, Loudvoice. You've got to tell your people the sundance is no longer allowed. We heard a rumour of a sundance. Any truth to that?

LOUDVOICE
Your rule makes no sense to our people.

AGENT
(offers LOUDVOICE a cigarette) Look. I don't make the rules. It's mostly those priests who insist the braves don't beat the tom toms, okay? The Mounties really don't care one way or the other.

LOUDVOICE
And you, Edwards?

AGENT
Me? I'm just doing my job. Remember when your people were starving out there. Now you harvest this field and I sell it in town – you're making a living. Anyone selling without a permit goes to jail in Fort Qu'Appelle. Now, I wouldn't want that to happen to anyone on my reserve.

LOUDVOICE
Yes, we have to go to town with you to sell the grain. The *Wapi'se'kow'we'as* sell as they please, to make money for their families.

AGENT
Now, Loudvoice. The "whitemeats" as you call us, own their land. They can do as they please. *(He hands pitchfork to LOUDVOICE, who seems tempted to use it as a weapon. Edwards is unfazed.)* You know that this equipment and the land you live on belongs to the Crown. And since I am an agent of the government, I am responsible for everything that goes on around here. So, my friend, get a move on clearing this field, or it won't be ready for seeding. Don't you have anyone to help you?

LOUDVOICE
Our children are at the industrial school. How can they work in the fields with us when you take them away, too?

AGENT
I have nothing to do with that. All I know is that if more of your people had character like you this would be a different place. Change, Loudvoice, you've got to learn to live with it.

FOOL
(to WESAKEYCHUK) Did you hear that?

WESAKEYCHUK
I have ears.

LOUDVOICE
I talked to some of your people. They tell me they moved here for freedom, and land. Because where they come from there is no freedom, no land. Maybe it is our people and the land that have fed your starving people. I know you think you found savages in rags…

AGENT
I'm telling you, Loudvoice. You keep your head out of the clouds, or you and your people are going to be a lot worse off than you are now. *(to audience)* We can't have these people roaming around hunting, scaring the settlers. I wouldn't be here if these people knew how to run things, on their own, in a civilized fashion, like our elected leaders. *(a beat)* Oh my God. I'd be out of a job.

LOUDVOICE
I'm sure you are a busy man and must be going, right?

AGENT
Yes, in fact, I do have some arrests to make... something to do with a sundance.
Fellow Agents, do your work!

WESAKEYCHUK
Now, Fool, now we get the real story, right?

Scene Six

The Indian AGENTS appear. They are masked figures, with costumes reminiscent of Edwards himself. They perform a choreographed chorus line number to "The Indian Agent's Song."

"Indian Agent's Song." Music and lyrics by Billy Morton.

AGENTS
We're gonna do what we want when we want to do it
Any old way you view it
We're gonna put 'em through it
We're Indian agents and if anyone asks for something
We're gonna tell them one thing
Then we're gonna do another

If anyone wants to see a friend
On another reservation
If we don't like the way they look
We're gonna kill their aspiration

We're Indian agents and if anyone asks for something
We're gonna tell them one thing
Then we're gonna do another

If anyone wants to make a trade
No ifs or ands or buts
Before we let the deal go down
We're gonna get our cuts first

We're gonna do what we want when we want to do it
Any old way you view it
We're gonna put 'em through it
We're Indian agents and if anyone asks for something
We're gonna tell them one thing
Then we're gonna do another

We don't care if they don't like us
We will do just what delights us
If you want to overcharge her
We don't care 'cause we're in charge here

We're gonna do what we want when we want to do it
Any old way you view it
We're gonna put 'em through it
We're Indian agents and if anyone asks for something
We're gonna tell them one thing
Then we're gonna do another

> *The Indian AGENTS roar, loud and threatening. They jump off the stage and into the audience, arresting and intimidating as they go.*

Scene Seven

> *Back at the Halls' homestead, a band of Sioux people are arriving at the hut and want to trade for food. FANNIE is again outside, where ELIZABETH and SALLY Hatfield are seated.*

SALLY
(standing) Oh my sweet lord. They're coming this way, I mean it they're coming! It's those warlike Sioux, just as he warned us…

ELIZABETH
Sally Hatfield, get a hold of yourself. Just stay calm. *(frightened in spite of herself)* Fannie! Get in the house this minute.

SALLY
Oh Lord, please look after us in our helplessness. Look after the children…

ELIZABETH
Sally get a hold of yourself. Get inside with the children. Excuse the mess, but get inside!

YUZICAPPI
(arriving) We would like to trade for food.

SALLY
(from inside the house) Mrs. Hall please be careful!

ELIZABETH
Mrs. Hatfield, would you get some flour, eggs and tea. It's all in boxes, there.

YUZICAPPI
What's wrong with that woman. Is she possessed by a spirit?

ELIZABETH
Yes. The spirit of loneliness, and fear. Please don't be scared of her, she means no harm.

> *SALLY places a box of foodstuffs down and returns quickly inside.*

YUZICAPPI
She should find herself or she will be lost out there.

STANDING BUFFALO
This is what we can offer you. Duck feathers and moccasins.

ELIZABETH

Fine. *(pause)* Isn't it illegal for you to be trading off the reserves with us?

YUZICAPPI

Our people are not on a reserve. We are searching for land, where we can make our home. Do you know what it is to be hungry, with no way to feed your family!

ELIZABETH

Look, I am sorry. To be honest, you people scare me.

STANDING BUFFALO

What do you have to be scared of? Do we bring guns to your house, or do we ask you to move from your home? Are your children starving?

ELIZABETH

No. They're not starving.

YUZICAPPI

These things he talks of are a part of our lives. People have brought guns to our home and pointed them at our wives and children. We have crossed into the land ruled by the Great White Mother... hundreds of miles from our grandfathers' graves.

ELIZABETH

I never thought about it. Not that way.

STANDING BUFFALO

How could you. There is never a time or place for our people to meet.

ELIZABETH

May I. Um. Offer you some tea, and hard biscuits?

YUZICAPPI

We will not risk entering the home of a white woman. We must remain on good terms with the ones who enforce your laws. We'll leave you now.

ELIZABETH

I see. Thank you...

The Sioux take the box of food and exit.

SALLY

Mrs. Hall... Elizabeth.... You are not going to trade away your children's supper for a few feathers!

ELIZABETH

I think the trade is more than fair.

She picks up the duck feathers and moccasins thoughtfully and goes into the hut. SALLY steps forward, gathers her hat and tattered parasol, and crosses to another stage as she speaks.

SALLY

(to the audience) The work never stopped, not in those early years. The fear stayed, too, for a long time, invading every nerve and fibre. Fear, every dawn, every dinner hour, for years. Only fear to break the monotony of loneliness... those long weeks

of isolation stretched out endlessly behind you and in front of you, like the barren prairie itself. *(suddenly angry)* And we went hungry too, sometimes! *(pause)* But the worst, the most unbearable hardship, were the winters...

> *Three gusts of winter wind—a sound effect—whip through the audience, "blowing" cast members towards another stage where LOUDVOICE stands strong against the wind.*

LOUDVOICE
My people came to the valley for winter shelter centuries before the Wa'pi'se'kow'we'as arrived. We gave you the skills to survive. And how do you return our gift of skills and knowledge! With lies, Indian agents, passes *(showing documents)* and permits!

> *ELIZABETH Hall appears outside the sod hut. She is carrying a basket of food and medicine.*

ELIZABETH
I finally understood – mostly understood. And I tried – not that I really could – but I tried to make up for the ignorance and prejudice of my people, and the greed of my government.

> *Enter YUZICAPPI. ELIZABETH places the basket at the feet of YUZICAPPI. They exchange a look. There is a cautiousness between them. ELIZABETH exits, then YUZICAPPI, in the opposite direction.*

Scene Eight

LEGENDWOMAN
I saw many more winters come, and go. The trains came to Fort Qu'Appelle in 1911. The town exploded with new prosperity...

> *Accompanied by the song "We've Come A Long Way," Fort Qu'Appelle townspeople appear with cut-out buildings springing into place and forming a train that moves through the promenade area. At the end of the train, and lagging slightly behind, is CHARLIE Sun, carrying his dry goods store. In the rhythm of a train some voices chant "Fort Qu'Appelle" continuously under the song.*

> *Fort Qu'Appelle Song: "We've Come a Long Way." Music and lyrics by Billy Morton.*

FULL CHORUS
Hey look what's comin'
Down the brand new track
The iron horse puffin'
With the smoke so black

Yes the trains are comin'
And it serves us well
Sure beats the old stage coach
Twenty miles from Qu'Appelle

Oh we've come a long way
And further yet to go
No matter how far we roam
We'll have the train to bring us home

Oh the town is boomin'
And we have the tools
We can build the buildings
And we'll fill the schools

We can see the future
And it's comin' fast
We can learn our lessons
Building from the past

Oh we've come a long way
And further yet to go
No matter how far we roam
We'll have the train to bring us home
Yes we'll have the train to bring us home
Yes we'll have the train to bring us home

SURVEYOR(S)
Fort Qu'Appelle… bound for glory as the future capital of the Province of Saskatchewan!

> *Enter the FOOL carrying the mudball. He is laughing uproariously, and approaches the LEGENDWOMAN, who is already on stage.*

FOOL
(laughing) So they made Regina the capital! The slough that ate the legislature! Now there's a good joke!

LEGENDWOMAN
(laughing with the FOOL, then suddenly serious) Listen, can you hear?

FOOL
Hear what?

LEGENDWOMAN
My mother is laughing too. She is happy that Regina saved her from the seat *(slaps FOOL on the bum)* of government.

FOOL
I see your point…

Scene Nine

> *It is the 1920s in Fort Qu'Appelle, at CHARLIE Sun's dry goods store. CHARLIE speaks as he carries on business with his customers.*

CHARLIE
(stocking shelves) I arrived in Canada when I was thirteen. Two hundred dollars it cost me, just to get in – head tax. But, that was a long time ago. Since then there have been a lot of changes in my life – the valley, Canada.

CUSTOMER 1
Morning Charlie. Tobacco, that's it. Cold today, isn't it? Warm in here, though.

CHARLIE
My store, my house. Sometimes I feel trapped by these walls. My wife does not speak English. I keep thinking what will this valley give or take from us.

CUSTOMER 2
(with goods in arms) Charlie, is my credit still good here?

CHARLIE
(boxing the goods and making a note of the transaction) I wish I could get credit with the Canadian government. Two hundred dollars… but now I can't even buy the land under my own store – it's against the law.

CUSTOMER 3
Hey Charlie, you going to donate for the curling bonspiel – like you do every year, eh?

> Enter the FOOL and WESAKEYCHUK. They are pushing each other to be the one to talk to CHARLIE.

WESAKEYCHUK
(pushing FOOL toward CHARLIE) Invite him! To the bonspiel!

FOOL
No, you invite him! Aren't you having a gathering in one of the communities… I don't know, somewhere in the valley?

WESAKEYCHUK
No, you see it wouldn't be right and all. It's very sacred and I don't know if he would understand the significance of the ceremony. Anyway, it's a long trip to the reserve.

FOOL
I know what you mean. Well, we'd like to have them over, but I… we wouldn't want them to feel out of place.

WESAKEYCHUK
(taking goods) Hey Charlie, I'm a bit short this week. Get you next time, okay?

> Exit FOOL and WESAKEYCHUK as an elderly SALLY Hatfield, extravagantly dressed, enters to buy pastries. A Métis woman named LUCIE holds the door for her.

CHARLIE
(to FOOL and WESAKEYCHUK) No, it's okay, really. We have social contact with the Chinese family up in Indian Head, and one at Balcarrres. *(now to Mrs. Hatfield)* Yes, Mrs. Hatfield, you've come all the way from Qu'Appelle? Something special?

SALLY
(handing him a list) Yes, for the party after the polo match tomorrow. I'll pick things up on my way home, thank you Charlie.

SALLY starts to go, bumping into LUCIE on her way out.

LUCIE
Oh, I'm sorry Mrs. Hatfield.

SALLY
(brushing herself off) That's quite alright. Good day.

Sally exits.

CHARLIE
You tell me, are my children going to feel this same way? (Pause while he watches LUCIE admiring his pastries.) You would like some of the turnovers, madame?

LUCIE
Just some cheesecloth, please. That will be fine.

CHARLIE
Yes, madame.

She carefully counts out the right amount of money.

LUCIE
Goodbye, sir.

CHARLIE
Yes, good day, madame. (watching her go) She must be from the mission.

Scene Ten

Focus shifts to a Métis home in the nearby mission community. MARIE is preparing food for the upcoming New Year's celebration. MARIE is thirty years old, and pregnant. LUCIE is on her way in with her shopping to help with the preparations. LUCIE is older, in her mid-forties. The two women kiss cheeks as a greeting. MARIE's hands are covered in flour and bread dough.

MARIE
Oh, la la, merde! (She has poured too much flour onto her board.)

LUCIE
Marie, you've started already. Here, let me do that.

She takes a pan of bread dough from MARIE's hands and carries it to a nearby table where it will rise.

MARIE
(kneading) Only three days left til the New Year. And you know by the time the people get here to our house it will be quite a crowd. Twenty loaves of bread to go, mon dieu!

LUCIE
(*putting her arms around MARIE*) That's why I'm here.

> *LUCIE unpacks supplies from her basket, dons an apron, and begins to prepare a cassoulet, ki'ni'ki'nik, or something appropriate.*

MARIE
(*taking a jar out of LUCIE's hands and looking at it*) So you did go to Fort Qu'Appelle...

LUCIE
Mmmm. Yesterday. Have you heard! There's a new shop opened up, run by a Chinaman? A Chinaman's store with the most beautiful looking pastries...

MARIE
(*puts the jar down, returns to vigorous kneading*) So, in Fort Qu'Appelle they buy their goods from a Chinaman? Haven't the time to bake their own bread in Fort Qu'Appelle, eh?

LUCIE
Marie, if you could see these pastries...

MARIE
Well, in the name of sweet Jesus, if the government ever gets off their rear ends to build us a road, then I could go to Regina to buy my pastries. I wouldn't have to shop with the wealthy... ladies... in Fort Qu'Appelle.

LUCIE
You know, I worry about that road. Here in Mission we feed ourselves. If we have a little extra, we go to the Fort for luxuries. What will happen when everyone can go to Regina to buy their vegetables...

MARIE
(*Suddenly excited, she wipes her hands on her apron and crosses to get papers from a desk.*) Our town.... Oh, the petition! Lucie, I saw the list of names, and everyone in town has signed except you...

> *Petitioners appear armed with clipboards, petitions and pens. The women are still in their scene.*

PETITIONERS
SIGN THE PETITION!

LUCIE
What petition?

MARIE
Where have you been, Fort Qu'Appelle? Look... (*pointing to the piece of paper in LUCIE's hands*)

PETITIONER 1
It says we want our town to be named Mission.

LUCIE
(*to MARIE*) Well, what else could it be named?

PETITIONER 2
They have to approve our name in Ottawa!

PETITIONER 3
Do you trust the government?

FULL CAST
NO WAY!

LUCIE
Look, Marie, old Mrs. Desjarlais hasn't signed it either. *(putting her coat on and leaving)* I'm going right now to get her to sign…

> *As LUCIE reaches the downstage edge of the stage, she raises the petition high above her head.*

LUCIE
Sign the petition!

FULL CAST
SIGN THE PETITION!

> *With fiddle accompaniment, LUCIE, MARIE and all the PETITIONERS descend into the promenade area and solicit signatures from the audience and cast members. The fiddle then segues into "Drops of Brandy."*

FULL CAST
BONNE ANNÉE! HAPPY NEW YEAR!

> *At least two lines of four couples have been created in the promenade area. With music, an abridged version of the traditional Métis dance "Drops of Brandy" is performed. Great shouts and whoops. Individual characters roam the audience with bottles, food, and hugs, which they share generously. The atmosphere is of a big, wild, elated party.*

> *As "Drops of Brandy" ends, the music segues into "Red River Jig," and two rounds of a solo jig is performed on one of the stages. The cast claps and cheers the dancer on. As the dancer leaves the stage, Father LEBRET appears from his "pulpit," and the Métis people arrange themselves in pews.*

LEBRET
You must heed the words of the church! You say that your people work hard all year. That you are allowed one day to celebrate. But the Métis New Year is a mockery! A mockery in the name of our Lord Jesus Christ. A shameful mockery of the sweet Virgin Mary. You know that I have never questioned the devotion of the Métis community. But I do question, and I will always question, conduct that the church views as inappropriate!

> *Still from his pulpit, he pulls out an empty mickey bottle and shakes it disapprovingly. The people in the "pews" stifle laughter. Among them are LUCIE and MARIE.*

MARIE
(to LUCIE) We should name the town "Little Chicago," eh Lucie?

LUCIE
Oh that would do wonders for our reputation in Fort Qu'Appelle.

MARIE
Come on, you know that we Métis do not drink any more than the Indians or the whites…

> *Raucous laughter from the pews. They then hush each other as they point to Father LEBRET descending sternly from his pulpit. He walks to downstage centre, removing a letter from his pocket. Meanwhile the churchgoers stand to form a group listening on the street.*

LEBRET
I've asked you to gather today, uh, on the subject of the name for the town. I know you had decided on a name for the settlement, but, well, in Ottawa they say there are already too many towns with the name of Mission. In the absence of another choice on your petition, I am pleased to inform you that the name on the mailbag which arrived this morning, is the new name for our community.

> *Silence.*

J.Z. LAROCQUE
Father Lebret, with all due respect, what is the name?

LEBRET
Well, you see, it was my name on the mailbag…

MARIE
Your name?

LEBRET
Yes. Lebret. It's official. The town is named Lebret. *C'est tout. Merci tout le monde,* I just wanted to let you know…

> *The crowd of listeners is furious. They disperse whispering angrily amongst themselves, but no one dares speak openly against the priest. Only MARIE and LUCIE remain onstage.*

MARIE
(holding the cross that she wears around her neck) Sacre, they will not destroy us! Never again will they ignore our wishes! For too long we have been forgotten and abused by the government. Separated from our Indian families. Forced to fend for ourselves. *(shouting)* We're on our own, we Métis, but never again—*Jamais!*—will they do this to us!

LUCIE
What more can we do? Everyone signed that petition! There's no use. Our town will forever be named for a useless priest that nobody likes.

MARIE
I'm not talking about the name! We have to organize the Métis people— everywhere—or they will keep treating us like the floor mat where they wipe their feet! Look, there's J.Z. Larocque. *Allons* – let's go see what he has to say.

> *J.Z. Larocque is now on a high platform.*

LUCIE
No, I'm going home.

MARIE
Allez, allez!

 MARIE runs off to join J.Z. Larocque.

J.Z.
That's my dream – "the Métis Nation of Saskatchewan." I won't let my children forget the events of the Red River. The land promised there was never delivered. We must stick together!

FULL CAST
THE MÉTIS NATION OF SASKATCHEWAN!

LEGENDWOMAN
So. They think they can shape their own lives. Forge their destiny. Are they right? In spite of everything, they have hope on their side. Hope is powerful. Hope drives your dreams. Your dreams… and mine. Without hope? Hope is what brought the Sanatorium to the valley. A place of healing. The healing place. The only place, so they say, where Indian and white were equal, brought together by the dread disease. But watch.

Scene Eleven

 At the sanatorium, DOCTOR Kyle is checking the chart of an ailing tuberculosis patient.

DOCTOR
Good. I see you've been getting more rest.

 Nurse ANNIE enters in a rush.

ANNIE
Doctor, I have to talk to you.

DOCTOR
Yes.

 ANNIE looks in the direction of the patient.

(taking a pulse) It's all right. What's on your mind.

ANNIE
It's the new patient in Room 9, Doctor. She needs to get a message to her son.

DOCTOR
(getting out his stethoscope) Yes.

ANNIE
Well, it's very important, you see, that he gets the message right away, and there's no way to get in touch with him…

DOCTOR
(thermometer) Yes.

ANNIE
Doctor, you see, your house is just on the edge of the reserve. When you drive home, you could, you know...

DOCTOR
(stops what he's doing) Drive onto the reserve?

ANNIE
Well...

DOCTOR
To deliver a message?

ANNIE
Well, yes. It would mean a lot to her. She's just arrived here, and she's lonely, and it really is very urgent...

> The DOCTOR has put away his instrument. Takes the patient's hand.

DOCTOR
You're doing beautifully. Remember to rest, ask for whatever you need, and I'll check in tomorrow at the same time.

PATIENT
Thank you doctor.

DOCTOR
You're welcome. And thank you. You make my work easy. Goodbye now. *(leading ANNIE toward the door)* All right. Yes, I think I can do that. *(pause)* It really is urgent, is it?

ANNIE
Yes. Well, I don't really understand these things – you know, their ways. But she's really upset.

DOCTOR
Yes, I see. What about, oh, you know, the woman who does the laundry, I forget her name. Doesn't she live out there?

ANNIE
No car, you see...

DOCTOR
No car?

ANNIE
She walks to work. But I know you're busy doctor... you know, well, we can try someone who's not as busy.

DOCTOR
No, no, if I can get very clear directions. I've never been out there. Is the road all right?

DOCTOR and nurse exit. Focus shifts to FOOL and WESAKEYCHUK.

WESAKEYCHUK
He won't go, you know.

FOOL
Well, why should he? It's asking a bit much, really. You know, our Indians are okay, but you can't blame a guy for being nervous about the reserve. I mean, you hear so many stories.

WESAKEYCHUK
(bitter) Yeh, stories.

FOOL
Hey, lighten up. This isn't the Depression you know.

LEGENDWOMAN
Oh yes it is.

WESAKEYCHUK
We're there, at the Depression? *(to FOOL)* When my people go starving, again?

FOOL
You think we don't suffer in the Depression?

WESAKEYCHUK
Yeh, those poor white farmers. They made their world work here. Their crops take over the prairie grasses. Prosperity at last. Then – the Depression. Hard times. Poor babies.

LEGENDWOMAN
So, did the hard times pull the people together?

FOOL
No, it took a war to do that!

WESAKEYCHUK
Indian and white, fighting together! For Canada!

LEGENDWOMAN
And after the war? Did the people pull together?

WESAKEYCHUK
Are you kidding? Indian veterans lost their right to be Indian, in exchange for – land!

FOOL
I didn't know that.

WESAKEYCHUK
Is that why they call you Fool?

FOOL
You think you're so bloody superior…

WESAKEYCHUK
Yeh. Brown Supremacist. It's a movement.

The FOOL advances threateningly.

WESAKEYCHUK
Hey, cheer up. This is 1945? White farmers are prospering. Indian farmers are getting by – things have been looking better lately. Too bad, because this is the year they blew up the sacred rock. They blew up the rock, to build some dams, to raise the water, to float their boats, to fish in the lakes… *(to the tune of "I don't know why she swallowed a fly")* "I don't know why they build dams so high…"

LEGENDWOMAN
(spoken) I guess they'll die.

Scene Twelve

The "PFRA Song", as a parade of vacationers marches through. They wear silly hats and sunglasses and carry oversized props such as a fishing pole, a giant ice cream cone, an inflatable raft, and a giant rubber duckie. The parade people drop garbage on the ground as they go through. Three native women, ANNETTE, ANTONIA and ALICE, follow behind the parade.

"The PFRA Song (Prairie Farm Rehabilitation Administration)." Music and lyrics by Billy Morton.

ALL
Where will we float our boat our boat
When we're on vacation
Where will we float our boat our boat
When we need recreation

MEN
When we come from Saskatoon
Or maybe from "Reginer"
We searched the province up and down
And there is no place finer

WOMEN
The valley's deep and picturesque
But there's much more at stake here
If cottages you want to have
We gotta have a lake here

ALL
Where will we float our boat our boat
When we're on vacation
Where will we float our boat our boat
When we need recreation

We'll get the old PFRA
To make a dam and bury
The farmland 'cause there's plenty left
Elsewhere on the prairie

Then we will float our boat our boat
Then we're on vacation
Then will we float our boat our boat
When we need recreation

Scene Thirteen

WESAKEYCHUK looks around at the new structure of the land. Onstage is the buffalo-shaped rock seen in the creation story in Act I.

WESAKEYCHUK
1945. This must be the right year. I am here to give the last offering for this buffalo. Today you will blow up. The day will be remembered by many people in the valley.

Enter FOOL laughing.

FOOL
Come on, it's a rock. It's not a shrine, for crying out loud.

WESAKEYCHUK
Gold is a rock. Like gold, this rock holds power for those who believe in it. Unlike gold, the power is for the human spirit.

FOOL
Yeh, yeh, I can buy that. But the rock is going to go. A lot can change in forty years, this is a new century! Time marches on. Don't get stuck in your damned circle going around and around.

WESAKEYCHUK
Oh yes, for you we're riding the tightwire of time – Genesis to Revelations! March on Time, until the earth blows up! *(beat)* One is never lost in a circle. In the circle, you can remember where you are from, by returning to the beginning.

FOOL
Fine. Whatever you like. But what are you going to do about the rock?

WESAKEYCHUK
Nothing. There is nothing to do. I've come here to watch.

A Cree MOTHER and her DAUGHTER approach.

FOOL
Who are these people?

WESAKEYCHUK
I don't know who they are. But watch.

MOTHER
Come here. Put your cloth in here. *(They give the offering to the rock.)*

DAUGHTER
We're going to get into trouble. At school we learn to follow the church, the true God.

MOTHER
I have no argument with the church or the people in town. But it's important that you know what to do – so you can live with your Mosom and Kokum. Does it matter if we get in trouble anymore?

DAUGHTER
But I believe that God exists, and He died on the cross.

> *MOTHER says a prayer in Cree.*

FOOL
Is that what you're talking about? The rock and its power?

WESAKEYCHUK
Maybe.

MOTHER
Come on, we have to go now. Remember that many of our people go to church and burn sweetgrass. This is not a problem for them. No one is right or wrong when it comes to this thing prayer.

> *As the MOTHER and DAUGHTER rise to leave, a Surveyor unreels a spindle to ignite the dynamite. The LEGENDWOMAN embraces WESAKEYCHUK. Suddenly understanding, the FOOL shouts to the MOTHER and DAUGHTER.*

FOOL
Get out of here! Run!

> *The Surveyor leans on the plunger to set off the explosion. The FOOL grabs the DAUGHTER and throws her out of the way, just in time, but he drops the mudball. The buffalo rock explodes with a flash and horrible noise that seems to go on forever. The LEGENDWOMAN screams in pain.*

LEGENDWOMAN
AS'TUM'OTA'NI'MO'SOM'WAK'EK'WA NO'KO'KUM'WAK'PE'WE'CHI'TAN!

> *Clouds and clouds of smoke. The smoke finally clears enough to see the Cree MOTHER lying dead, with her DAUGHTER mourning over her, rosary in hand. The FOOL watches in horror as LEGENDWOMAN lifts the DAUGHTER to lead her offstage. The DAUGHTER is droning "Holy Mary, mother of grace, Holy Mary, mother of grace...." WESAKEYCHUK notices the mudball on the ground. It has been split in two. He picks up one half, and kicks the other half at the FOOL. He then leaves after LEGENDWOMAN.*

> *The FOOL is devastated. He dejectedly picks up the mudball half, then stands motionless, holding it in both hands. He is the picture of the sad clown as a Surveyor drags the body of the MOTHER offstage.*

Scene Fourteen

Shift to Annette arriving at work. Also arriving at their separate workplaces are the two other domestics.

ANNETTE
There was a time when I did not have to work outside the reserve. Before the flooding of the hay fields...

ANTONIA
Putting on my boots and walking to work.

ALICE
Make sure that you leave on time so you're not late.

The women arrive at the door(s), enter, and meet an invisible woman employer. They continue the conversations as if they are together.

ANNETTE
When you arrive, it's good morning, how are you. The weather's not too bad now that it's summer. Yes, I'll get to the floor right away.

ANTONIA
(to the employer) Me, I'm fine. Yes I'll watch the baby while you are outside. *(to others)* I watch other people's kids more than I see my own.

ALICE
Morning, Ma'am. *(to others)* I don't get along very well with these people. No ma'am, I was not talking back. Yes ma'am, I fed the chickens before I came in. No ma'am, I did not forget that today is laundry. Yes, I told my husband I would be late tonight.

They begin to clean the house by sweeping the floor and washing it. They move to the windows.

ANNETTE
My husband and I used to have a good little farm till they built the dams a couple of years ago.

ANTONIA
You know, some white farmers lost their land too. We used to sell our hay to the RCMP for years. Now my husband works on the farm next to the reserve – when there is work.

ALICE
Then each year after the dam was built the land would disappear, little by little.

ANNETTE
Before the dams, the men would start at the different farms along the lake. They would cut the hay. That was hard work, but it was fun too.

ANTONIA
Then bale it. Haul it in big red racks. I remember, they would come into the house all dirty and dusty from the soil.

ALICE
We did our own work and we benefitted from that work. No ma'am, I was talking to nobody. Yes ma'am, I have been doing my work.

The women come together at this point. They start to gather the clothing and do the wash by hand. One woman pours hot water into the tub of clothes. The next woman feeds the wringer by hand. The third woman grabs the cloth and hangs it on the clothesline.

ANNETTE
I often wonder what the old people would think. Here we are, we had to stop hunting because there is no game. Now we have to stop farming because there is no land.

ANTONIA
Sometimes I think we lost more than land when the dams came. I think we lost a deep sense of the community.

ALICE
The young people could look at their parents with pride and enjoyment. Now the kids see parents leaving the reserve every morning to do work for other people.

ANNETTE
But we all know that nothing lasts forever.

ANTONIA
Nobody told us again about the change to our land.

ALICE
There was no compensation for the land swallowed by the water.

The women have finished their work. They put on their coats and their boots, and wait for payment for the week.

ANNETTE
Good night ma'am. We'll see you next Monday. Enjoy your weekend. No the kids won't be coming back from school this week.

ANTONIA
We'll see you later. My kids? No, the kids are too far away to come home every weekend.

ALICE
Good night.

The three women join up for the walk home.

ANNETTE
The walk home always seems easier. Maybe it's because you get paid at the end of the day.

ANTONIA
When I walk home I think of nothing. I just look at the sun and the beautiful colours the summer sky brings. I think of freedom.

ALICE
I don't like the walk here or home. I'm always thinking of how now, I have given everything. We gave you our land. We gave you our rights. Then the dams – and we give you our land again. And we gave you our children! *(pause)* And now, I give you myself. *(remembering)* My children. You know, I fooled my kids into going to the residential school. I am sorry babies. I love you.

The women leave the stages and go to their homes.

Scene Fifteen

WESAKEYCHUK enters atop a huge tractor, wearing a Cargill hat. The FOOL sits cross-legged and glum on the hood of the tractor. Both are dressed in contemporary fashion. Each has his own half of the mudball.

WESAKEYCHUK
Look, this is great. Do you see what they can do with these things now? Look, weeds!... *(sprays weeds played by children, weeds wilt)* and check out the fertilizer! *(sprays again, straight lines of wheat pop up)*

FOOL
Sure, spray chemicals all over the earth. We're all gonna die anyway, right?

WESAKEYCHUK
Oh, look who's got a conscience, all of a sudden. Seems to me you thought this was all pretty funny a little while ago...

FOOL
People are dying! A way of life—a culture—has been shoved aside, for progress! Now more progress, and another way of life...

WESAKEYCHUK
Whaddaya mean, "another way of life"? – oh, you mean Agri-Culture! Forget it, Fool, it's Agri-Business now. Get with the times! It's inevitable, remember?

JACK Tompkins enters from across the playing area.

JACK
Get off my tractor, thief!

WESAKEYCHUK
(taunting) Are you sure it's *your* tractor, Mr. Farmer?

JACK
Okay, okay, so it belongs to the bank. Just get off. *(He heads threateningly toward the two clowns on the tractor.)*

WESAKEYCHUK
(getting nervous) Come on, Fool, I think he means it.

The FOOL pays no attention, still depressed. WESAKEYCHUK drags the limp FOOL off the tractor as JACK climbs into the tractor and heads through the audience to his home. His brief drive is accompanied by one chorus of "The Tractor Song."

"The Tractor Song." Music and lyrics by Billy Morton.

It works like a charm
It don't run on blood
It will never lose in the sloughs and the mud
I dearly love my tractor painted green
Yes, I dearly love my tractor painted green

Scene Sixteen

JACK gets off his tractor in front of his house. Inside, his wife JANET is reading her grandmother's diary. LEGENDWOMAN, WESAKEYCHUK and the FOOL watch from above.

WESAKEYCHUK
(singing loudly after the song has ended) I John Deerely love my tractor painted green...

LEGENDWOMAN
(indicating JACK and JANET) Watch, both of you.

JACK enters.

JANET
Appalling!

JACK hangs up his hat, then looks out the window. He is silent.

JANET
(still reading) That's terrible!

JACK
I've been to the bank, Janet.

JANET
Jack, listen to this...

JACK
Did you hear me?

JANET
Jack, my grandmother, Elizabeth Hall was one of the last white people to see a sundance performed!

JACK
I don't give a damn!...

JANET
Jack!

JACK
…a hoot. I don't give a hoot about your Dances With Wolves!

JANET
(closing the diary) I know you don't. That's the problem.

JACK
The problem is, we are about to lose our farm, and you would rather sit there and feel sorry for people we don't even know!

JANET
And why don't we know them, Jack. Tell me that.

JACK
We don't know them because they live on reserves. We live on our farm, breaking our backs to make the loan payments, working the soil, *plus* taking an off-the-farm job! Those people, they don't have to mortgage their land…

JANET
Because they don't own their land!

> *A standoff. JANET breaks the ice.*

We're both working off the farm, right?

JACK
Exactly!

JANET
Because we can't make a living from the grain, right?

JACK
Right… we have to put food on the table so we don't starve, right?

JANET
Yes. *(pause)* Do you remember Mrs. Bear, who used to clean my mother's house? She had the same complaint. "Can't make a living from farming anymore. Not since those dams were built. That's why I'm here, minding you."

JACK
Not a nice thing to say to a child.

JANET
Well she was telling the truth.

JACK
The truth is, Janet, I've been to the bank. They're calling in our loan…

> *Pause.*

JANET
It's really happened. We're going to lose our land. What are we going to do?

JACK
Well maybe you should quit feeling responsible for other people's lives.

JANET
We're all responsible, for everything.

JACK
Our land is everything!

Scene Seventeen

Focus shifts back to the LEGENDWOMAN, WESAKEYCHUK and the FOOL, still with their halves of the mudball. The FOOL is glum. WESAKEYCHUK is dancing elatedly.

WESAKEYCHUK
Yes, yes, yes, yes!

FOOL
(angry, leaping down the steps from the raised stage) I give up! Get me away from this place! You people are cruel!

WESAKEYCHUK goes down the steps on the other side, intercepting the FOOL on the lower stage. In this scene, the TRICKSTER and the FOOL do somersaults, cartwheels and shoulder rolls that launch them into threatening poses.

WESAKEYCHUK
You people – are hypocrites! You deserve everything you get and more!

FOOL
Look, I know we horned in on your territory. But now you want everyone to pay for it! You want people to die, to starve, commit suicide?

WESAKEYCHUK
Don't talk to *me* about suicide! Who has the highest suicide rate in the country? Tell me that.

FOOL
Yeh, so what are you going to do about it?

WESAKEYCHUK
No, what are *you* going to do about it? Why don't you just go home?

FOOL
Why don't you just go home!

Pause.

WESAKEYCHUK
Now that's funny.

Pause.

LEGENDWOMAN
We're almost there. Can you feel it? Almost there! Watch this.

The FOOL and WESAKEYCHUK turn to watch.

Scene Eighteen

Enter MONA, an Aboriginal woman. She is dressed stylishly, and is carrying a briefcase and a lot of groceries. She is returning home from her job with the tribal council.

MONA
(calling) Hello!

No reply. MONA puts down the groceries and the briefcase, and checks her make-up in a mirror. Her husband FRED enters, home after travelling across Canada. He carries a briefcase and a suitcase and wears a suit and bolo tie. He walks into his home, kisses MONA, and takes out a bottle of champagne.

FRED
Good news, Mona. Just a little more red tape, and Ottawa is going to turn over land entitlement.

MONA
That's ironic, isn't it? The band council will be a landlord.

FRED
Ha ha ha. Cute, Mona. You won't ever let me off the hook, will you? *(begins opening the Champagne)*

MONA
No way. Not until you smell the coffee and see the buffalo. In the paper you said "We'll develop this land as we see fit" – remember? You said...

FRED
I was misquoted.

MONA
(mocking) Oh, so I suppose you also didn't say, "Nobody can own the land. The land owns herself."

FRED
What I said was, "Now they will have to admit who owns the land."

MONA
Is that what you told me, or is that what you told the paper?

FRED
Mona, welcome to the white man's world. This is 1992, remember?

MONA
I'm not asking anyone to live in the past. But nobody knows... what is the band going to do with the land? Some people want to put their money into projects that are sensitive to the land.

FRED
Yeh. We thought of that. Sure. I hear what you're saying.

MONA
Remember. Piapot and Starblanket – they never threw away their beliefs. Even after the signing of treaties. They were truly Indian.

FRED
(angry) Now you're saying I'm an apple.

MONA
I didn't say you were. I said remember.

FRED
Even great chiefs like Starblanket had to join in eventually. When the people were starving. Economics, Mona. We have to make the tough choices to survive.

MONA
Look at us! We're doing all right. We don't have to make bad choices, do we?

FRED
We have to take care of ourselves, you know!

MONA
We have to take care of others too! Balance. All I said was "remember…"

Scene Nineteen

FOOL
Remember what? There's nothing worth remembering around here. Just pain – too much pain! We should just give up–

WESAKEYCHUK
Okay. Jokes. What do you call a white man surrounded by a hundred Indians? A bingo caller!

The FOOL gets it. WESAKEYCHUK turns serious.

WESAKEYCHUK
How about this one. Why did the Indian cross the road?

FOOL
(eager to laugh) I don't know.

WESAKEYCHUK
Death wish.

FOOL
I don't get it.

WESAKEYCHUK
You know, suicide. What he really wants is to die, hit by the white man's car.

FOOL
You're kidding.

WESAKEYCHUK
You believed it! You see, you think you understand now, you really felt something. But you'll believe anything. You don't really know, how could you? So you just believe these stories, about life on a reserve! Like that doctor guy...

FOOL
So? Are you saying we make these things up? I know what goes on out there.

WESAKEYCHUK
"Lighten up."

FOOL
Sure...

WESAKEYCHUK
Hey, do you play games? It's a guessing game. *(gets out handgame bones)*

FOOL
(malcontent) A game. Right. Sure.

WESAKEYCHUK
Look it's easy. *(tosses off bones to FOOL)* Okay, see your bones. One striped, one plain. I have the same. Your job is to match bones.

FOOL
Okay, I get it.

WESAKEYCHUK
Fool! Ready?

> Hand game drumming and singing. WESAKEYCHUK starts a dance as he hides the bones in a blanket.

FOOL
Wait! What are you doing, jumping around like that? How can I guess when you do that?

WESAKEYCHUK
Hey bro, I am an Aboriginal dude. Heavy on the original. When I play I got to move and sing. Come on, guess!

FOOL
(flustered) Striped left and plain, right. *(song cuts out)*

WESAKEYCHUK
(switches the bones to match) Amazing. Truly amazing.

FOOL
No hard feelings. It's quaint. I know these primitive games.

WESAKEYCHUK
Think so? Okay, let's make a bet. Two outta three.

FOOL
For what?

WESAKEYCHUK
Everything.

FOOL
Everything?

WESAKEYCHUK
The mudball. Both halves.

FOOL
Old stuff. The mudball is worthless now.

WESAKEYCHUK
So you can't lose, right? Come on, both halves.

FOOL
Okay, the mudball.

    Hand games song.

WESAKEYCHUK
HO! *(song cuts out)*

FOOL
Hah?

WESAKEYCHUK
I choose, Ho. *(shows bones)*

FOOL
You're wrong, Aboriginal dude. This is kind of boring.

    Hand games song. They circle each other.

WESAKEYCHUK
You're right. Why don't you come out to the reserve for some excitement.

FOOL
Hey, I know lots of people who work on the reserves these days. Police, social workers. Doctors. Teachers. Consultants.

WESAKEYCHUK
IN-sultants. The point is when we meet it's always because of work. That's our relationship. We work, you work. Good workers, those Indians.

FOOL
Do you want me to feel guilty? Ask for forgiveness? Apologize? It's not my fault...

WESAKEYCHUK
Akosi! Choose!

FOOL
Left plain and right striped. *(song cuts out)* Damn. Wrong.

    Hand game song. They circle again.

FOOL
(challenging) I'll come and visit, okay? But you have to invite me. And tell me what I'm… s'posed to do.

WESAKEYCHUK
Do nothing. Just visit.

FOOL
Yeh, right, just, like, watch hockey on TV or something.

WESAKEYCHUK
Whatever.

FOOL
HO! HO! HO! *(song cuts out)*

WESAKEYCHUK
(showing bones) Merry Christmas…

FOOL
I can't believe it! Okay, double or nothing.

WESAKEYCHUK
(taking the FOOL's half of the mudball) Story of my life. Two outta three…. Fair's fair.

> *LEGENDWOMAN appears.*

LEGENDWOMAN
Trickster! Is that the story you want to tell? We're so close.

> *Pause.*

WESAKEYCHUK
I was jus kidding. Here, Boss. *(gives a mudball half to the FOOL)* But be careful when you call me Indian giver.

FOOL
You cheated, didn't you?

LEGENDWOMAN
Fool! Don't lose your chance.

> *FOOL and WESAKEYCHUK then look to each other a bit warily. Each has one half of the mudball.*

FOOL
You were right, Bonehead.

WESAKEYCHUK
Yeh, well, you were right too, Butthead.

LEGENDWOMAN
No, you are both wrong. And you are both right.

> *WESAKEYCHUK and the FOOL hold up the two halves of the mudball.*

WESAKEYCHUK
I want to try something. *(holds out his half of the mudball)*

FOOL
(holding out his half) Me too.

> *Pause.*

WESAKEYCHUK
You are White.

> *Pause.*

FOOL
Yes. *(beat)* You are Brown.

> *Pause.*

WESAKEYCHUK
Yes. *(beat)* You are human.

> *Pause.*

FOOL
Yes. *(beat)* You are human.

> *Pause.*

FOOL AND WESAKEYCHUK
YES.

> *They fit together the two halves of the mudball. As the two halves touch, a beautiful, other-worldly music begins.*

ACT III

From the hilltops a candlelight procession emerges and approaches the playing area. There are many children. The children lead the way.

LEGENDWOMAN
(with the whole mudball) It is a new era, and it is an old era. We have come full circle.

The spirits of the valley appear. These are characters from Acts I and II. Only their faces are lit.

MCKAY
In the beginning, there was a need.

MAS'WA
In the beginning, there was no need.

SKYWOMAN
In the beginning, there was equality.

DESJARLAIS
(a joke) And then, along came the Métis.

ELIZABETH HALL
There has been oppression.

YUZICAPPI
(with Elizabeth) There has been kindness.

ANNETTE
There has been fear.

SALLY
(with Annette) There has been ignorance.

MRS. PRATT
Our ancestors.

KOKUM
Remember.

LEBRET
The church.

J.Z.
Remember.

ALL
WE REMEMBER.

PRATT
Forgiveness.

LOUDVOICE
(angry) Forgiveness! We must never forget!

ALL
(*whisper*) WE WILL NEVER FORGET.

LEGENDWOMAN
My mother is with us.

> *WESAKEYCHUK and the FOOL appear. They are dressed in their original Act I costumes.*

WESAKEYCHUK
Your mother this, your mother that… who is your mother, anyway?

FOOL
Oh, don't play the fool.

WESAKEYCHUK
(*smiling*) A'ko'sai. (*extends hand*)

> *They shake hands.*

FOOL
That's it, then.

> *They leave separately.*

LEGENDWOMAN
My mother is the land, and I am my mother. I am the land. I am the valley. I am your ancestors, and I am the church. I am my mother, and she is what makes us human. She is all of this, and none of this. She divides us. She makes us whole. She is real, and you are her dreams. Listen!

> *As the procession reaches the promenade area, one voice begins to sing. The processors and all other cast members walk onto all stages, listening.*

> *A Cappella Soprano: "One Voice Calling." Music and lyrics by Billy Morton.*

One voice calling across the ages
Joined by another, they speak of the past.
Soon the voices of thousands gather
Leaving the quarrel, together at last
Just like a harmony chorus sounding
Through past and present and time yet to come
We must remember that all things living
Are equal in every way under the sun
Close the circle, the Play is done

> *Accompaniment comes in for another verse of "Dreamtime."*

So now here we stand beneath the open skies
Remembering the truth is seen through many eyes
Reasons to believe existing everywhere
Becoming clearer when we take time to care
We are together we are tonight

ALL
Tell me what you see when you gaze into the night
Dancing overhead it is the northern lights
Marching back and forth across a field of blue
An echo from the past calling out to you
Welcome to Dreamtime, welcome tonight
Welcome to Dreamtime, welcome tonight

> *Segue into "Fire in the Valley."*

Gather the people
Gather their strength
Gather the natural forces
Strong we will stand in the wind and the rain
We'll ride with the power of horses

CHORUS
There's a fire in the valley tonight
There's a flame and it shifts with the weather
There's a fire in the valley tonight
And it's pulling the people together

> *Repeat chorus.*

> *With the music to "Fire in the Valley," two massive puppets, the dove and the eagle, fly to opposite ends of the playing area. They circle each other, and us. A lone voice and then full cast cry "A'ko'sai" at the conclusion of the song.*

> *Music for the round dance. Cast and crew step off stages into the audience for the round dance. Audience, cast and crew: everyone dances together. A gathering. A celebration. A beginning.*

> *The end.*

Letters in Wartime

Kenneth Brown and Stephen Scriver

STEPHEN SCRIVER is known for his best-selling collection of hockey poems, *All Star Poet!* (Coteau, 1981), and has published three other books of poetry: *Between the Lines* (Thistledown, 1977), *More All Star Poet!* (Coteau, 1989) and *Under the Wings* (Coteau, 1991). His poetry has also been anthologized in *Number One Northern* (Coteau, 1976), *Diversions* (Alberta Education, 1978), *Contexts* (Gage, 1983), *The Maple Laugh Forever* (Hurtig, 1982), *100% Cracked Wheat* (Coteau, 1983), *A Sudden Radiance* (Coteau, 1988), and *In the Clear* (Thistledown, 1998). Stephen, who served as Sports columnist for *The Sports Line* in Edmonton between 1995-96, has also had poetry included in *88 Years of Puck-Chasing in Saskatchewan* (Schafer, 1977) and Ken Dryden's *Home Game* (M&S, 1989). In addition, his work in documentary film has been widely seen on History Television, especially "Missing On Way Back," which won a City of Regina Heritage Award and a Houston Film Festival Bronze Medal. He also helped research "Mountain of Gold" (History Television, 1999) and "Disasters of Canada" (History Television, 2000-01) six-part series. *Letters in Wartime* was his first serious foray into drama. He lives in Edmonton, where he has recently retired after 32 years of teaching, and lives with his wife of 33 years, Barbara, a midwife. They have three children and five grandchildren.

KENNETH BROWN is one of Western Canada's most prolific writers for the theatre. Of his eight one-man shows, four have had national broadcasts in Canada and one in Germany, *Sparks* (*Feuer und Flamme*) and *North of America* (*Nach Manitoba)* have been translated into German, while *Life After Hockey* has been translated into French and German. As an actor, he has toured to nearly every place in the country large enough to support a theatre, and has toured in four countries abroad. Ken was trained at the National Theatre School and holds an MA from the University of Alberta. His teaching work at Grant MacEwan College in Edmonton has gained him friends and colleagues across the country, and lately he has devoted much time to directing and developing the works of young playwright-actors like Sheldon Elter (*Metis Mutt*), the Ribbit collective (*Be A Man, Be a Man With Girls*), and the up-and-coming Janel Snider. He also directed and developed *Boy Groove*, Chris Craddock's brilliant boy band play. His most recent one-man show, *Lewis Lapham Live*, was based on the editorial writings of the brilliant Harper's editor who is one of the Bush Administration's most eloquent critics. Ken lives and works in Edmonton.

Introduction to Letters in Wartime
Stephen Scriver

Kenneth Brown and Stephen Scriver were veterans of the hockey wars when they first met in 1990. Brown had written, produced and acted in his spectacularly successful one-man play, *Life After Hockey*, while Scriver's best-selling collections of hockey poems, *All Star Poet!* and *More All Star Poet!* were staples in Canadian schools and dressing rooms.

It was another connection, however, that brought them together creatively. They were the sons of veterans, and in their first conversations they discovered they both had been profoundly disturbed by the CBC production of the McKenna brothers' documentary, "The Valour and the Horror." As Brown put it: "The film angered not a few veterans of the war, who felt that their sacrifices and those of their comrades, were degraded by the film's apparent message: that the policy of bombing Germany, promoted by 'Butcher' Harris, had little strategic effect on the war's outcome." They felt a response was necessary.

At the 1993 Edmonton Fringe Festival, the idea was hatched that they would write and stage a play in response to "The Valour and the Horror" at the 1994 Fringe. *Letters In Wartime* was the result.

The writing process was collaborative at two stages. The play was first mapped out scene by scene. Brown, who had trained as a pilot, claimed the flying scenes, while Scriver, the researcher, provided much of the play's historical spine through incident and anecdote. Both men were ardent story collectors and tellers, and many of the names and events in the play were based the recollections of veterans they had met. Foremost among these was their friend, the late actor Wally McSween, who flew Lancaster and Halifax bombers twenty-eight times over enemy territory in World War II. One of the great pleasures for the writers was having Wally attend several productions of the play.

After going their separate ways to write, Brown and Scriver came together again in the editing phase. Both men agree that the brutality and honesty necessary for the blue pencil process forged what has become an enduring friendship.

The obvious choices to play the roles of Allen and Moira for the first production were, of course, Kenneth and Michele Brown. Michele's pregnancy, however, necessitated the search for a new Moira, and Elizabeth McLaughlin came on board. During the first reading of the play, Elizabeth revealed that her uncle had not only been an RCAF Spitfire pilot during the war, but had been a prisoner of war at Stalag Luft 3, the POW camp from which The Great Escape was carried out.

The first production at the 1994 Edmonton Fringe Festival was staged, appropriately enough, in the Strathcona Legion Hall, and during eleven performances, including four in holdover, the audience response was tremendous. Colin McLean, the respected Edmonton drama critic, picked it as the finest production of that year's Fringe. It went on to win the drama community's Elizabeth Sterling Award for the best new Fringe work of 1994.

In the initial programme notes, Brown observed: "My personal reasons for wanting to do this play all have to do with honouring the superlative heroism of the Canadian men and women who traded their hard but simple provincial lives for years of privation and death. As they came of age, so did the nation.

"War is not good. I've never met a real warrior who thought it was. In the words of the late Roger Davies: 'Modern warfare is a prolonged industrial accident.' But I believe that wars bring out great qualities in people, and that there are some wars that have to be fought. The conflict against the Third Reich was one. Canadians accepted this terrible duty and fought."

Scriver added: "My hometown, Wolseley, SK, was less than 1000 souls, of whom over 100 served in WWII, and 21 sacrificed their young lives. Being surrounded by vets, including my Dad, I learned to be a good listener, a collector of stories, and when I joined my own struggles on the hockey rink, a storyteller. I am thankful to have been given the chance to share some of the stories I collected. I have looked after these stories, and they will look after me."

As of the publication of this play, it has been staged five times: 1994 Edmonton Fringe (Ad Astra Productions and THEATrePUBLIC), Edmonton, 1995 (Workshop West), Morrisburg, ON, 1995 (Upper Canada Playhouse), Alberta Tour, 1997 (THEATrePUBLIC), and Kelowna, BC, 2003 (Sunshine Theatre Productions).

— • — Selected Bibliography – Stephen Scriver — • —

Stage Plays – Published

Letters in Wartime. Ad Astra Productions and THEATrePUBLIC. Edmonton Fringe, 1994.
> *Letters in Wartime.* With Kenneth Brown. In *The West of All Possible Worlds: Six Contemporary Canadian Plays.* Ed. Moira Day. Toronto: Playwrights Press of Canada, 2004.

Letters in Wartime. (copyscript) With Kenneth Brown. Full-length. Toronto: Playwrights Guild of Canada, c.1994.

Filmscripts

- "Wings of Courage" (researched and wrote). First aired on History Television. June, 1999.
- "Birdman" (researched and wrote). First aired on History Television. November 1998.
- "Missing on Way Back" (researched, wrote and co-produced). First aired on History Television. November 1997.

Poetry – Published

- *Under the Wings.* Regina: Coteau Books, 1991.
- *More All Star Poet!* Regina: Coteau Books, 1989.
- *All Star Poet!* Regina: Coteau Books, 1981.
- *Between the Lines.* Saskatoon: Thistledown Press, 1977.

— • — Selected Bibliography – Kenneth Brown — • —

Stage Plays – Published

Letters in Wartime. Ad Astra Productions and THEATrePUBLIC. Edmonton Fringe, 1994.
> *Letters in Wartime.* With Stephen Scriver. In *The West of All Possible Worlds: Six Contemporary Canadian Plays.* Ed. Moira Day. Toronto: Playwrights Press of Canada, 2004.

> *Letters in Wartime.* (copyscript) With Stephen Scriver. Full-length. Toronto: Playwrights Guild of Canada, c.1994.

Alma's Night Out. THEATrePUBLIC. Edmonton Fringe, 1986.
> *Alma's Night Out: A Play in One Act* In *Riding on the Roar of the Crowd: A Hockey Anthology.* Ed. David Gowdey. Toronto: Macmillan of Canada, 1989.

Life After Hockey. THEATrePUBLIC. Edmonton Fringe, 1985.
> *Life After Hockey* One-act In *Five From the Fringe: A Selection of Five Plays First Performed at the Fringe Theatre Event.* Ed. Nancy Bell with Diane Bessai. Edmonton: NeWest Publishers, 1986.

> *Life After Hockey.* (copyscript) Full-length version. Toronto: Playwrights Guild of Canada, c.1986.

> *La Vie Après le Hockey.* [French translation of *Life After Hockey*]. Trans. Michel Garneau. Available through CEAD [Centre des Auteurs Dramatiques.]

Stage Plays – Unpublished

- *Uncle Van* (Canadian version of Uncle Vanya). THEATrePUBLIC. Edmonton Fringe, 2002
- *The Old Curiosity Shop* (Adapted from Dickens). THEATrePUBLIC. Edmonton Fringe, 2001
- *Garneau Kid.* THEATrePUBLIC. Edmonton Fringe 2000, Shadow Theatre 2001
- *Joseph Andrews* (adapted from Henry Fielding). THEATrePUBLIC. Edmonton Fringe, 1996.
- *Joseph Andrews* (adapted from Henry Fielding). (copyscript) Full-length. Toronto: Playwrights Guild of Canada, c. 1998.
- *The Bridge* THEATrePUBLIC. Edmonton Fringe, 1995.
- *The Bridge: A Play in One-Act.* (copyscript) Toronto: Playwrights Guild of Canada, c. 1995.
- *My Father's House: A Mythic Journey.* THEATrePUBLIC. Edmonton Fringe, 1992.
- *My Father's House: A Mythic Journey.* (copyscript) One-act. Toronto: Playwrights Guild of Canada, c. 1992.

- *Cambodia, a play for people who find television too slow.* Adapted with Brian Fawcett, from Fawcett's book *Cambodia, a book for people who find television too slow.* THEATrePUBLIC. Edmonton Fringe 1990.
- *The Cambodia Pavilion* [full-length version] THEATrePUBLIC 1991.
- *North of America.* THEATrePUBLIC. Edmonton Fringe, 1988.
- *North of America.* (copyscript) Full-length. Toronto: Playwrights Guild of Canada, c. 1993
- *Sparks: An Anti-Romantic Comedy.* THEATrePUBLIC. Edmonton Fringe, 1984.
- *Sparks: An Anti-Romantic Comedy.* (copyscript) One-act. Toronto: Playwrights Guild of Canada, c. 1984
- *Bombs: A Play About Nuclear Anxiety for Young Audiences.* With Keith Thomas. Theatre Network. Edmonton. 1982.
- *Bombs: A Play About Nuclear Anxiety for Young Audiences.* (copyscript) With Keith Thomas. One-act. Toronto: Playwrights Guild of Canada, c. 1993.

Reviews of Letters in Wartime

Arslanian, Araxi. "Letters About People, Not History." *VueWeekly* 9-15 November 1995: 11.

Kennedy, Janice. "Morrisburg Playhouse Salutes Small Towns." *Ottawa Citizen* 8 July 1995: F1

MacLean, Colin. "Letters Moving." *Edmonton Sun* 3 November 1995: 10.

MacPherson, Margaret. "Wartime Loss of Innocence Chronicled: Workshop West Theatre Expands Award-winning Play." *See* October 1995.

Mandel, Charles et al. "Final Day Fringe." *Edmonton Journal* 21 August 1994: F4

Mauthe, Rene. "Poignant Tale of Letters." *Edmonton Examiner* 10 November 1995.

Morash, Gordon. "Yarn Driven by Love and Anxiety: Play Based on Wartime Letters Set to Hit the Stage at the Fringe and Capture Your Hearts." *Edmonton Journal* 7 August 1994: E5.

Nicholls, Liz. "Love and War: Letters in Wartime Chronicles a Relationship Scarred by the Second World War." *Edmonton Journal* 2 November 1995: C1.

---. "McSween's Talents, Spirit Will be Missed." *Edmonton Journal* 21 February 1996: B1.

Staples, David. "Rusty Died for his Country but There's No One Left to Care." *Edmonton Journal* 21 August 1996: B1.

The technical advisor about wartime flying was Wally McSween,
himself a former Lancaster pilot,
to whose memory we dedicate this publication of Letters in Wartime.

Letters in Wartime had its first professional production by Workshop West Theatre at the Kaasa Theatre in the Jubilee Auditorium, Edmonton, Alberta, in November 1995 with the following company:

Allan   John Ullyatt
Moira   Tanis Dolman

Director: David Mann
Stage Manager: Cheryl Millikin
Sound Design: David Clarke
Lighting/Set Design: Melinda Sutton

— • —

The premiere production of *Letters in Wartime* was a co-production of Ad Astra Productions and THEATrePUBLIC at Strathcona Legion Hall, Edmonton Fringe Festival, Edmonton, Alberta, in August 1994 with the following company:

Allan   Kenneth Brown
Moira   Elizabeth McLaughlin

Director: Jim DeFelice
Stage Manager: Rob Trousdell
Production by S. Scriver, R. Trousdell & Co.

— • —

A later production by THEATrePUBLIC toured within Alberta. It starred Kenneth Brown as Allan and Michele Brown as Moira.

Characters

Allan Staunton
Moira Lyons

Letters in Wartime
by Kenneth Brown and Stephen Scriver
——— • ——— • ———

Prelude

Glenn Miller's "Moonlight Serenade."

On stage, two acting areas:

Stage right, a 1940s period writing desk and chair, behind which is an armchair beside a side-table upon which is a radio. The radio is practical, and will play occasional news reports. There is also a coat rack.

Stage left, a military-style steel writing desk and chair. A little downstage and to the left of this is a trunk marked "Staunton, A.W." Out of this box come ALLAN's changes of clothes. ALLAN also has a coat rack.

At centre-stage is a third acting area, which represents the train station in Scene One, and the street in front of the chapel in Scene Two.

As the lights come down, a collage of sound: Chamberlain announcing "Peace In Our Time," Hitler giving his "Germany for the Germans" speech, the announcement of the invasion of Poland, Britain joins the war, Canada's declaration, the song "The Siegfried Line," Vera Lynn singing "The White Cliffs of Dover," Churchill's "Some chicken! Some neck!" speech to parliament, sound bytes from Dunkirk, announcement of Pearl Harbour, Roosevelt's "Infamy" speech; Christmas 1941, message from Mackenzie King.

The collage resolves in the music, "We'll Meet Again," and the sound of a steam train arriving at the station. The sound of steam huffing under:

ACT I – First Movement: Beginnings

Departure.

ALLAN
Well.

MOIRA
You look swell. In uniform.

ALLAN
No wings yet, though.

MOIRA
No.

ALLAN
It's too bad about the University. Maybe you'll get a chance to go back next year.

MOIRA
Well, Mom and Dad need me right now.

Short pause.

ALLAN
Peter will be all right. I'm sure you'll be hearing something.

MOIRA
Yes…

ALLAN
Missing in Action doesn't mean dead. Hong Kong must be complete chaos, and who knows how the Japanese are dealing with their prisoners. I mean, you know, administration, and so on. They can't even pronounce our names. He'll make it just so I can rib him about dating his sister.

MOIRA
Will you see Norman, do you suppose?

ALLAN
No, I don't think so. Hardly any chance of being put on the same base. I think the conductor's waving.

MOIRA
I'm glad you asked me to come and see you off.

ALLAN
Are you? You look pretty in that dress. More than pretty. How about a kiss?

MOIRA
Not in front of everyone.

They kiss. Pause.

ALLAN
I meant to tell you. About that Saturday. What I said, in the car…

MOIRA
I don't want to think about…. What I would feel if…. Just promise me…?

ALLAN
What?

MOIRA
Don't promise me anything.

ALLAN
Promise me.

MOIRA
What? *(beat)* What??

ALLAN
Promise me you'll write. And take good care of yourself.

l to r:
Elizabeth
McLaughlin,
Kenneth
Brown

*photo by Thomas
Turner,
courtesy of
THEATrePUBLIC*

MOIRA
Yes, I will. I will. For you.

The sound of a steam whistle. They kiss. Black.

— • —

Light. Two chairs. He sits writing. She recites a letter she has composed:

MOIRA
(writing) Dear Allan. Wouldn't you know it? I'm hardly home from the train station and I can already feel how much I'm going to miss you. I have so much I want to tell you.

Pause. She can't think of anything to write.

When we kissed…. In front of all those people in the station. I felt like we… had wings.

Pause. She speaks to herself:

I felt like Andromache: "She stood beside close to him, letting her tears fall, and clung to his hand, and called him by name…." Why did I have to wait till he was leaving to feel that?

She writes:

Dr. Wilmot was wonderfully kind when I told him I wouldn't be at his lectures anymore. He said he had been grateful to have one enthusiastic Classics student. He gave me a copy of Homer's *Iliad.* "This book may be old, but it's not out of date," he said.

We have heard...

ALLAN AND MOIRA
(together, he reading, she writing) ...from Norman's family that he has been posted to a Spitfire squadron, isn't that dashing? And no, you have no need to be jealous. Must close now. Mother is just coming in from her church meeting...

ALLAN
(reading) Best love...

MOIRA
(writing) Best.... Love,

ALLAN AND MOIRA
(together) Moira.

ALLAN
"Best love." Best. Love.

He hesitantly smells the envelope. It smells good.

Does that mean she *sends* me best love, or that I *am* her best love? And what does she mean, I have no need to be jealous? SPITfires! God.

He takes pen in hand, prepares to write.

(to himself) Is this supposed to be a... love letter...?

Pause.

I don't know how to write a love letter.

(writes) "Dear Moira: It was good kissing you..." Jesuus. *(Pause. He tries again.)* "Southern Alberta is very flat around here." Jesus!

He takes a breath, tries again.

Well, here we are, pounding the pencils and trying to be good students. Since we arrived, they've done everything they can to convince us of two things: first, that we are no longer civilians, and second, that whatever it is we are, we're no damn good at it. We certainly don't seem to be pilots – I don't think that anyone plans to trust us with an airplane during our military careers. Instead, they're teaching us the theory, 'though what value that's going to be in a dogfight against the Germans isn't exactly clear. Maybe we're supposed to bore them to death.

At night, when the lights go out, some smart-ass will yell out, "anybody from the West here." Some enthusiastic Westerner will yell out, "I'm from the West," and then all the Easterners will yell, well I won't say what they yell, but what they mean is "fornicate the West!" Whatever they call this training, it isn't for polite society.

Anyhow, the food is good. And there's lots of it, which is a pleasant change. In fact, I'm going to close this letter now because we have a mess call coming up.

Pause.

Look, I know that Norman and you had this understanding…

(to himself) Understanding…

— • —

He erases. He writes.

Glad to hear that Norman is doing so well. *(He is anything but glad.)* And hello to whoever… *(erases)* "Whomever. Best Wishes,

ALLAN AND MOIRA
(together) Allan.

MOIRA
(to herself) Norman. Who I haven't heard from since September. "Best Wishes"?

She writes:

Dear Allan… *(erases)* My Dear Allan… *(erases)* My Dear Friend… *(erases)* My Dear Friend Allan… *(erases)*

Dear Allan,

It was good to get a letter from you so soon. I'm sure it's hard to get time to write. I'll bet you're all very dashing as you march around, keeping up the local girls' morale.

(to herself) I hope that's the only thing you're keeping up. *(laughs, then:)* Oh my.

(writing) How well I know what you mean about plentiful food. All my life it seems I've been scrimping and getting along with nearly nothing. I don't know what we'd have done during the thirties if Dad didn't hunt and Mom hadn't been a crackerjack gardener. Starved, I suppose. Still, I never want to taste moose meat again for the rest of my life.

The Japanese have taken Bahrain. Their progress through Malaysia has been startling. Thank God the Germans have decided to take on Joe Stalin, I hope they're as frozen as we are here.

ALLAN
(writing) Elementary Flying Training School,
High River, Alberta

Dear Moira,

I don't think I chose the right service. Maybe I should re-muster for the Army. Had my first training flight in a Tiger Moth this morning, with a hard-bitten old (well, thirtyish) pilot who would prefer to be flying a Hurricane against the Germans. We took her up to seven thousand, and then he says, "down we go," and pulled over into a spin. It was like the movies, the world spinning in front of the windscreen. I had vertigo like crazy.

I feel like an idiot at the controls, nothing makes sense. They tell me this should change. If it doesn't, I'll be washed out and end up a tail-gunner in some hulking great bomber.

The prairies are so beautiful from the air. You can see all the mountain ranges from seven thousand feet, the world looks so perfect, you can't believe this training is for killing people.

MOIRA
(writing) January 31st, 1942

Dear Allan,

The Russians are holding their own against the Germans on the Don River. If the weather is anything like it is in Alberta, I'll bet they're regretting that Hitler ever got the second front idea. And speaking of second fronts, I've been thinking about going out to work. Dot wants to get an apartment somewhere in Edmonton, near the base. I haven't told Dad yet about either plan. He's very old-fashioned about women working. You're not, are you? And once he hears about me moving out, he'll hit the roof. So I'm taking it one step at a time.

By the way, how DO you feel about women working?

ALLAN
(writing) Dear Moira,

In response to your previous question: just fine. In fact, I'm all for a fellow being supported and lazing about while the women do the work.

Soloed on Saturday. I feel like a million bucks, I greased the landing with the whole gang watching. I'm starting to feel like this flying stuff could be fun. If all goes well, I'll be finished EFTS in a few weeks, and then I might get some leave. How about a date with a dashing Spitfire pilot? I've been doing a lot better on aerobatics. I think they might believe I'm fighter pilot material.

(to himself, delighted) I scared the crap out of myself this morning. Austin and I were bullshitting each other about flying under the bridge down near Nanton. They say the span is only fifty feet, and the deck is only twenty-five odd feet above the water. So Austin says, "Staunton, you wouldn't have the guts to fly under that span," and I told him to follow me if he had the guts. We chased each other once we got out of sight of the tower. The guys are always doing that, pulling fake dog-fights, practicing Immelman turns on each other. In a Tiger, you feel the wind in your face, it's like flying in the Great War, you pull that stick over and roll her, and you feel just like Billy Frigging Bishop.

We finished by finding our way to the Old Man River. We flew down low into the valley, following the contour of the river. I was pretending it was a train line somewhere, and I was machine-gunning a Kraut munitions train.

I was side slipping around curves, turning the Moth on its side, pulling up to clear obstacles and letting the engine bite into the air. If I had made one mistake, I'd have been dead. I loved it.

MOIRA
(writing) February 10th, 1942

Dearest Allan,

I don't know how to tell you this except to tell you – the Feniaks just got a telegram saying that Norman has been confirmed Killed in Action. It didn't give many details, something about him being shot down while strafing a train in France.

It seems like a nightmare. I've seen the notices for others in the *Journal*, but the names have never meant anything until now. A memorial service will be held on March 3rd. I hope you can get home. I don't want to go through this without you.

Please write soon. I think about you constantly,

Love,
Moira

ALLAN
(writing) Dear Moira,

I can't tell you how sorry I am to hear of Norman's death. I will be home in three weeks for a few days before Service Flying School. Please keep me posted about the memorial. Let me know if there's anything I can do.

I have been posted to train on dual-engine aircraft, which probably means bombers.

MOIRA
(interrupts, speaking to herself) Thank God, he's being posted to bomber training. Surely he'll be safer in bombers.

ALLAN
(to himself) Because they're losing bomber crews at such an incredible rate.

(resuming his letter) I remember Norman with great admiration. He was a real leader and a man of deep conviction. It sounds corny, but I believe he gave his life in a struggle for democracy.

I am committed to taking up his battle if I can.

(to himself) And I will never fill his shoes.

— • —

Edmonton. ALLAN and MOIRA are outside the chapel after Norman Feniak's memorial service. MOIRA is preoccupied. She is thinking of Hector and Andromache. ALLAN is trying to work up his courage to propose.

MOIRA
It was a nice lunch…

ALLAN
Uh?

MOIRA
Did you get a chance to speak to the Feniaks?

ALLAN
Ya.... Mrs. Feniak couldn't even look at my face... just kept staring at my buttons...

MOIRA
"Funerals are for the living. The dead care not that we mourn for them."

ALLAN
I'll bet Norman was wearing his dress blues the last time she saw him. *(short pause)* Moira, I can't wait to get over there.

MOIRA
I know. Thank God the Americans are in it now... there's bound to be a second front soon. Germany can't survive with the Russians on one side and us on the other.

ALLAN
(looking at his watch) Four hours... train leaves at nine.... Look, Moira, I... we... Brantford's a long way off and I was wondering... will you write?

MOIRA
(sensing his real intentions) Of course I will... you'll have another leave after Service Flying School. Don't *you* forget to write, okay?

ALLAN
Sure... do you mind if we walk home?

MOIRA
Four hours... you'll want to see your folks.

ALLAN
Ya, but it's just... God, Moira, there are some things I want to say.

MOIRA
Not here, okay? Let's walk.

> *They link arms. MOIRA and ALLAN address the audience, as if remembering the scene from the future:*

While we walked, it started raining...

ALLAN
I had the ring right in my pocket.

MOIRA
I could tell he was crying. But he'd put out his hand and say, "It's sure coming down, eh?"

ALLAN
For two weeks I'd planned how I'd ask her. But it wouldn't have been fair.

MOIRA
I knew what he wanted to say.

ALLAN
Her letter said, "I think about you constantly…"

MOIRA
But I just kept seeing Norman's face, like we used to know him, not a care in the world…

ALLAN breaks away from MOIRA.

ALLAN
Next leave, after Brantford, there'd be time to think, to get it right…

ALLAN takes his place back at his desk.

MOIRA
(to audience) That's when I decided, if I was going to lose another man it wouldn't be sitting at home, hoping for a letter, dreading a telegram. There was a place for me somewhere.

Black.

— • —

When lights return, ALLAN and MOIRA are in their own spaces. He is writing from Service Flying Training School in Brantford. She is in Edmonton.

ALLAN
(writing) March 20th, 1942
Brantford, Ontario.

Dear Moira,

Service Flying Training School has been a real eye-opener. We're working at a much higher intensity. Right now, I am training on Ansons. The Anson is a funny sort of aircraft that looks like a flying school bus, but is very forgiving to fly.

ALLAN, shaken, confides to the audience:

Williamson was making a blind approach under the hood. No one really knows what happened. He was coming in with no problem, textbook approach, when the starboard wing lifted. No apparent reason. Maybe he panicked, stopped believing the instruments. But the port tip caught the runway, the plane sort of bounced onto its nose, then started to cartwheel. It was like watching a ride at some macabre carnival. We all ran out to the crash, lifted the aircraft off its back. The fuel was leaking out. We were terrified. But no fire. Just Williamson, his neck broken, and the instructor, whose face was pretty badly smashed up, and who never stopped cursing a blue streak at us all the time we were lifting him out, his shin bone sticking right out through his trousers.

ALLAN nervously takes out a cigarette and lights it.

MOIRA takes out a cigarette and lights it.

MOIRA
(to the audience) What's good for the gander is good for the goose. Dad says it's unladylike, so I chew a lot of Sen-Sen before I go home.

ALLAN
(butts out his cigarette, to audience) I didn't used to smoke. But at I.T.S. our Flight Sergeant used to stop for smoke breaks. Anybody who didn't smoke would have to work while everybody else sat around. You don't have to hit me over the head with no ball-peen hammer.

— • —

ALLAN
But the worst part is the swearing. At Manning Depot, it was obvious that those who didn't pepper their vocabulary with every four-letter word weren't tough enough to make the grade.

I was shocked! Jesus, I was a lamb! But by the time of that first leave, I got off the train and there was Mom. I ran up and threw my arms around her.

"MOM!" I yelled, "Fuck, it's good to see you!"

He shakes his head in self-mocking disgust.

MOIRA
(writing) Dear Allan,

I've taken a job up at Blatchford Field in Edmonton, where I can get near the war effort. There's going to be a lot of flyers there, so it's a way to stay close to you as well. My father's opinion is, "You should be at home helping your mother." He's afraid of what might happen to his little girl out on the base with all those dashing young airmen.

There are boys from all over the world.

(to herself) And God are they good-looking. I mean, some of them are. *(pause)* No. They all are. *(She laughs.)*

(writing) It's a long trip from the farm every morning. The train lands me downtown at seven-thirty, and then it's a dash to the streetcar which gets me to the airfield just before eight. My job is fun, and that's the main reason I'm doing it. Well, that and the money – thirty cents an hour! Get this – I'm driving a transport truck at the field. At first I thought that they weren't going to accept me because I'm a woman, but then I realized that more than half the drivers are. Say what you want, but the war has made some room for us, and I'm glad of it. I'm enjoying myself at work, at least now that the weather has gotten warmer, and very much enjoying the looks on people's faces when they ask me what I'm doing and I tell them I'm a truck driver.

ALLAN
(writing) Dear Moira,

Well, well. The home front mustn't be a very safe place any more with you behind the wheel. But seriously, I'm not a bit surprised that you're doing what in peacetime would be considered a man's job...

MOIRA
(interrupts) "What in peacetime...?" Just you wait.

ALLAN
(writing) In the press, they're always trumpeting on about "Heroic Soviet women taking their places on the firing line." Sooner or later, I guess women will even be flying operationally. Though not in my lifetime, I hope.

MOIRA
(responds) Dear Smarty pants,

For your information, I am enclosing a newspaper article from the *Journal*.

ALLAN
(reading the clipping) "Recent aptitude tests have shown that women actually do better than men at jobs requiring manipulation dexterity."

(to himself) They faked the tests.

MOIRA
(writing) June 13th, 1942

Dear Allan,

Maybe it was poor timing, but tonight at supper is when I told my parents that Dot and I are getting an apartment in Edmonton. I don't think my folks think much of Dorothy, my dad made a few remarks that were very insinuating. Because Dot wears make-up, I suppose, or because she doesn't mind what she says to anybody. That's part of the reason I want to make this move. Our house is like a permanent funeral with Peter missing; Mom looks terrible, and Dad is taking it just as hard, though he tries not to show it.

> *She confides to the audience:*

Dad feels guilty it's Peter and not him.

I think he's drinking an awful lot.

— • —

MOIRA
(writing) You must be getting near the end of Service Flying School. Any plans about your leave? I know a certain girl who'd love to go out dancing with you.

(She confides.) I'd like to do more than dance with him.

(writing) Can't wait to see you,
Love and a few kisses. A few hundred, that is.

> *The RCAF Air Force March is heard. ALLAN puts on his dress tunic.*

ALLAN
(*writing*) Dear Moira,

I've been posted overseas! That's the good news. The bad news is, the posting is taking effect immediately. It's a rotten piece of luck for us, but the fact is, they're starting up a brand new Canadian Bomber Group, and I want to be in on the ground floor.

I'll let you know how it is in dear old Blighty. I'm sorry, Moira, I was looking forward to seeing you, but there's a war on.

Keep writing.

Love,
Allan

> *ALLAN stands at attention, on parade. He salutes, proudly.*
>
> *MOIRA reads his letter. It makes her furious. She crumples the paper and throws it away.*

MOIRA
"There's a war on!"

> *Pause. She picks the letter up. She sits.*

— • —

MOIRA
(*writing*) Dear Allan,

I know how much it means to you to finally get into it.
I'd have liked to have seen you with your wings.

(*to herself, angrily*) But you had to rush into the goddamned war.

(*writes, hiding her anger*) I will miss you desperately. (*erases the last word*) I will miss you very much.

Love,
Moira

Second Movement: Letters Overseas

ALLAN
(*writing*) My first letter from overseas and I'm in ecstasy having received your four letters this morning...

MOIRA
(*to audience*) ...four?

ALLAN
(writing) I could tell there were a couple missing…

MOIRA
…more like a dozen…

ALLAN
(writing) …but things being the way they are, I'll just have to be patient. Some of the boys haven't received a thing, and they look so low when they see me poring over your letters again and again.

To top it off, a parcel arrived this morning from the T. Eaton Co. with wool socks, tooth powder, shaving soap, and a flashlight! I'm not sure what I'm allowed to tell you in letters, but if we mention anything specific, it'll get a quick clip from the censors…

MOIRA
(to herself) "Loose lips sink ships."

ALLAN
But here's a laugh for you! The ship we were on was packed with onions.

MOIRA
(directly to ALLAN) Onions!

ALLAN
(directly to MOIRA) Yes, onions! In every nook, onions! Under every bunk, onions! On the deck, between the depth charges, in the mess hall, underfoot everywhere, bags and bags of onions! But at least we were going too fast for any U-boats to catch us…

MOIRA
(writing) I know… your sister wrote me a note. Being in signals, she had the information, and she wrote, "It's nice that Allan will get to see the late king's wife." *The Queen Mary*, of course! Fastest ship in the world!

ALLAN
(writing) I wasn't supposed to say where I made that last phone call from, though.

MOIRA
New York! She added at the bottom: "Have a Happy New Year!" underlining the "N" and the "Y". If it hadn't been October, I might not have caught on.

ALLAN
It's "hurry up and wait" for us right now. Marching during the day and getting acquainted with what the English sarcastically call beer in the evenings. Don't worry, I'm taking it easy in that area. I'm eager to be posted. I'll have more news later, but all I can tell you right now is the food is terrible, the fellows are great, I'm sure to be active soon, and most of all, I love you with all my heart.

All my love,
Allan.

MOIRA
(*writing*) November 11th, 1942

Dear Allan,

Today is Armistice Day. We all went down to the cenotaph this morning. Your dad was there, stumping along with the rest of the Great War vets. They are starting to look old, and the ranks are thinning. One wonders what they are all thinking as the news from Europe, Africa, Russia, and the South Pacific covers the headlines. Are they dying to be in it? Or do they feel relief. One thing I do know: that simple ceremony means so much to me, especially with Norman gone, and Peter, about whom we still have no word. I don't think anyone had a dry eye. For a country with so little military tradition, we sure have sacrificed a lot of our people.

— • —

MOIRA
(*to herself*) The women who were waiting for the boys to come back home after Vimy are still waiting for their life to start.

Not me.

ALLAN
(*writing*) Number Three Personnel Receiving Centre is in Bournemouth, a former resort area on the south coast of England. Our digs are quite spiffy. We've taken over the hotels in the area.

MOIRA
(*trying to make sense of ALLAN's visibly censored letter*) "There's little holiday spirit left, though."

ALLAN
(*writing*) There's little holiday spirit left, though. The beaches have been mined and strewn with barbed wire waiting for the German invasion. Bofors guns are stationed every half-mile or so and manned by Home Guard, who take a few useless shots at any Jerries who stray too low going to and from raids...

MOIRA
(*reading*) "We're earnestly resented by the locals."

ALLAN
We're earnestly resented by the locals, who remember better days without us Canucks crowding their pubs and tennis courts.

   MOIRA, puzzled, holds up ALLAN's letter, which is full of the holes the censor has cut in it.

MOIRA
(*dryly*) He's in the silent service!

(*writing*) My dearest Allan,

Apartment life is quite interesting, especially with a roommate like Dot. She's what we call a real cut-up around here.

— • —

MOIRA
(to audience) I just wish she'd warn me when she's bringing a fellow home…

ALLAN
(writing) My dearest Moira,

I'm still waiting for word on posting. In the meantime, we're often at loose ends to keep from getting bored to death.

(to audience) Getting drunk in the middle of the day was a new experience. Then it was going at it two days in a row. So was waking up with a head the size of the Macdonald Hotel and staggering to roll call. Luckily, they don't expect us to march anymore, so we're generally cut loose before noon.

(writing) I've done a couple of courses at a base near here. Some of the lucky dogs with over 500 hours have been posted. Guys like me with under 400 will have to wait our turn. Your neighbour, J.B., went yesterday.

MOIRA
J.B.… Jimmy Banes!

ALLAN
(writing) I think about you constantly…

(to audience) …especially when I see the shining faces of the English girls… birds, they call them here. They think us quite a novelty. We string them along with stories about shoot-outs against tribes of wild Indians on Jasper Avenue, and buffalo runs down Saskatchewan Drive. Jimmy Banes's favourite line is, "Some day, honey, you'll have to come to Alberta and tour my gopher ranch."

(writing) Dot sounds like a lot of fun…

(to himself) …like a case of round heels and loose panties…

— • —

MOIRA
(writing) I was home on the weekend. Mom and Dad are well, and asked about you. I wasn't able to get over to see your folks this trip…

(to herself) His Dad is going to drive me nuts. He never fails to come up with something about the last war or Allan's certain death. Last time it was: "Well, Moira, dear, when all is said and done, I know he'll go clean." Just what the hell does he mean by that?

ALLAN

(*writing*) Thanks for keeping in touch with Mom and Pop. I know this has been hard on them both...

(*to audience*) The old man is probably driving her nuts. I don't think he will ever get his mind past the Great War. I can see him holding forth about Vimy. It's always...

MOIRA AND ALLAN

(*together*) "Two steps out of the trench and the bastards blew it clean off!"

MOIRA

(*to audience*) God, it's more than I can stand.

ALLAN

(*to audience*) My first action turned out to be from a distance. Me and two of my new buddies, Johnny Gregoire and Bev Smillie, were out for a stroll along the beach one morning when we heard what sounded like fireworks. It turned out to be two Kraut Stukas who had the bad luck to be spotted by a couple of Spitfires. The Spits came down on them out the sun; it was like sparrows on crows – a few bursts and the show was over. Only one of the Krauts got out. He opened his chute and we could see him picked up by coastal patrol a couple of minutes after he hit the drink. We ran almost two miles to get a look at the Jerry as he came off the boat.

What did he look like? Nothing special... just a chap... blond, kind of short, sturdy. No arrogance, no sneer or "Heil Hitler" as he passed us. He just looked at our tunics, for a second into our eyes. All I saw was relief. His war was over.

We walked back in silence. I was thinking: "Jesus Christ, there's a war on! Those bastards were shooting real bullets at one another...

When we reached the lobby, a fellow from down the hall yelled over, "Hey Staunton, did you hear about Jimmy Banes?"

I shook my head, figuring with Jimmy, it had to do with too much booze or skirt.

"He was killed a couple of days ago. Training flight. Burnt to a crisp."

ALLAN walks to his desk, begins composing a new letter.

Dear Mr. and Mrs. Banes,

I had the privilege of rooming with your son, Jimmy, when we arrived overseas...

MOIRA

(*writing*) April 18th, 1943

Dearest Allan,

I've received a promotion! Eat your words, flyboy! I'm now on fuel trucks or what we call bowsers, but you probably know the term. I call it a promotion because it's a lot closer to the action. I'm fueling up mostly trainers – Harvards, Ansons, and the odd Tiger Moth...

ALLAN

(*writing*) Dearest Moira,

Sorry I haven't written sooner. I've been through a lot of changes lately and been kept busy with my training. I can't tell you where I'm based, or even what kind of airplane I'm now flying. Suffice to say that the plane is not from the house of York, if you read your Shakespeare.

MOIRA

(to herself) Not from the house of York... Lancaster! He's flying Lancasters?

(writing) I dropped in on the Feniaks last weekend. They asked about you. They took me up to Norman's room and it would bring you to tears to see how Mrs. Feniak has kept it as if Norman was still in high school and expected home any moment for lunch. By the look Chester gave me I could tell he was distressed. I hope she gets on with things soon.

ALLAN

(continues) Always happy to receive your letters. News from home is swell, even if it's just about how many eggs your mother picked on Saturday.

Thanks loads for the cigs. Believe me, nine hundred a month isn't too many.

The enclosed snap is of our crew. I've written their names on the back and where they're from. The guy with the Stetson is our Wireless Air Gunner, "Cowboy." He's always bragging about how many Krauts he's going to shoot down... *(short pause)* The short guy on the left, Roy Toane, was our rear gunner. He isn't with us anymore.

Was at the pub last night, we're not flying, due to a... little mishap. After our next op, we're due to go on leave for a while, and I'm going to take the train down to London, poke about in the big city and see Saint Paul's and all that.

I think of Norman often.

Much love...

(to audience) My first op on a Lancaster last night. Scotty gets up beside me in the cockpit. I look at him: "Scotty, do you know how to start one of these fucking things?" "Don't yooou?" he asks. "Hell no," I tell him. When I did my checkout, the training officer landed the goddamned thing and I got in while it was still running. We did a few circuits and bumps, and then he got out and said, "Looks like you've got it, off you go."

So Scotty and I, our first operational flight, we don't know how to start the goddamn airplane. We figured it out eventually, and got off okay. But does that plane fly, like a fighter after the Hallybag and the Wimpy.

Unfortunately, we had a brush with Jerry over the target.

A Folke Wolf 190 caught up to us after we had released our bombs. The first I knew that we'd been attacked was when I noticed she was yawing to port, and then the rear turret fired. When Roy didn't talk to us, our mid-upper, Sandy Smith, crawled back to the rear turret and tried to force the door. He couldn't. The kite was shot up badly, I had no port rudder control. We got down all right using a series of right-hand turns, which the controller wasn't pleased about, but a kite in one piece, even full of holes, is better than a mess on his runway, I guess.

all that isn't said ends up as reportage

As we shut down, Sandy jumped out and hurried round the back with the erks. What a mess. The perspex was shattered. Roy was lying in a pool of blood, unconscious, but he came to as we were lifting him out of the turret. His left eye was simply dangling from the side of his face. I don't know how he was enduring the pain. I guess you just do.

The odd thing is, Roy managed to shoot the guy down. On his first pass, the German was apparently just trying to knock out the rear gunner. I suppose he thought he'd succeeded, and seeing the turret, you could see why. For one thing, Roy's guns were jammed in one position. So the Kraut, thinking he'd have all night to chop us up, flew right past Roy's gun-sight, and Roy pulled the trigger. Said he could see the tracer flying right into Jerry's cockpit. The 190 rolled over and fell away, then Roy blacked out.

They say they may be able to save most of the vision in the other eye, but they'll have to sort of rebuild the left side of his face.

We'll be assigned a new tail gunner in a day or two.

— • —

MOIRA
(*writing*) July 6th, 1943

You won't believe it! The old hometown just went over 100,000! Of course it's all the Americans that have moved in to help build the highway to Alaska.

The whole city has a new look. A lot of their money has been put into rinks, tennis courts and the like, and renovating some older buildings, like the Jesuit College. I can't wait to go to one of those new hamburger emporiums with you.

But you sure can't mistake the Yankees. They don't seem to go anywhere without making some sort of noise. Maybe it's their cars, their swagger, their pockets full of money, but mostly it's the attitude they have that we should all be very grateful they're here.

Your Dad says it was the same in 1917 when they landed in France. Mayor LaGuardia of New York visited in July and the *Bulletin* reported that he said Edmonton was "a most attractive city… from the air." Imagine the nerve!

(*to audience*) Dot just loves the Yanks. She says Huck Finn's a hell of a lot more fun than Oliver Twist. I didn't even know Dot read.

(*writing*) Your folks invited me to picnic with them last week, and a number of their troops had taken over most of Borden Park. I can't say I was impressed with their behaviour.

(*to audience*) …or the behaviour of some of the local girls who hung on them like scarves. But there really is something about young men in uniform. They kept looking over my way, I'm sure because they feel that any unattached woman is fair game.

— • —

MOIRA
(to audience) "Jesus Christ on skis," Dot tells me, "you don't know what you're missing, honey!" What she doesn't know is that I get to chat up boys from almost anyplace over at the field. I'm usually dressed in coveralls, but that doesn't stop them from leaning out of their jeeps to see what they can see. The Yanks are bad, but nothing like the Aussies.

ALLAN
(writing) September 28th, 1943

Dear Moira,

When you mentioned the Yanks working at home in your last letter, you probably heard me laugh right over the Atlantic. You ought to see them here.

Up until now, we've kind of had the run of the place. The Brits accepted us as their poor cousins from the colonies. The Americans of the United States Army Air Force, known as the 8th, act like they own the place. They get paid about twice what we Canadians do, and about three times what the Brits do.

There's always a gang of them bellied up to the bar, throwing five-pound notes around and making fun of everything English.

But we get our own back sometimes. They wear a lot of medals on their tunics, which by the way are pink, of all colours. Anyhow we have a guy in our squadron, ex-Mountie, who likes to approach some Yank in a bar and gaze with mock-awe at the victim's chest and say, "Gosh, look at that beautiful medal. What'd you get that for, eating your breakfast?

(to himself) What really bothers me is that the sons of bitches travel in hordes, so you're sitting in some pub chatting up a bird and thinking you're making progress, when about fifty of them will come in and take the place over. Right away the bird knows that she can graduate from bitter to Scotch, and you know you've either got to talk faster, or dig deeper.

> *ALLAN suddenly feels the cold. He puts on his tunic, his battle-dress, and his greatcoat. He's still cold.*

— • —

ALLAN
(writing) Your package arrived in time for Christmas. A welcome sight, and thanks for wrapping it so well. It keeps the contents out of "enemy" hands.

MOIRA
(writing) So glad to hear my parcel arrived. The cigarettes aren't hard to get, but finding that prepared chocolate was a stroke of luck.

(to audience) Dot picks it up from one of her Yankee boyfriends. I don't want to know the details.

(writing) I surprised Mom and Dad by bringing Dot home for Christmas dinner. I think they expected the worst, but believe it or not, she brightened the place up,

just what the doctor ordered. After dinner she traded farming stories with Dad, and then got everyone into a singsong at the piano. When she sang "I Wonder Who's Kissing Her Now," you could have knocked Mom and Dad over with a feather. They'd really taken a liking to her by the time we left.

(to audience) We didn't want to miss the dance.

ALLAN

(writing) The prepared chocolate is "bang-on" as they say here. Just add water and mix. A real hit with the guys! If you ever find more...

MOIRA

(calling offstage) Dottie! Who's on for tonight? *(to herself)* Oh, Christ, I can't believe I said that.

ALLAN

(writing) The five-day I wangled in early December was great! I took in the sights of Edinburgh.

— • —

ALLAN

(to audience) Queen Street! Eight blocks of pubs that do us more damage than the Luftwaffe ever could. The legend is that no one has ever had a drink in every pub and lived to tell the tale. I tried. I failed. But it was an historic piss-up. A ten-hour blur, a League of Nations of laughing, singing, slap-on-the-back, hail fellows well met, the shoulder flashes announcing Brits, Canucks, Yanks, Norwegians, Free French, Poles...

I started at one end with my right pocket full of half crowns. A shilling a beer, a shilling a gin, the change going into my left, so I was listing badly to port by the time I admitted defeat. It was in a pub where a Canadian artillery sergeant had taken over the piano, and we settled in to endless choruses of...

ALLAN sings ditties from the following songs, in various accents: "Don't Sit Under the Apple Tree," "Good Night Irene," "Red River Valley," and especially "Rum and Coca-Cola."

He suddenly feels ill.

How I ended up in the hostel, facedown on my pillow, I'll credit to that angel who hovers over sweethearts, fools, and drunks.

(writing) I'm not suffering from lack of things, and I know you are making sacrifices at home, too.

MOIRA

(to audience) Sugar was just cut from three-quarters to half a pound a week, tea and coffee by half, and meat...well, I'm lucky Mom and Dad are on the farm. Canning season was hard on Mom last year, so Dad butchered a bull and I traded meat to some of the girls for their sugar rations. The sign in the store says: "Loyal citizens do not hoard." What are they going to do, shoot me?

Third Movement: Lies and Valentines

MOIRA
(writing) February 14th, 1944

Dear Allan,

I'm so glad about the good news from the South Pacific. The Americans are really giving it to the Japanese, and with any hope, there will soon be a new front. The really big news, though, is that it's just Valentine's Day, and so I'm sending you this by way of a Valentine, and asking, "will you be mine?"

(re-reading) "Will you be mine…?" Jesus.

(erasing, then writing) Your letter certainly perked up my spirits, just what I needed as I was home on the weekend and made the rounds to see your parents and then over to the Feniaks. Your Mom and Dad were fine, except that your Dad complained bitterly about rationing, somehow wondering aloud why a veteran of the Great War had to make sacrifices again.

ALLAN
(writing) Dear Moira,

Well, another year passes, and we're still at it. It seems we've been going at this forever, I really don't know how the Krauts can keep it up, fighting a war on three fronts, because they are, whatever the papers say.

I'm in London, managed to wangle a 3-day leave. As I write to you, I'm just preparing to go out for another night on the town, would you believe it? "Where to?" some conductor will ask. "Piccadilly," I'll say, just like I was saying, "Jasper and First." Still haven't been in St. Paul's, but I've been past it twice a day. Leave ends tomorrow, and I'm attending a little party tonight put on at the home of one of the foreign diplomats, one of the perks we get for being shot at."

(to audience) She had a strange manner about her, and I don't just mean about her accent. As though all the time she spent with me she was really half thinking of other things.

— • —

She is Polish, and she speaks with a heavy Slavic rumble. Very alluring. But that didn't stop this Brit colonel from sidling up to me and whispering, "Nice, but a bit colourful, what?" I didn't know what the hell he was talking about. "Jewish," he says.

The CO introduced me and told her I was from Western Canada. "I suppose you, how you call it, lasso leetle beefs?" she says. I'm trying to be clever, I say, "No ma'am, I don't lasso little beefs, I just put up with them from the crew."

Which just goes to show you should never crack jokes with foreigners. "Mr. Cowboy," she says, "I want you should dance with me tonight." So I did. It was very good. We parted at the end of the night, but she gave me her address.

MOIRA
(writing) There was a big dance out at the field last night, everyone was there. I didn't want to go, but Dot convinced me. You've got to meet her, she's as crazy as a bedbug. Mart Kenny's band was playing – who says we're making sacrifices? I did have one or two drinks, but nothing untoward happened.

Oh I must tell you about the nice Norwegian pilot I met. He came up to me suddenly and explained in his broken English that I reminded him of his sweetheart back home.

(to herself, confessional) Ingvar Norqvist. He's a Norwegian. Very tall, and blond. He flies. He's in training on the base. He's onto Harvards now. He speaks English almost like an Englishman. Those long vowels. *(imitating)* "How do you do?"

He escaped Norway in 1940, skiing out part of the way, and then he and three friends took a small open boat into the North Sea. He was eighteen at the time. His life is like a novel. They killed his brother. *(beat)* He is so sad.

Dot introduced us at the dance. She is terrible. "Ingvar, this is my friend Moira. Did you know Moira means fate in Greek?" With a terrible glinting smile at me.

We danced. He is awkward, doesn't have a feel for swing at all. I had to teach him. He held me very close. He needs something. So do I...

I think I'm in love.

— • —

ALLAN
(writing) Dear Moira,

This last leave spent in London one of the most interesting times I've had since coming over.

(to audience) I spent the whole thing in her apartment. We screwed like maniacs.

MOIRA
(writing) "Work at the base is hum-drum. Dot says hello."

(to audience) Dot is pregnant.

ALLAN
(writing) London is all blacked out of course, so at night there's an almost eerie darkness on the streets, and people walk around like ghosts, with their voices low, as though the Germans could hear them.

(to audience) Walking home you can hear all the pros and the tarts, also known as Piccadilly Commandos, in the doorways. Christ, I swear half this city is gone completely nymphomaniac, they do it in doorways, up alleys, they'd use the phone booths if they thought they'd fit.

MOIRA
(writing) I went out to a big V-bond party with some friends.

(to audience) I left with Ingvar. We siphoned some gas from my truck. We drove out to Cooking Lake. It was... very romantic.

ALLAN AND MOIRA
(together, to audience) Why do all of his/her letters sound so phony?

ALLAN
(writing) Of course, London isn't in anything like the danger it was in during the real blitz, but they're taking no chances, and the squareheads still make the occasional raid to prove their bomber forces are still in it. Even though they're not, of course, ha, ha, compared to what we're doing to them. You can't imagine what it's like, from twenty-five thousand feet, watching a city get pulverized by a thousand-bomber raid. And I don't cry for the Krauts. They asked for it, and we're giving it to them.

I wanted to visit St. Paul's as I told you, on the last leave, but once again it seemed damn hard to get around to it. The war... has done funny things to people, me included.

MOIRA
(to audience) I wrestle with it constantly... my shame and my desire. Even though Allan doesn't deserve this, I do...

(writing) You might be interested to know that I'm now in charge of transport operations for the entire field. My responsibilities include allocation, scheduling, filling in for sick drivers when the need arises. Yesterday, the base CO told me I was doing an excellent job. I like working, and I like the money it brings.

The war... has changed this little city very much. I wonder if you'd recognize it.

ALLAN
(writing) I wonder if you'd recognize me.

MOIRA AND ALLAN
(together) If I should appear to have changed when next we meet, please don't be too shocked.

MOIRA
(to herself) Oh, drat it all! *(erases her last remark)*

ALLAN
(to himself) Fuck. *(erases his last remark)*

MOIRA AND ALLAN
(together) Well, I'll close,

Love,
Allan/Moira

— • —

ALLAN
(to himself) People don't know what it's like to go into hell one night and be pissed on champagne the next. They don't know how insane it is, how fucking funny, how... extreme. My 29th op tonight. Hanover. If I live, I'm going to tell the CO to put me up for another thirty. Then a fortnight in London. I'm going to stay drunk. And stay with her.

MOIRA
(tries to write a "Dear John" letter) Dear Allan,

I have not received a letter from you for several weeks now. I don't know what this means, but I pray to God that it doesn't mean you're injured or ki– missing. I have to tell you that I have been remiss in writing because...

(to audience) Because why? Because everything has changed in our little lives. Because I've been working at my own job, a difficult, responsible job. Because everything is so much more important than one individual. Because I can't stand knowing whether or not you're dead at the moment I'm writing these letters.

(writing) I've been remiss in writing because... I've been doing a great many other things. And because I've been doing some other dating. I recently met a Norwegian pilot who's in the Commonwealth Air Training Plan here. He's going to be finished soon, and then he will be leaving, posted somewhere in Europe. He is a very nice fellow, Allan, and I...

I can't write this.

She crumples up the unfinished letter, throws it away.

Fourth Movement: On Ops

ALLAN
(to the audience) Dusk falls. The nervous lorry ride out to dispersal. Our Lanc, D for Dumbo, is way out at the end of the runway, so we're last to get off the truck. Charlie goes and pisses against the rear wheel. We used to bug him about it, ask him why he didn't wait till we were all in the aircraft so we wouldn't tread in it. Now, after twenty-nine ops with only one casualty, nobody bugs him any more.

The flight engineer and I go round the kite and check the tire pressure, the oleos, the control surfaces and cables. Every now and then you hear about some poor bastard who didn't take off his rudder or elevator locks. Smoke and tar at the end of the runway.

When I first saw the Lanc I thought she was kind of ugly. Like a great big insect with bulbous protrusions all over her. But when you see her from some angles. From behind, quarter-view, you see how beautiful those fat wings are, even the huge tail surfaces, you can feel the power of her design, the perfect utility of what she was designed to do. And what she was designed to do is hanging in the bomb bay. Thousand pounders to break things apart, gas and water mains, then incendiaries to set the whole thing on fire. And four big beautiful Merlins to bring you back safe.

I pat the left rudder, then the right, pound on the back of the rear turret, and then walk once clockwise completely around the plane. Don't ask me why, I just do it. Then I get in. Climbing up to the cockpit over the main spar isn't easy with all your kit. The guys try not to think about what it would be like to try to get to the rear exit with the aircraft hit and spinning in the dark. I strap myself in, plug in the oxygen, usually pull a few deep breaths to clear the head. We check oxygen supply and intercom, and I ask everybody to report standing by. When I've finished the cockpit check, I signal the ground crew: Start 'em!

The noise of airplane engines, growing in volume, as the lights fade on ALLAN, suspended like a statue of a man, going forward to an uncertain future.

ACT II

ALLAN is in his airplane.

ALLAN
(shouting the first words) START EM!

> *The noise of the engines begins. It continues, all the way till the end of this speech.*

Four engines, port to starboard. Set revs for 1000 rpm, let 'em warm up, then check pitch control for each engine at 2800, throttle back to plus six thrust and check mag drop.

We taxi out, feeling the low bounce of the wheels carrying the heavy weight of the bomb load. Control the speed with the handbrake, steer with the outer engines. Before turning onto the runway, final runup check: trim, revs, flaps, mag drop, pressure. Okay. Onto the runway. There's a flare from the hut. All right, boys? This is it. Line her up, apply the brakes and give her all four throttles. I wave the engineer away, I'll do this one myself. The noise builds, unbelievable nearly, the Merlins howling. She's bucking to move. I let off the brakes and she begins to roll, slow and lumbering at first, but gathering speed rapidly. Christ, the torque is pulling us to starboard, I roll back the port outer throttle and she corrects herself. The tail wheel lifts off and I have some control with the rudder now. Quick glance at the airspeed. 85... 90. She gently lifts her wheels off the deck and the bumping stops. I hold her low to get the ground effect, build up airspeed. Pull up the nose, now, she wants to fly, up she climbs at 165 knots. What a feeling. God.

The ground disappears rapidly now, it's nearly dusk. We climb to set course altitude, joining the first off and waiting for the others. Check the time. Right. Steer one zero five by the gyro. We're on our way. Now the routine starts. Nav? ETA to turning point, please. Two hours, twenty minutes. We're gradually climbing to tonight's bombing height, 23,000. I fiddle with the trim, feel the urge to piss, suppress it, try to relax.

First crisis, flak from the Dutch coast. Jerry never fails to get a shot at us. We're flying over eight-tenths cloud and the bastards are still uncannily accurate. They have radar control, and their predictors work very well. I begin to weave gently, maybe a useless exercise. At least it's something. For chrissake keep an eye out, guys. Our biggest danger is running into one of our own kites.

— • —

We reach the turning point over Arnheim and try to fool the Germans by making a turn onto our main target. As if Jerry is fooled. Christ there's eight hundred bombers in the stream, Jerry isn't stupid, he knows exactly where we're headed. Into the fucking Ruhr valley again. Into the valley of death. There's a goddamn garden party waiting for us. The searchlights form a reception line. Security is now a joke. You wait for one of the blue lights to cone you. The flak is all over the sky now. A burst close enough that I swear I can hear it over the engines, and the mid-upper reports that he can hear the shrapnel against the fuselage. I'm fighting the control column now, the turbulence from all the explosions. There's enough light that we can catch occasional silhouettes from the rest of the bomber stream.

O Christ, they've found us with the blue light. God, the cockpit lights up like somebody was using a blowtorch in here. Jesus, the rest of the lights will cone me in a second, and then we're dead. Dive straight into the light, hard port rudder, full left aileron. We're going downhill fast, 22 thousand, 21, 20, 19, 18. The light is still incredibly bright, I can't see a fucking thing. Somebody is screaming into the intercom. Shut up, you asshole, SHUT UP! I jink left, then right… I lose the bastard! But now I'm diving nearly out of control, airspeed exceeding 325, Jesus, with a full load of bombs. Have to haul her out. Pull off the power, and I'm hauling back with all my strength. It's like wrestling an elephant. The trim! I roll it back all the way. Down to three thousand feet, and the nose is just starting to come up. Holy Christ, we're not going to make it. We're below the surrounding hills! Something inside my brain shuts down. I'm not aware of any fear, anywhere, just me and this control column. Pull!

The plane starts to come out of the dive, and I'm pressed down into my seat by the G-force. The blood is draining out of my head, I'm half-dizzy. We are going to make it, we are going to make it. The nose comes up at last, I can hear something creaking. God bless the people that built this airplane!

God, we're starting to climb up! We need power: I run the throttles up. Two of the Merlins roar, one coughs, one chokes completely. Jesus H Christ. Jock, get that port inner started again! Somebody's mumbling in my headset, Jesus it's Jimmy in the tail turret, he's saying Hail Marys, the Catholic sonovabitch. Jimmy, shut up for chrissake.

Jock has the engines all going now and we're climbing. Give me a course to target, Ed. No, I'm not going to jettison and go home, they won't even give us credit for the mission. How will they know? *I'll know.* Besides, there's the cameras. We'll join the bomber stream late and drop from twenty thousand. George, bring that bottle up here, will you, I have to piss something terrible.

As we approach Essen, there's no doubt about the location of the target. The whole horizon is one big conflagration Christ, we're pounding the hell out of it tonight. The flak is terrible. Two miles to port, there's a flame in the sky where someone has an engine on fire. The fireball is gradually descending. Jesus Christ, boys, get out before it goes. I hope to God it's nobody I know. Flak everywhere, occasionally you can see tracer.

The bomb aimer takes control of the aircraft. All I have to do is the only thing every nerve ending is screaming at me not to do: fly straight and level and give the bastards a perfect target. I slump down in my seat, so I can't see, and fly blind where the bomb aimer wants me. Charlie is very good. He's leaning over his sights in the nose, talking calm and low. I hold her steady as I can. Open bomb doors! Bombs away! The aircraft lurches upward, freed of five tons weight. We have to hold course for another two minutes for the cameras. I've got the wind up seriously now, the flak gunners seem to be getting our range. Fifteen seconds more and we'll turn to port and dive away from this shit.

O CHRIST we've been hit. Like a giant bashed us with an almighty hammer. ENGINEER WHAT'S GOING ON. Everyone report. Oh Christ it's Sandy in the mid-upper, he's caught some flak, SHUT UP GODDAMN YOU STOP SCREAMING. Something is vibrating like crazy, my hands are being nearly shaken off the yoke, and now I see the flame licking out of the starboard inner HIT THE FIRE EXTINGUISHER and feather SHIT the hydraulics have packed in the goddamn prop can't be feathered and we're yawing to starboard. What am I thinking? Dive starboard... the engine fire is like a beacon to the fighters. I crank the column over, mush through a 30 degree turn and start praying she doesn't spiral on me with God knows what damage to the control surfaces. But she comes out flat and level oh you beautiful bird. I trim the rudder to keep us flying straight against the pull of the extra port engine. GIVE ME A COURSE, Ed, tell me how to go home, straight home. God knows how much fuel we've lost or how much we need. I settle in for two and a half hours of being shaken by this wounded airplane. Jock has stopped the fuel flow to the dead engine, and is figuring out how to juggle his reserves. The mid is mercifully not on intercom now, he's been given morphine and is lying over the main spar.

Now the battle of nerves, flying a wounded kite all the way home, the Krauts can track you on radar, they know you're travelling slow, and will have some speed merchant in a Mess 410 after you. Your watch becomes your enemy, you keep looking at it occasionally expecting half-hours to have passed and discovering that only minutes have.

After an hour you want to smoke, you want to sleep. Your attention wanders. I talk to the guys every few minutes, get them to check in, get them to keep watching. This is the time of awful danger, you need to close your eyes, you think it's over. The first glimmerings of light on the horizon behind you. Perfect cover for the fighters coming up from below. I'm scanning the sky for cloudbanks to duck into if we're attacked. Of course, for once, the weather is ideal.

North Sea now, no flak opposition on the coast, I wonder why. Don't let us into that terrible cold sea. But the Merlins purr. We cross the coast. My left leg is shaking on the rudder. Crash positions, boys! We're given a circuit, of course the air is full of Lancs trying to get down. I tell them we've got wounded, and they put us first. Next crisis: the landing gear. Jock and I look at each other, cross fingers, select "down." We get greens, thank Christ. The flare path. Set her down, fly her on, God knows what speed she'll stall at with this damage, keep it over a hundred. We bounce once, twice, the port outer quits suddenly, we swing left. Images of the ambulance racing along the runway, the fire wagon. We leave the tarmac, the wheels dig into the grass, we slow down, slew sideways, the right tire explodes, this is all happening in slow motion, the oleo collapses, the wing digs in, I'm thrown left against the windows. We stop spinning. I reach over and shut the engines down. We're home.

The lights go down on the image of ALLAN, slumped in his chair. On the other side of the stage, MOIRA, in silhouette, takes off her blouse. She gestures to someone to be quiet. She lights a cigarette, and laughs. She sighs.

Black.

Fifth Movement: Fibre, Moral and Immoral

MOIRA and ALLAN, writing.

MOIRA
June 7th, 1944.

Dear Allan…

ALLAN
Dear Moira…

MOIRA
Oh, God, what great news about the invasion of France…

ALLAN
I have looked at a page of history. The second front has finally been opened on the beaches of Normandy…

MOIRA
We have lived with constant dread about the outcome of the war for three and a half years, but at last we can feel that there is some end in sight, and that our side is going to win.

ALLAN
We flew three raids yesterday, bombing German positions… at least we hope they were German positions, and the incredible array of ships, tanks and men was beyond imagination.

MOIRA
Everyone home was glued to the radio as Lorne Green read the news from the front. It is said that the Canadians are at the forefront of some of the fighting.

ALLAN
Everything was under a cloud of explosives, shellfire, and smoke from the ships trying to cover the men in the landing craft, but you could see, here and there, groups of men running up the beach, some of them collapsing like little tin soldiers…

MOIRA
Mother says we ought to pray for them, but I can't…

ALLAN
Canada has a whole division at Juno beach, and our guys have done well, I understand. We're not in their good books, though…

MOIRA
My own faith in God has been so shaken by the events of this war, I can't bring myself to pray.

ALLAN
One of our crews was ordered to fly in and drop antipersonnel bombs on some water tower, and after they finished their drop, they flew over a second water tower where the Germans actually were…

MOIRA
Gordon Priggit, Don Howard, John McConnogh, Jimmy Banes, Norman Feniak...

ALLAN
The guys feel sick, but what can you do?

MOIRA
I don't know who to be mad at. The Nazis are just indistinct characters in funny helmets. I'm mad at Prime Minister King, who's always trying to get his picture taken with Roosevelt and Churchill. And I look at all those pictures of guns and tanks and planes, and I think, those things aren't made for free, someone's getting profit out of them. And I wonder, if no one was making any money out of this war, would it have been going on so long?

She silently re-reads what she has written, then crumples it up. She starts again.

Dear Allan,

Oh, God, what great news about the invasion of France. At last, we can feel that there is some end in sight, and that our side is going to win...

ALLAN
(writing) Dear Moira,

I am writing to everyone back in Canada, to you, and to my folks and friends, to let you know that I will not be coming home within the foreseeable future. I have finished my first tour of duty...

MOIRA
(reading) His *first* tour of duty?

ALLAN
(writing) ...and I have volunteered for a second tour. I will probably be promoted, but I can't say that this is my motive. To tell you the truth, I can't exactly say why I want to stay over here. I wish I could tell you it was for patriotic reasons, but it's not.

(to himself) When I think about getting off the train in Edmonton, Alberta, and facing all those people. People who think that we're heroes. Last week, over Dortmund, we saw three of our kites go for a Burton in one minute. All flamers. Smitty, our Wireless Air Gunner, starts singing "it could happen to you, it could happen to you," and we're all nearly out of control. I think Charlie was on the verge of shooting him. I screamed at him to shut up, finally somebody hit him. When we got back, everyone hopped on the truck, but no Smitty. He wouldn't get out of the aircraft. I thought he was embarrassed, so I went back into the plane to get him. "Come on, Smitty," I told him, "nobody's going to blame you." He started crying. "I can't get onto that truck with them, Skipper," he says, "you see, I've shit myself, and I stink to high heaven."

MOIRA
(writing) Dear Allan,

The news of the D-Day invasion kept us glued to the radio here for weeks. I have been following the tracing of the battle lines on my European Atlas, at least as far as can be made out from the news broadcasts. The other day I was at The Bay looking for some shoes, and I heard two of the salespeople refer to our troops in Italy as the D-Day slackers. Can you imagine?

(to audience) The invasion is driving Ingvar out of his mind. He can't wait to be posted over there. When he talks about the Germans, his eyes turn pale, and if anyone even mentions Quisling, he stomps out of the room.

He is bound to be posted soon. What in God's name will happen if Ingvar is still here when Allan comes home?

ALLAN
(writing) Dearest Moira,

I must tell you about a funny experience that happened to me at a party in London several months ago. At the party I met a Polish woman, who had apparently once been very rich in her own country, but all her family's money was confiscated because they're Jewish. She asked me if I lassoes beefs, and I told her I didn't lasso any beefs, but that I'd been putting up with some from the crew, which I thought was kind of smart, but she didn't get the joke at all. Anyway, I thought it was kind of funny.

He looks up. He crumples the letter, discards it.

— • —

ALLAN
(to audience) The hell of being CB'd is not being able to get away... to get to London... her apartment... to lose myself in clean sheets... the smell of the perfume in her hair.

The worst of it is too much time to think... about how you're gonna get it... about that shell fragment grazing your ear from behind and knocking the compass off your panel... about the 109 pilot waving as he flew by your nose too low on petrol or ammo to make another pass... and you wonder what would've happened if you'd lifted off the tarmac half a second earlier, or if the armourers had squeezed one more 500-pounder into your bay, or if the 109 hadn't used up his ammo ripping the shit out of another kite.

MOIRA
(to audience) I get a little sick of them hanging around me when Ingvar isn't around. I should have known there'd be some who figure they can step in and take his place... when I reject them, they look at me like I'm diseased... piss on them.

ALLAN
(to audience) Oh, Bomber Command is real good with statistics. What they give us is big numbers of Kraut night fighters shot down and low ones on how many of our kites have gone for the chop. Shit, even those of us who're only sober half the time can figure it out. An air crew that lasts more than ten ops is pushing the odds.

And Christ, if we'd destroyed as much of Germany as Harris claims, there'd be nothing left but a huge hole from the Rhine to Berlin.

MOIRA
Even the dances don't seem so glamorous any more... those fresh young faces that once fascinated me... now they're just guys you'll never see again after six weeks.

ALLAN
I just hope it's quick... Like R-Robert over Stuttgart, floating along fifty yards off my starboard wing.... A kite one second... ka fuckin boom... garbage the next.

— • —

MOIRA
It really gets me when these guys who've been in Canada since '39 strut up with their brass all polished and expect you to lift your skirt. Christ, I've got to clean up my mouth. I still see Dot once in a while. God, the joys of motherhood. She came to a couple of dances afterwards, but the news was out.

ALLAN
I just don't want to have the North Sea rushing into my face, or a stray shell winging me, taking the controls out of my hands with six other guys depending on me.

MOIRA
(reading) "Allied airmen who parachuted into three unnamed places in central Germany Monday were killed by agitated people." Oh, Allan...

ALLAN
...or having to bail out... that's the worst. Who knows what happened to Norman. Even if he did get out of his kite, he could've ended up hanging in some town square for all we know. I keep having this dream, a dream that even a bellyful of gin can't drown. I'm falling into the blackest of holes when above me my chute opens... FOOMP... I look up... there's no chute... it's my first flying instructor, screaming at me... "Incompetent asshole! You screwed up again!" ...I look down and in the distance I see D-Dumbo hit the deck in a ball of flame. My crew's in that fire... I can hear them screaming.... Shit, my intercom's still on! I'm floating down... there's a crowd of people... they're reaching for me... I wake up...

MOIRA
We've got Paris now. You'd think they could let up on the German cities. It's got to be almost over. Oh, to lose you now...

ALLAN
"Cowboy" used to brag that he'd hidden his asthma from the M.O. when he'd enlisted. Last month they caught him with his face in a hole in his mattress. He was pounding on it, inhaling the dust till he was coughing blood. He's on his way home with L.M.F. across his discharge: Lack of Moral Fibre...

But you look around and see the rest of them coping. You drown the hours in the mess, sing the songs, tell the stories, and wait... eventually you coax her into the air and head for the Fatherland.

MOIRA
(*writing*) Dear Allan: The news from the front gets better day by day. Our boys in Holland, the Yanks across the Rhine, the Russians pushing to Berlin.

ALLAN
(*writing*) Sorry to have forgotten your Mother's birthday. Please give her my best. (*pause, then*) Do you remember Elmer Swanson from school?

MOIRA
(*to herself*) The Air Training program officially closed on the 31st, so it looks like I'll be back on Civvie Street soon.

ALLAN
I ran into him in London. He was in the Commandos from D-Day on and with the first Canadians over the Rhine. They came upon one of those German internment camps at a place called Bergen-Belsen. It had been used for Jews and anyone else the Nazis didn't feel was suited to the master race.

MOIRA
(*writing*) You may have some idea of the extent of the Training Plan. With it closing, we will suddenly find ourselves in a little provincial backwater again. My friend Ingvar, a Norwegian flyer that I have mentioned in another letter, is going to be posted any day now.

ALLAN
(*writing*) The few living were skeletons. The rest... thousands... were piled up like firewood. The survivors who knew English told of slave labour, torture, summary executions on the whim of the SS...

Believe me, you don't want to hear the rest.

MOIRA
(*to audience*) And I will be left here, watching a small yellow airplane fly into the sun.

Sixth Movement: Finding a Way Home

ALLAN
(*writing*) Dear Moira,

I'm kind of curious about what you're up to. I haven't heard from you for a while, and I'm wondering about this Norwegian flyer you've mentioned. Maybe I shouldn't write this, but I can't help but be curious. Write me a letter when you feel like it. It's been a strange time.

I probably won't be able to mail this for a while, security reasons. But I'm curious.

Affectionately yours,
Allan

MOIRA
(*thinking aloud*) "Affectionately yours?" (*pause*) He knows.

(writing) Dear Allan,

I received your letter today several weeks after it was written, and I can't make out the postmark. I wrote you about my pleasure on hearing that the end is at last in sight. I have to tell you that I don't know what you mean to imply with your remarks about Norwegian flyers, but I just want you to start considering what kind of pot you have on to boil before you start calling the kettle black.

ALLAN
(reading this, mutters) She knows.

MOIRA
(writing) March 8th, 1945

Dear Allan,

I have been procrastinating about writing this letter for several weeks. I feel cheap and cowardly about it, but I can't change the facts. For several months, I was seeing a young man who was with the BCATP here. His name is Invar Norqvist. He is a brave decent person and at this point I feel he's been more decent than me.

— • —

MOIRA
(to audience) He was like some Norse god. He was quiet and confident, and sometimes he flashed with anger. He had seen too much. Once, he told me what happened the day they escaped Norway. Sneaking house-to-house in the dark, and climbing down the city walls onto the frozen lake. The barking of the dogs, and the wild pursuit. Seeing his own brother collapse, shot dead, right beside him...

He was so hurt, so tender. So full of grim purpose. They all knew. No doubt about it. The times we left the dances early. The looks I asked him to conceal. He asked me to be strong. I pretended I was, and I became what I pretended. My mother fears what's happened, but she knows she has no authority now to forbid anything. I guess I could tell her that I'm still technically a virgin, but that would be getting pretty technical. *(laughs)* My father says nothing, but somehow I think he understands.

On the train platform, we didn't even kiss. It was his choice, he didn't want to compromise me. To tell the truth, it was so much like a scene from "Casablanca" that I wasn't absolutely sure we weren't in the movies. I wished him luck, and told him... I know it sounds corny, but I told him I hoped Norway would soon be free. He didn't take it as a joke. He gave me a parting gift: I don't know where he found it.

   She holds up a book.

The Odyssey. In Greek. Someday, I'm going to read the whole thing. He gave me so much, without promising me anything.

Goodbye, my darling, Ingvar.

We will always know.

We will always remember.
Goodbye.

MOIRA
(writing) Allan, I feel like I have broken a promise to you, even if we never promised each other anything but to be faithful correspondents. For weeks at a time, I wondered if you were dead. But I have gone on living, as I must go on living, without him, and now probably without you. If you can take me as I am...

— • —

MOIRA
(to herself) No. I won't make any promises. I will never make any promises again.

ALLAN
(writing) May 1st, 1945

Dear Moira,

I am sorry that I have not written sooner. I finally received today your letter of March 8th. It had gone astray during the past few weeks, which have been very eventful ones for me. I must tell you that I am in no position to judge you about the Mr....

(to himself) The Norwegian Romeo. Whatshisname...

MOIRA
Norqvist.

ALLAN
(writing) Norqvist. I know you have been mad at me, and I want you to brace yourself for the truth. You were right. I have had another involvement here in England. I'm sorry to be so blunt, and I'm not expecting you to be anything but mad, and I'm not expecting you to want to keep seeing me if I make it back. These two years have been hard enough without someone's affection, and letters simply wouldn't suffice. I fell in love with another woman, a Polish girl who had seen incredible suffering because she was Jewish.

MOIRA
(looks up, snaps) As if I should care about *her* suffering!

ALLAN
(continues) Her name was Grazina Mankowitz.

MOIRA
(to herself) Was?

> *MOIRA continues reading ALLAN's letter.*

She was a strange, sad young woman who was carrying a terrible burden. She was guilty of the crime of being alive, when almost everyone around her had been killed by the Nazis. She bore this without complaint until the news came out of

Bergen-Belsen. When Grazina heard what the SS did to her own family, it was more than she could bear. She killed herself.

I write you these facts not so that you will forgive me, but so that you will understand something of what has been going on over here. If you still choose to continue corresponding, I will be very glad, and if not, I will understand.

I'm sorry this note is so blunt and to the point. I remain,

ALLAN
(*writing*) Your affectionate friend,
Allan

> *She folds up the letter, pauses, puts it in her bodice. Pause. She takes out the letter and begins reading it to herself again.*

— • —

ALLAN
(*to audience*) The last night she was alive, we were together in London. I think she was waiting until she could say goodbye. We went walking, and she took me into St. Paul's. I had never made it there, and it was sort of a joke between us. We went into the old cathedral, and we sat in one of the pews at the side. She kept staring at the images of Christ, the crucifixion. "I don't understand you Christians," she told me. "You worship this Jewish man who told you to abandon your money, to serve God, and to turn the other cheek when somebody strikes you. And you do this." And she handed me the telegram. From some friend of a friend who had been with her mother and her little sister at the end in Bergen-Belsen. Her whole family.

I became angry. At the Germans, at her family for dying, at her for shoving it in my face like that. I told her that it wasn't our fault, that we were the ones who were trying to stop the Nazis. We fought in the Cathedral, she told me the meanest things she could think of, about my family, my lovemaking, everything. We sat whispering in the church until the sexton came up and insisted we leave.

I walked her home, told her I'd stay with her, wanted to keep her company. She wouldn't let me. We said goodbye. I said, "I'll come tomorrow before my train up North." She sort of smiled and kissed me and let herself in. I slept at the "Y" that night. When I went round in the morning, the police were there. She had been found in her kitchen. The police said it was a lucky thing no one had come in with a lighted match. The funeral was yesterday. I had to miss it. We had an op.

Seventh Movement: War's End

MOIRA
(*writing*) My Dear, Dear Allan,

At last I understand what Dr. Wilmot meant by a Bacchanal. I have been to one today.

ALLAN
(writing) We got the news in the officers' mess and by the time we got outside, the erks were already streaming off the base into the cities. They'd just dumped their breakfast trays onto the floor and bolted.

MOIRA
(writing) All of Edmonton, it seems, showed up downtown today to celebrate. I want to cherish that memory as long as I live. There was of course an official parade, and a ceremony over at the Legislature. But that wasn't the real celebration.

ALLAN
(writing) I caught a truck into York. Men of all ranks screaming, laughing, hugging like maniacs… I lost my hat, but didn't care. Some Nervous Nellie who mentioned the Pacific theatre was lucky to escape with a bloody nose.

MOIRA
(writing) The real celebration was along Jasper Avenue and on 101st street, where people simply went out of their minds with joy. The whole street was filled with people. They were hanging out of the shop windows, and out of the upper floor of the King Edward Hotel. They had climbed all the lampposts and they commandeered the streetcars, scores of young men sitting on top of the cars, I was afraid they'd be electrocuted.

ALLAN
(writing) The civilians of York went crazy. For them it was the end of six years of anxiety, bombs, telegrams, rationing, and putting up with damn foreigners.

— • —

MOIRA
(writing) People were drinking in the streets and shouting like maniacs. Someone would begin a song, and thousands of voices would join in. At one point, someone started a chorus of "The White Cliffs of Dover," and grown men around me were crying.

ALLAN
(writing) If you didn't want to be kissed by strangers or filled with free beer, you may as well have gone home. It was one big blur of relief and happiness.

MOIRA
(writing) But the best part of all, my darling, was the thought that you wouldn't be flying over Germany any more…

ALLAN
(writing) I was in love with the world…

MOIRA
(writing) …or at least not being shot at if you were.

ALLAN
(writing) I thought of you.

Short pause.

MOIRA

(writing) I have seen lots of pictures of the devastation of Germany by Allied planes. I feel terrible for the families who lived in those hulks of buildings, but most of all I just want you home and safe. But perhaps I'm getting ahead of myself. There is still talk that Canadians will now be transferred to the South Pacific to fight the Japanese. God how I hope that it will not be you. We have very much to talk about when you get home. Mostly I want you to know that I'm dying to see you, and that I hope you're feeling the same way.

Whatever has happened, we must try to be happy.
I can't wait to hear from you.

ALLAN

(reading MOIRA's letter) Best Love, Moira.

— • —

ALLAN

(to audience) I'm luckier than most I guess,
Roy with his mangled face, and all the dead.

What will become of the Germans? Their whole country is turned into rubble. Of all us guys, experts in this terrible trade? They say there's going to be some jobs in commercial aviation, but I don't have much desire to fly.

I have seen my friends and colleagues explode, or burned, or mangled. And you make this hole in your mind, where they all go. A little crater in your mind, and you build a fence around it, and that's where they are, the ones who never came back in the morning.

And what am I going to tell you about my life here, the rush of fear, the deliciousness of survival. About the fierce needs of the survivors.

I don't think I'll ever be able to hear a sermon or a lecture for the rest of my life without thinking: no this isn't the way it is, this isn't real life they're talking about, they don't understand anything that's half so sacred as the huge crater in my mind where all my friends went.

I just don't know how I'm going to find my way back home.

MOIRA

(to audience) The war was tragic and terrible. So much death, so much loss. No way to measure the suffering. We are tortured by doubt about Peter. The Japanese apparently didn't treat their prisoners very well.

(to herself) The war was fun. We were part of the world for a while, and we learned a lot. "Eat your ice cream while it's on your plate," says the poet. And the war taught us to do that.

(as though in answer to an inquiry) What will I tell my daughters? That I was one of the lucky ones. That they should never give up what I gained. That they should love and be happy.

I'm building a home in my heart. Perhaps we'll be able to live there.

— • —

MOIRA
(writing) Dear Allan,

I don't understand what is happening. The Americans have dropped a single bomb on some place called Hiroshima and apparently destroyed the entire city.... It's a very chilly thought.

Everyone is sure Japan will now have to capitulate. At last, the suspense about Peter will be over.

I'm dying to see you.

> *ALLAN rushes to don his dress uniform.*

ALLAN
(writing) I'm coming home! With the Japs out of it, the conversion of our squadron has stopped. Thank God it's over.

MOIRA
(writing) Oh, joy, Allan, he's alive, and he's coming home! We've heard that Peter is among the survivors. He was unable to communicate with us, but he's alive! I'm so delighted for Mother, and Dad looks ten years younger.

ALLAN
(writing) The best news is that I won't be "shipping out." I've been chosen to fly one of our Lancs back.

(to himself) Jesus, get to the point...

(writing) Moira, I've been doing a lot of thinking...

MOIRA
(to herself) I want to see him before I write another word.

ALLAN
(to himself) I think I have to do this in the flesh.

Final Scene: Homecoming

MOIRA's parents' farm.

ALLAN crosses the stage, for the first time coming into MOIRA's acting area. She comes forward to him, as though finding him unexpectedly on her porch.

ALLAN
The train was early. I walked from the station.

MOIRA
Come in. Mother's not home. Do you want…?

They are both standing.

You must think I'm a hypocrite.

Pause.

I'm sorry. It was too hard for me alone.

ALLAN
Me too. I mean, I'm sorry too.

MOIRA
You survived. You look older. Bigger.

ALLAN
You've grown up.

MOIRA
We all have. *(beat)* Do you have plans?

ALLAN
I'm going to go back to University. They're offering settlements. I'll study something bland, calm. Maybe accounting… dentistry. I want to have a nice house somewhere in a small town. I want a garden, and maybe a cottage on a lake somewhere. I want a family, four kids, two boys, two girls, who will be fat and smiling and spoiled.

MOIRA
Yes…

ALLAN steps to her.

ALLAN
I want you to take this ring, and to put it on your finger, and to say, Allan Staunton, I promise to be your wife, for ever and ever, till death do us part.

He offers her the ring. It is the ring he had in his pocket the last time they saw one another.

MOIRA
Wait. I want you to say, I will not blame you, and I will try not to blame myself, for everything that these times have made us do to ourselves…

ALLAN
I don't…

MOIRA
…or I will not marry you.

ALLAN
I will not…

MOIRA
…blame you…

ALLAN
…blame you…

MOIRA
　　…and I will try not to blame myself…

ALLAN
　　　　…and I will try not to blame myself…

MOIRA
For everything these times have made us do to ourselves.

ALLAN
I may have nightmares.

MOIRA
That's all right.

ALLAN
I mean, for a long time.

MOIRA
That's. All. Right.

　　　ALLAN puts the ring on her finger.

Allan Staunton, I promise to be your wife, forever and ever, till death do us part.

ALLAN
Let's begin.

MOIRA
Yes, let's begin.

　　　Lights out.

　　　The end.

Einstein's Gift

Vern Thiessen

photo by Nicholas Seiflow

VERN THIESSEN has written for stage, radio and television for more than sixteen years. His plays have been seen across Canada, including *Blowfish* (National Arts Centre; Northern Light Theatre, Edmonton), *The Resurrection Of John Frum*, (National Arts Centre; Manitoba Theatre Projects, Winnipeg), *Apple* (Workshop West Theatre, Edmonton; Touchstone Theatre, Vancouver), and *Dawn Quixote* (Quest Theatre Calgary; Geordie Productions, Montreal; Globe Theatre, Regina.) His short plays *Valentine* and *Interest* have been produced at the Drilling Company in New York City. He wrote the screenplay for "Samurai Swing," a short film that won the 1998 National Screen Institute Drama Prize, and has since played film festivals across North America as well as CBC television nationally.

Both *Apple* and *Chaos* are winners of the prestigious Alberta Play Competition, and *Apple* is also the winner of the 2001 Elizabeth Sterling Haynes Award for Outstanding New Play. Thiessen has served as Playwright-in-Residence at Workshop West Theatre (where he founded the Playwrights Garage Development Program), the University of Alberta, and the Blue Heron Arts Centre in New York City. *Apple*, *Blowfish* and *Einstein's Gift* are published by Playwrights Canada Press.

Thiessen is Artistic Associate of Play Development at the Citadel Theatre, and has served as President of the Playwrights Guild of Canada – a national service organization representing professional playwrights across Canada.

Original Foreword to Einstein's Gift

Russell E. Bishop, Ph.D.
Departments of Laboratory Medicine & Pathobiology, and Biochemistry
University of Toronto

Vern Thiessen tells me that we were in a pool hall in 1996 on Edmonton's Whyte Avenue when I suggested he write a play about Fritz Haber. I honestly don't recall the location, but that fact alone suggests Vern is probably correct. I do recall suggesting that he should call the play *The Haber Process*, but Vern quickly told me that part of the motivation for writing a play is to sell tickets. We scientists often read journals that only other scientists read. One of these is a British journal called *Nature*, which, in addition to publishing research articles, regularly reviews scientific books and biographies about other scientists. I stumbled across the *Nature* review on the biography by Dietrich Stolzenberg that chronicled the tragedy of Haber's life and told Vern it would make a good play. To this day, I'm surprised that Vern took my suggestion so seriously.

Anyone who has taken an introductory university course in chemistry is probably familiar with the Haber Process for the fixation of atmospheric nitrogen. The Haber Process illustrates some fundamental principles of physical chemistry. It earned Haber a Nobel Prize in chemistry in 1919, in large part because it led to the development of nitrogenous fertilizers. Most members of the public probably have never heard of Fritz Haber. I am a biochemist and, as a student, I had to learn about Fritz Haber, but I had little concept of his life.

In Haber's time, scientists were afforded a remarkable amount of respect, no doubt owing to a public perception that scientists could do no wrong. An enzymology professor at the University of Alberta, Neil Madsen, used to show his students a slide that portrayed Emil Fischer (one of Haber's contemporaries) walking at the front of a parade alongside the Kaiser himself. Professor Madsen was trying to emphasize the status that chemistry had achieved in Germany at the dawn of the twentieth century. It must have been a very different experience to be a successful scientist in Haber's time. He probably never imagined for an instant that his work would ever have negative consequences. Today, scientists are not only expected to cure diseases and discover clean energy sources, but they are also held tacitly responsible for much environmental decay and the threat of nuclear annihilation.

The perception that basic research must be regarded as value-neutral owes much to the fact that the benefits of science, both good and bad, cannot always be predicted. I suppose that this dictum also holds true to some extent for every-day life events. That people choose to place their faith in a higher power at all must reflect, at least partially, a need to believe that unpredictable life events will somehow turn out positively. Theologian John F. Haught argues in his book *God After Darwin: A Theology of Evolution* that conflicts between science and religion owe much to the rooting of traditional theology in Greek philosophy's metaphysics of the eternal present. Modern science provides us with cosmic and biological evolution because it is rooted in a materialist metaphysics that accounts for both present and past. Haught suggests that modern theology would do well to ground itself in a metaphysics of the future, which can then embrace the facts of cosmic and biological evolution as a part of God's promise for eternal novelty. A little spiritual guidance from this viewpoint certainly won't hurt modern science's effort to keep its own objectives from going awry. That Fritz Haber had to deal with issues of his own religious beliefs certainly does highlight this conflict. But, we should be careful before we attempt to attribute any adverse consequences of Haber's research to his own personal conflicts with religion. To what, then, could we attribute Haber's discoveries that helped feed the world?

In 1994 (two years before Vern and I first spoke of Haber) I had the pleasure of studying at the Max Plank Institutes, one of Germany's scientific research centres. I even gave a seminar in Berlin at the same institute that had been set up under Haber originally as the Kaiser Wilhelm Institute. I distinctly recall walking by the same building where Vern later discovered letters of correspondence between Haber and Albert Einstein. Here, Vern managed to discover a perfect foil for Haber, which vaulted the play to a level that I had never quite imagined. Their friendship also provided Vern with a title: *Einstein's Gift*. In case you don't know it, the German word "gift" actually means "poison" in English. The irony in that should become apparent once you read the play.

Original Postscript to Einstein's Gift
Vern Thiessen

I am not a scientist, nor am I an historian, and I apologize to Herr Haber, Herr Einstein and all the other historical people I refer to in this play. I am a playwright, a storyteller, and I lean my crutch heavily on Aristotle's dictum: "History is *what* happened; drama is what *may* have happened." I have taken pains to capture the *geist* of Fritz Haber and his compatriots with as much historical accuracy as possible, but without being a slave to it. Frankly, I don't care much about breaking what some consider the sacred seal of historical fact. I hope only that I have captured the essence of Haber's tragedy. As Einstein himself put it: "Haber's is the tragedy of the German Jew, the tragedy of unrequited love."

I began researching this play in the fall of 1996, after hearing about Fritz Haber through Dr. Russell Bishop (see Foreword). As material on Haber is scant (especially in English), I travelled to the Archiv zur Geschichte der Max-Planck-Gesellschaft in Berlin. With the help of Uta Siebeky and her staff, I gained access to previously unpublished material, almost all of it in German. What drove me to keep working on the play (through seven years and over a dozen drafts) was the same question the central characters struggle with in this play: "What do I believe?" I believe we are all like Einstein and Haber at some level. Even if we are not all brilliant physicists or ambitious chemists, I believe we all have hopes and dreams, and conversely, that we all wrestle with doubt. And if we follow Einstein and Haber's lead, we will see this doubt—and crises of faith—as a gift.

Nevertheless, I cannot shy away from the question most frequently asked about the play: "how much of it is historically accurate?" And so, I offer a few historical tidbits to compare and contrast with the fiction of the play:

Friedrich Jacob Haber was born in Breslau on December 9, 1868. He was baptized in November, 1892 (early 1900s in the play), by the Archdeacon Dr. Auffahrth at St. Michael's Evangelical Lutheran Church of Jena. Most sources concur that Haber converted to Christianity for little more than practical reasons. Anecdotes of friends and family represent Haber as a careerist, easily prone to moodiness and arrogance. But they also praise him as charismatic, passionate, and inspirational. His students considered him an excellent teacher, and fellow workers revelled in his ability to hold court, write playlets, and improvise poems on almost any occasion. Haber's Uncle Ludwig was indeed killed by a Samurai warrior in Japan in 1874.

Both Einstein and Haber considered each other a good friend and colleague. Although their relationship was heartfelt and respectful, it was often strained and oddly formal. Neither Haber nor Einstein addressed each other in the familiar German "du," even after corresponding for years (e.g. Haber writes "Dear Einstein" and not "Dear Albert"). Haber did help Einstein on several occasions and Einstein reciprocated when he could. Although Haber and Einstein never actually duelled, they sent postcards back and forth on which are written nothing but mathematical formulae (suggesting an exchange, or battle, of ideas). The two men saw each other more often than I indicate in the play, and corresponded regularly. They probably met around 1911 (1905 in the play), and continued writing to each other after Einstein left Germany for Princeton in 1933. Einstein's gift of the Kipa and Tallis is my invention, although Haber did reconvert to Judaism at the end of his life, before dying in Switzerland in January, 1934. Einstein's final letter to the Haber family after Haber's death is heartbreaking and speaks to a true friendship and love between the two men.

Otto is loosely based on Otto Sackur, a colleague of Haber's killed in an explosion in 1915 while developing chlorine gas. He *never* had any fascist leanings (that I know of), and thus I have used his first name only, simply as inspiration.

Clara Immerwahr was the first woman to graduate from the chemistry department of Breslau University. She worked closely with Haber in the early years of their marriage, and Haber even dedicates an early book to her: "To Clara, my silent partner." Nevertheless, I suggest a close collaboration between her and Haber nearer to fiction than fact. They married in 1901, and had one child, Hermann. Clara committed suicide about two weeks after the chlorine release. She tried a test shot with Haber's revolver, then proceeded to shoot herself in the heart. The thirteen-year-old Hermann discovered her. According to one anecdote, she lived another twenty minutes before dying. Some sources suggest her despair over the chlorine release contributed to her suicide, while others point to the possibility of a genetic mental illness. Hermann too killed himself, in 1946, at the age of forty-four.

Lotta Nathan was born in 1889. Her mother died of cancer when she was eleven. She wanted to be an actress, but her father forbade this. After a brief foray at medical school, she worked secretarial jobs at libraries and newspapers. Eventually she became a "Girl Friday" at the German Club, a gathering place where famous personalities of the day discussed politics, art, science and literature. The first meeting between Charlotta Nathan and Haber (the umbrella section) is taken directly from her autobiography. Lotta's wit, charm, easygoing nature, and love of life were in stark contrast to Clara's stern and obsessive character. Haber and Lotta actually met earlier than I have depicted, and were married by 1917. Their trip around the world (1924-25) took place *after* the gold in seawater experiment (approx. 1920-24), which I have pushed into the late 20s/early 30s for dramatic purposes. Haber and Lotta had two children, Ludwig (often known as Lutz) and Eva. Haber and Lotta divorced in 1927, although they kept in close contact with each other. Lotta died in 1978, in Switzerland.

Haber was present (and responsible) for the chlorine release at Ypres in April, 1915. He did not get along with General Deimling, although his relationship with Colonel Peterson was quite good. Correspondence between Haber and Minister Rust—including Haber's daring resignation letter—forms the basis of scenes between the two men. Haber was overseeing work by his juniors (Hase and Flury) on the pesticide Zyklon (versions A, B and C) as early as 1920, but again I have pushed this a decade later for dramatic purposes. Thankfully, Haber died before discovering what the Nazis did with his work. It is the final, horrible irony of Haber's life: that Zyklon, a pesticide meant to improve agriculture, was developed into a gas used to kill untold numbers of Jews at Auschwitz. Among the victims were some of Haber's own in-laws and cousins.

Although more material has become available on Haber over the past several years, comprehensive information in English is still scarce. In German, I suggest *Fritz Haber: Chemiker, Nobelpreistrager, Deutscher, Jude* by Dietrich Stolzenberg, by far the most comprehensive and authoritative text. Both Charlotta's autobiography *Spiegelungen der Vergangenheit*, and *Der Fall Clara Immerwahr: Leben für eine humane Wissenschaft* by Gerit von Leitner, were of great help. In English, *The Story of Fritz Haber*, by Morris Goran, is heavy on good anecdotes, but light on basic facts. *Einstein in Berlin*, by Thomas Levenson, has some good sections on Haber. Other suggestions are: *Enriching the Earth: Fritz Haber, Carl Bosch and the Transformation of World Food Production* by Vaclav Smil; and of course *The Poisonous Cloud*, written by L.F. Haber (Haber's son Lutz). Lastly, I recommend *The Great War and Modern Memory* by Paul Fussel. Although it has no real information on Haber, it was key in helping me understand the horror and historical significance of World War One.

— • — Selected Bibliography — • —

Stage Plays – Published

- *Einstein's Gift*. Full length. World Premiere at Citadel Theatre, Edmonton (March 2003.) Also at Theatre and Company Kitchener (April 2003.) Workshopped at On the Verge (Ottawa), May 2001; Citadel Theatre, Edmonton, Feb. 2000; Toronto Jewish Theatre Committee, May 2000; Banff PlayRites Colony, Sept. 1999; Playwrights Theatre Centre, Vancouver, May 1999.
    Einstein's Gift. In *The West of All Possible Worlds: Six Contemporary Canadian Plays*. Ed. Moira Day. Toronto: Playwrights Canada Press, 2004.

    Einstein's Gift. Toronto: Playwrights Canada Press, 2003.

- *Apple*. Full length. Premiere at Workshop West Theatre, Edmonton April 2002. Also: Borrowed Time Theatre, Regina (July 2002) and Touchstone Theatre, Vancouver, March 2003. Commissioned by Workshop West Theatre. Workshopped at Springboards New Play Festival, Workshop West Theatre Edmonton in April 2000; New Play Festival (Playwrights Theatre Centre), Vancouver, May 2001; Blue Heron Arts Centre, NYC, July 2001; Original Sin Productions workshop, NYC, Oct. 2001; NJ Rep, November 2003.
    Apple. Toronto: Playwrights Canada Press, 2002.

- *Blowfish*. Full-length. Co-produced by Northern Light Theatre, Edmonton and the National Arts Centre, Ottawa, Nov. 1996.
    Blowfish. (introduction by John Murrell). Toronto: Playwrights Canada Press, 1998.

Stage Plays – Unpublished

- *Interest*. One Act. Produced by The Drilling Company, NYC, November 2002.
- *Valentine*. One-act. Produced by The Drilling Company, NYC, November 2001. Readings at ATP Brief New Works, March 2002 and Springboards, April 2002.
- *On The Line*. One-act (theatre for young audiences.) Produced by Quest Theatre, Calgary, January 1998.
- *Dawn Quixote*. One-act (theatre for young audiences.) Produced by Quest Theatre, Calgary, January 1995; Globe Theatre, Regina, October 1996; Geordie Productions, Montreal, winter 1996/97.
    Dawn Quixote. (copyscript) Toronto: Playwrights Guild of Canada, c 1995.
- *I Fell in Love with an Eel*. One-act. Produced by University of Alberta, Edmonton January 1991. Death and Taxes Theatre, Toronto, Winnipeg and Edmonton Fringes, 1991.
    I Fell in Love with an Eel. (copyscript) Toronto: Playwrights Guild of Canada, c 1991.

- *The Resurrection of John Frum.* Full-length. Produced by the National Arts Centre, Ottawa, April 1990; Theatre Projects, Winnipeg, November 1991; Landlock Theatre Cross-Canada tour, 1999.

  The Resurrection of John Frum. (copyscript) Toronto: Playwrights Guild of Canada, c. 1990.
- *The Courier.* One-act. Produced by: Agassiz Theatre, Winnipeg, April 1987; Winnipeg Mennonite Theatre, October 87; Theatre Centre, Toronto, May 88; Edmonton Fringe, August 88; Lakeland College, Lloydminster October 93, Winnipeg Fringe, July, 97.

  The Courier. (copyscript) Toronto: Playwrights Guild of Canada, c 1987.

Radio and Screen Plays

- *Back to Berlin.* 6 minutes. Commentary. Produced on "First Person Singular" by CBC Radio. Aired nationally, November 1999.
- *Samurai's Swing.* 18 min. Drama. Produced by Irresponsible Films, Inc., Aired nationally on CBC Television. 1999
- *Entrance 23.* 30 min. Film. Drama. Produced by University of Alberta/NAIT, April 1993.
- *The Courier.* 50 min. Drama. Produced by CKUA Radio, April 1992.

Periodicals

- "The Generation X of Canadian Theatre." *Theatrum* 33 (April/May 1993): 12-13.
- "Moher is More." *Theatrum* 29 (June/July/August 1992): 25-26.
- Book reviews of *Bordertown Café* (Kelly Rebar), *The Mail Order Bride* (Robert Clinton), and *The Chinese Man Said Goodbye* (Bruce McManus). *Prairie Fire* 11:3 (Autumn 1990): 98.

Reviews of *Einstein's Gift*

Bergman, Brian. "People: Telling Sad, Scary, Scientific Tale." *Maclean's* 117.2 (12 January 2004): 51.

Byles, Ileiren. "*Einstein's Gift* a Clock-Stopper." *St. Albert Gazette* 1 March 2003: 28.

"Edmonton's Citadel Premiere's Play on Scientist Who Invented Poison Gas Weapon." *Canadian Press Newswire* Toronto: 18 February 2003.

Gladstone, Bill. "Out of Town." *Canadian Jewish News* 13 February 2003. 33.7: 33.

Hall, Jamie. "People." *Edmonton Journal* 17 February 2003: B2.

Horton, Marc. "Three Nominations a First for Local Writers." *Edmonton Journal* 21 October 2003: A1.

—. "Seven-Year Struggle Yields Huge Gift for Thiessen." *Edmonton Journal* 13 November 2003: C1.

MacLean, Colin. "New Play is a Question of Faith: *Einstein's Gift* Looks at a Forgotten Man." *Edmonton Sun* 18 February 2003:40.

Morrow, Martin. "Another Dr. Frankenstein." *Globe and Mail* [Toronto] 4 March 2003: R2.

Nicholls, Liz. "Citadel Commits Itself to Developing New Plays: New Artistic Associate to Nourish Canadian Talent." *Edmonton Journal* 14 April 2001: C4.

—-. "The Brain Behind *Einstein.*" *Edmonton Journal* 26 February 2003: C1.

—-. "Brave Examination of Genius Corrupted: Thiessen's Newest Play is Seldom Cautious in Tracing Path to Damnation." *Edmonton Journal* 1 March 2003: E6.

—-."The Party's the Thing When Theatre Folks Gather." *Edmonton Journal* 5 July 2003: E4.

—-. "The final act." *Edmonton Journal* 28 December 2003: B1.

Rousseau, Isabelle. "Chaos Theory: *Einstein's Gift* is Strong on Ideas but Messy on Stage." *See* 6-12 March 2003.

Rubinstein, Dan. "Misfits of Science. Themes of War, Religion, Ambition, Love Whirl Like Electrons Inside Fascinating *Einstein's Gift.*" *VueWeekly* 6-12 March 2003: 45.

Production Notes

Staging and Conventions:

Einstein's Gift is a memory play of sorts, and Albert should be present on stage for the entire performance, leaving only for the most practical reasons. In the original production, Albert became a kind of puppet master, assisting characters with props and occasionally, reacting to the scenes being played out. Individual producers/directors are encouraged to experiment with this convention without detracting from the "present" scene being played. Although Albert is seen in two different guises (i.e. the older Albert as narrator; the younger Albert who actively participates in scenes) only one actor should play both "parts" of Albert.

In the "fencing scene" and the "sidewalk scene", I have tried (to the best of my abilities) to chart out the formulas for the actors. I recommend directors/producers consult with a local chemist for more information.

The original production featured live music, inventive staging, and a highly theatrical design that never detracted from the rather straightforward story of Haber and his compatriots. In the spirit of the scientists portrayed, I encourage actors to be as passionate as possible, and directors/designers to be as imaginative as they wish.

The play should flow from scene to scene with few—if any—blackouts. The play should run no longer than 2 hours and 15 minutes, plus intermission. This version of *Einstein's Gift* went to print shortly after the World Premiere and second production. Producers are advised to contact the playwright's agent for the most up to date version of the text.

Pronunciations:

Outside the pronunciations below, German dialects are *NOT* to be used:

Jena	YAY-na	Rust	"u" as in "oo" in book
Deimling	DIME-link	Clara	"a" as in father
Bernard	BAIRN-hart	Immerwahr	IMMER-vahr
Reichstag	RYKS-tog	Ludwig	LUDE-veeg
Haber	"a" as in father	Jacob	YA-kob
Charlotta	Shar-LOTT-a	Charlottenburg	shar-LOTTEN-berg
Peterson	PAYTER-soan	Delphinus	Del-FY-nus
Karlruhe	KARLS-roo-ih	Knorr	Nor

Suggested Multiple Casting:

ACTOR 1 (male: Haber)
ACTOR 2 (male: Albert)
ACTOR 3 (female: Clara, Singer)
ACTOR 4 (female: Lotta, Soldier in Act 1)
ACTOR 5 (male: Otto)
ACTOR 6 (male: Deimling, Rust)
ACTOR 7 (male: Deacon, Peterson, Gestapo, Soldier in Act Two)
The Company plays all smaller roles.

Einstein's Gift received its World Premiere at The Citadel Theatre, Edmonton, Alberta, in February 2003. It was performed on the MacLab Stage with the following company:

Albert	James MacDonald
Haber	Michael Spencer-Davis
Otto	Julien Arnold
Clara/Cabaret Singer	Stephanie Wolfe
Peterson/Soldier/Rust	Philip Warren Sarsons
Deacon/Deimling/Gestapo	Paul Morgan Donald
Lotta	Daniela Vlaskalic
Live Music	Paul Morgan Donald, and the company
Assistants, Train Porter, Guests, etc.	The Company

Director: David Storch
Set and Lighting Designer: Bretta Gerecke
Costume Designer: Narda McCarroll
Composer/Sound Design: Paul Morgan Donald
Assistant to Sound Design: Aaron Macri
Stage Manager: Gina Moe
Assistant Stage Manager: Tracey Byrne
Apprentice Stage Manager: Kristopher Heuven
Science Advisor: Dr. Mike Joyce
Research Dramaturges: Ben Unterman, Sarah Polkinghorne

For the Citadel Theatre:

Artistic Director	Bob Baker
Managing Director	Tammy Fallowfield
Director of Production	John Raymond

— • —

Einstein's Gift was subsequently produced at Theatre and Company, Kitchener, Ontario, in April 2003. In the cast were: Mike Peng, Alan K. Sapp, Andrew Lakin, Kathleen Sheehy, Elana Post, Raymond Louter and Robin Bennett. Directed by Stuart Scadron-Wattles. Set and Costume Design by Dennis Horn. Lighting by Renee Brode. The production was Stage Managed by Anna Graham and Assistant Directed by Linda Bush.

Characters

Albert Einstein	a physicist
F.J. Haber	a chemist
Otto	Haber's assistant
Deacon Auffarth	a Lutheran minister
Clara Immerwahr	Haber's first wife
Peterson	a Commander in the German army
Deimling	a General in the German army
Soldier	in the Ypres trench
Singer	at the German Club
Lotta Haber	Haber's second wife
Bernhard Rust	Minister of Education
Gestapo	Guard to Rust

Assistants, Train Porters, Guests, etc.

Setting

Act One: USA, 1945; Germany, 1905-1915

Act Two: Germany/Switzerland, 1919- 1934; USA, 1945

Songs and Translations

Latin translation by Gwen DeFelice, used with permission. Translations and adaptation of Haber and Goethe poems by Vern Thiessen. The songs "How We Wish We Were Kids Again" (1921) and "A Little Yearning" (1930) are both by Friederich Hollaender. English lyrics by Paul Morgan Donald and used here with permission.

Dedication

To my parents, for keeping the faith.

Einstein's Gift
by Vern Thiessen

— • —— • ——

_____ **ACT I**

An explosion of light and sound. ALBERT, 66 years old, shields his eyes. Then, he speaks to the audience.

ALBERT
(smiles) Was a time....

Was a time women spoke music. And men thought poetry. When hope equalled work, and work equalled faith and the world's equation balanced.

Was a time I thought the world was a watch, its hands smooth as a symphony, its workings well-oiled, its balance poised and true.

Was a time I thought I could do no wrong. When every colleague coddled my mind. When every prize was draped in pomp and platitudes. When every country honoured me. When every word I spoke, every oath I swore, every thought I formed was recorded for ages to come, for all time.

Was a time... I believed.

— • —

Church bells. Holy Michael's Lutheran Church. The ARCHDEACON with paper and writing instrument. ALBERT watches unnoticed.

DEACON
Name?

ALBERT
(to audience) An ambitious young man.

HABER
Friedrich... Jacob... Haber.

DEACON
"Jacob".... Jewish?

ALBERT
In Germany.

HABER
Is that a concern?

ALBERT
In 1905.

DEACON
On the contrary. Such a wonderful occasion when a Son of Abraham decides to become a child of Christ. Date of birth?

HABER
December 9, 1868.

DEACON
Done. You will sign here and here.

HABER
Very good then.

DEACON
But. Before we proceed. I must ask you a few questions.

HABER
…Alright.

DEACON
Why is it you want to be baptized.

HABER
Do you doubt my intentions?

DEACON
There are many who take this most holy oath merely in the name of convenience.

HABER
This is anything but a convenience Herr Deacon. My work, my future depend on–

DEACON
Your future as a Christian is the subject.

HABER
But–

DEACON
Anything beyond that is irrelevant, to myself and to God. Now then, why do you want to be baptized?

   A long pause.

Why do you ask Christ to come into your heart?

   A long pause.

I'm trying to make this easy for you, Herr Haber. If you cannot answer these simple queries–

HABER
I will not lie.

   Pause.

I cannot.

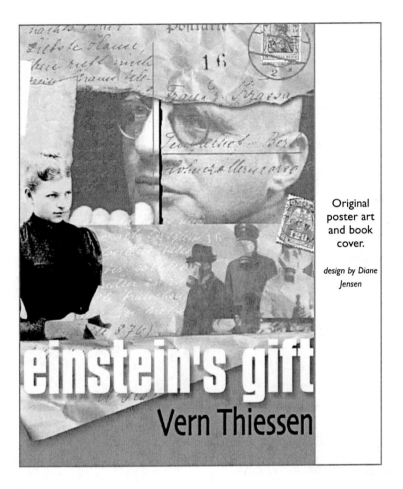

Original poster art and book cover.

design by Diane Jensen

DEACON
I see.

HABER
You know why I'm here.

DEACON
I believe so yes.

HABER
You know my predicament.

DEACON
I do.

HABER
I am Jewish and–

DEACON
I am a minister of this faith, Herr Haber. I have made a vow to uphold it.

Pause.

HABER
I understand.

Pause.

I… I thought perhaps…

Pause.

Thank you.

He starts to leave.

DEACON
One moment, one moment…

HABER turns.

Tell me. What is it you believe.

HABER
What do I…?

DEACON
If I – if we… could find some place where your beliefs and that of Christ come together…

HABER
I believe in science.

DEACON
…science…

HABER
(with passion, but not arrogance) I believe, I believe science reveals truths not understood in any other way. You see?

DEACON
Perhaps, but…

HABER
Do you know The Law Of Multiple Proportions, Herr Deacon?

DEACON
I can't say I…

HABER
If two elements unite to form more than one compound, the different masses of one element that combine with a fixed mass of the other element are in a ratio of small whole numbers.

DEACON
I don't follow.

HABER
It has beauty. Like a poem or a, a Bible verse. Dalton taught us how small God's world is; Galileo taught us how large it is; Newton taught us why your stained glass is as beautiful as it is. I believe in science. And to be a scientist, is to search the soul of God.

DEACON
You can never know God, Herr Haber.

HABER
Not to *know* God, but to glimpse into His mind. For the briefest of seconds, to think what He thinks, to breathe what He breathes, to see through His eyes. A flash in time, when inspiration comes, or insight is gained, or forgiveness is granted, or courage is gathered, or humility is felt. And then to act on it, to do good, to make it live, to, to give people something to believe in. We don't want to be God, but we all try to be more *like* God, do we not? Is that not what we two believe? Is that not faith? Is that not holy?

Pause.

DEACON
Perhaps it is.

> *HABER kneels. The ARCHDEACON performs the baptism, the water bathing HABER's cheek.*

— • —

OTTO
Haber!

HABER
Otto!

OTTO
Catch!

> *OTTO throws HABER a foil. Both men begin stretching. ALBERT watches.*

ALBERT
An ambitious young man. A faithful friend. The turn of a century.

HABER
Otto, my friend, did I ever tell you the story of my dear Uncle Ludwig?

OTTO
Which one?

HABER
I have only one Uncle Ludwig.

OTTO
No, which story.

HABER
Uncle Ludwig was in Japan. Eighteen hundred and seventy-four. At tea with a Samurai, he was, when the topic of the worlds preeminent warriors arose. The Samurai claimed the Japanese were superior, whereas Uncle Ludwig, having fought in the Franco-Prussian War, naturally believed Germans to be the ultimate fighting machines.

OTTO
Naturally.

HABER
They argued well into the evening, late into the night, and early into the next morning. Finally, the Samurai challenged Uncle to a duel, at which Ludwig not only threw down his gauntlet, but also suggested they exchange weapons. The Samurai laughed, for Uncle Ludwig carried a pistol, whereas he, the Samurai, had nothing but a sword. Uncle insisted, and weapons were exchanged. But before the Samurai had a chance to cock the hammer, Uncle Ludwig swung the sword over his head, and with one quick, efficient movement, cleft the Samurai in twain. Right down the middle.

OTTO
Good lord!

HABER
On hearing this, my father said: "Ludwig, that stunt took a lot of character." To which Uncle replied: "Brother, to be German is to *have* character."

OTTO
(laughs) Well said Uncle Ludwig!

HABER
Have I told you that story before, Otto?

OTTO
Oh yes. But last time it was the tragic tale of Uncle Ludwig dying at the hands of the savage Samurai. Which is true?

HABER
Does it matter? *En garde.*

   They take positions.

ALBERT
A young man arrives. Checks his watch. Clears his throat.

   A younger ALBERT steps into the scene.

Good day, I hope I'm not...

OTTO
Ah! Haber, I completely forgot to – we have a visitor come on business. Haber, this is Herr Albert Einstein. Herr Einstein, this is Doctor Friedrich Haber, our brilliant new chemistry instructor.

HABER
(correcting) Professor.

OTTO
Oh yes. As of last Tuesday, Assistant *Professor* Doctor Haber, of our University of Jena.

ALBERT
Congratulations Herr Haber. Your work with Knorr is very impressive. I'm particularly interested in how this study of nitrogen gas–

HABER
There once was a Switzerland Jew
Who surprised the whole world with his view
Through amazing insight
He discovered that light
Was not what we thought we all knew.

OTTO
(laughs, applauds) Bravo Haber! Well done!

HABER
(bowing) Thank you Otto.

ALBERT
Yes, well, unfortunately only one part of the poem is factually correct.

HABER
Only *one*? And what was that *one* part? You are Swiss, are you not?

ALBERT
A citizen yes, but I was born here, in Germany.

HABER
But you gave up that privilege.

ALBERT
It was no privilege for me. The Prussian school system was far too strict; it didn't allow children like myself–

HABER
The Prussian school system is considered the best in the world. I myself would not have come as far as I have without the Prussian school system.

ALBERT
Imagination is more important than knowledge.

HABER
Is it. Well then, was it your amazing insight then, I managed to get factually correct?

ALBERT
I make no claim to that. I am a physicist. My job is to think.

HABER
To think.

ALBERT
Yes.

HABER
Nothing more.

ALBERT
Well…

HABER
Go into physics Otto: You'll be paid to day-dream.

OTTO
Haber…

ALBERT
Chemistry I find, how shall I put it… tedious.

HABER
Oh?

ALBERT
Unimaginative.

HABER
Really.

ALBERT
Boring, frankly.

OTTO
Perhaps we should go in, it's getting rather hot.

HABER
Tell me Einstein: these new theories on light, what purpose will they serve?

ALBERT
Purpose?

HABER
What will they do.

ALBERT
They are ideas Haber. They don't do anything on their own.

HABER
You have no interest in the outcome?

ALBERT
Interest, yes, but the practicalities are out of my control. The role of the scientist is to think, not to tell the future.

HABER
That's not enough. It is not enough to sit in our labs, day in, day out, and stew and experiment and think and dream. It is not enough. We must also apply. Your theories may change the way people see things, but they will do little for, say, the starving farmer, who can't fertilize his field.

ALBERT
Nor are they meant to.

HABER
Then what *use* are they.

OTTO
Gentlemen.

ALBERT
What use is a, a painting Herr Haber, or a concerto, or even your clever, if ill-scanned, limerick? To give insight. To challenge perception. To feed the soul.

HABER
It is the farmer's stomach we should be feeding.

ALBERT
I am as concerned for the farmer as you are, Herr Haber, I like to eat. My study on light may well affect the farmer, or the businessmen or the artist. It may. But is not in my realm.

HABER
Very well then. What *was* the one thing I got factually correct.

ALBERT
I am a Jew.

HABER
Ah! Of course.

ALBERT
As are you.

HABER
A fact I've forgotten, Herr Einstein.

ALBERT
Forgotten a fact? Religion isn't a coat to be shed.

HABER
Neither is nationality.

ALBERT
And is nationality why you've chosen to be baptized?

OTTO
I just mentioned it in passing, Haber, I didn't think–

HABER
We are at the dawn of the 20th Century. Christianity is, for better or worse, the norm. Otto, for example.

OTTO
Me?

HABER
A prime example of the upstanding young Christian.

OTTO

I am no more a devout Christian than–

HABER

Than Einstein is a devout Jew, am I right?

ALBERT

I consider myself a deeply religious non-believer, but–

HABER

–then you see my point–

ALBERT

–I have no plans to convert.

HABER

Because you live in Switzerland. Yes? I can assure you, Herr Einstein, I have no more interest in the Christian faith than I do in any other. But in this country, a baptism certificate is, unfortunately, one more piece of red tape necessary in acquiring a full time professorship. Another form to fill out, another exam to take, another test to pass. It is a matter of fact, that is all.

He pulls paper from his pocket and hands it to OTTO.

Here. From Martin Freund in Vienna. I wrote asking for work. Read the last line, read it.

OTTO

"Take my advice seriously Haber. They don't want Jews in this position."

HABER

I've studied with the best: with Bunsen in Heidelberg, with Lunge in Zurich, with Liebermann in Charlottenberg, and now with Knorr. I'm making strides, Einstein, you said it yourself. If I can continue my work on nitrogen, if I apply it to a practical purpose, I might discover something that may help the starving farmer or the businessman or the artist. Not just a new idea, but a new way of doing. But I need a proper lab, I need a full position. I can't move forward, I can't do my work on a measly part-time assistant professorship in this stinking little town.

ALBERT

Why not move then, why not–?

HABER

Move?! This is my home, this is my – My father came to this country with nothing. Not a Mark.

ALBERT

I know, many Jews suffered the same–

HABER

One day my father and I were walking home from Schul. A friend came running: "the Kaiser has made a decree! Jews can own land, they can stay as long as they like." The Kaiser was a rational man. He knew we were good people, worked hard. He gave us freedom. And in return, he asked only one thing. That we be Germans. That we love this country.

ALBERT
Germany is a piece of land–

HABER
–it is my *country*–

ALBERT
–nothing but a piece of land–

HABER
–It is my *home*–

ALBERT
–but your faith is nearly 6000 years–

HABER
(erupting) I won't have it! I won't throw away my work, my life, my home because of this, I won't!

    Pause.

But enough. Tell us Einstein. What brings you to Jena?

ALBERT
Me?

HABER
I'm sure you didn't come to discuss my personal affairs.

ALBERT
Yes, well…

OTTO
Herr Einstein has come to ask a favour.

HABER
A favour?

OTTO
Of you.

HABER
Of me? Now the truth comes out.

OTTO
He is looking for contacts.

HABER
I am not a physicist, I don't–

ALBERT
But you, you *know* people, you have a good reputation for talking to everyone, and I'm, I'm not good at–

OTTO
Herr Einstein was hoping you could furnish…

HABER
Names?

ALBERT
Yes

HABER
Of people.

ALBERT
Yes.

HABER
With influence.

OTTO
Yes.

Pause.

ALBERT
I could mention you. Or not. Whatever your preference.

HABER
I see.

Pause.

We'll duel for it.

He picks up the foils.

OTTO
A duel! *(laughs)*

ALBERT
I beg your pardon?

HABER
If you win, I'll give you names. If not, you shall attend church with me on Sunday.

ALBERT
I'm not good at games. The only thing I play is the viola.

HABER
Nonsense.

ALBERT
I'm a pacifist.

OTTO
A what?

HABER
Good God, next you'll be telling us you eat no meat.

ALBERT
I don't believe in violence as a means to settle disputes.

HABER
Einstein, you are more Christian than I will ever be!

ALBERT
You don't understand, I–

HABER
(throwing the foil to ALBERT) What would our beloved Bismark say to this, eh Otto? If all Germans acted like Einstein, we'd have lost all Prussia. *(to ALBERT)* Did you know that my Uncle Ludwig viciously killed a Samarai warrior?

ALBERT
Haber, I–

HABER
(striking a fencing stance) En garde.

> They fence. HABER is quite good. After a few passes, they break.

Well, well, not bad. Your Prussian school training didn't do you so bad. Let's see how you do battle on two fronts.

ALBERT
No, really, I–

HABER
(going on the attack) If the radiant energy emitted by a blackbody is infinitely divisible, what value can it have within a given range?

ALBERT
The energy emitted by a blackbody must always be an integral of a quantum and never less.

HABER
(pressing) What is the energy a single electron possesses when radiation with a frequency of one times ten to the fifteenth strikes sodium metal?

ALBERT
Four point one electron volts.

HABER
(thrusting) Light is a wave!

ALBERT
No! Its energy is only dependent on its frequency and therefore light is also a particle!

> ALBERT scores a hit.

HABER
Ah!

> HABER drops his foil, clutching his cheek. OTTO rushes over.

OTTO
Haber!

ALBERT
Are you alright?

HABER
Fine.

ALBERT
I'm sorry, I didn't mean to–

HABER
Not to worry.

ALBERT
But when you categorically stated that light…

HABER
Yes, yes, yes. Only a nick.

>   *Pause.*

Otto.

OTTO
Yes Haber?

HABER
Assemble a list of my best contacts.

>   *Pause.*

ALBERT
Thank you, thank you.

OTTO
Come by tomorrow, Herr Einstein.

ALBERT
Yes, well…

>   *ALBERT wanders off, watching throughout.*

OTTO
How are you?

HABER
Uncle Ludwig would be proud.

— • —

>   *The University. CLARA Immerwahr—in her late 20s—delivering her dissertation to various guests.*

CLARA
** *Homines et feminae liberales, hospites honorati et conlegae insignes…*

>   *HABER enters, stands beside OTTO. CLARA pauses briefly, then continues:*

In conclusione…

OTTO
Where've you been?

HABER
Running late. How is it?

OTTO
Fantastic.

ALBERT
An ambitious young woman. A brilliant chemist. Her dissertation in Latin.

HABER
Latin? They scrapped that rule years ago.

OTTO
She insisted.

CLARA
(with above) …*velim dicere mentem futuram nostram facultatis dissolvi aeris, plumbi, argenti vivi et cadmiae habiturium esse sine dubio vim magnam, non solum in industria sed etiam in pensis quotidianis domi. Vobis gratias ago.* **

    Applause and cheers from guests.

OTTO
We ought to say our congratulations.

HABER
I need to get back to the lab.

OTTO
Nonsense. There's food and dancing and–

HABER
But I wasn't here, I…

OTTO
What's this? The overly-confident Herr Assistant Professor Doctor Haber shy about meeting a colleague? Shame on you.

    OTTO leads the way.

HABER
Otto!

OTTO
Doctor Immerwahr, my congratulations.

** Translation of Latin: Gentlemen, Ladies, honoured guests, and distinguished colleagues… In conclusion… …I would like to stress, that our future understanding of the solubility of copper, lead, quicksilver, and cadmium, will undoubtedly have far reaching impact, not only on industry, but also on everyday tasks in the home. Thank you.

CLARA
Thank you.

OTTO
"The future understanding of copper and cadmium."

CLARA
(correcting) "As they relate to everyday tasks in the home."

OTTO
An excellent dissertation, well researched, and very practical.

CLARA
You are too kind.

OTTO
And the first woman to graduate from this University! I'm sure you'll brighten up conversations considerably.

CLARA
Hopefully the conversations will have more to do with chemistry and less with my being a woman.

OTTO
Of course. Doctor Immerwahr, surely you've met Herr Assistant Professor Doctor Haber, newly promoted last week?

> They lock eyes.

CLARA
So you're the man.

HABER
(coy) Well…

CLARA
The applications of nitrogen gas, yes?

HABER
I'm making small discoveries.

CLARA
(teasing) "Discoveries?" No, no. You are making *observations* that, just at the right moment, you might properly utilize.

HABER
Yes, well…

> A small orchestra strikes up a Viennese waltz.

OTTO
I'll let you two get acquainted.

> He exits.

CLARA
Shall we dance?

HABER
I beg your–?

CLARA
I've already broken down one barrier today, I may as well break another.

HABER
I must warn you, a man is either a good chemist or a good dancer. The same man cannot do both.

CLARA
That may be true of men, Herr Professor, but women are trained to be good at everything. Shall we?

He bows. They dance.

HABER
Congratulations on your dissertation.

CLARA
Thank you.

HABER
It was most… illuminating.

CLARA
Was it.

HABER
Yes.

CLARA
Which part.

HABER
(struggling) Well. Your use of… Latin, as a language of presentation, was, especially–

CLARA
I saw you come in.

HABER
(pause) Ah.

CLARA
Near the end.

HABER
My deepest apologies. I do hope you will forward a copy to my office immediately. But on one condition.

CLARA
What's that?

HABER
That you submit your paper in German. My Latin is rusty to say the least.

CLARA
Of course. *(touching it)* Your cheek.

HABER
Eh?

CLARA
A nick.

HABER
Ah.

CLARA
Evidence of a run-in with Herr Einstein?

HABER
How did you–?

CLARA
News travels.

HABER
It was nothing. I let him win.

CLARA
Did you? Brilliant man, Einstein.

HABER
A brilliant *mind*. With no understanding of the real world.

CLARA
Oh?

HABER
Einstein's physics is all in his head and highly limited.

CLARA
The future of science is in its application.

HABER
Yes.

CLARA
Applying science to a *practical* purpose.

HABER
Yes, yes!

CLARA
Science for a greater humanity.

HABER
Exactly!

The number ends. CLARA grabs two drinks and hands one to HABER.

I must say I am intrigued by your name, Doctor Immerwahr.

CLARA
Clara, please, we are colleagues.

HABER
Very well Clara, call me Fritz.

CLARA
And what intrigued you about my name, Fritz.

HABER
Immer-wahr. It means "always true."

CLARA
Yes.

HABER
Is it?

CLARA
What?

HABER
True?

CLARA
My name?

HABER
No, you. Are you… always true?

CLARA
I try.

HABER
That is admirable.

CLARA
And what about your name.

HABER
It means nothing. An old name of Jewish stock.

CLARA
You're Jewish, then?

HABER
No.

CLARA
Christian?

HABER
No.

CLARA
What then?

HABER
A little of both.

CLARA
(smiles) I didn't think that was possible.

HABER
Above all, I am a German.

CLARA
I see. There seems to be a lot of that going around.

HABER
We live in a great country, why not be proud of it.

CLARA
So: born a Jew, professionally a Christian, and German by character.

HABER
Exactly.

CLARA
And spiritually?

HABER
Spiritually? *(quietly, intensely)*
"Do my eyes not look into your eyes,
And does it not flood
Your head and your heart
Floating in eternal mystery
Seen and unseen all around you?
Then call it what you like:
Happiness! Heart! Love! God!
Its name is mere sound and smoke,
Clouding the light of Heaven."

CLARA
(pause) Goethe.

HABER
Yes.

CLARA
Beautiful.

HABER
Yes. Beautiful.

— • —

ALBERT
Was a time women spoke music. And men thought poetry. When hope equalled work, and work equalled faith and the world's equation balanced. Was a time

ambitious young men and women sat under stars, shared their dreams, drank deep their future...

Moonlight through a window. CLARA and HABER with wine, staring at the night sky.

CLARA
(drawing it in the air) And that?

HABER
(unsure) Ursa Major?

CLARA
Very good. And that?

HABER
Ursa... Minor?

CLARA
Well done. And there?

HABER
Pisces.

CLARA
(laughing) Pisces? Does that look like a fish to you?

HABER
How am I supposed to know? They taught me how molecules are strung together, not the stars.

CLARA
And here I thought you knew everything.

HABER
(a challenge) Alright then. Which constellation is that?

CLARA
Which.

HABER
That.

CLARA
Where?

HABER
You see, right where my finger—

CLARA
Those stars there?

HABER
Yes.

CLARA
Hm.

HABER
Ah ha! I've got you!

CLARA
Delphinus.

HABER
Del...?

CLARA
Delphinus. Poseidon decided to make Amphitrite his wife. But she fled to Mount Atlas, eager to preserve her virginity.

HABER
Did she.

CLARA
But Poseidon was relentless. He sent every man and beast to search for her, including the dolphin. The dolphin looked everywhere for Amphitrite, and finally, found and captured her. And do you know what happened? Poseidon married her, decreed the dolphin sacred, and placed an image of it among the stars: *(She points.)* one star for its mouth; five for its fins; one for its back; and two for its tail. You see? Delphinus.

HABER
Well. Now I know everything.

HABER is very close.

Marry me?

Pause.

CLARA
I don't know.

Pause.

Will you search for me?

HABER
I...

CLARA
Will you?

HABER
I...

CLARA
Will you? Because if you don't.... If you stop searching, if you stop working, if you stop trying to know, you will lose me. Do you understand?

HABER
Yes.

CLARA
Do you?

HABER
Yes.

CLARA
Do you?

>   *Pause.*

HABER
Yes.

CLARA
Good. Now come to my bed. Come.

— • —

>   *A train station. A PORTER brings in bags. OTTO helps ALBERT with his coat.*

OTTO
(to PORTER) Thank you.

ALBERT
(to audience) A faithful friend. A burning passion. To believe in something.

OTTO
Have a good trip.

ALBERT
I will. Write to me?

OTTO
(surprised, but pleased) If you wish…

ALBERT
These past few months have been helpful and I'd like to stay in touch. Thank you.

OTTO
Don't thank me, thank Haber.

ALBERT
Yes, well…

OTTO
Do it in person. I'm dining with him tomorrow evening.

ALBERT
Time is ticking, and I'm already overdue at home. Besides, I wouldn't be welcome.

OTTO
Nonsense. Haber thinks you're brilliant. It's your work he finds, how shall I put it, "useless."

ALBERT
All's well then, for I find his work to be brilliant, and Haber himself to be, how shall I put it, "stupid."

OTTO
Herr Einstein–

ALBERT
Albert, please.

OTTO
Come now Albert. You admire him, you do, despite everything.

ALBERT
Perhaps. Perhaps there's something about his narrow-minded, arrogant, infuriating character that I find… interesting. And you. You think that highly of him?

OTTO
I do.

ALBERT
You believe that strongly in him.

OTTO
I'm a research assistant, Albert, that's all. But Haber… he shares his ideas with me, he takes my work seriously, he listens to what I have to say.

ALBERT
If you want to advance Otto–

OTTO
I don't need to advance. I don't need titles. I just need to feel I'm making a difference. And believe me, Haber will make a difference.

ALBERT
(skeptical) Hmm.

    A train whistle. They shake hands, and ALBERT heads off.

OTTO
(calling after) A new science for a new century.

— • —

    Night. CLARA asleep at her desk, surrounded by papers. HABER enters quietly, gently kisses her neck.

ALBERT
Was a time. Was a time she slept, surrounded by secrets. Ideas darkening her dreams, formulae fermenting her mind, thoughts locked deep inside her…

HABER
…Clara…?

CLARA
(starts) Wha–

HABER
Shhh…. It's alright…

CLARA
(breathing hard) …what, what time is it?

HABER
…late…

> *He holds her, and after a time, she calms.*

…my dear Frau Haber…

CLARA
…my dear Herr Immerwahr…

> *They kiss.*

HABER
You should be in bed.

CLARA
I know. But I have news that will excite you.

HABER
What a coincidence…

> *He takes out a letter.*

…for I have news that will excite you.

CLARA
Really.

HABER
Yes.

CLARA
Me first.

HABER
No me.

CLARA
No!

> *Pause.*

Me.

HABER
Very well.

CLARA
Our child has arrived.

Pause.

HABER
You're not… are you…?

She shows HABER a manuscript. He stares at it.

Oh! For a second I thought…

CLARA
No.

HABER
That wouldn't be a bad thing, would it? To have a—

CLARA
Read.

HABER pages through the manuscript.

HABER
…fabulous…

CLARA
I rewrote the equation in Lecture Two.

HABER flips through the pages, reads.

HABER
…fantastic…

CLARA
And you botched a footnote at the end of Seven.

HABER flips ahead, reads.

HABER
You're brilliant.

CLARA
(dismissing it) Yes, yes.

HABER
You *are*. You should be published on your own.

CLARA
Now. About your lecture tomorrow—

HABER
You should. Sitting at that desk, night after night…

CLARA
Fritz, we have to—

HABER
Double-checking calculations, rethinking formulas…

CLARA
It's late, if we don't start now—

HABER
You deserve more, you deserve–

CLARA
Stop it!

> *Pause.*

HABER
What's wrong. Clara.

> *She hands him a letter. He reads:*

"Dear Frau Doctor Haber: Although your credentials are satisfactory–"

> *CLARA grabs it from him and rips it up.*

Clara…

CLARA
I'm receiving as many rejections for being a woman as you do for being a Jew.

HABER
Christian.

CLARA
Oh please.

HABER
Clara, I know this is hard. But we're in this together, yes? Together, our star rises. We both believe in the same thing, we do. Don't we.

> *Pause.*

Don't we?

> *Pause.*

CLARA
…yes. Now you.

HABER
Eh?

CLARA
Show me.

HABER
(pause) Oh…

CLARA
Come now.

HABER
It's nothing, it's–

CLARA
Show me!

She grabs the letter from him, reads as he speaks.

HABER
It, it came today. Completely without warning. An offer. At the University of Karlsruhe. I, I heard about the posting, and I, I...

    Pause.

CLARA
When?

HABER
Next month.

    CLARA is silent.

I know it's...

    CLARA is silent.

I know you must...

CLARA
My friends are here. My family is here.

HABER
I know. But think about it Clara: A full professorship. No more late nights, no more editing.

CLARA
I like the late nights, I like the–

HABER
Excellent reputation, cutting-edge work, better labs...

CLARA
We have good labs, we have–

HABER
Imagine Clara: Picnics on the Rhine...

CLARA
...no...

HABER
...theatre in Freiburg...

CLARA
...no...

HABER
...walks in the forest–

CLARA
No!

    Pause.

HABER
Clara. Please.

Pause.

Please. I need you.

Pause.

Please.

She stares at him.

— • —

ALBERT with his viola, completing a frantic arpeggio.

ALBERT
September 10, 1908. Dear Otto: Congratulations to you and Haber on your new positions at Karlsruhe.

I take it from your letter Haber is making some headway. Tell your Christian master to watch his back. I hear Nernst is working on a similar project in Hamburg. I hear Nernst is nearly complete.

Poise the balance. Wind the mainspring. Now is your chance.

ALBERT plays again, furiously.

— • —

A street. HABER and CLARA walking swiftly. OTTO is trying to keep up and take notes at the same time.

HABER
No, no, no! Don't guess Otto! We'll never get anywhere if you keep making these ridiculous guesses in the name of science!

OTTO
You're pouring a large pail of facts over my head; I need time to sort through them, to, to–

HABER
This isn't sleepy little Jena any more, Otto, it's Karlsruhe.

OTTO
I know.

HABER
And now I find out that damn Nernst is all over me.

OTTO
…I know…

CLARA
And if we don't keep up with Nernst, we can kiss our hard work goodbye.

OTTO
But we've been at it since six this morning. Can we not talk at a restaurant?

HABER
Otto: we could have starvation across Europe if something isn't done soon.

OTTO
I know.

CLARA
In five years, there won't be any dinner to eat if something isn't done.

OTTO
I know, I know.

HABER
Then be a scientist. Review the facts. Both of you. Now: How does a farmer fertilize his field?

OTTO
Animal waste.

HABER
And the problem?

CLARA
Not enough.

OTTO
Difficult to import.

CLARA
Expensive.

OTTO
Time consuming.

HABER
Now what if… what if none of those options existed, how would the crop survive?

OTTO
The soil.

HABER
How?

CLARA
It naturally reduces nitrogen to ammonia.

OTTO
But that's too slow, it takes years–

HABER
So then we need to find another source of ammonia, yes?

OTTO
(*frustrated*) There *is* nowhere else. You can't–

HABER
The air.

OTTO
No.

CLARA
Why not? Air contains nitrogen. If we–

OTTO
We've already been through this. It's ridiculous. You can't fix it, you can't magically turn that nitrogen into ammonia.

HABER
But if we could.

CLARA
A process of fixing nitrogen.

OTTO
This is crazy…

HABER
Use it as "artificial" fertilizer.

CLARA
Cheaper.

HABER
Plentiful.

CLARA
No need to import.

HABER
A process with a practical use.

OTTO
But that's my point, the process doesn't exist, you can't–

HABER
Wait…

> HABER *digs out chalk from his pocket.*

CLARA
Fritz…?

HABER
Wait.

> HABER *gets on his hands and knees.*

OTTO
What are you doing?

HABER
Come here, come here, both of you! Here. Air consists of...

They kneel down. HABER writes on the sidewalk. The following happens at break-neck speed:

$$N2 + O2 + Ar + CO_2$$
$\downarrow$

CLARA
Nitrogen, Oxygen–

OTTO
Argon, Carbon...

HABER
But what if, what if we combined Nitrogen with Hydrogen...

As he speaks, HABER continues writing:

$\downarrow$
$$N_2 + H_2 \rightarrow NH_3$$

And then balance the above:

$$N_2 + 3H_2 \rightarrow 2NH_3$$

(to self) Will it go...?

HABER continues under the above equation:

$\triangle$ Gf   0   0   -16 kj/mol

CLARA finishes it:

$\triangle$ Gf   0   0   -16 kj/mol $\triangle$ Gf = -32

(to self as he adds the next) ...will it generate heat...?

$\triangle$ Hf   0   0   -46 kj/mol

CLARA finishes it:

$\triangle$ Hf   0   0   -46 kj/mol $\triangle$ Hf = -92

OTTO
The Nitrogen won't come apart, not at room–

HABER
But if we apply pressure, or temperature or a catalyst...

During the following OTTO and CLARA quickly sketch the beginnings of a chart that, if completed, would look something like this:

Pressure

Temperature	300	400	500
400	48%	55%	61%
500	26%	32%	38%
600	13%	17%	21%

NH_3 Yield

OTTO
100 atmospheres.

HABER
No no! 200 atmospheres… at a temperature of, say…

OTTO
200 degrees.

HABER
No, no, that's too low! 200 atmospheres at 500 degrees, and we, let's say we used a, a catalyst, say…

CLARA
Iron filings.

HABER
Perhaps, but–

OTTO
Copper.

HABER
No! *Think* you two, think!

> *Pause.*

Aluminum.

OTTO
(scoffs) Aluminum? Do you realize how expensive–!

CLARA
But how do we get the Nitrogen?

HABER
Distill it.

OTTO
But where do you get the hydro–

HABER
Sh, sh…

> *He writes:*

$$CH_4 + H_2O \rightarrow CO_2 + H_2$$

Then balances it:

$$CH_4 + 2H_2O \rightarrow CO_2 + 4H_2$$

Long pause as they stare at it.

OTTO
Huh.

CLARA
Hm.

HABER
Well?

CLARA
I'm not sure.

OTTO
Doubtful.

HABER
I say... possible. Back to the lab.

CLARA
But Fritz–

HABER
Come come! We'll create a series of experiments to test it.

HABER begins to leave. Turns back to them. They stare at him.
Well?!

He exits. CLARA runs after.

OTTO
But... what about dinner?

— • —

ALBERT with his viola. HABER addressing various crowds.

ALBERT
1909:

ACTOR A
"Haber Awarded Goethe Medal."

HABER
I am proud to have created a scientific process of nitrogen fixation. But nothing we create is of any value for its own sake – its advantage to mankind must be the ultimate measure.

ALBERT
1910:

ACTOR B
"Haber Creates New Collaboration With

ACTORS A & B
Science And Industry."

HABER
A method of mass production must be determined if ammonia synthesis is to be useful and the world is not to go hungry. Let science and industry work together. It is not enough to know, we must also apply!

ALBERT
1911:

ACTOR C
"Haber Named Director of Government Institute in Berlin."

HABER
We have saved Europe from starving. We have made science useful. And now, we open an institute dedicated to a trinity of purpose:

HABER & ACTORS A, B, & C
Science, industry and government.

ALBERT
Well well. If there isn't a Prophet among us.

— • —

Outside the Kaiser Wilhelm Institute.

HABER
Einstein.

ALBERT
Ah. My dear Herr *Director* Professor Doctor Haber.

HABER
Otto mentioned you'd be by. How long has it been?

ALBERT
Let's see… three years.

HABER
Six at least.

ALBERT
Six? Are you sure?

HABER
At least. And look at him Otto. Six years, and still wearing the same coat.

ALBERT
Am I?

HABER
Otto showed you around?

ALBERT
He did.

HABER
And?

ALBERT
The tennis court looks like fun.

HABER
(to OTTO) The best facilities in the country and he talks of the tennis courts.

ALBERT
There's more to life than science, isn't that right, Otto?

OTTO
Perhaps.

HABER
So Einstein, what brings you to Berlin. In need of more contacts, are you?

OTTO
Haber, really.

ALBERT
Something less taxing.

OTTO
A space to work is all, yes?

ALBERT
Just for a few weeks, before I leave for the Crimea.

HABER
Well. I'm sure we can make room. On one condition.

ALBERT
And that is?

HABER
Otto reminds me you play the viola.

OTTO
(to ALBERT) A passing mention, I…

ALBERT
I'm not very–

HABER
I'd like a concert for the staff.

ALBERT
Very well. I have a Tchaikovsky ready.

HABER
I'd prefer Bach.

ALBERT
Fauré.

HABER
Beethoven.

ALBERT
Rossini.

HABER
Good God Einstein, have you no Germans in your repertoire?!

ALBERT
(smirks) I'll dig something up.

HABER
Otto, set up a fully-equipped lab in the south building.

ALBERT
I don't need a–

HABER
And arrange for a full-time researcher.

ALBERT
That won't be–

HABER
And a secretary to address the paperwork.

ALBERT
Really, that's not–

HABER
And gather the staff to meet our "famous" guest.

ALBERT
Otto, you must stay, I insist.

> *OTTO looks to HABER.*

OTTO
Sorry Albert. My "duty" calls.

> *OTTO leaves.*

ALBERT
You work him too hard.

HABER
(oblivious) He's not complaining. I'll show you to your office.

ALBERT
Alright.

HABER
Where's your briefcase?

ALBERT
I…

HABER
You didn't lose it.

ALBERT
As a matter of–

HABER
I'll send Otto to–

ALBERT
No no I–

HABER
(calling) Otto!!

ALBERT
I don't carry a briefcase!

> *Pause.*

HABER
Einstein, how is it that you have revolutionized theoretical physics without a briefcase?

ALBERT
Haber.

HABER
This astounds me.

ALBERT
This… *(his head)* …is my laboratory. And this sweater, is my lab coat. And this… *(He takes out a sandwich from his pocket, gives it to HABER, and holds up the wrap paper.)* This paper, is my note book. The only thing I need from you is a pencil.

HABER
A pencil.

ALBERT
Yes.

HABER
Well I don't know, I may have to pull a few strings.

> *An awkward chuckle between them. HABER hands the sandwich back.*

ALBERT
Here, take half.

HABER
No no, I couldn't.

ALBERT
No please, Mileva made it 'specially.

> *HABER takes it. An ASSISTANT in lab coat enters.*

ASSISTANT 1
Excuse me, Herr Director Doctor Professor Haber.

> *He/She hands HABER a number of forms to sign. He does so, carefully. ALBERT is not impressed.*

Thank you, Herr Director.

> *The ASSISTANT leaves. HABER and ALBERT sit under the shade of a tree and eat.*

HABER
So.

ALBERT
So.

HABER
How is Mileva?

ALBERT
We're divorcing.

HABER
Oh?

ALBERT
Yes.

HABER
Why?

ALBERT
Because.

HABER
That simple.

ALBERT
No, that complex.

HABER
Yes. I know what you mean.

ALBERT
Why, your wife...

HABER
Clara.

ALBERT
Clara, yes, she...?

HABER
Obsessed. Every detail of my work. Every experiment, every lecture, every paper must be perfect or she flies into a rage. The other day, she came to my office in the middle of the day. My office! I told her you can't do that. It's just not done. But she insists.

ALBERT
They want what we have, and they can't have it. Yes?

HABER
But it's different with me. Before we married, she, she was–

ALBERT
An Immerwahr, yes?

HABER
No. She was a chemist.

A different ASSISTANT enters.

ASSISTANT 2
Excuse me, Herr Director Doctor Professor Haber...

More signing of forms. ALBERT finishes his sandwich.

Thank you. Herr Director.

The ASSISTANT leaves.

ALBERT
Tell me Haber. How is it possible you practice any science here, what with all this "administration."

HABER
You still believe science to be some kind of "philosophy," don't you?

ALBERT
Science is for science.

HABER
But how can that be. Science must serve a useful purpose, the greater good. I've proven that. We must judge it on what it *does*.

ALBERT
I am interested in what a man thinks and how he thinks, and not what he does or suffers. How is goodness measured, Haber, when it changes from second to second, from person to person, from country to country? No, we must practice science and leave goodness to God.

HABER
You are wrong.

ALBERT
I am right.

HABER
You are wrong.

ALBERT
I am right.

    Pause.

And yet, here we sit, together, passing the time.

    Pause.

HABER
So. The Crimea.

ALBERT
A study of gravitation yes.

HABER
And then?

ALBERT
Paris.

HABER
Paris?

ALBERT
I'm working on a new theory with–

HABER
But how can you.

ALBERT
How can I what?

HABER
France.

ALBERT
Yes.

HABER
There's talk of a war.

ALBERT
Oh that. Don't worry. It won't happen.

HABER
Nevertheless, we must be prepared.

ALBERT
You cannot simultaneously prevent and prepare for war, it defies all possible logic.

HABER
Why is it you insist on this ridiculous notion of pacifism.

ALBERT
Because wars kill people, all they do is–

HABER
There you go. More naive statements that bear no relation to reality.

ALBERT
My reality does not include spilling blood, no matter what the cause.

HABER
But your country is–

ALBERT
I am a Swiss citizen, I am not–

HABER
Your language is German, your culture is–

ALBERT
We are not talking about a country–

HABER
Of course we are, we are talking about–

ALBERT
You are wrong Haber, not the country.

HABER
What will you do for your cause!?

ALBERT
You are not Germany Haber!

HABER
What will you do–!

ALBERT
Haber–!

HABER
What!

ALBERT
Nothing!

 Pause.

I am a scientist.

HABER
No. You are a coward.

— • —

Night. CLARA, smoking, working at her desk. HABER enters, lights a lamp.

CLARA
It's two in the morning.

HABER
I know, I–

CLARA
Where have you been.

HABER
I'm sorry, I…

CLARA
I've been waiting since seven.

HABER
Clara…

CLARA
I've been here all day.

HABER
Please, can we–

CLARA
Re-working these calculations. Look at them.

She frantically digs through papers.

Here. And here. Errors. Mistakes. You can't do this.

HABER
I'll deal with it later.

CLARA
No no–.

HABER
I said we'll–

CLARA
You expect me to sit here, every single day, correcting your shoddy work, and even then you can't be home at–

HABER
I am tired! Can you not see that?!

Pause.

CLARA
(cool) What is it? What.

Pause.

HABER
There's going to be a war.

CLARA
(weary) ...oh God...

HABER
They've... they've asked me to form a new organization.

> *Pause.*

Chemists, meteorologists, industry people. The need for munitions will be high. They don't think they can...

> *Pause.*

If, if we can find a reasonable way to release chemicals...

CLARA
...Chemicals?

HABER
Simply transfer the work on ammonia to chlorine and...

CLARA
...oh no...

HABER
...create a practical method to release–

CLARA
No.

HABER
I know. I know what you're thinking. I know. But if we don't develop this, the British, the French, they will. We have to make strong choices. We have to be brave.

CLARA
You call this bravery?

HABER
If it brings a quick end to the war, if it saves a thousand lives, then yes, it is bravery. Do you think those men will care when an artillery shell flies overhead? They won't even blink. But the smell of chlorine gas, that will shock everyone. The fear of chlorine will be worth two thousand shells.

CLARA
I was under the impression we were using science to help people.

HABER
Clara, I am to be the first chemist in the history of Germany to run a war department. Privy Council to the military. Me.

CLARA
You'll never convert yourself to what they are Fritz. Never. No matter how many religions you adopt, no matter how many government officials you bow to, or medals you win, or discoveries you make, you'll never be a real German. In their eyes, you're one thing and one thing only.

HABER

I'll prove it to you, I'll prove that my science–

CLARA

This is *my* science. My work is your work, your work is mine. Mine. And now you are betraying all that.

HABER

We still believe the same thing, we still believe–.

CLARA

You don't believe in anything. You can't bear to look at yourself and see what it is you truly believe. You don't have the courage. But you have the gall, you have the audacity, to take everything I believe in, to rob me of the only thing I own, to sacrifice it on the altar of "country," of "nation," of "Germany."

HABER

No one is forcing you to work on this. If you don't like it, work on other projects, work on–

CLARA

Why. Why would I do it. Why would I ever work on *anything* ever again. Why would I open a notebook ever again. Why would I write an equation ever again. Why would I create an idea, or nourish a theory, or ask a question, or search for a solution, or bother to *think* ever again, when my husband… when my husband has taken my faith and turned it into something terrible. When my husband's belief is butchery. When my husband's religion is murder.

> *HABER raises his hand to hit her.*

(fierce) Don't. *(pause)* Don't.

— • —

> *OTTO, putting on his uniform. ALBERT with a letter.*

OTTO

(cheery) November 3, 1914. Dear Albert: thank you for your letter. But I can't agree with your description of this war as "diabolical." We are a great nation. We must defend our interests and not let this threat go unanswered.

ALBERT

(to audience) The greatest threats in war are men without faith.

OTTO

Watch Albert. The war will be over before year's end, Germany will score an easy victory, and we will earn the respect of the entire world. As Haber said to me yesterday: "Science will prevail. Science for the greater good."

— • —

HABER is getting into military uniform, preparing to leave. CLARA sits in silence.

HABER
All the bills are taken care of.

Pause.

I've arranged for someone from the Institute to drop by every few days. You won't be so lonely.

Pause.

Why don't you work. Eh? It's not like you not to–

CLARA
(quietly) Don't.

Pause.

Don't touch me.

HABER
Clara.

CLARA
If you're going, go.

HABER
I love you. I do.

CLARA
You love your uniforms and titles, that's what you love, Herr *Privy Council* Director Professor Doctor Haber.

HABER
Please.

CLARA
I will leave you. You know that. If you do this, you will lose me.

A knock and OTTO enters in uniform. He salutes HABER.

OTTO
Message from Colonel Peterson. Weather conditions tomorrow look to be perfect. A great day for Germany, Haber.

HABER
Excellent.

OTTO starts to leave.

CLARA
Don't do it Otto.

HABER
Clara.

CLARA
(to OTTO) Don't go with him, you don't–.

HABER
That's enough.

CLARA
You don't believe in the same thing, you don't–.

HABER
I said that's enough!! (to OTTO) Wait in the car.

    OTTO exits. HABER collects his things.

I'll be back in a few days.

CLARA
What? No bow, no kiss, no goodbye poem?

    HABER sees his revolver and goes to pick it up. She takes it first.

HABER
Clara.

CLARA
You're not leaving.

HABER
Clara, don't be…

CLARA
You can't do this. You can't. You can't.

    Pause.

HABER
I'll be home when I can.

    He leaves. She stares after him, then down at the gun.

— • —

    A trench at Ypres. The chronic sounds of warfare. HABER and OTTO enter. PETERSON salutes.

HABER
(eager) Colonel Peterson.

PETERSON
Herr Privy Council Haber.

HABER
A beautiful day.

PETERSON
For some.

HABER
How is Johnny today?

PETERSON
Quiet. When the French are quiet, they're scared; but when the Canadians are quiet, it makes me nervous.

HABER
Is everything ready?

PETERSON
(to OTTO) Bring the report from the Gas Batteries.

HABER
(to OTTO) And inform General Deimling I've arrived.

OTTO
Jawohl.

He exits.

HABER
Problems?

PETERSON
Two days ago, our men were laying your chlorine gas flasks.

HABER
And...?

PETERSON
An incoming artillery shell ruptured the containers.

HABER
(pause) Casualties?

PETERSON
Twenty dead.

HABER
Good God.

PETERSON
God was not good on that particular day, sir. My brother was in that unit.

HABER
I'm sorry.

PETERSON
With all due respect sir, I believe the Front is a dangerous place for college professors.

HABER
Forgive me Colonel, but I am Privy Council first, a chemist second, and a professor third.

PETERSON
Chemists, physicists, and weatherman did not win us the Franco-Prussian War.

HABER
No, but imagination, ingenuity and bravery did.

PETERSON
My grandfather fought in that war, and he had all three. What he didn't need was chlorine gas.

HABER
Perhaps not. Perhaps he used a pistol, something soldiers seven hundred years earlier would have thought barbaric.

PETERSON
The soldiers don't trust things that haven't been proven. They don't like to see friends killed by their own weapons. They don't want something they can't understand and can't control. All these "modern" weapons are destroying the valour and the honour of being a soldier.

HABER
If you don't believe me to be brave Colonel, and you don't believe in my invention, then consider me to be the imagination of this regiment. I am here to help you, work with you, make your job easier. I only want for us all to get home faster. Is that clear?

PETERSON
Yes, sir.

HABER
Anything else?

PETERSON
Some of the men, sir, they wonder about...

HABER
About what.

PETERSON
About your faith. Sir.

HABER
My faith?

PETERSON
Yes, sir.

HABER
And what do you tell them?

PETERSON
I tell them you are a "Christian," sir.

HABER
I am.

PETERSON
Of course. Sir.

Enter OTTO.

OTTO
General Deimling is on his way.

PETERSON
Good.

OTTO
The Gas Batteries have reported…

HABER
Excellent.

OTTO
(hesitant) Haber. There isn't… there's doesn't appear to…

HABER
What is it.

OTTO
There are no reserves in place.

HABER
What?

PETERSON
After the accident, General Deimling instructed no extra men be used in this operation.

OTTO
But without extra men to back up the chlorine release–

PETERSON
(to OTTO) Report from the weather station.

OTTO
If we can't back up the first wave of men–

PETERSON
I said report from the weather station!

Pause.

OTTO
Jawohl.

He exits.

HABER
(to PETERSON) What is the meaning of this.

DEIMLING enters. HABER, PETERSON salute.

DEIMLING
Haber. Peterson.

HABER
Herr General Deimling. I have, only now, been informed that we have no reserves.

DEIMLING
After that disaster, I won't risk any more men.

HABER
Forgive me sir, but at this late date, I think it imprudent to change the battle plan, we must have men to back up the chlorine release.

PETERSON
We can't ask our men to put their faith in the direction of the wind.

HABER
The only way is a mass release of chlorine *and–*

DEIMLING
Observe the attack and determine the chlorine's effectiveness, that is all.

HABER
Herr General, the purpose of the chlorine is to create havoc in the enemy's trench, so that the first wave may advance and take the enemy's position. But if there are no extra men to follow, the attack will fail. We may simply kill enemy soldiers without advancing our cause.

PETERSON
Herr General, I insist–!

HABER
The entire strategy–!

DEIMLING
Strategy is none of your business! You are here to perform a little demonstration, Haber, nothing more. Do your "science," and leave the strategy to me.

> *Enter OTTO.*

OTTO
Wind shifting to West/North West at four kilometers per hour.

DEIMLING
Perfect conditions. This is what you've been praying for, isn't it Haber?

> *HABER is silent.*

Isn't it?

> *HABER is silent.*

You have a choice: Release the chlorine on enemy lines without full reserves. Or if you do not, I will see to it personally that you be court-martialled, stripped of your rank, and dismissed from your post. Don't forget who you are, Haber, and where you come from. Because we haven't.

> *Long pause.*

HABER
(to PETERSON) On my signal.

OTTO
But Haber.

PETERSON
(to OTTO) Tell all divisions to stand by.

OTTO
Haber, why are you–?

HABER
Be quiet.

OTTO
The entire possibility of breaking through the line will fail–

HABER
–that's enough–

OTTO
–why would you want to kill people, why would you want to–?

> HABER hits OTTO with the back of his hand.

HABER
Don't question me again.

> OTTO is stunned.

PETERSON
(to OTTO) Tell all divisions to stand by.

> OTTO stares at HABER.

OTTO
…jawohl…

> OTTO exits.

DEIMLING
Well done Haber. I'm sure a promotion to Captain will be in order, no matter what the outcome. Now then. We will meet in my barracks at 20:00 hours. Agreed?

PETERSON
Jawohl.

> HABER stares.

DEIMLING
Haber, are we agreed?

HABER
(quietly) Jawohl. Herr General.

DEIMLING
Good.

DEIMLING and PETERSON exit. HABER gives the signal and it is passed down the line. A cloud makes its way over no-man's-land. OTTO and ALBERT appear separately. As ALBERT reads the letter, the SOLDIER crawls to HABER, barely visible in the dying light.

OTTO
Ypres. April 22, 1915. Dear Albert:

ALBERT
Dusk. Chlorine billows over the land. Peterson sends the men over the top, their dark gas masks tight over pale faces. They make their way behind the vapour, and drown in the growing dark. The last rays of setting sun catch the chlorine, turning it a yellow-green ochre. Beautiful. In a way.

The sounds of chaos. Then silence – the SOLDIER's gasping the only sound.

Then, out of the early evening pall, a lone soldier, crawling on hand and knee over no-man's-land. He falls, gasping for breath, ten metres from our trench. "Give me your hand."

OTTO
–says Haber.

ALBERT
"Give me your hand!" The soldier reaches his fists forward, a cloth jammed in his mouth. Haber inches his body out low over the edge of the trench. There's gunfire, but it's high, and he manages to grab the soldier's hand and pull him in. A boy...

OTTO
–no more than sixteen.

ALBERT
A faulty gas mask...

OTTO
–he never stood a chance.

ALBERT
Haber drags him onto his thigh, rests his head on his shoulder, pulls the cloth from his mouth. The boy gasps for air. Black blood flows from his nose, down his chin, gathering in Haber's lap.

OTTO
"Who are you?"

ALBERT
–says Haber. And the boy's eyes roll open, blinded by chlorine.

OTTO
"What is your name?"

ALBERT
The boy heaves air into his destroyed lungs.

SOLDIER
(gasping) Help me.

ALBERT
–he says.

SOLDIER
Help me.

ALBERT looks to OTTO.

OTTO
Of all people, he asks Haber for help. Haber.

OTTO vanishes. CLARA appears, holding HABER's revolver to her heart.

CLARA
...esse sine dubio vim magnam, non solum in industria sed etiam in pensis quotidianis domi...

HABER
Oh God.

An explosion of light and sound. CLARA, HABER and the SOLDIER disappear. ALBERT shields his eyes.

ALBERT
Oh God.

ACT II

Rain. The German Club. 1918. ALBERT enters.

ALBERT
…Was a time…

He takes a seat. A cabaret SINGER performs an upbeat number: "Oh, How We Wish We Were Kids Again." CHARLOTTA—in her early 20s—at the hatcheck counter, reading a newspaper.

SINGER
(sings) "Not so long ago we Germans thirsted after blood.
We had half the world in trenches crawling through the mud.
Remember all our victories? Good God we had a streak!
Ya, we were the big guys then, but now our future's bleak.
From Charlemagne to Tamberlaine
We've always "bayne" the heroes.
Where's our luck? How come we're stuck
With such a bunch-a zeroes?
When will we awake n' see
We should make a vacancy:
The status quo just has to go in Germany!
Oh, how we wish that we were kids again,
How kind we were back then, when we were young.
Back then we played at war on soft green grass
And fought with make-believe, not poison gas.
And now that we have seen the truth of war
We're not the same as we were before.
Oh how we wish that we were kids again
To be naive again. Believe again. Achieve again!"

Near the song's end, OTTO and HABER enter. OTTO is older and sullen, almost unrecognizable. HABER—now in his 50s—wears top hat, tails and pince-nez. He shakes out his umbrella.

LOTTA
Rain, rain, rain.

HABER
Yes.

ALBERT
A rich older man.

LOTTA
Drowning.

HABER
Yes.

ALBERT
A beautiful young woman.

LOTTA
Drowning in rain and work.

ALBERT
Berlin: December 1918.

She takes their coats.

HABER
(aside, to OTTO) Find a table.

OTTO
Where?

HABER
Where I can't be seen.

OTTO exits.

LOTTA
Your umbrella?

He bows deeply with the umbrella. She giggles.

HABER
And what is so funny?

LOTTA
Bowing ended with the war.

HABER
That much out of the fashion, is it?

LOTTA
Yes. Along with taste, wit, kindness, charm…

HABER
In that case, *(bowing again)* I lay this umbrella at your heart and myself at your feet.

LOTTA
Hmm, I'd prefer it the other way around.

LOTTA takes the umbrella.

HABER
And what is it *you* are doing here?

LOTTA
I *work* here. Upstairs in the office.

HABER
I thought this club was open only to men, whether you work here or no.

LOTTA
Times change.

HABER
What are you doing down here, if you work upstairs?

LOTTA
The check girl's sick.

HABER
Oh.

LOTTA
Knocked up by a soldier.

HABER
Oh.

LOTTA
Gone for an "operation," if you know what I mean.

HABER
Good God.

LOTTA
The war's changed a lot of things.

HABER
Indeed.

LOTTA
They say there'll be another in twenty years.

HABER
Do they?

LOTTA
I read it in the papers. They say we only lost the war because we didn't have enough supplies.

HABER
And what else do the papers say?

LOTTA
There's the revolt in Russia...

HABER
Ah yes.

LOTTA
There's going to be some kind of treaty with the Allies...

HABER
Yes, I've heard that.

LOTTA
And you know that Haber?

HABER
Haber...

LOTTA
You know...

HABER
Haber…

LOTTA
Poison gas.

HABER
Ah yes! And what do the papers say of him?

LOTTA
The Nobel Prize.

HABER
That a fact?

LOTTA
'Though France and the Unites States will boycott it.

HABER
Really.

LOTTA
Don't know why. He's not getting the prize for chlorine gas, he's getting it for that thing, you know, what's it called–

HABER
Nitrogen Fixation.

LOTTA
Saved millions from starving. Five years ago the world thinks he's a savior, and now…

HABER
Yes, the war certainly did change things. *(with disdain)* This "music" for instance.

LOTTA
Too modern for you?

HABER
Give me a good old-fashioned waltz anytime.

LOTTA
It speaks to people, this music, about their lives.

HABER
Vulgar, like their clothes. Or lack thereof.

LOTTA
(teasing) Too much sex in this "new" world?

HABER
Beg your pardon?

LOTTA
Sex.

HABER
Are we talking of love?

LOTTA
Love, sex, it's all the same.

HABER
It certainly is *not*.

LOTTA
What's the difference then?

HABER
Love, my dear Fräulein, is about creation. Sex is about completion.

LOTTA
(laughs) Very good.

HABER
(teasing) And I, for one, have always found the creation more pleasing than the completion.

LOTTA
Have you now? Well then, you must "please" your wife a great deal.

HABER
(pause) Well…

LOTTA
No?

HABER
No… I…

LOTTA
Not married?

>   *She grabs his hand. No ring.*

HABER
She… died. Years ago.

LOTTA
Oh. I'm sorry. What happened?

>   *HABER is silent. A sultry cabaret number begins: "A Little Yearning."*

Dance?

HABER
To this?

LOTTA
Come.

HABER
But you're working, mustn't you–?

LOTTA
The customers can wait.

HABER
(coy) I must warn you, a man can be a good dancer, or a good–

LOTTA
Come, before the song ends.

> *They dance. HABER is awkward. She pulls him close. OTTO watches them, grimly. The singer dances in with a man. HABER sees them. They become CLARA—her shirt stained with blood—and the dead SOLDIER, gasping for air. Their dance transforms into an old fashioned waltz. HABER breaks away.*

Are you alright?

HABER
(short of breath) Otto!

LOTTA
What's wrong?

OTTO
Haber?

HABER
(to OTTO) Take me home.

LOTTA
Is he…?

OTTO
Haber, are you alright?

LOTTA
Haber? You're…?!

HABER
(to OTTO, quietly) Take me home, please, I…

> *OTTO leads him out. LOTTA looks after.*

LOTTA
You're… Haber…

— • —

ALBERT
Was a time…. Was a time he was born into a new world. So new, he didn't even know her name…

> *LOTTA at work, typing.*

HABER
I must apologize.

LOTTA
Herr Haber!

HABER
It was unfair to withhold that information from you.

LOTTA
If I had known you were–

HABER
But I must be careful. England has named me a war criminal and there are many people who would like to see me, well…

LOTTA
Hanged?

HABER
Yes. You aren't one of them I hope?

LOTTA
No. Are you better?

HABER
Thank you, yes. Now, may I enquire as to your name?

LOTTA
Charlotta Nathan. From Berlin.

HABER
Charlotta.

LOTTA
Are you being familiar with me, Herr Haber?

HABER
I am. For I am telling you, that from this day forth, I will have my daily coffee with no one but you.

LOTTA
Well, Herr *Captain* Director Professor Doctor Haber, I thank you for offering me the honour and privilege of having coffee with you. Though whether or not you have the privilege of going with me, is still up for debate.

HABER
What's to debate?

LOTTA
Really, Herr Captain–

HABER
Fritz.

LOTTA
I barely know you, calling you by your familiar name–

HABER
Fritz.

LOTTA
–is a great impropriety.

HABER
Fräulein Nathan, are you being more old fashioned than the ancient Prussian soldier standing before you?

LOTTA
No, no, I merely–.

HABER
Then with your permission, I will call you Charlotta.

LOTTA
I quite like Lotta.

HABER
I quite like "Lo." *(pronounced "low")*

LOTTA
No, Lotta.

HABER
Fine, Lotta then. Now before I go.

He presents her with flowers.

LOTTA
Oh my–!

HABER
And to accompany them, a poem.

He hands her the poem.

"Put them at your desk side
See them now and then
Flowers are to women
What women are to men."

LOTTA
Herr Captain…

HABER
Ah, ah! Fritz.

LOTTA
This is all – you shouldn't – I can't very well–

HABER
Isn't that the way you young people do things these days?

LOTTA
Yes! No! I…. Why are you doing all this?

HABER
I…

Pause.

Have you ever had a, a second chance. To do something differently? To do it better?

LOTTA
I think so. Yes.

HABER
Well then. We have something in common.

She smiles.

The Kranzler Café. Three o'clock. Coffee.

— • —

OTTO throwing books into a briefcase.

OTTO
My resignation is on your desk.

HABER
For God's sake Otto, it's not in my control. The Committee only allows me one guest.

OTTO
And so you take that woman, that, that child?

HABER
Don't talk about Lotta as if–

OTTO
If Clara were alive–

HABER
If Clara were alive, *she* would be coming with me and not you.

OTTO
You're an embarrassment.

HABER
Am I. The Nobel Prize, you call that–

OTTO
Germany is desperate for heroes, no matter how tarnished they are.

Pause.

What did we do Haber?

HABER
What do you mean?

OTTO
What did we do. Out there.

HABER
I, I don't know what…

OTTO
We promised them victory, promised greatness. And what did we give them? Nothing. We left them with nothing to believe in. Nothing.

HABER
That's not true.

OTTO
People are hungry Haber. They have no food, they have no money. And what are we doing about it? Eh? Resting on our laurels. Claiming victory when there was none. Travelling the world while our country suffers.

HABER
Otto.

OTTO
Go ahead. Forget your science, forget your friends, forget.

    Pause.

Maybe I'll forget too.

— • —

    ** *OTTO alone. He pulls a letter from his pocket. Simultaneously, ALBERT pulls a letter from his pocket.*

ALBERT
"Returned: Address unknown."

    ALBERT pulls another letter.

Returned: unknown…

    And another.

Unknown…

    ALBERT looks to OTTO. OTTO exits.

— • —

    The sea. LOTTA with no shoes and dress hiked up to her knees. She skips along the strand. HABER, fully clothed, tries to keep up.

LOTTA
Let's play!

HABER
(out of breath) Lotta!

** This scene was cut from the Premiere production, and is optional.

LOTTA
We'll splash in the sea, we'll build castles in the sand, we'll have sex in the surf!

HABER
I can't.

LOTTA
Why not?

HABER
Because. I…

LOTTA
(mocking) Because what. Because you have *work*? You *have* no work! You're on vacation! You're FREEEEE!

    She runs. He follows.

HABER
I'm too old for this…

LOTTA
What do you want?

HABER
What?

LOTTA
You won the Nobel Prize. You're a famous scientist. You can have anything.

HABER
I want…

    Pause.

I want to be re-born in your eyes.

LOTTA
Are you proposing marriage?

HABER
And if I did?

LOTTA
I'd consider it.

HABER
Consider it?

LOTTA
This isn't like it was twenty years ago. I don't need a husband.

HABER
But there are things we need to work out.

LOTTA
Like what.

HABER
You are Jewish and I am Christian.

LOTTA
(bored) Fritz...

HABER
Christianity is important to one's advancement.

LOTTA
No, it was important to *your* advancement.

HABER
But Lotta–

LOTTA
Catch me.

HABER
Eh?

LOTTA
Catch me!

> She runs again. He runs after, catches her and pulls her down into the sand. They kiss, hold each other. She turns his head to the sea.

Look out there. What do you see?

HABER
Ideas, thoughts, dreams. Bobbing in the sea, like sails on the horizon. At first small, drifting here and there, barely moving, only the setting sun to light their way. But when they come ashore, they grow big and strong, rugged and weather-beaten. And if you show respect, they will let you ride them for a while, see the world the way they see it. And those are the ships you wait for all your life.

LOTTA
Yes. They are.

> HABER picks up a handful of sand.

HABER
If I could make bread from the air... why can't I mine gold from the sea.

— • —

> ALBERT with his viola. HABER addressing various crowds. LOTTA at his side.

ALBERT
1920:

ACTOR A
"Haber in Sweden to Accept Nobel Prize."

HABER
I thank the committee for its bravery and foresight at such a sensitive time in Germany's history. Nothing we create is of value for its own sake – its advantage to mankind is the ultimate measure.

ALBERT
1923:

ACTOR B
"Haber Speaks at Japanese Conference."

HABER
50 years ago, my Uncle Ludwig nearly died at the hands of one of your Samurai warriors. But like our great German nation, he battled back, and won the respect of the Samurai. For to be German is to have character!

ALBERT
1927:

ACTOR C
"Haber South Sea Project Shrouded in Secrecy."

HABER
I am now embarking on a highly sensitive, multi-year project that by its very nature will benefit Germany and all of mankind. It is not enough to know, we must also apply!

ALBERT
Well, well. If it isn't the Second Coming.

— • —

HABER is packing.

LOTTA
Tell me.

HABER
No.

LOTTA
I have a right to know.

HABER
I can't.

LOTTA
I have a right to know why my husband's spending God knows how long sailing to South America. Now tell me.

Pause. He relents.

HABER
You must promise. Not even the housekeeper can know.

LOTTA
My lips are sealed.

HABER
There was a Dutch scientist, Arrenhuis.

LOTTA
Yes?

HABER
He calculated there were six milligrams of gold per one tonne of sea water. Up to now, no one's tested his work. No one.

LOTTA
I see.

HABER
The Allies will kill this country with their Versailles reparation payments. 20 Billion Gold Marks. With interest. It will be nineteen hundred and eighty-eight before the debt is paid. 1988! But if I can find a way to extract gold from seawater…

LOTTA
I see.

HABER
We can help the country rebuild, and provide a new source of mining technology. But it must be kept secret. Any leaks could affect the gold markets. Better to keep things calm.

LOTTA
I want to come.

HABER
We've spent two years travelling the world, and I never left your side once. Not once. Do you really want to spend another nine months on a hot smelly boat?

LOTTA
I want to spend it with you.

HABER
No.

LOTTA
Fritz–

HABER
I said no!

She is hurt.

I'll miss you, you know that. But I'm nearly sixty. This may be my last chance. If I'm to do this, I have to do it now. I have to do it alone.

She moves close, kissing his neck.

LOTTA
Here I'll be. Waiting. Thinking of nothing but you. Your breath on my neck, your warm body next to–

HABER
(pulling away) Lotta.

LOTTA
(frustrated) What.

HABER
Please.

LOTTA
What's the–?

HABER
I'm not young anymore.

LOTTA
Well I am.

> ALBERT *enters, holding his viola case.*

ALBERT
Excuse me. I didn't…

HABER
Einstein.

LOTTA
Please, come in.

ALBERT
Perhaps I should come back another time.

LOTTA
No, no, please. We've been expecting you. *(to HABER)* Ah hem.

HABER
Ah. Einstein, this is my wife Charlotta. Lotta, this is Albert Einstein.

LOTTA
A great honour.

ALBERT
When I meet the wife of the great Haber, then the greatest honour is mine.

> *He kisses her hand.*

LOTTA
May I take your coat?

ALBERT
No thank you.

LOTTA
Your hat.

ALBERT
No thank you.

LOTTA
Your violin case.

ALBERT
Thank you, but no.

HABER
Hasn't changed a bit. Wins the Nobel Prize and carries no luggage.

ALBERT
Carrying no luggage is easy; winning the Prize is much more difficult, as you well know.

LOTTA
I'll make some coffee.

ALBERT
No, please stay, I wouldn't–

LOTTA
It's no trouble.

> *She exits. An awkward pause.*

HABER
So.

ALBERT
So.

HABER
How long has it been?

ALBERT
Ten years.

HABER
Fifteen at least.

ALBERT
Fifteen? Are you sure?

HABER
At least.

ALBERT
Yes, well…

> *An awkward pause.*

HABER
So. To what do I owe this visit? More contacts, another office space to let, another–

ALBERT
No. No, I.... I'm giving a fundraising concert at the New Synagogue. I thought you and your wife might like to come.

HABER
That may be why you're in Berlin, Einstein, but I am positive it's not why you're here.

> *Pause.*

ALBERT
I've been trying to reach Otto.

HABER
Otto?

ALBERT
Yes, but my letters to him have been returned. So I thought perhaps you...

HABER
Otto left the Institute a long time ago.

ALBERT
Oh?

> *Pause.*

HABER
Yes.

> *Pause.*

If locating Otto is the reason you're here, I'm afraid–

ALBERT
There are a number of reasons. The concert, for one. Number two, to accept my German citizenship.

HABER
Einstein a German?

ALBERT
The new government offered, and as a sign of support for the Weimar Republic, I've accepted.

HABER
How convenient.

ALBERT
And lastly...

> *He hands a piece of paper to HABER.*

HABER
What is it.

ALBERT
A petition. Signed by fifty of Germany's top intellectuals.

HABER reads.

Demanding Germany immediately end conscription and the military training of young men in keeping with the Versailles Treaty. Your name would be a great addition.

Pause.

You have always helped me Haber. I've always counted on you.

HABER
With science, yes; with politics, no.

ALBERT
This is not about politics.

HABER
Really Einstein.

ALBERT
This is about humanity.

HABER
And here I thought "science was for science."

ALBERT
If *you* sign, then others–

HABER
Lunacy.

ALBERT
The war was lunacy. You know it, I know it, why not let others know it. You have always said your work is toward a practical purpose, now use it. Take a risk. Tell people what you really believe.

HABER
There are considerations, there are compromises, there–.

ALBERT
There are principles.

HABER
My principles lie in the science and its application; this political nonsense will help neither.

ALBERT
Thousands died from exposure to chlorine–

HABER
Don't.

ALBERT
Thousands!

HABER
You don't need to remind me–

ALBERT
You saw it with your own eyes, you saw it–

HABER
I did what I did, and that's the end of it! We can't turn back the clock no matter how much we try. Now. If we find a way to pay these awful reparations, a strong Germany will rise, and we'll never be forced to use chemical weapons again. But we must have a trained army at the ready.

ALBERT
But Haber, if you sign–.

HABER
We must defend ourselves. The enemy–

ALBERT
The enemy is within; National Socialism–

HABER
Hitler is a thug; the radical fringe of–

ALBERT
He is a patriot, just like you.

HABER
I will not apologize for loving my country. You, on the other hand, belong to a country only when it suits you; you care about something only when you're at its centre; you're loyal only when it advances one of your pointless causes. Pacifism…

ALBERT
Sign the petition.

HABER
Internationalism.

ALBERT
Sign it.

HABER
Zionism.

ALBERT
Sign it!

HABER
No!

He rips up the petition. ALBERT stares at him, horrified. HABER calms himself.

I… I'm sorry…

— • —

LOTTA composing a letter. ALBERT with his viola. HABER at sea, working. An assistant brings him various beakers. HABER examines them, then takes notes in a book.

LOTTA
My dearest Fritz...

ALBERT
Was a time he sailed the South American seas, searching for gold where there was only the horror and holiness of water. The eternal ocean, where time is forever stopped.

LOTTA
My dearest Fritz: Everything has become cold here since you left. So cold, even time feels chill.

ALBERT
"National Socialists Ride Wave to New Heights."

LOTTA
Employment has sunk to murky depths; the price of bread rises like an unending tide.

ALBERT
"The Rising Tide of Reform."

LOTTA
The winds are changing, dear husband, and you must soon sail home.

ALBERT
"Gold in Seawater.... A Failure."

HABER examines the last container, dejected. He shakes the assistant's hand: a thank you and a goodbye. Then, he closes his book.

— • —

Packing crates. HABER enters with suitcases, tired. He stares into the dark room. A woman sits in the shadows, smoking.

HABER
(to the woman) Lotta?

CLARA
It's two in the morning.

HABER
I know, I–

CLARA
Where have you been?

HABER
I'm sorry, I...

CLARA
I've been waiting since seven.

The woman stands. It is CLARA. LOTTA enters, cautiously.

LOTTA
…Fritz?

CLARA vanishes.

Thank God you're home, thank God…

She goes to him; she weeps.

HABER
What is it, what's wrong–?

LOTTA
It isn't safe here, it isn't, there's no–

HABER
Calm down. Calm down. Now tell me what happened.

LOTTA
Two days ago. I came home. On our door. Painted in black. "Jew." "Jew."

Pause.

HABER
A stupid prank.

LOTTA
They're selling Nazi newspapers on the corner. They're closing down the Jewish shops.

HABER
Thugs. Besides, I'm baptized, there's nothing–.

LOTTA
But I'm not! They don't care about that anymore Fritz. They don't care. They don't care what you've done. All they care about is what you are.

Pause.

I've sent everything to Basel.

HABER
Switzerland?

LOTTA
I've rented a house, we'll find you work, we'll–

HABER
I've been gone nearly a year, I can't just leave, I can't just…

LOTTA
We can't stay here. We can't.

HABER
This is my home, I can't just–

LOTTA
You think I don't love this place as much as you? You think I *want* to leave? I was born here. My family has been here for generations. My brother and my father died for this country. But not for this. Not for this. I won't live another war. I won't.

>   *Pause.*

HABER
I'll come up with something. I know I will. One month. That's all I need. One more month.

LOTTA
I'm not an equation Fritz.

>   *Pause.*

Don't make me do this without you. Please.

>   *She starts to go. He holds her.*

HABER
You can't go. You can't. You can't…

>   *She holds him. Then, she kisses his head.*

LOTTA
My dear Herr Captain.

>   *She exits.*

— • —

>   *HABER in his office, preparing a class.*

ACTOR A
1930:

ALBERT
Hitler captures 107 seats.

ACTOR B
1932:

ALBERT
Hitler captures 36% of the popular vote.

ACTOR C
1933:

ALBERT
Hitler sworn in as Chancellor.

>   *A GESTAPO bursts in, ushering in RUST.*

RUST
Herr Haber.

HABER
Excuse me, what are you–

RUST
(smiles) I am Bernhard Rust, Minister of Education.

HABER
Ah!

They shake hands.

RUST
I am sorry to interrupt your work, Herr Professor. But I would like a word.

HABER
I'm sorry, it will have to wait. I have a class in–

RUST
It's quite important Herr Professor. I'm sure your students will understand.

HABER
Very well.

RUST
Thank you. Tell me, what are your views on education?

HABER
Have you come to discuss philosophy?

RUST
Your views on education are of great interest to the government. You are, after all, one of our leading scientists, one of our shining stars.

HABER
My views on education…

RUST
As they relate to the state.

HABER
As they relate to the state. Very well. Education is the striving for insight, for higher purpose, for the attainment of culture and spirit. In my view the State exists to preserve and protect this culture, which is held in trust by education.

RUST
(chuckles) Very good Haber, very old fashioned, very… Prussian. Unfortunately, this government no longer holds that view of education.

HABER
Oh?

RUST
No. We believe education to be, foremost, the sacrifice of the individual to the community. The old system reduced everything to personal gain. But education

under National Socialism is to be an uplifting one. This... egoism in science must go.

HABER
Then we must agree to disa–

RUST
Whether you agree or not is immaterial. I've come to tell you it is so.

    Pause.

I understand you're working on something new.

HABER
Yes. Is there a–?

RUST
After your... misfortune with gold in seawater, many people thought–

HABER
I'm not one to flinch at failure, Minister.

RUST
I am glad to hear it.

HABER
I am working on a new chemical that will change the face of agriculture.

RUST
Another nitrogen fixation?

HABER
Zyklon. My assistants have been conducting preliminary tests.

RUST
And its use?

HABER
A pesticide.

RUST
Nothing more?

HABER
Zyklon will have a major impact on farming around the world. That is not a *nothing* Herr Minister, that is a very big *something*.

RUST
Of course. You are a recognized genius when it comes to the practical uses of science. We encourage you to continue.

HABER
Thank you. Now if–

RUST
Lastly, I am here to tell you about the laws that were passed two days ago.

HABER
I don't think I–

RUST
Let me fill you in, as they will be of great interest to you.

The GESTAPO hands papers to RUST who hands them to HABER. HABER looks them over.

GESTAPO
The Law of the Restoration of the Civil Service has now come into effect. The following are to be immediately released from their posts. Number one: those without proper qualifications or who are political appointees.

HABER
No worries of that, everyone here–

GESTAPO
Number two: Those not unreservedly serving the new state.

HABER
What exactly does that–?

GESTAPO
Number three: those of non-Aryan descent.

Pause.

RUST
Of course, you would be exempt.

HABER
I should hope so.

RUST
The law allows exemptions for war veterans.

RUST motions and the GESTAPO hands him a file.

But I see from your list of employees, Herr Haber, a large number of non-Aryan names.

HABER
And what do you expect me to do Herr Minister, fire them?

RUST
That is exactly what I expect.

Pause.

HABER
But that's, that's impossible, I can't fire three quarters of my staff!

RUST
I am here to inform you of the law, and to tell you that the government expects the law to be carried out. We are the main funder of this Institute. I would hate to see its worthy status, how shall I say, diminished.

HABER
Herr Minister–.

RUST
Unfortunately, I have other business to attend to. I'll let you get to your class. Heil Hitler!

GESTAPO
(automatic) Heil Hitler!

> RUST salutes. So does the GESTAPO. HABER does nothing.

RUST
I said, Heil Hitler, Herr Haber.

> Very slowly, HABER half-heartedly raises his hand. RUST smiles, and exits with the GESTAPO. HABER turns. CLARA is at his desk, studying his work. She looks up at him.

— • —

> ALBERT packing his viola in its case. HABER enters.

HABER
Einstein.

ALBERT
…Haber?

HABER
May I come in?

ALBERT
You may.

HABER
I trust I'm not – you look like you're…

ALBERT
My train leaves in an hour, but–

HABER
Ah, well, perhaps I'll–

ALBERT
No, please, come, sit.

> HABER does.

What can I do for you?

HABER
I wanted to…

> Pause.

I need your…

> *Pause.*

I was hoping you'd…

> *Pause.*

ALBERT
…yes?

HABER
I was hoping you might speak at the Institute's bi-weekly Colloquium.

ALBERT
Me? Speak at your Colloquium?

HABER
I realize you're busy, but I thought–

ALBERT
I would love to, Haber. But I will be gone.

HABER
Oh?

ALBERT
And if you're smart, you'll be gone too.

HABER
What, what do you mean?

ALBERT
You've heard.

HABER
What.

ALBERT
The fire. At the Reichstag.

HABER
Ah. That.

ALBERT
Arson.

HABER
Arson, who says it was–?

ALBERT
Hitler blames the communists; others blame Hitler.

HABER
Propaganda.

ALBERT
Is it.

HABER
Nothing more.

Pause.

ALBERT
I'm sorry Haber, I can't help you.

HABER
Really, Einstein, one little fire and you, what, you run away with your tail between your legs?

ALBERT
Where have you been Haber? Eh? Where have you *been*? Stuck in that office with your nose in budgets and God knows–

HABER
That's not true I–

ALBERT
Germany is sick Haber. Everyone knows that, everyone but you.

HABER
Fine fine, the National Socialists are acting somewhat strange, I admit to that, but there's no need to panic, there's no need to spread the kind of silly propaganda you–.

ALBERT
I do not spread propaganda Haber. I collect facts. Twenty percent of our university instructors are Jewish and only seven percent are full professors. This is not propaganda. This is fact.

HABER
I know that, you don't need to tell *me*–

ALBERT
Public cartoons making racist comments about me appear in national newspapers. This is not propaganda. This is fact. My work is denounced as "Jewish-Communist Physics." This is not propaganda. This is fact. And you stand there, you stand there and tell me to my face I am spreading propaganda? You stand there and tell me the Nazis are "acting strange?"

HABER
Einstein–

ALBERT
Haber, listen to me. I beg of you. Listen.

Pause.

Great spirits have always met with violent opposition from weak minds. You know that better than I. Weak minds cannot understand it when you or I don't thoughtlessly submit to prejudice, but honestly and courageously use our minds.

No, listen to me, please.

We are intelligent beings Haber. We require a new way of thinking if we are to survive. And I for one cannot think in the environment in which we are presently living. I cannot think in a land which is hostile to the intellectual. I cannot think in a land that equates science with pessimism. I cannot think in a land which refuses to let its people see certain motion pictures, or read certain books, or listen to certain music. I cannot think in a land that does not allow me to think. National Socialism is a contempt of the mind. This government has undertaken to set itself up as a judge of truth and knowledge and I tell you it will be shipwrecked by the laughter of the gods. Trust me.

HABER is silent.

Come with me, Haber.

HABER
I can't.

ALBERT
Why not.

HABER
Because.

ALBERT
Because why.

HABER
Because I–

ALBERT
Why?

HABER
Because this is my home! Because this country is my home! Because I have given everything to it. And you, you think with one turn of my hand, I can wave goodbye to it? I won't let them steal it from me. I won't.

Pause.

ALBERT
Goodbye Haber.

HABER
Einstein, please–

ALBERT
I have to go.

HABER
I, we need you, Germany needs you–

ALBERT
For God's sake Haber. If they're burning the Reichstag; if they're burning the house where the laws of this country are to be kept and protected, then nothing will stop them from burning *your* house. Open your eyes.

ALBERT leaves. HABER stares after.

— • —

RUST's office.

RUST
(smiles) Haber.

HABER
Herr Minister.

RUST
Right on time. Have a seat.

HABER
I prefer to stand.

RUST
(pause) Very well. Have you given any thought to what we discussed last week?

HABER
I have thought of nothing else.

RUST
And...?

HABER
I have a proposal. I trust we can reach some kind of compromise. It seems a, a waste, to let so many talented people go.

RUST
There is more "talent" available in the country I am sure.

HABER
That I doubt. I pride myself on having the best staff on the continent, let alone the country.

RUST
And your proposal is?

HABER
You are concerned with a certain, a certain kind of person on my staff, yes?

RUST
To the point, Herr Haber.

HABER
I have a way of alleviating your concern. I will request certain members of my staff to be baptized.

Pause.

RUST
...baptized?! *(He laughs.)*

HABER
Yes, and if they agree, then they, they can claim to be Christians, you see, and circumvent your concerns.

RUST laughs louder.

In return, you will allow them to remain employees of the Institute. Would this not be satisfactory, Herr Minister?

RUST
(chuckling) My dear Haber. To think that, that the government would not be able to distinguish... oh my.... That may have worked for you thirty years ago, Herr Haber, but I'm afraid not today. Not today. No, no. They must go.

HABER
But surely we can–

RUST
I'm sorry Haber. There is only one solution here. Fire them.

HABER
And if I do not?

RUST
(sincere) Let us not even discuss such a possibility. Eh? Because the thought of firing *you* is very unpleasant to consider.

OTTO enters.

OTTO
I'm sorry Herr Minister, I didn't realize–

RUST
No no, you're just in time. Haber, have you met–?

HABER
Otto. What are, what are you doing here?

OTTO
Pleased to make your acquaintance. Herr Haber.

Pause.

RUST
Otto joined the department, what was it, last month, was it not?

OTTO
Yes, Herr Minister.

RUST
He's been keeping us... informed regarding your research on Zyklon. Haven't you?

OTTO
The new government will help make Germany great again.

RUST
With any luck, Zyklon will be the new chlorine, isn't that right Otto?

OTTO
But more successful.

HABER
Otto.

OTTO
Government and industry working together.

HABER
No.

OTTO
For it is not enough to know, we must also–.

HABER
Don't!

RUST
Herr Haber, I really don't think–

HABER
You are making a big mistake, a very big–.

RUST
No. You are making the mistake.

HABER
Driving away the greatest minds in Germany.

RUST
I don't need you to–

HABER
Einstein, Brecht, Mann,–

RUST
We don't need Einstein, we don't need Brecht–!

HABER
These are the very people who made this country what it is.

RUST
All we want is true Germans!

HABER
Then I suggest you replace the Führer, Herr Minister, because he is from Austria; and I suggest you replace Herr Rudolph Hess because he is from Egypt; and I suggest you replace–

RUST
You are fired. Do you hear me, as of today–!

HABER
You cannot; for as of today, Herr Minister, I resign.

He grabs a pen from RUST's desk, and quickly scrawls out a letter.

For more than thirty years, I have chosen my colleagues. Me. And I have chosen them first and foremost on the basis of their intelligence and their character. And not on the basis of their grandmothers and grandfathers. Here. Here is what you want. Here is the resignation of a non-Aryan. Here.

He throws the letter at RUST and starts to leave.

OTTO
Jew.

HABER freezes, then turns.

HABER
I am a War veteran, I am a Nobel prize winner, I–

RUST
A Jew is a Jew is a Jew! You cannot convince me that you are anything else but a Jew! You think because you won a prize, people will revere you? You think because you fought a war people will care? Fire your workers and rip up this ridiculous resignation letter–

HABER
I will not.

RUST
–or I will revoke your citizenship and see to it that you never set foot in Germany ever again!

HABER
You wouldn't–!

RUST
Why wouldn't I?

Pause.

Eh? Why wouldn't I?

Pause.

(to OTTO) Go to the Institute, find Herr Haber's office, and take what you need.

OTTO
Yes, Herr Minister.

HABER
(to OTTO) Don't do this Otto, don't–

RUST
(to OTTO) You may go–

HABER
You don't know what you're doing, you don't–

RUST
(to OTTO) I said you may go!

OTTO salutes and leaves. Pause.

Otto tells me Zyklon is an effective killer of lice. Is that so?

CLARA appears.

CLARA
(a ghostly whisper) The future of science is in its application…

RUST
He tells me, in high concentrations, Zyklon can be quite, quite… fatal.

The gasping SOLDIER appears.

CLARA
…science for a practical purpose…

RUST
I'm sure Zyklon will be very useful at the new work camps the government plans to establish.

CLARA
…science for a greater humanity…

RUST
Don't you think? Herr Captain Director Doctor Professor Haber?

HABER
You are poison! You are poison a hundred times worse than any I ever dreamt of!

RUST
I highly suggest Herr Haber, that you seek asylum, in another country, as quickly as possible.

RUST vanishes. HABER stumbles, a holocaust growing in his mind.

HABER
(broken) Oh God. What have I… what have I done…?

HABER collapses. CLARA and the SOLDIER vanish.

— • —

ALBERT with a package. LOTTA greets him.

ALBERT
Switzerland. 1934. An old man arrives.

LOTTA
Thank you for coming.

ALBERT
When did he get here?

LOTTA
Last month. They took everything. His office, his…

ALBERT
Yes. Rabbi Weizman told me.